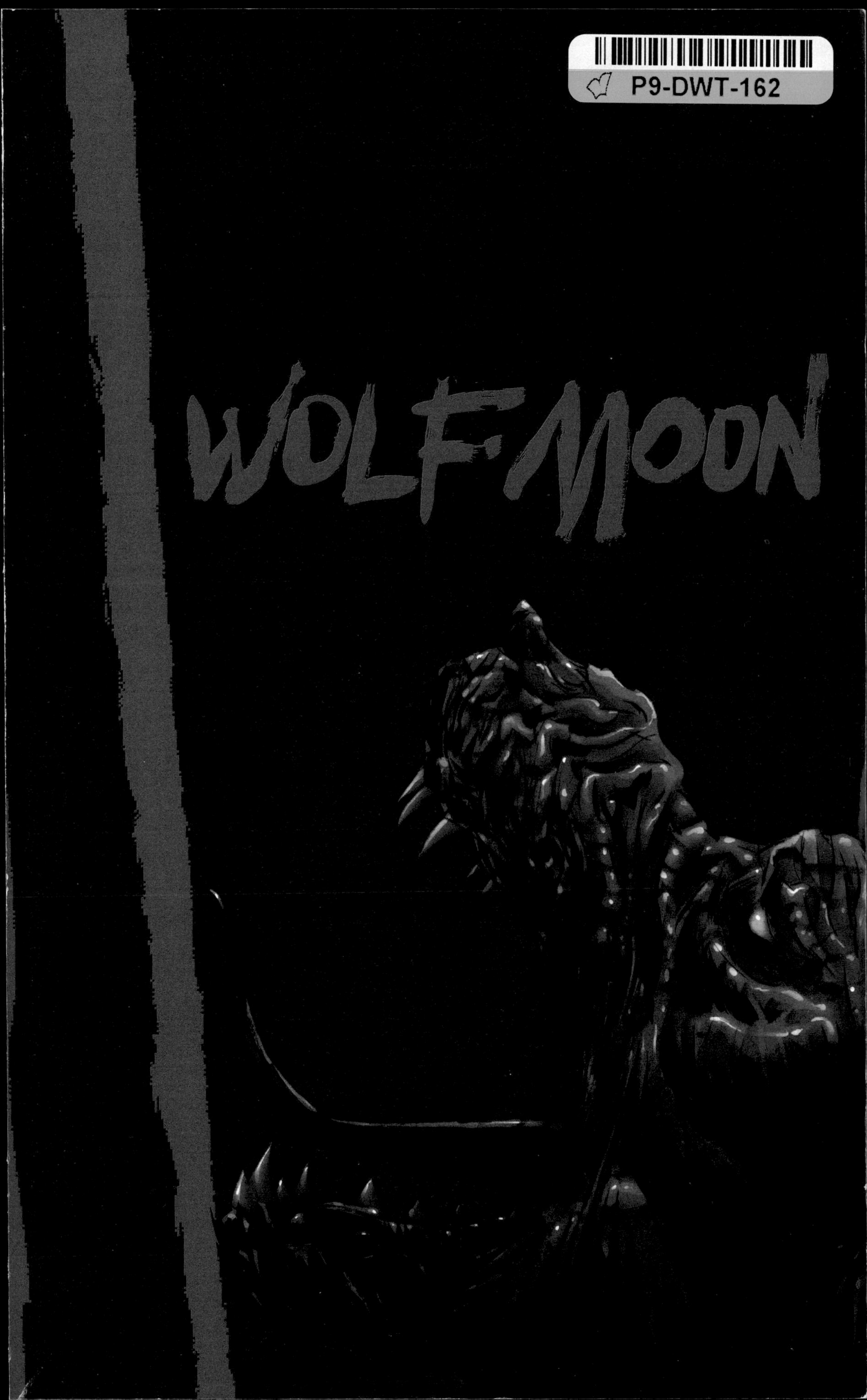
WOLF MOON

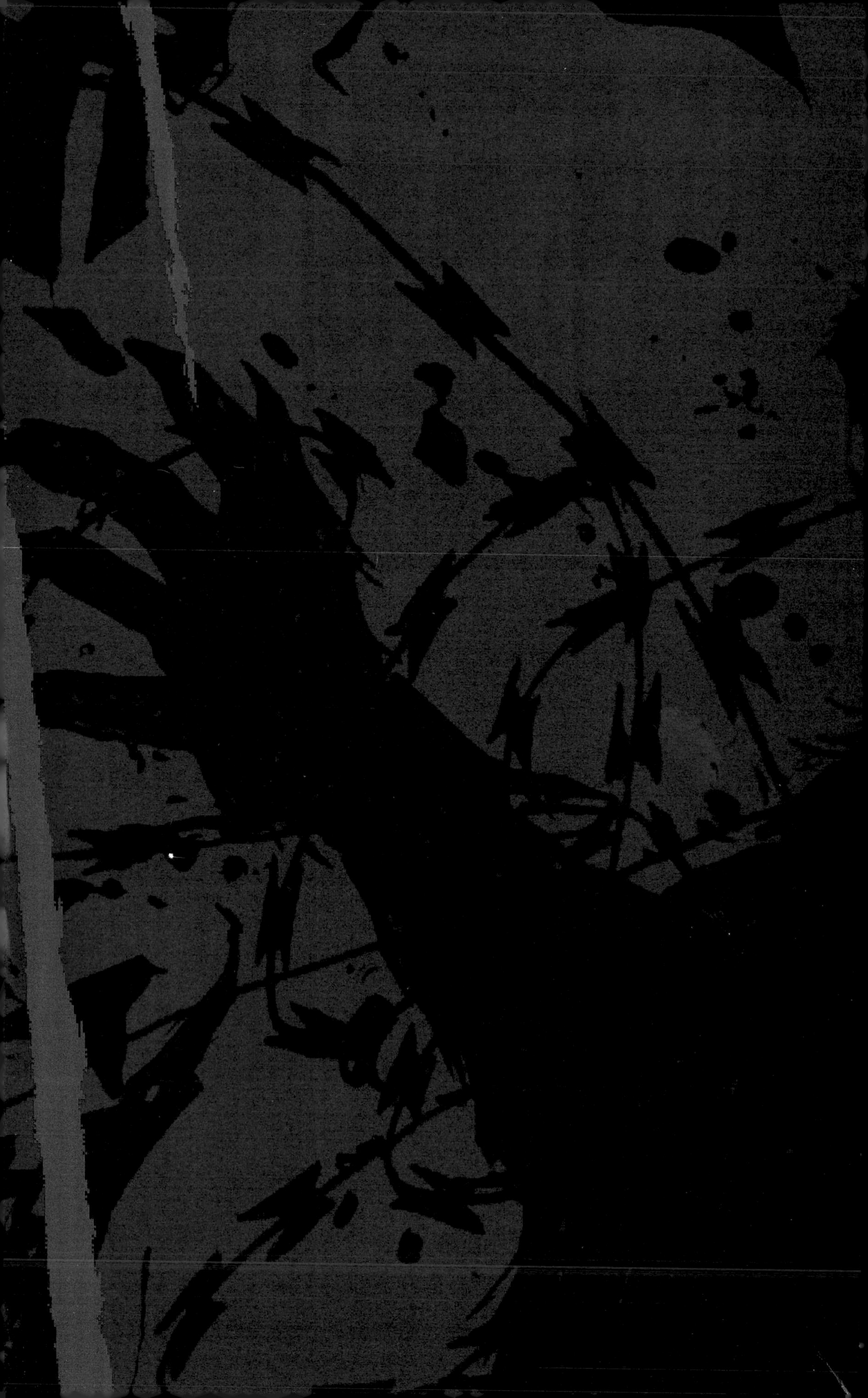

# WOLF MOON

**CULLEN BUNN**
Writer

**JEREMY HAUN**
Artist

**LEE LOUGHRIDGE**
Colorist

**TRAVIS LANHAM**
Letterer

**LEONARDO MANCO** and **TRISH MULVIHILL**
Cover Art

**JAE LEE (#1) RYAN KELLY (#2)**
**JILL THOMPSON** and **LEE LOUGHRIDGE (#3)**
**LEANDRO FERNANDEZ (#4) MARGUERITE SAUVAGE (#5)**
**LEONARDO MANCO** and **TRISH MULVIHILL (#6)**
Original Series Covers

**WOLF MOON** CREATED BY **CULLEN BUNN** and **JEREMY HAUN**

SHANNON ERIC DENTON GREG LOCKARD Editors – Original Series
JEB WOODARD Group Editor – Collected Editions
SCOTT NYBAKKEN Editor – Collected Edition
DAMIAN RYLAND Publication Design

SHELLY BOND VP & Executive Editor – Vertigo

DIANE NELSON President
DAN DIDIO and JIM LEE Co-Publishers
GEOFF JOHNS Chief Creative Officer
AMIT DESAI Senior VP – Marketing & Global Franchise Management
NAIRI GARDINER Senior VP – Finance
SAM ADES VP – Digital Marketing
BOBBIE CHASE VP – Talent Development
MARK CHIARELLO Senior VP – Art, Design & Collected Editions
JOHN CUNNINGHAM VP – Content Strategy
ANNE DEPIES VP – Strategy Planning & Reporting
DON FALLETTI VP – Manufacturing Operations
LAWRENCE GANEM VP – Editorial Administration & Talent Relations
ALISON GILL Senior VP – Manufacturing & Operations
HANK KANALZ Senior VP – Editorial Strategy & Administration
JAY KOGAN VP – Legal Affairs
DEREK MADDALENA Senior VP – Sales & Business Development
JACK MAHAN VP – Business Affairs
DAN MIRON VP – Sales Planning & Trade Development
NICK NAPOLITANO VP – Manufacturing Administration
CAROL ROEDER VP – Marketing
EDDIE SCANNELL VP – Mass Account & Digital Sales
COURTNEY SIMMONS Senior VP – Publicity & Communications
JIM (SKI) SOKOLOWSKI VP – Comic Book Specialty & Newsstand Sales
SANDY YI Senior VP – Global Franchise Management

Logo design by TOM MULLER

WOLF MOON



DC Comics, 4000 Warner Blvd., Burbank, CA 91522
A Warner Bros. Entertainment Company.
Printed in the USA. First Printing.
ISBN: 978-1-4012-5774-3.

Library of Congress Cataloging-in-Publication Data

Bunn, Cullen, author.
Wolf Moon / Cullen Bunn, writer ; Jeremy Haun, artist.
pages cm
ISBN 978-1-4012-5774-3 (paperback)
1. Werewolves—Comic books, strips, etc. 2. Graphic novels. I. Haun, Jeremy, illustrator. II. Title.
PN6727.B845W65 2015
741.5'973—dc23
2015014469

PEFC Certified
Printed on paper from sustainably managed forests and controlled sources
PEFC
PEFC/29-31-75
www.pefc.org

# INTRODUCTION

The Wolf doesn't simply reshape flesh and blood.

It reshapes lives.

When I first set out to write this story, that was the idea at the front of my mind. It was an idea that had been with me, on some level, since I was a child.

I had a nightmare when I was five or six years old, and to this day I can still remember it in vivid detail. In the dream, I stood outside the farmhouse my family called home. It was night, and the moon was bright and seemingly too close to the world. Watching the house, I could see bulky, shaggy shadows behind curtained windows and just past the screen door that rattled and creaked in its frame. I heard growling within. Somehow, I knew that everyone in the house — my parents, my brothers, my sister — had turned into werewolves.

That nightmare — one of the earliest I can recall — has haunted me for years. Maybe that's why werewolves have always been one of my favorite monsters. Maybe that's why I find movies like *The Wolfman* and *An American Werewolf in London* and *Dog Soldiers* and *Ginger Snaps* so rewatchable. Werewolves are terrifying, but not necessarily because they're hulking brutes with fangs and claws. They're scary because of everything they can take from you.

In my nightmare, I knew that if I walked through the creaky door, I'd be torn apart — by my loved ones! The werewolf "curse" took everyone I loved away from me. What's worse, it made them want to kill me.

A werewolf, on its snarling, fur-covered surface, is frightening enough. It's fast, vicious and lethal. It can track you down and smell your fear. It's virtually unstoppable unless you have a silver bullet — and while gun shops often sell cheesily labeled "zombie-stopper" rounds, the werewolf's poison is in short supply. Finally, the werewolf looks human by day. It might be your mail carrier, your priest, your boss, or even your spouse.

That last part — the bit about the creature being "one of us" when the full moon's not aglow — is what really makes the werewolf terrifying.

Imagine turning into the beast. You might try to hide, to seclude yourself out of fear of what you could do to those around you. You might wonder if you have the strength to end your curse — and your own life — if you could just get your hands on one of those aforementioned silver bullets. You might be forced to ride along as a helpless passenger while the monster uses your transformed body to harm those around you. Your husband. Your wife. Your parents. Your friends. Your kids.

I can flee from a wolfman. Hell, if I've been training for a 5K, I might even have a slim chance of escaping the creature. But the dread, the guilt, the sense of loss... those things are inescapable, no matter how fast you run.

So, what makes the werewolf truly monstrous for me is that it destroys everything it touches. It kills innocent people. It wrecks the lives of those who are close to it. And it crushes its true victim — the person who plays host to the monster — with guilt and loss. Those are the fears I wanted to draw out in WOLF MOON.

I also wanted the opportunity to explore those fears with as many characters as possible, which is where the idea of the wolf "jumping" from person to person came from. In your typical werewolf story, the full moon rises, the werewolf goes on a rampage, the hero finds a silver bullet (or a silver-tipped cane), and the monster is vanquished. I wanted a monster that was a little more difficult to track, one that moved from host to host, seemingly at random. I thought that it might make for an interesting cat-and-mouse scenario.

More important, though, I also thought that such a monster might leave behind a trail of previous hosts — men and women who had been touched by the Wolf, poor souls whose lives had been completely upended by this brush with the supernatural. And each one of those people might have a different reaction to it. Some might be overwhelmed by grief over what they had done. Some might be consumed by rage. Others might long to feel oh-so-powerful again.

As I was brainstorming the idea, I stumbled onto some folktales that fed directly into the kind of story I wanted to tell. (What, after all, is a werewolf story without a healthy dose of lore?) While I wanted to introduce some new ideas to the lycanthrope legend, I also wanted the book to be true to the "feel" of the horror stories that had come before. That was a moment of pure joy for me, a moment when everything came together and I was able to forge ahead and write this yarn.

Still, it almost didn't happen. After I had written the entire series, and after several issues had already been drawn, the book fell into limbo. It sat on a shelf, maybe to never see the light of day. The years of waiting were torture for me, because I didn't just want to write the story — I wanted people to read it! Thankfully, Vertigo swooped in to save the day, and I think that they are absolutely the best publisher for a book like this.

There's a lot of bloodshed and violence in these pages. It's a brutal story at times. But there's also a haunting sense of dread and grief and loss — an atmosphere that could only have been achieved through the work of my wonderfully talented partners. Jeremy Haun draws a mean (really mean) werewolf, and colorist Lee Loughridge can dance the tightrope between mood and vivid gore like nobody's business. Their collaboration on my little nightmare brought both its visceral and its psychological horror to life.

From childhood dream to unpublished comic book (with various titles, including *Wandering Wolf* and, at one time, the kind of dreadful *Shapewalker*) to seeing print through one of the comics imprints I respect the most... it's been a crazy (dare I say shapeshifting?) ride. I hope you enjoy how it all turned out.

— CULLEN BUNN
AUGUST 2015

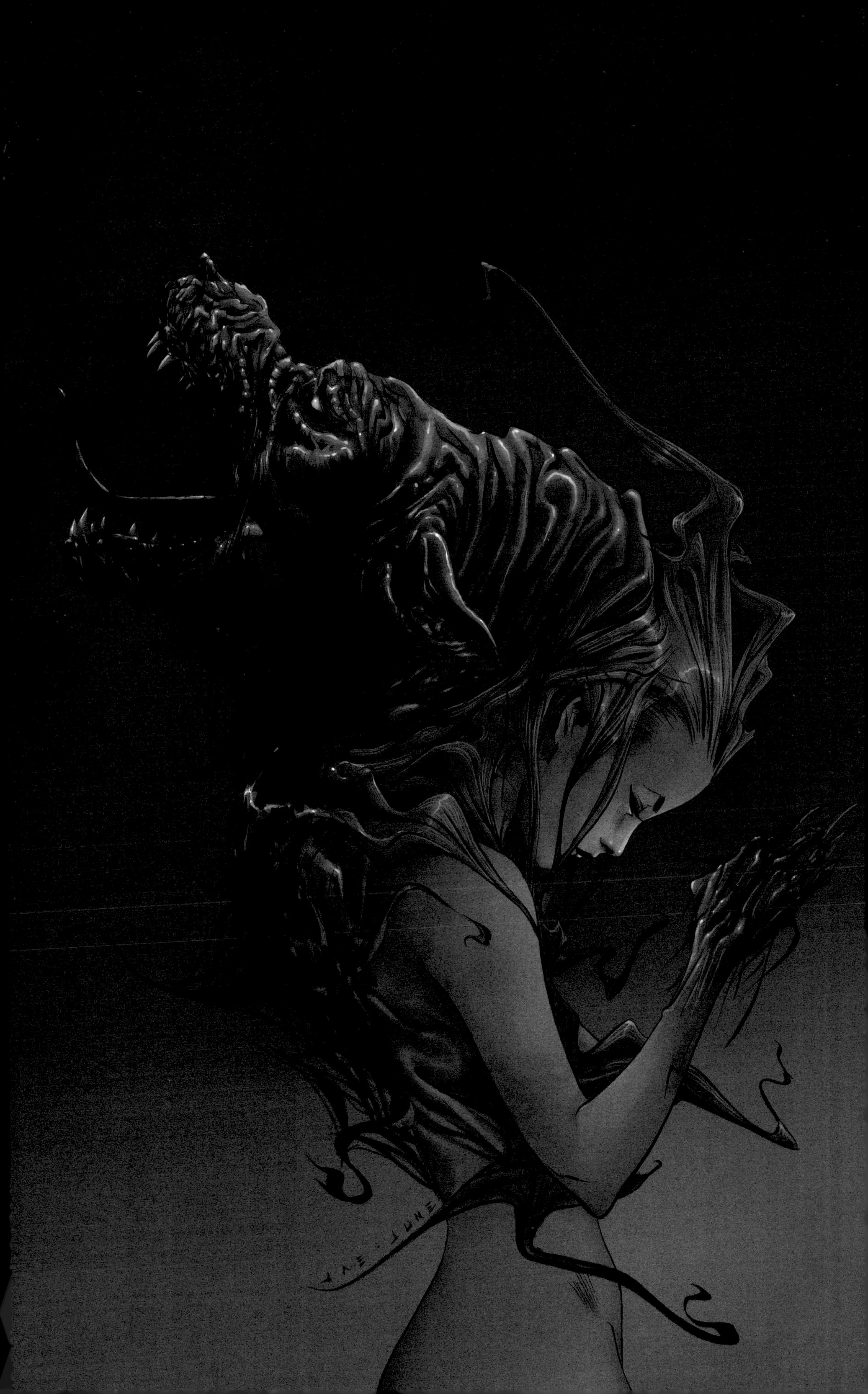

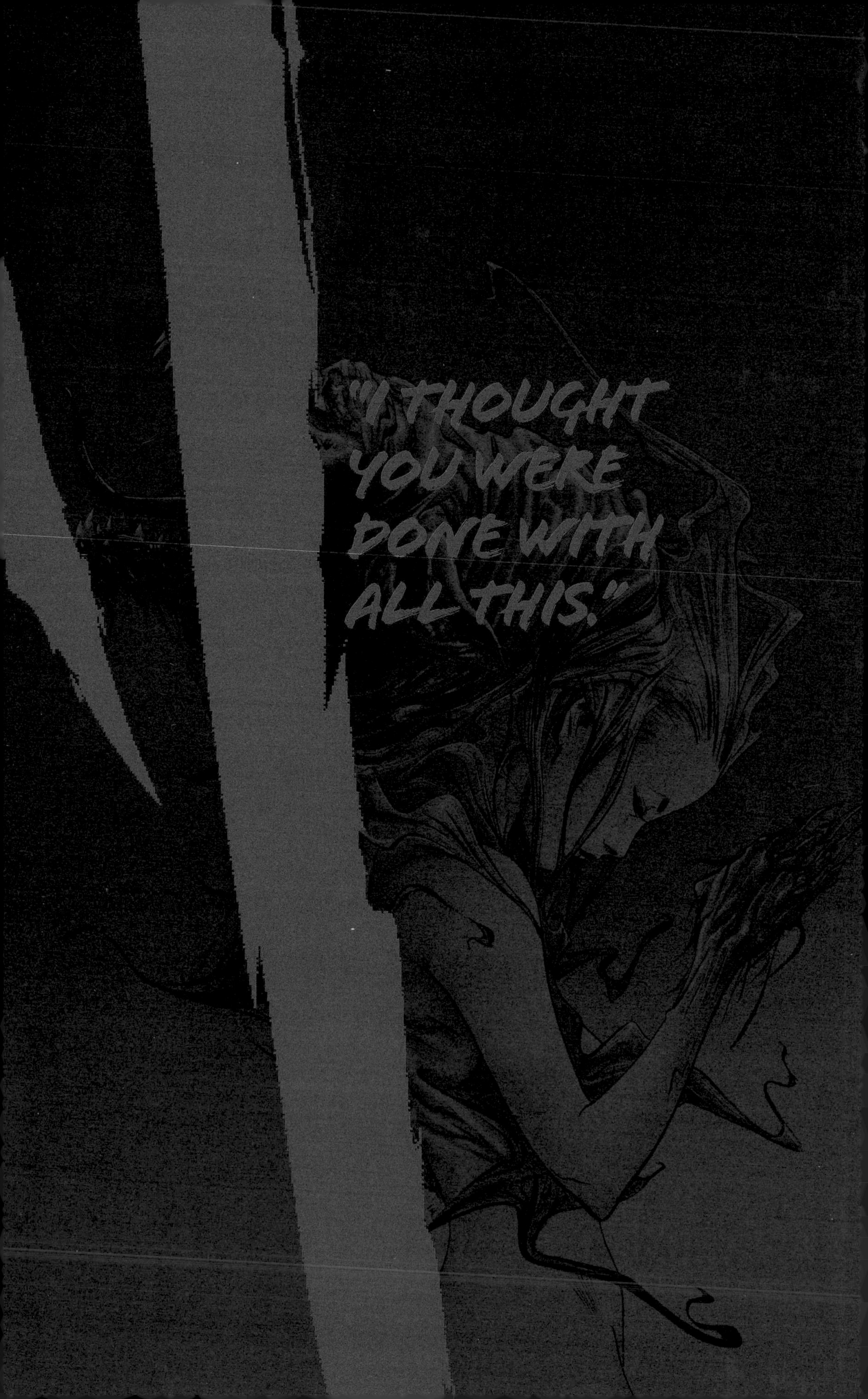
"I THOUGHT YOU WERE DONE WITH ALL THIS."

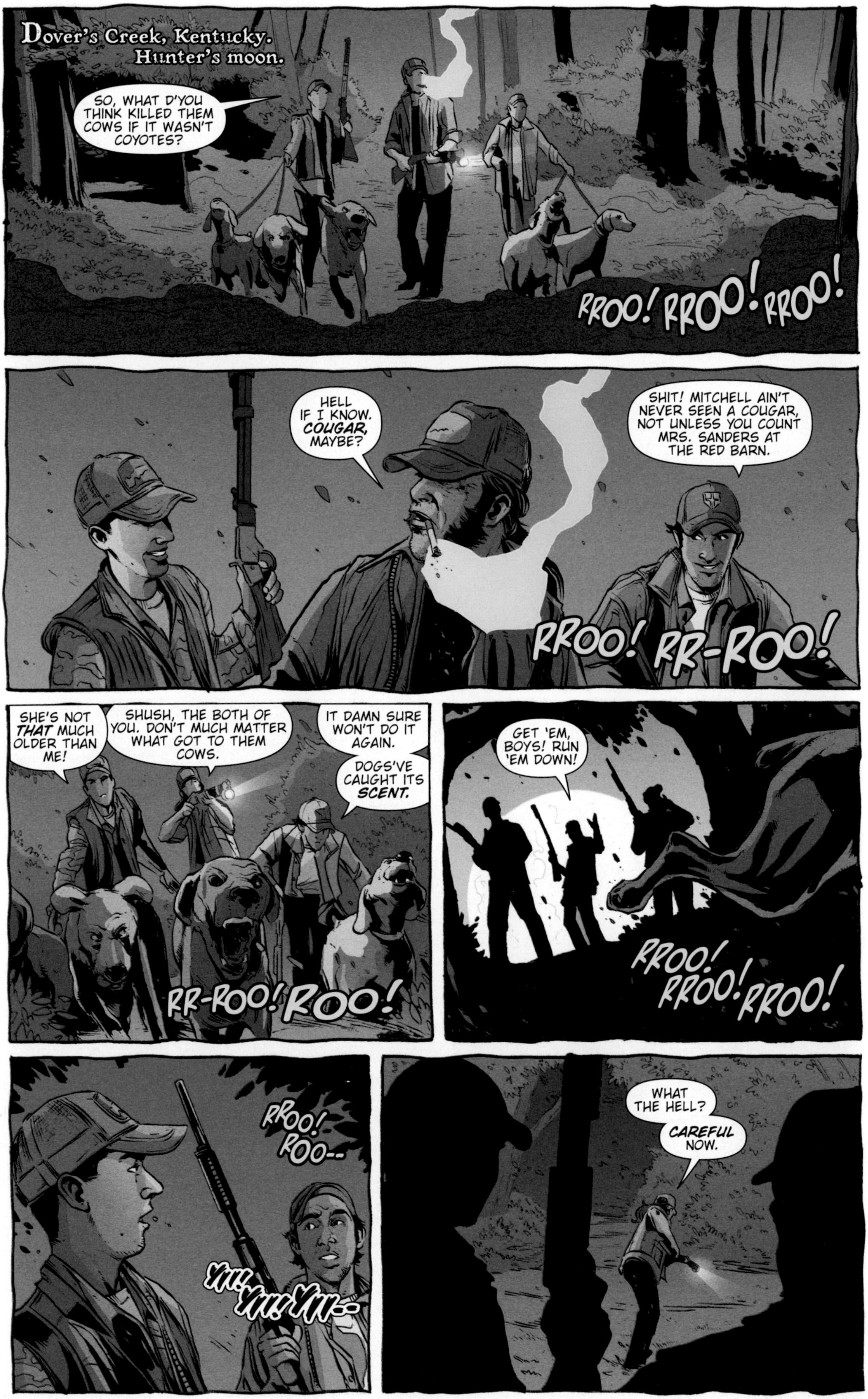

Dover's Creek, Kentucky.
Hunter's moon.
SO, WHAT D'YOU THINK KILLED THEM COWS IF IT WASN'T COYOTES?
RROO! RROO! RROO!
HELL IF I KNOW. COUGAR, MAYBE?
SHIT! MITCHELL AIN'T NEVER SEEN A COUGAR, NOT UNLESS YOU COUNT MRS. SANDERS AT THE RED BARN.
RROO! RR-ROO!
SHE'S NOT THAT MUCH OLDER THAN ME!
SHUSH, THE BOTH OF YOU. DON'T MUCH MATTER WHAT GOT TO THEM COWS.
IT DAMN SURE WON'T DO IT AGAIN.
DOGS'VE CAUGHT ITS SCENT.
RR-ROO! ROO!
GET 'EM, BOYS! RUN 'EM DOWN!
RROO! RROO! RROO!
RROO! ROO--
YI!! YI!! YII--
WHAT THE HELL?
CAREFUL NOW.

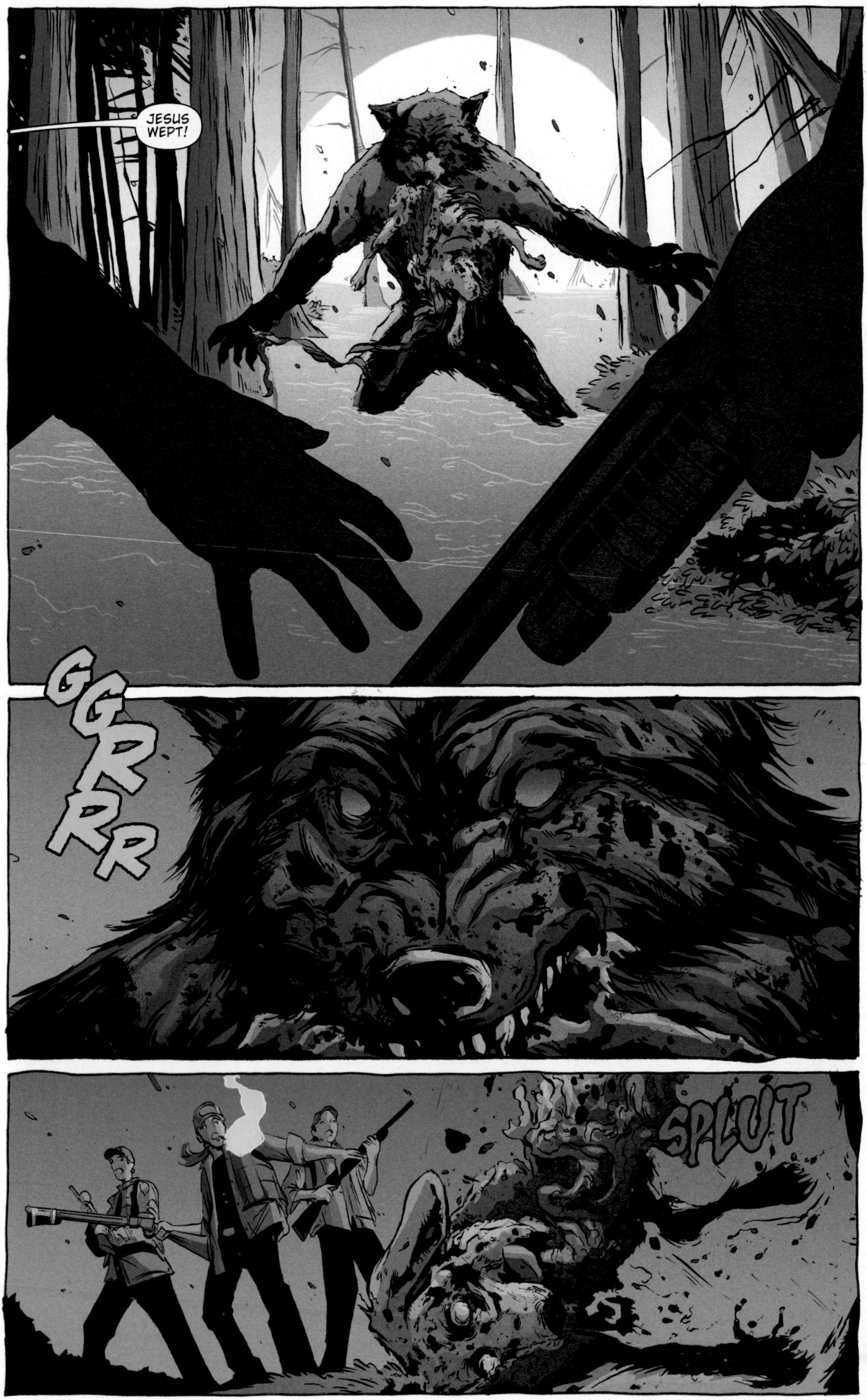
JESUS WEPT!
GGRRR
SPLUT

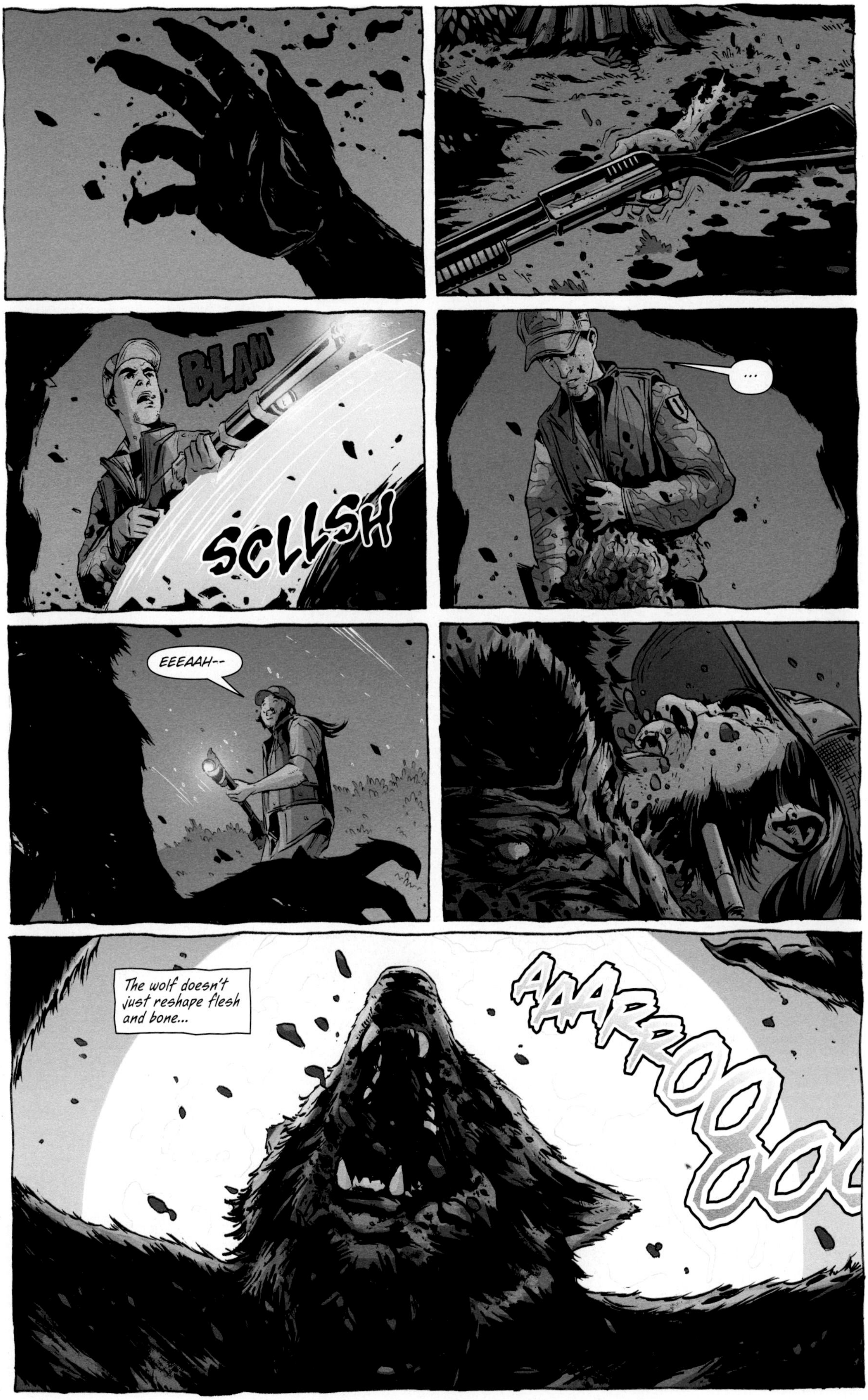
BLAM
SCLLSH
...
EEEAAH--
The wolf doesn't just reshape flesh and bone...
AAARROOOOOO

...It reshapes _lives._

Rockford, Illinois.

DILLON...

YOU'RE **PACKED.**

I'M **LEAVING.**

OH.

I...I GUESS I THOUGHT YOU WERE **DONE** WITH ALL THIS.

THE LAST COUPLE OF MONTHS WERE **NICE,** WEREN'T THEY? I LIKE YOU STAYING HERE INSTEAD OF RUNNING OFF AT THE FIRST SIGN OF--

THE TRAIL WENT COLD FOR A WHILE, BUT THERE'S **SOMETHING** GOING ON.

**KENTUCKY** THIS TIME.

I CAN GET THERE BY TONIGHT IF I LEAVE NOW.

| News alert: | Grizzly attack |
| | Incident in KY |
| Re: | Wolf |
| News alert: | Cattle mutilation |
| News alert: | Someone you should talk to? |
| Re: | Lunar cycle |
| News alert: | Ammunition |
| Re: | |

IT MIGHT BE ANOTHER **WILD-GOOSE CHASE,** BUT IT MIGHT...

IT MIGHT BE MY CHANCE TO KILL THIS THING.

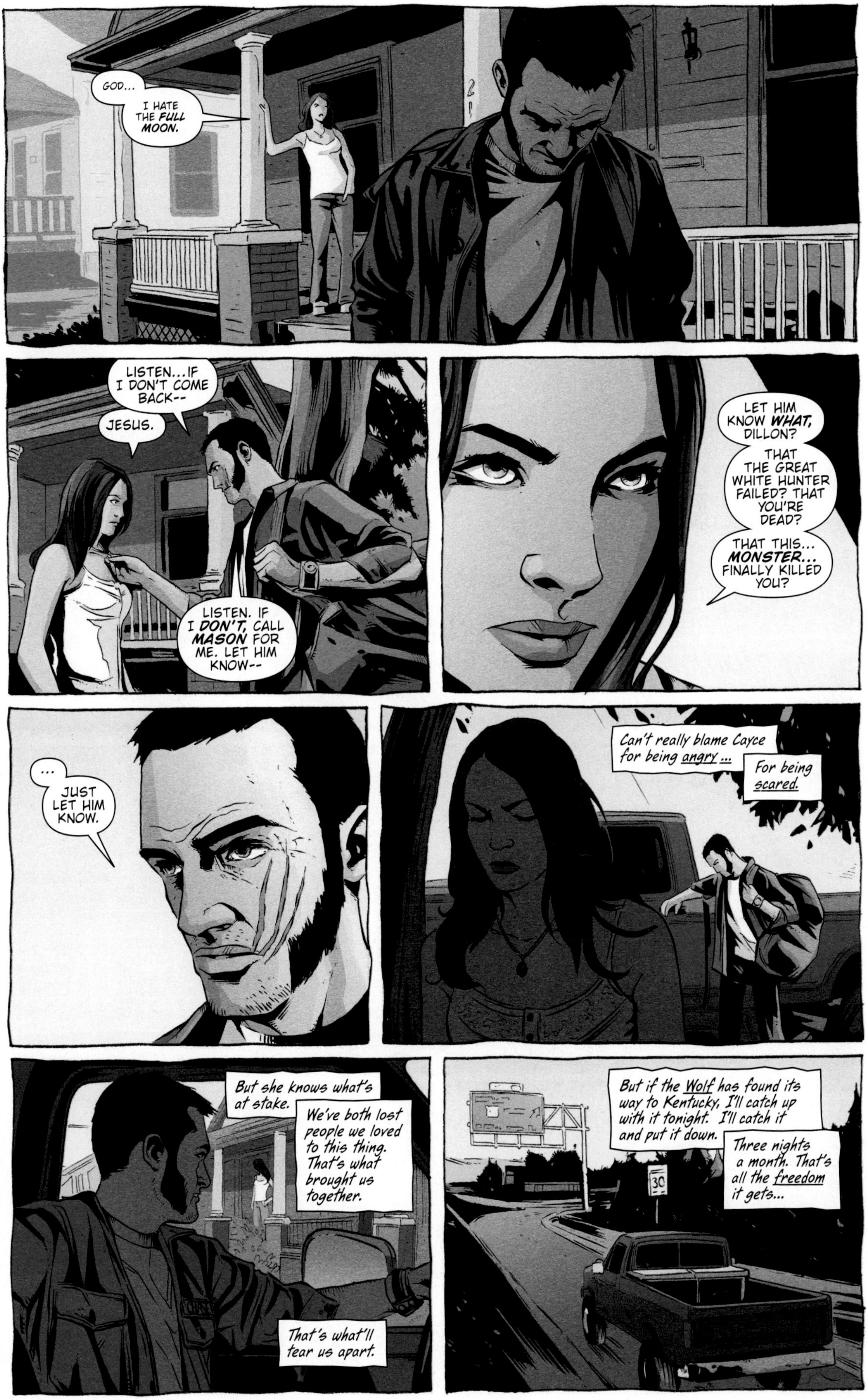
GOD... I HATE THE FULL MOON.
LISTEN...IF I DON'T COME BACK--
JESUS.
LISTEN. IF I DON'T, CALL MASON FOR ME. LET HIM KNOW--
LET HIM KNOW WHAT, DILLON?
THAT THE GREAT WHITE HUNTER FAILED? THAT YOU'RE DEAD?
THAT THIS... MONSTER... FINALLY KILLED YOU?
... JUST LET HIM KNOW.
Can't really blame Cayce for being angry ...
For being scared.
But she knows what's at stake.
We've both lost people we loved to this thing. That's what brought us together.
That's what'll tear us apart.
But if the Wolf has found its way to Kentucky, I'll catch up with it tonight. I'll catch it and put it down.
Three nights a month. That's all the freedom it gets...
30

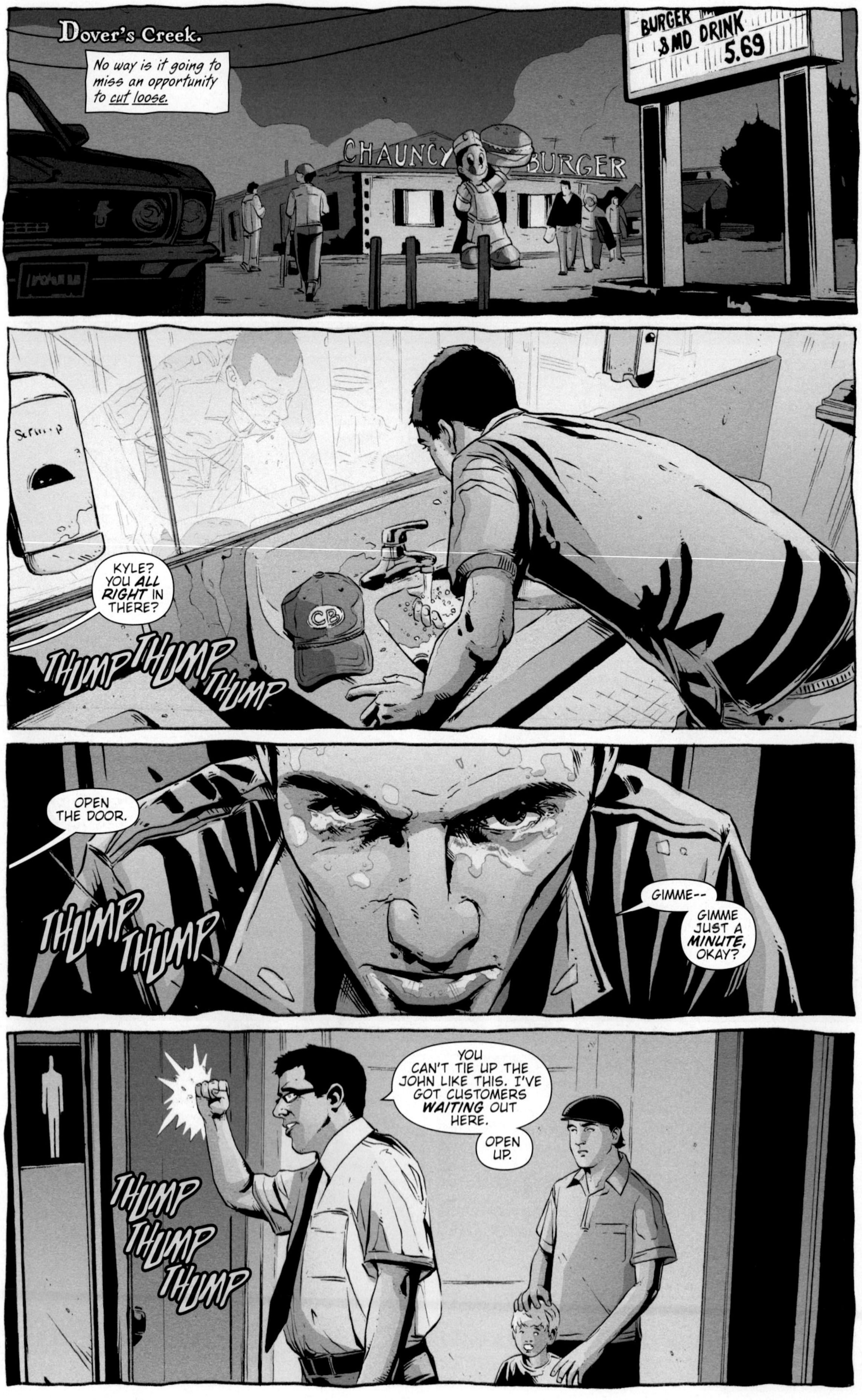

Dover's Creek.
No way is it going to miss an opportunity to cut loose.
BURGER
$MD DRINK
5.69
CHAUNCY BURGER
KYLE? YOU ALL RIGHT IN THERE?
THUMP THUMP THUMP
OPEN THE DOOR.
THUMP THUMP
GIMME--
GIMME JUST A MINUTE, OKAY?
THUMP THUMP THUMP
YOU CAN'T TIE UP THE JOHN LIKE THIS. I'VE GOT CUSTOMERS WAITING OUT HERE.
OPEN UP.

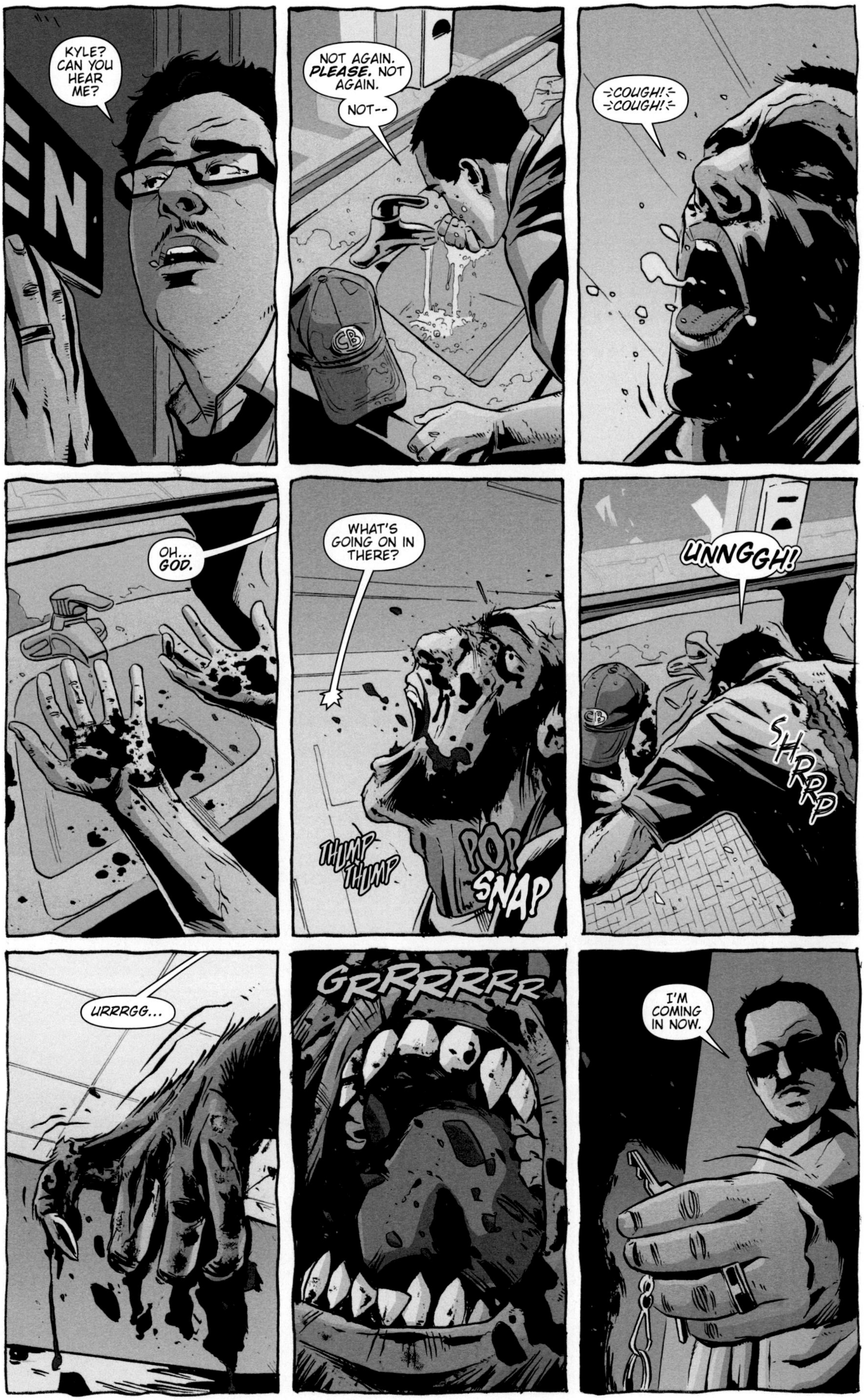
KYLE? CAN YOU HEAR ME?
NOT AGAIN. *PLEASE.* NOT AGAIN.
NOT--
COUGH! COUGH!
OH... *GOD.*
WHAT'S GOING ON IN THERE?
THUMP THUMP
POP SNAP
UNNGGH!
SHRRP
URRRGG...
GRRRRRRR
I'M COMING IN NOW.

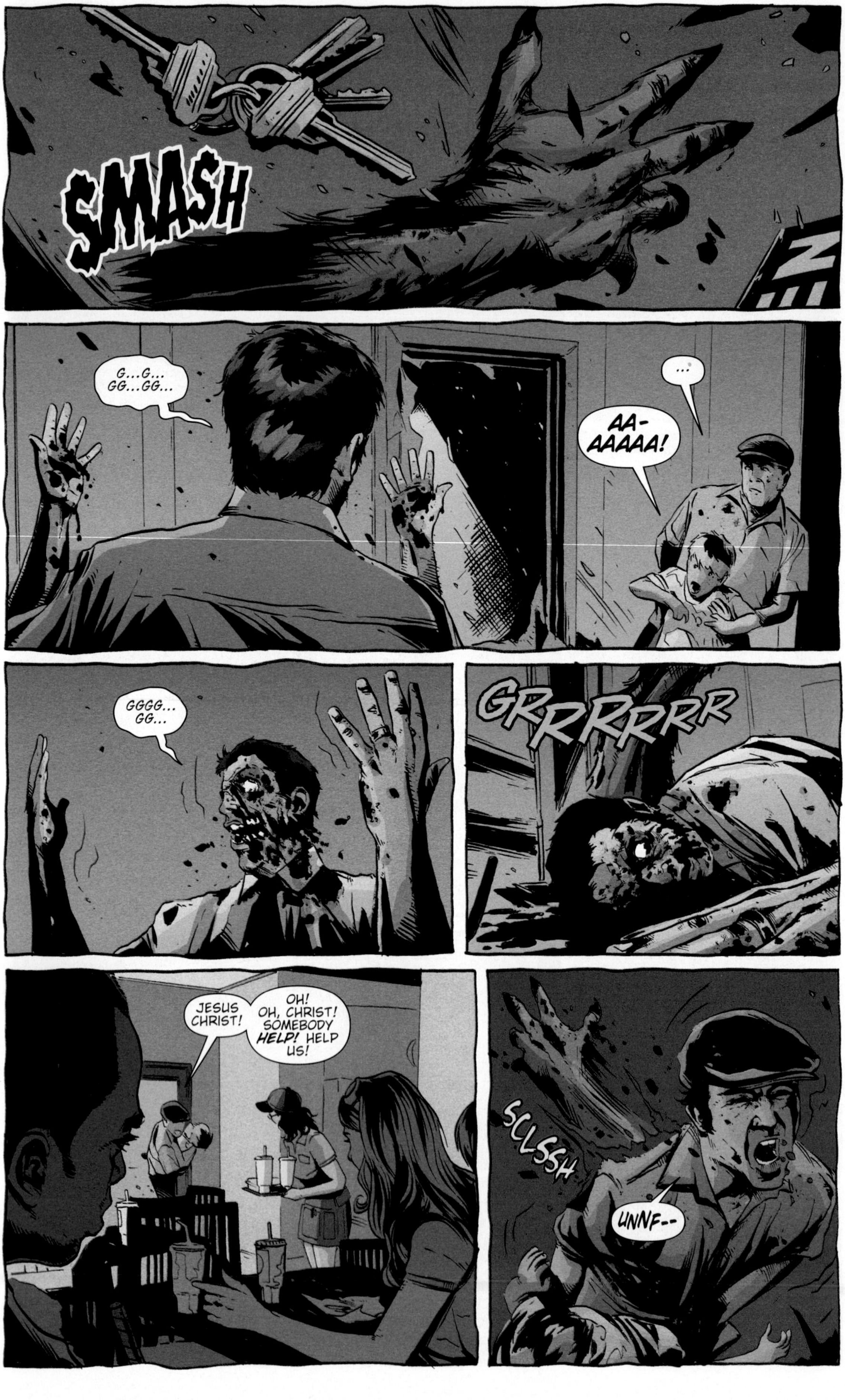
SMASH
G...G...
GG...GG...
...
AA-
AAAAA!
GGGG...
GG...
GRRRRRRR
JESUS CHRIST!
OH! OH, CHRIST! SOMEBODY **HELP!** HELP US!
SCLSSH
UNNF--

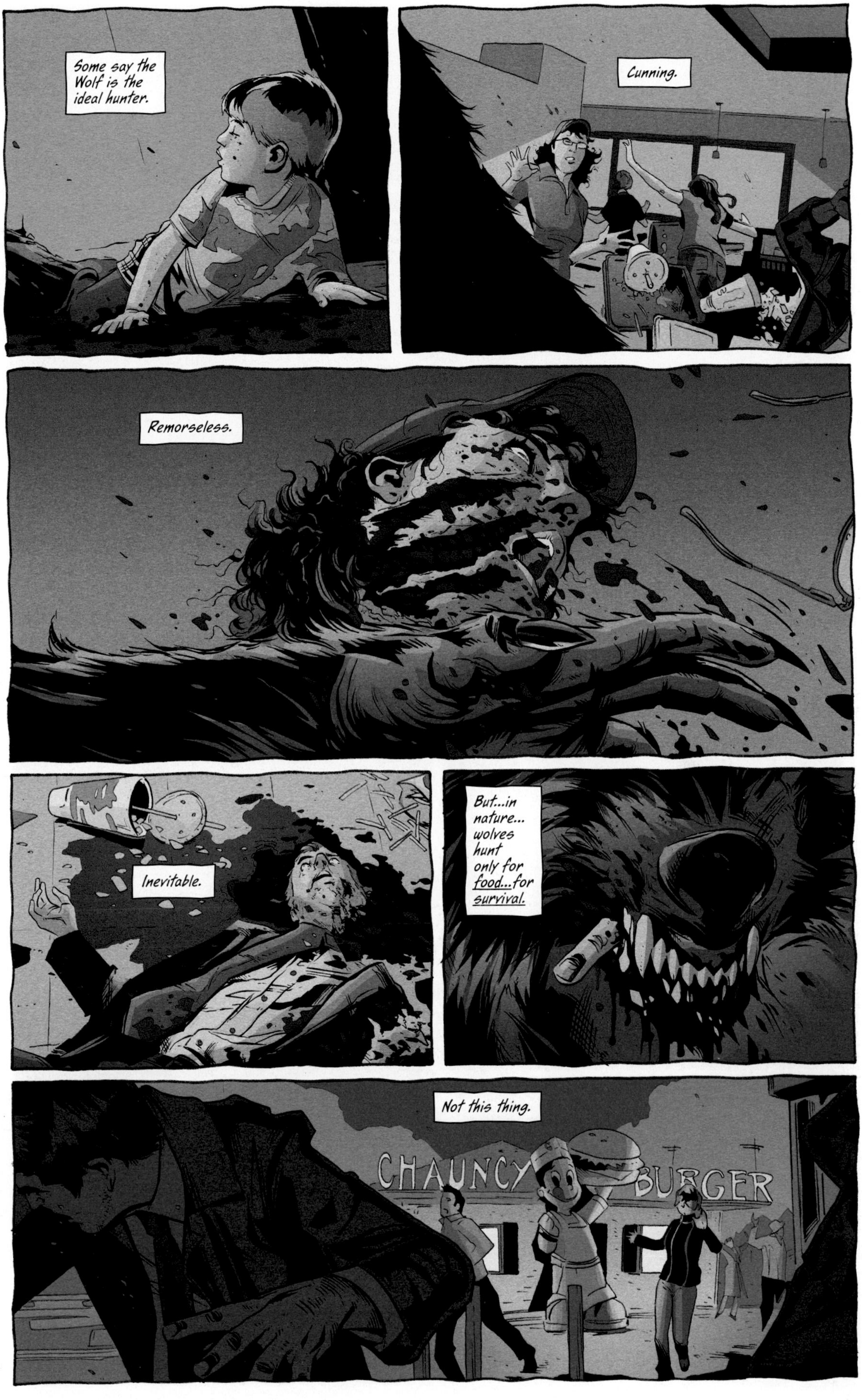
Some say the Wolf is the ideal hunter.
Cunning.
Remorseless.
Inevitable.
But...in nature... wolves hunt only for food...for survival.
Not this thing.
CHAUNCY BURGER

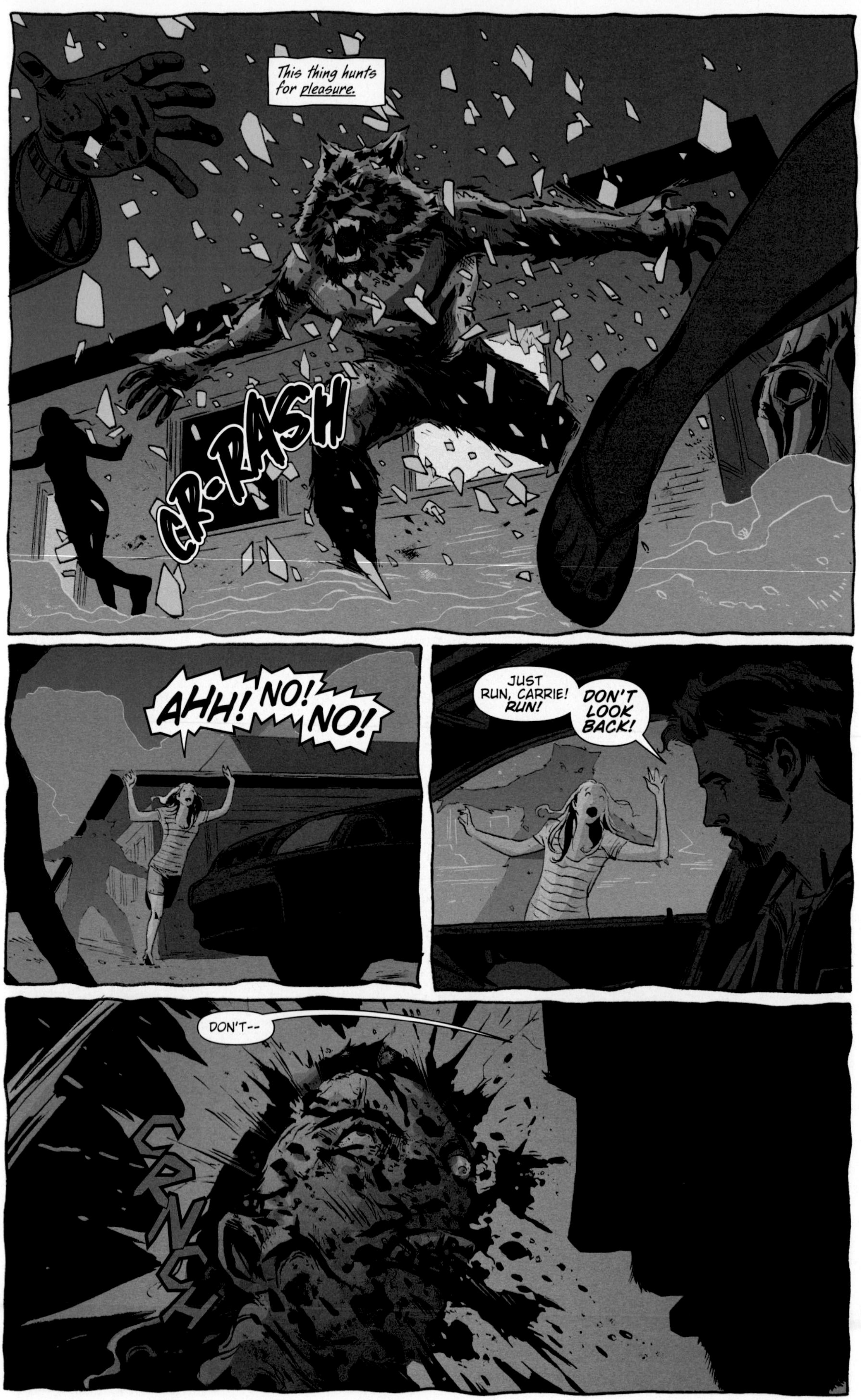
This thing hunts for pleasure.
CR-RASH
AHH! NO! NO!
JUST RUN, CARRIE! RUN!
DON'T LOOK BACK!
DON'T--
CRNCH

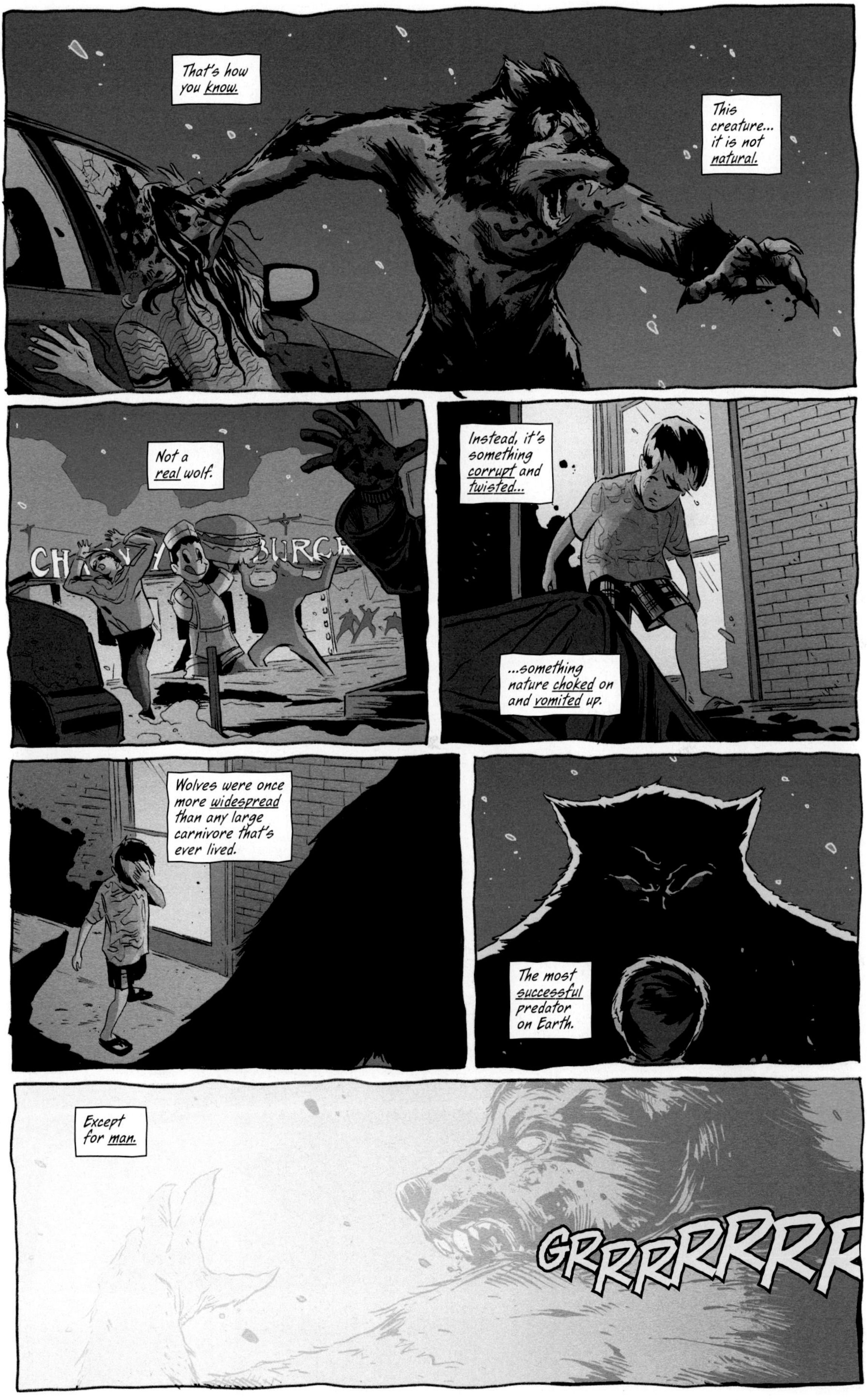
That's how you know.
This creature... it is not natural.
Not a real wolf.
CH BURG
Instead, it's something corrupt and twisted...
...something nature choked on and vomited up.
Wolves were once more widespread than any large carnivore that's ever lived.
The most successful predator on Earth.
Except for man.
GRRRRRRR

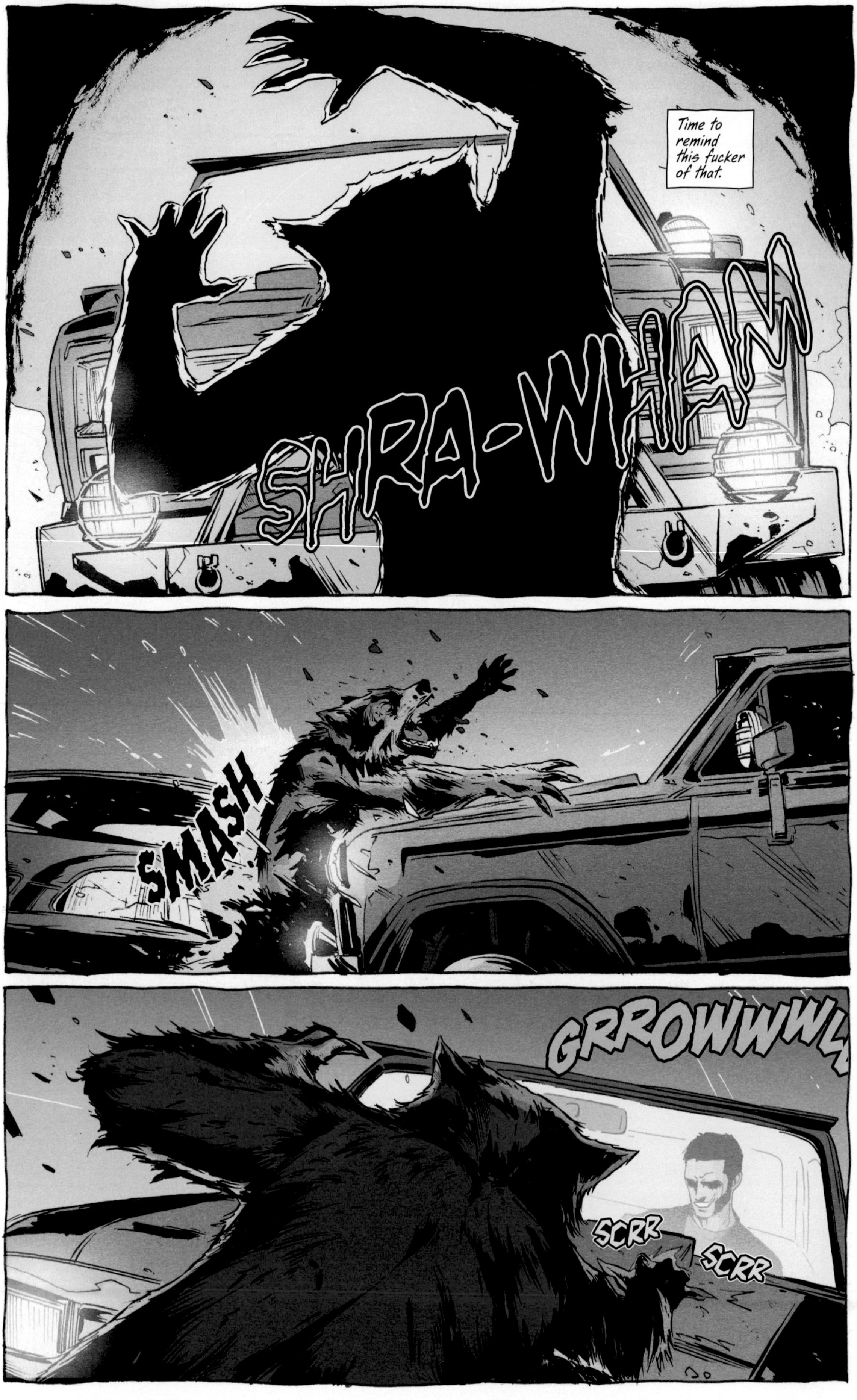
Time to remind this fucker of that.
SHRA-WHAM
SMASH
GRROWWWLL
SCRR
SCRR

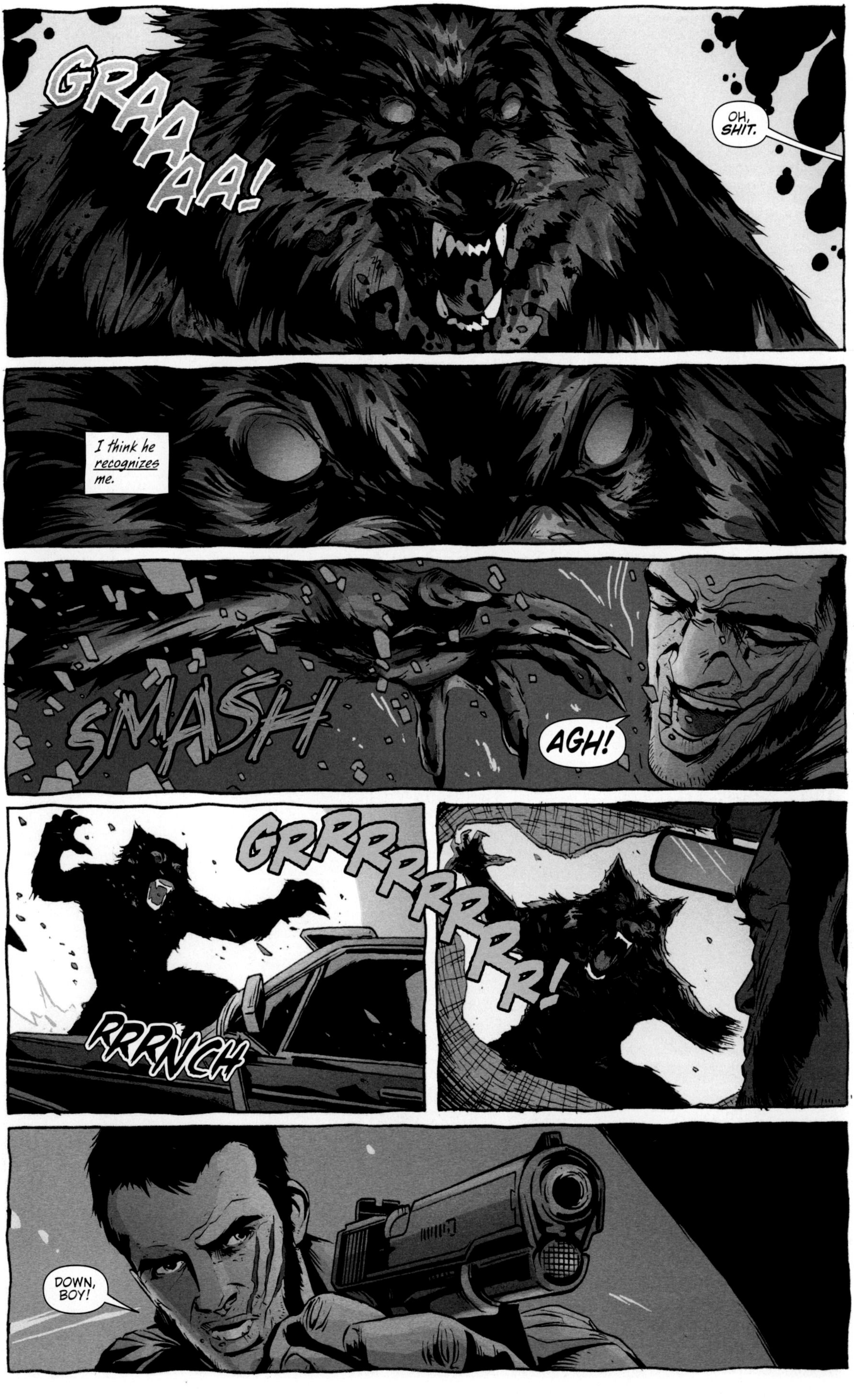
GRAAAAA!
OH, SHIT.
I think he recognizes me.
SMASH
AGH!
GRRRRRRRRR!
RRRNCH
DOWN, BOY!

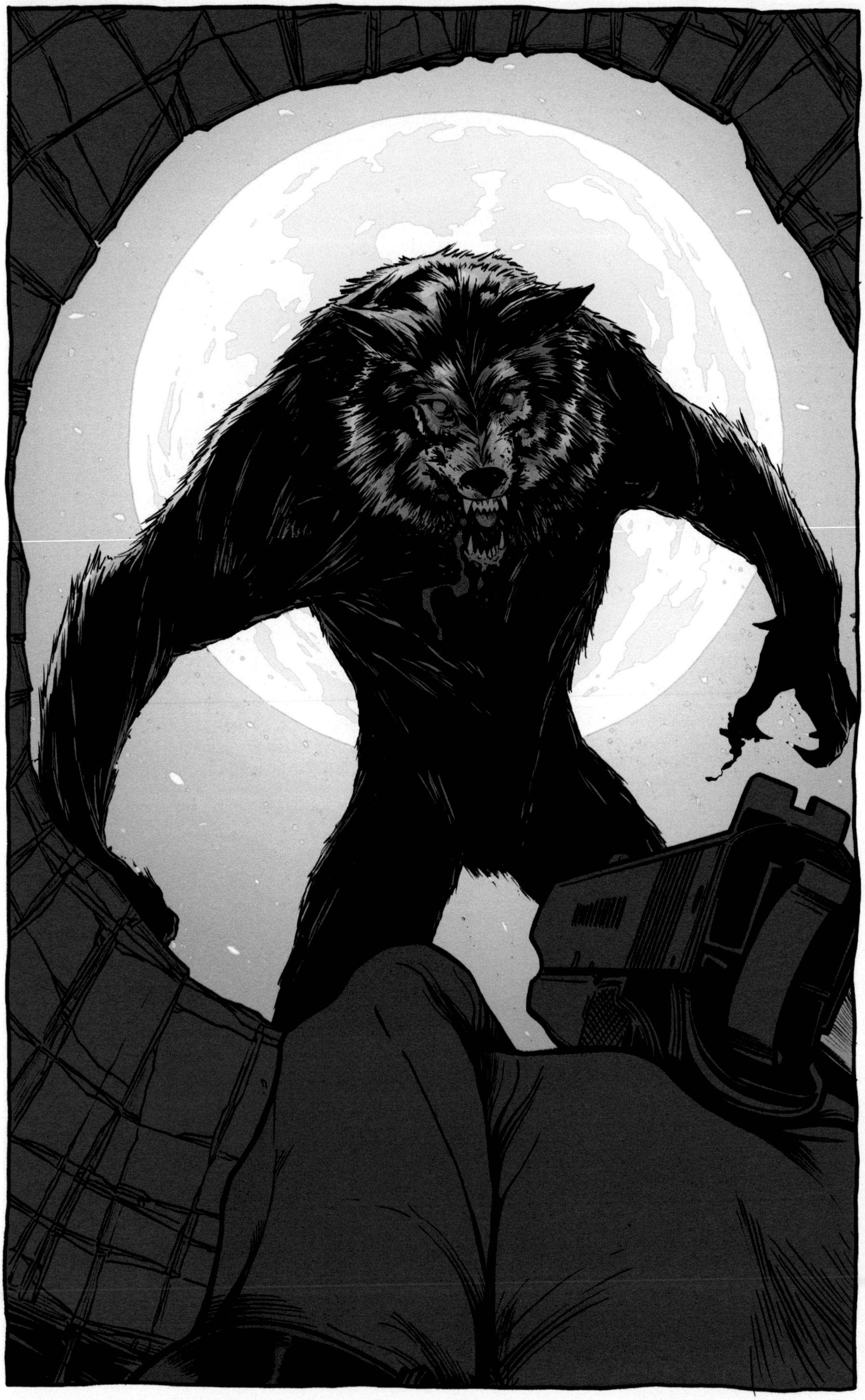

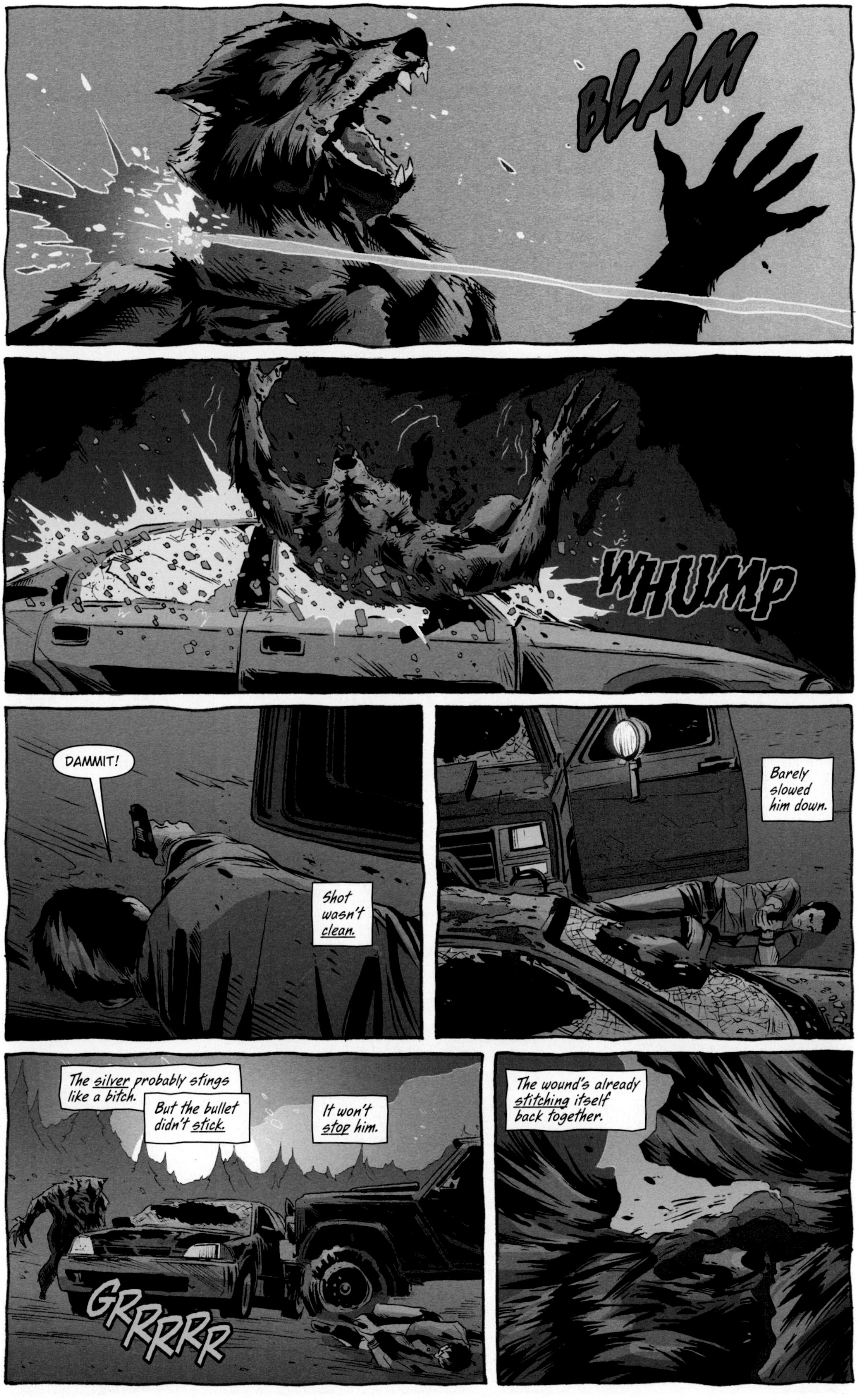
BLAM
WHUMP
DAMMIT!
Shot wasn't clean.
Barely slowed him down.
The silver probably stings like a bitch.
But the bullet didn't stick.
It won't stop him.
GRRRRR
The wound's already stitching itself back together.

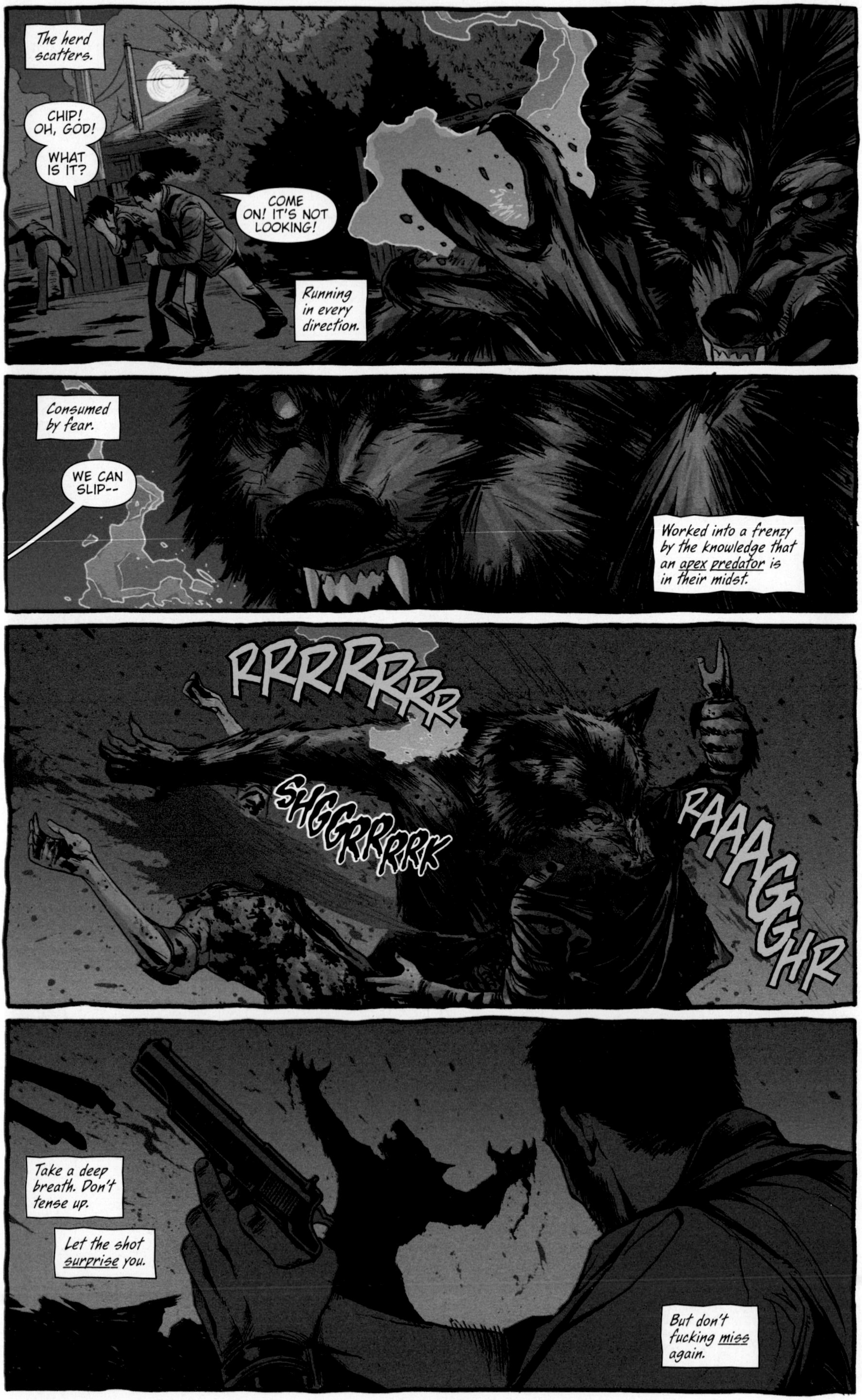
The herd scatters.
CHIP! OH, GOD!
WHAT IS IT?
COME ON! IT'S NOT LOOKING!
Running in every direction.
Consumed by fear.
WE CAN SLIP--
Worked into a frenzy by the knowledge that an apex predator is in their midst.
RRRRRRRR
SHGGRRRRK
RAAAGGHR
Take a deep breath. Don't tense up.
Let the shot surprise you.
But don't fucking miss again.

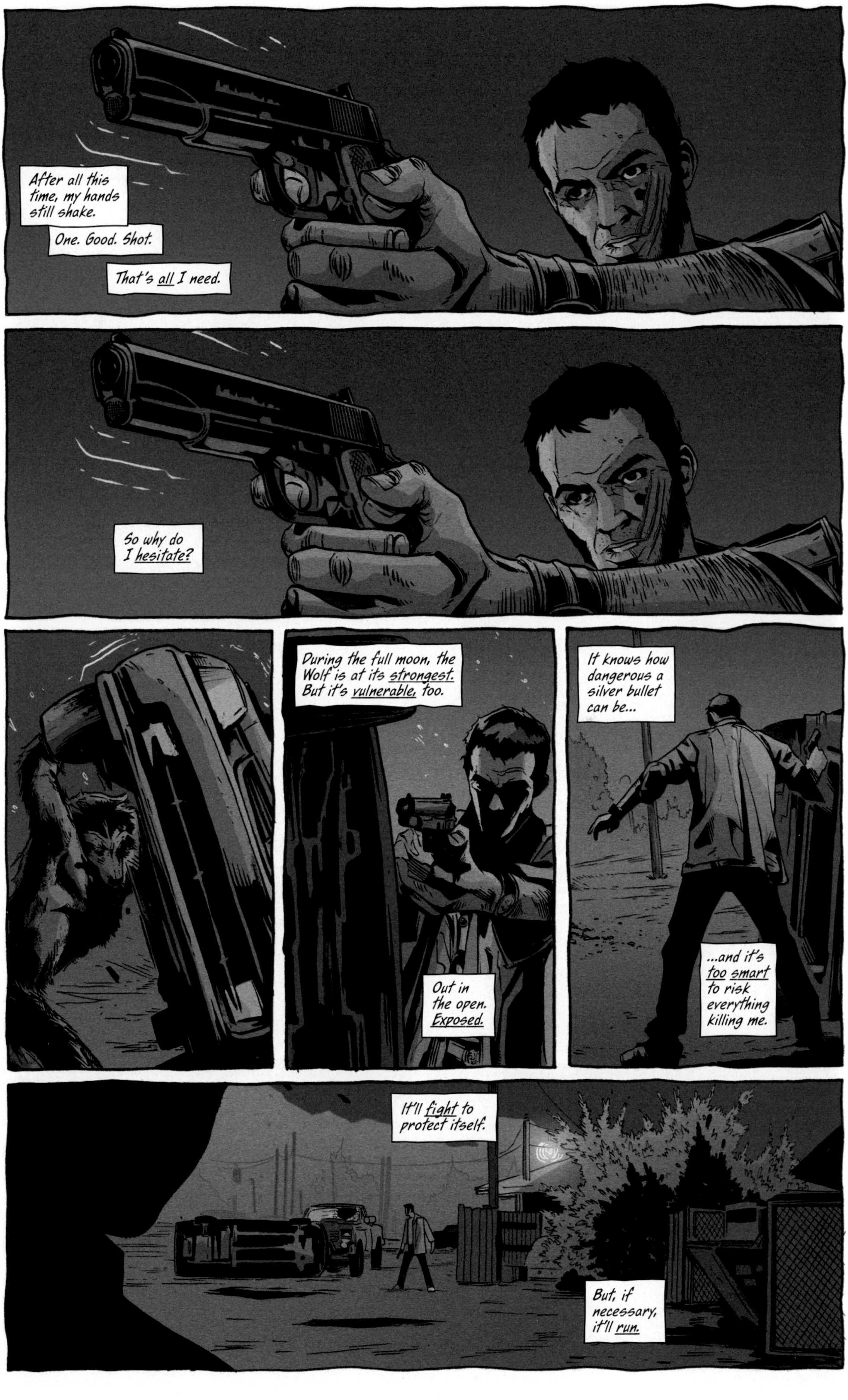

After all this time, my hands still shake.
One. Good. Shot.
That's all I need.
So why do I hesitate?
During the full moon, the Wolf is at its strongest. But it's vulnerable, too.
Out in the open. Exposed.
It knows how dangerous a silver bullet can be...
...and it's too smart to risk everything killing me.
It'll fight to protect itself.
But, if necessary, it'll run.

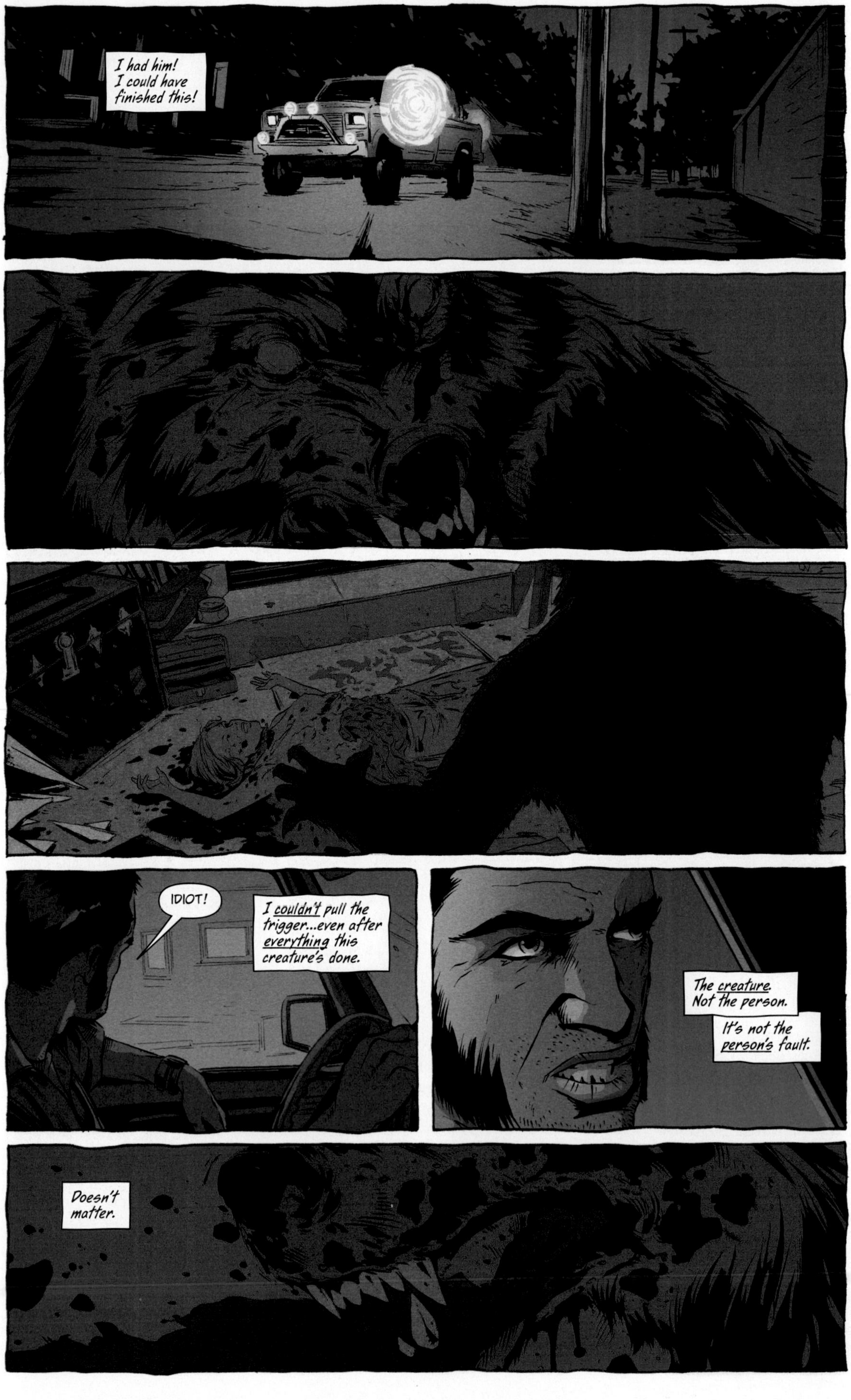
I had him! I could have finished this!
IDIOT!
I couldn't pull the trigger...even after everything this creature's done.
The creature. Not the person.
It's not the person's fault.
Doesn't matter.

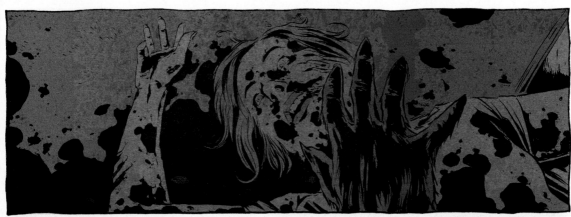

Last night of the cycle.

Haven't been this close in months.

There's no telling how long it will be before it surfaces again.

GONE FISHING

And all it needs to do is avoid me until...

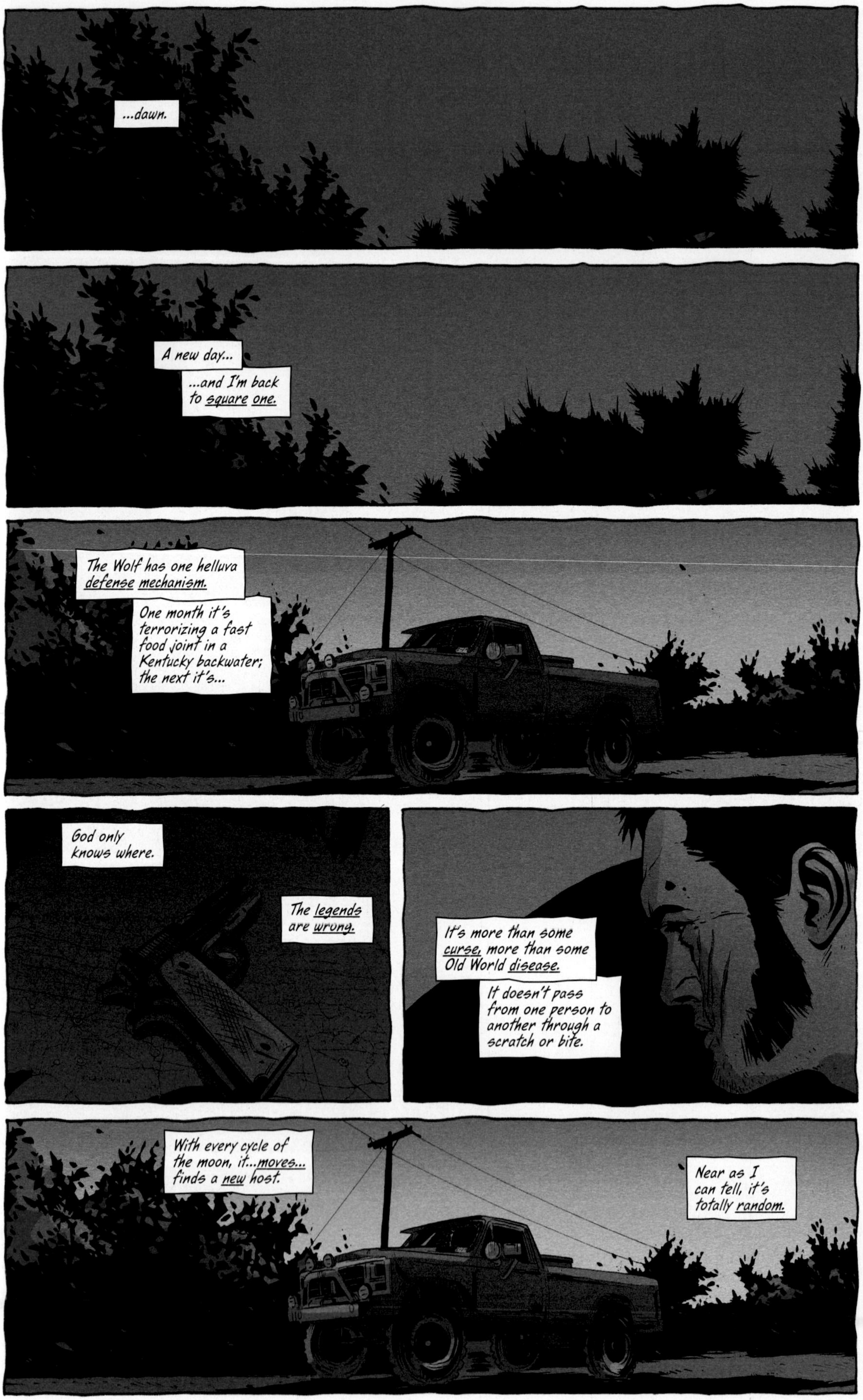

...dawn.
A new day...
...and I'm back to square one.
The Wolf has one helluva defense mechanism.
One month it's terrorizing a fast food joint in a Kentucky backwater; the next it's...
God only knows where.
The legends are wrong.
It's more than some curse, more than some Old World disease.
It doesn't pass from one person to another through a scratch or bite.
With every cycle of the moon, it...moves... finds a new host.
Near as I can tell, it's totally random.

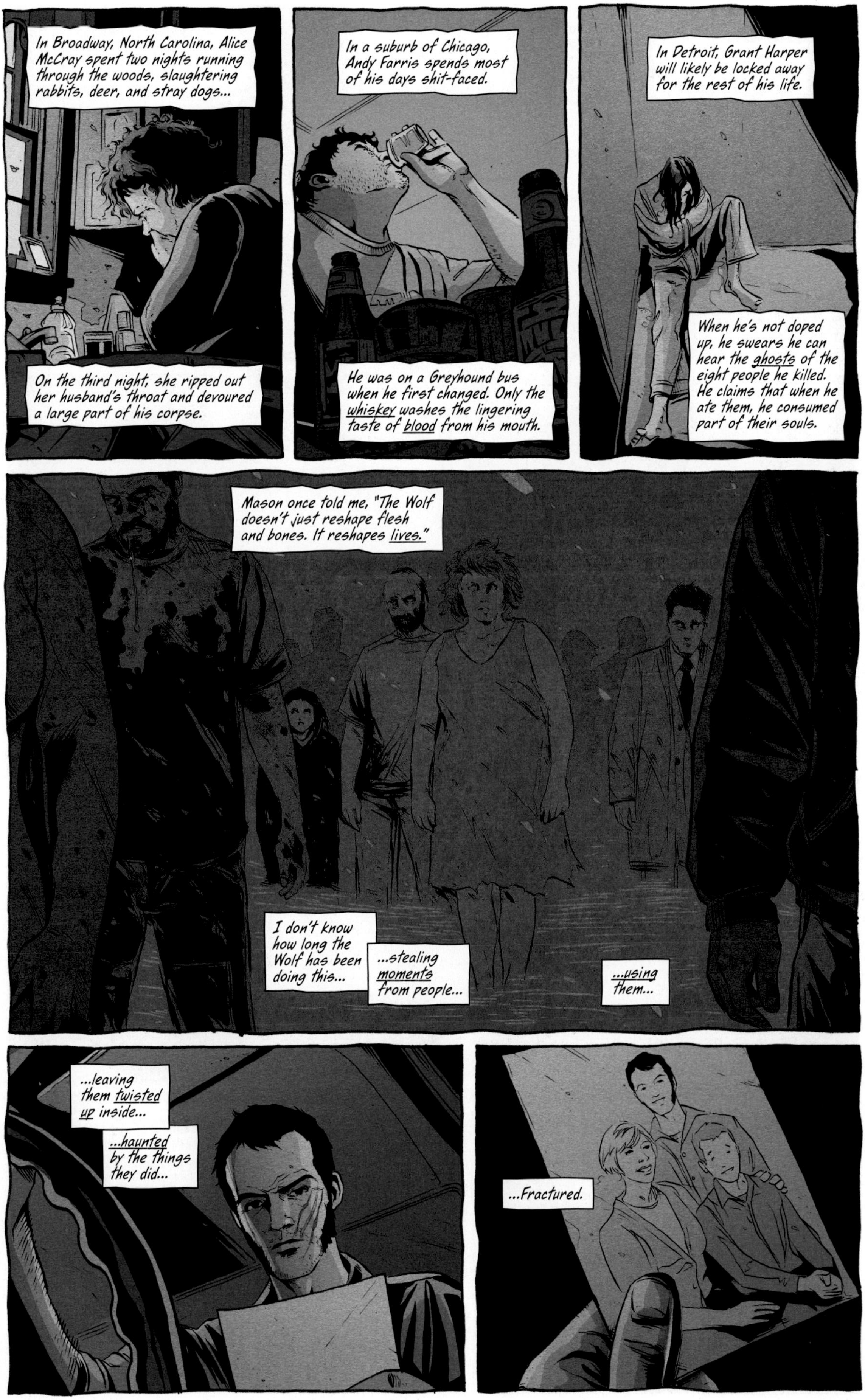
In Broadway, North Carolina, Alice McCray spent two nights running through the woods, slaughtering rabbits, deer, and stray dogs...
On the third night, she ripped out her husband's throat and devoured a large part of his corpse.
In a suburb of Chicago, Andy Farris spends most of his days shit-faced.
He was on a Greyhound bus when he first changed. Only the whiskey washes the lingering taste of blood from his mouth.
In Detroit, Grant Harper will likely be locked away for the rest of his life.
When he's not doped up, he swears he can hear the ghosts of the eight people he killed. He claims that when he ate them, he consumed part of their souls.
Mason once told me, "The Wolf doesn't just reshape flesh and bones. It reshapes lives."
I don't know how long the Wolf has been doing this...
...stealing moments from people...
...using them...
...leaving them twisted up inside...
...haunted by the things they did...
...Fractured.

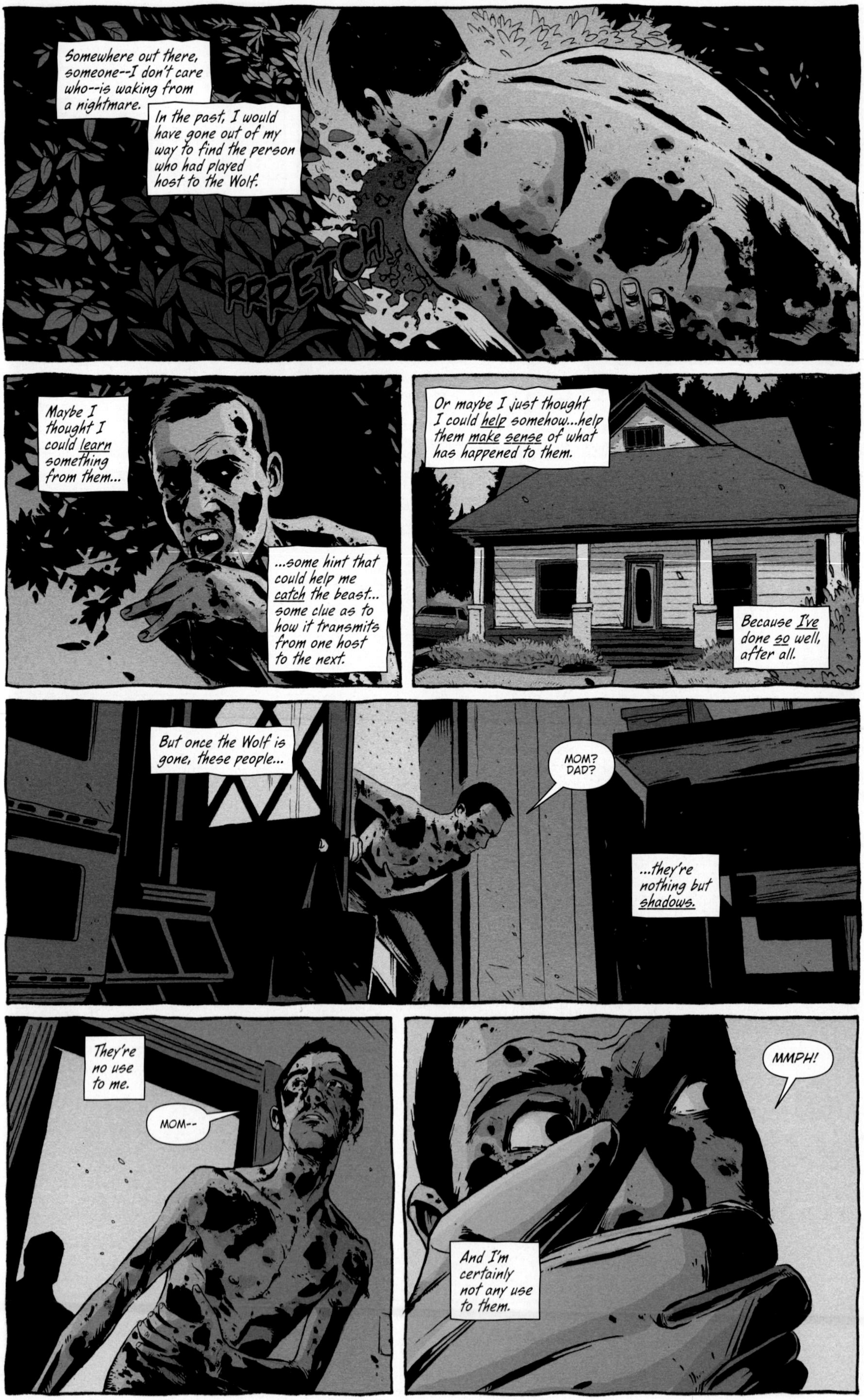
Somewhere out there, someone--I don't care who--is waking from a nightmare.
In the past, I would have gone out of my way to find the person who had played host to the Wolf.
PRRETCH
Maybe I thought I could learn something from them...
...some hint that could help me catch the beast... some clue as to how it transmits from one host to the next.
Or maybe I just thought I could help somehow...help them make sense of what has happened to them.
Because I've done so well, after all.
But once the Wolf is gone, these people...
MOM? DAD?
...they're nothing but shadows.
They're no use to me.
MOM--
MMPH!
And I'm certainly not any use to them.

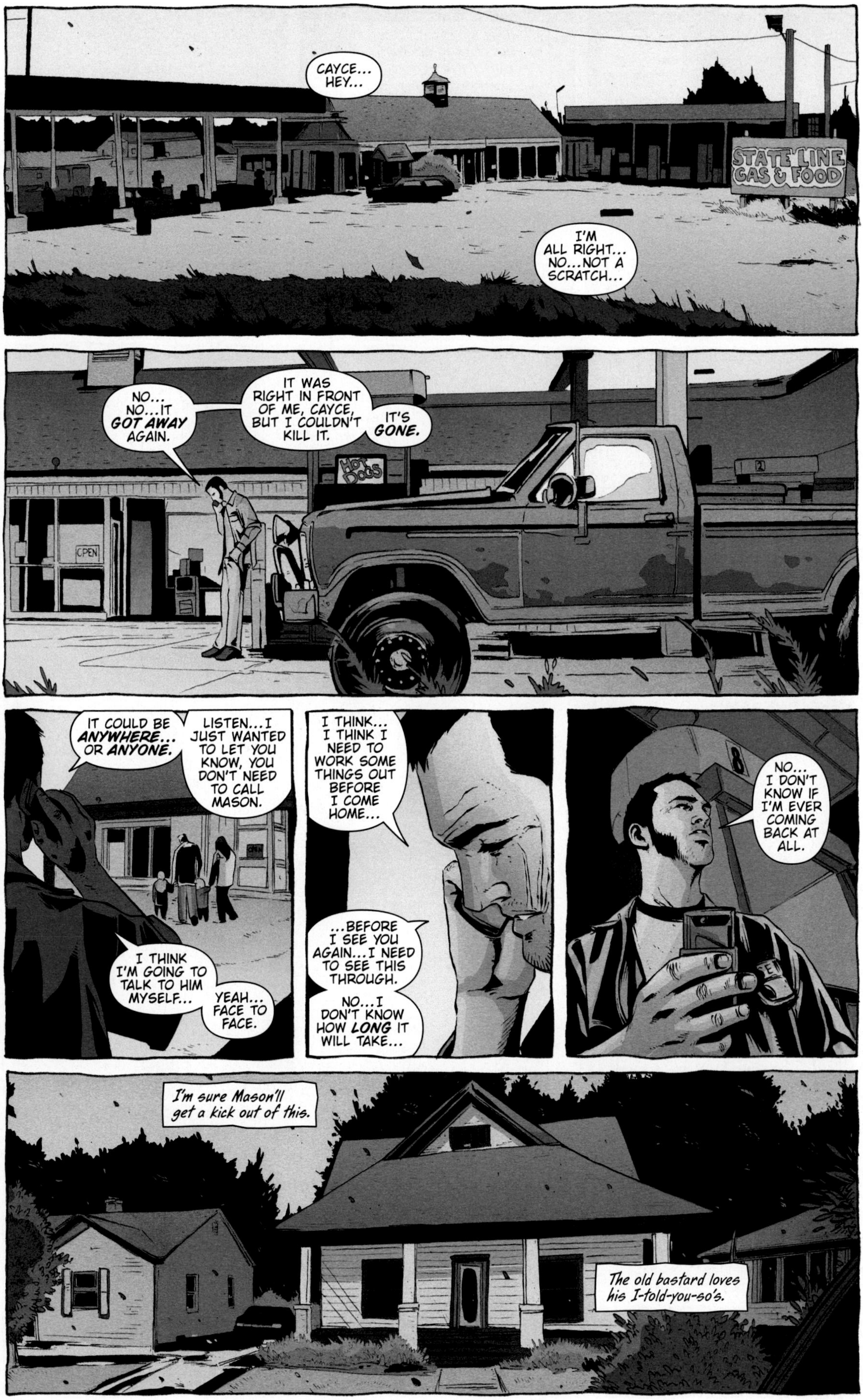

CAYCE... HEY...
STATE LINE GAS & FOOD
I'M ALL RIGHT... NO...NOT A SCRATCH...
NO... NO...IT **GOT AWAY** AGAIN.
IT WAS RIGHT IN FRONT OF ME, CAYCE, BUT I COULDN'T KILL IT.
IT'S **GONE.**
HOT DOGS
OPEN
IT COULD BE **ANYWHERE...** OR **ANYONE.**
LISTEN...I JUST WANTED TO LET YOU KNOW, YOU DON'T NEED TO CALL MASON.
I THINK I'M GOING TO TALK TO HIM MYSELF...
YEAH... FACE TO FACE.
I THINK... I THINK I NEED TO WORK SOME THINGS OUT BEFORE I COME HOME...
...BEFORE I SEE YOU AGAIN...I NEED TO SEE THIS THROUGH.
NO...I DON'T KNOW HOW **LONG** IT WILL TAKE...
NO... I DON'T KNOW IF I'M EVER COMING BACK AT ALL.
*I'm sure Mason'll get a kick out of this.*
*The old bastard loves his I-told-you-so's.*

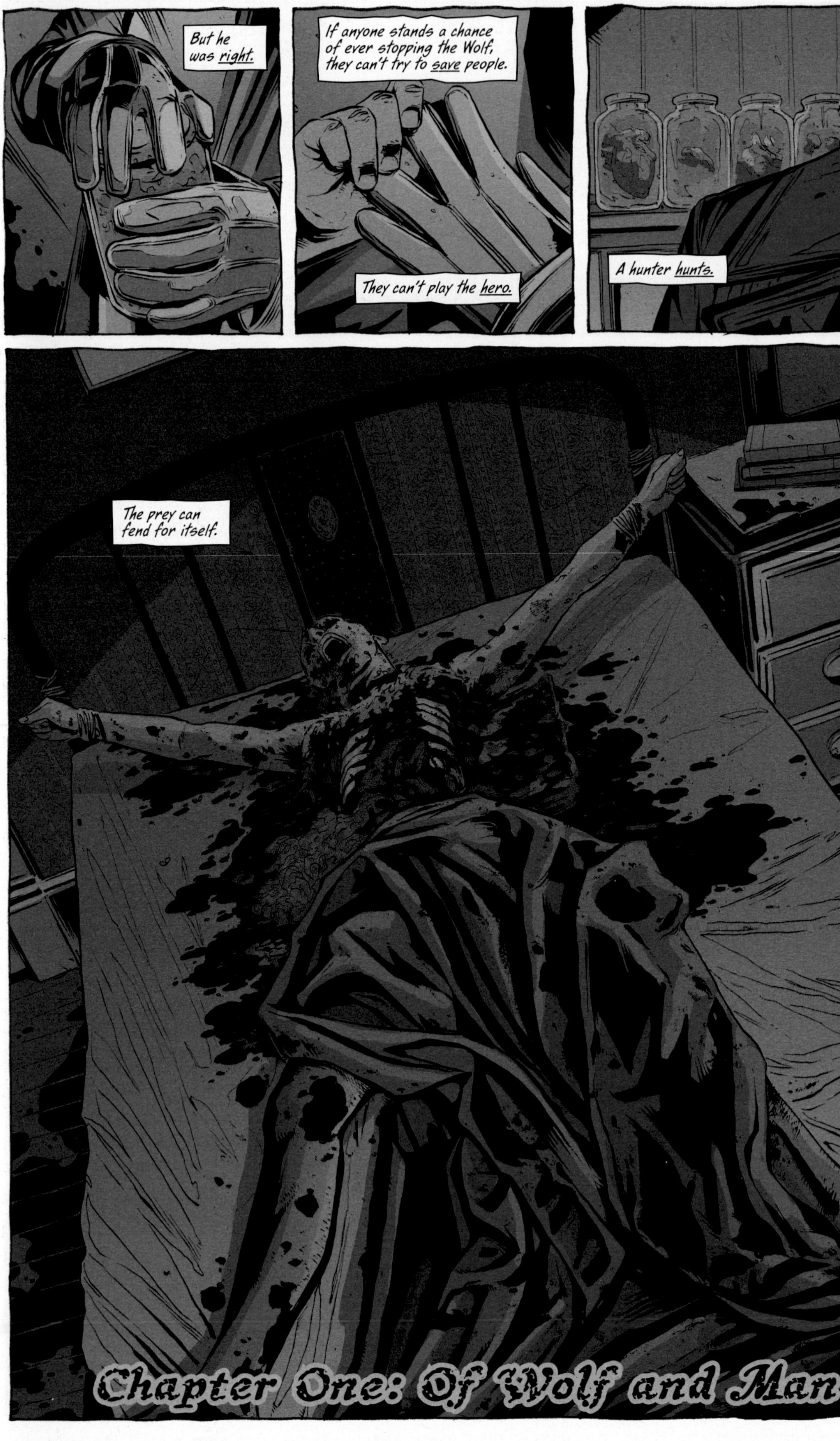

But he was right.
If anyone stands a chance of ever stopping the Wolf, they can't try to save people.
They can't play the hero.
A hunter hunts.
The prey can fend for itself.
Chapter One: Of Wolf and Man

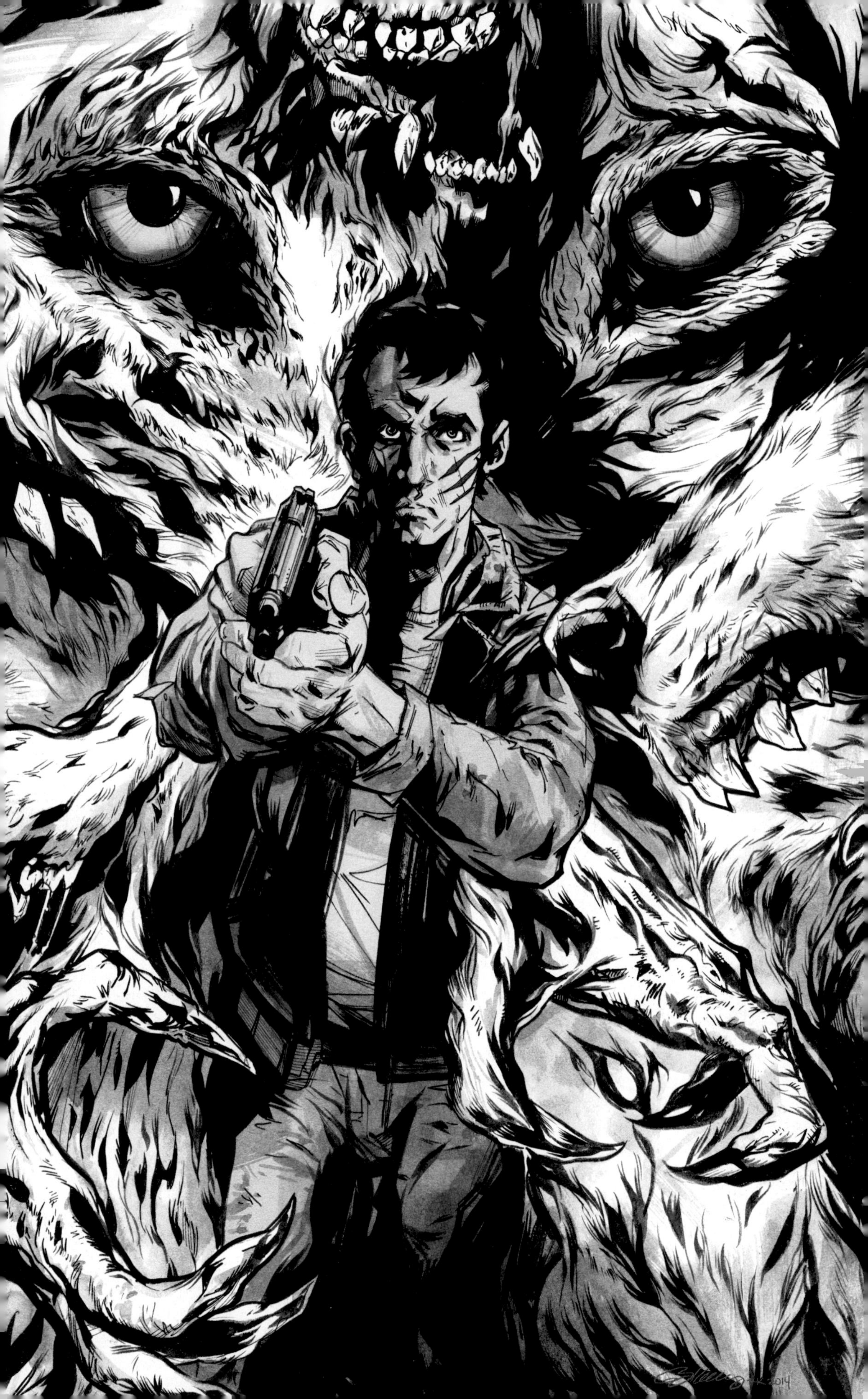

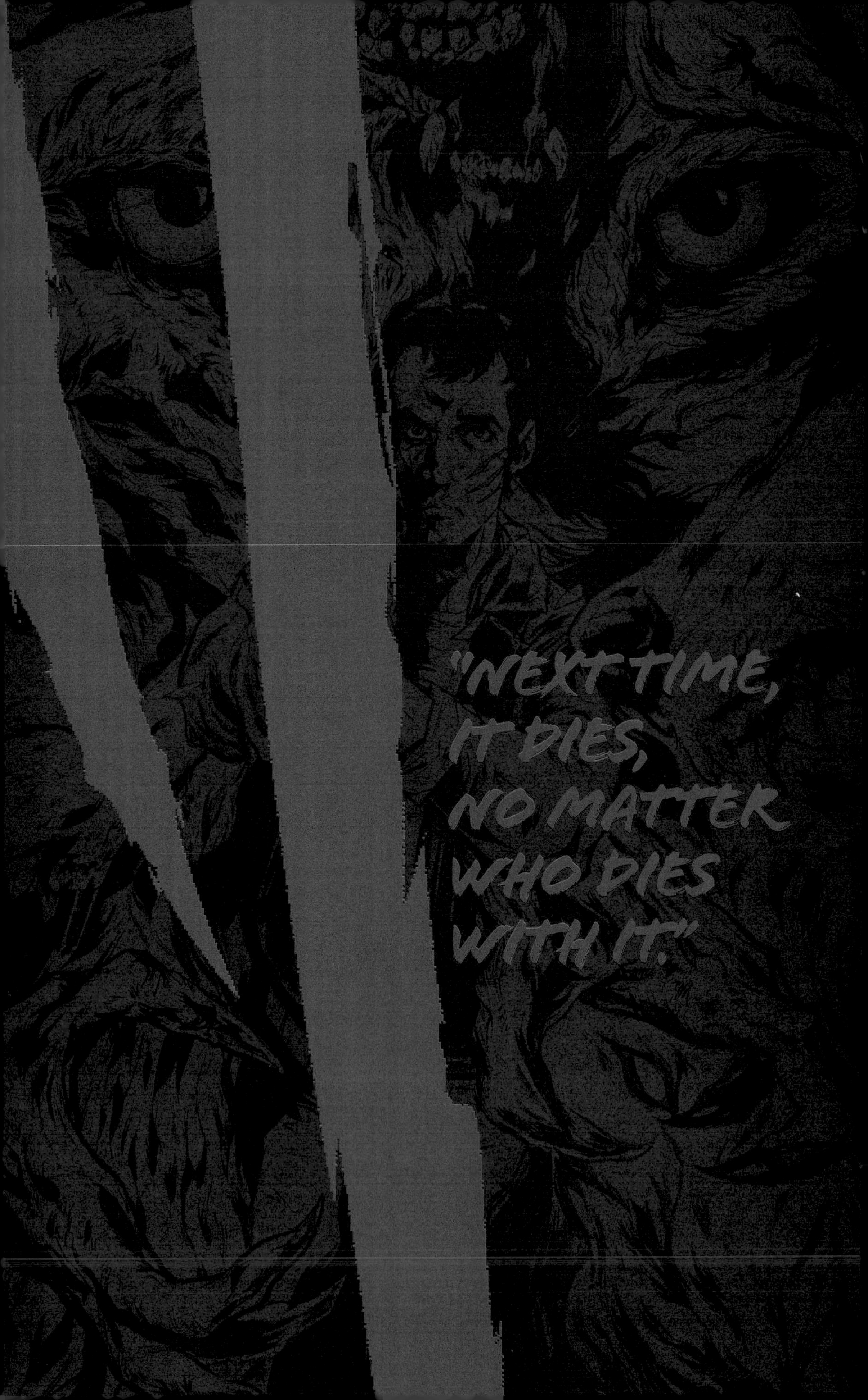
"NEXT TIME,
IT DIES,
NO MATTER
WHO DIES
WITH IT."

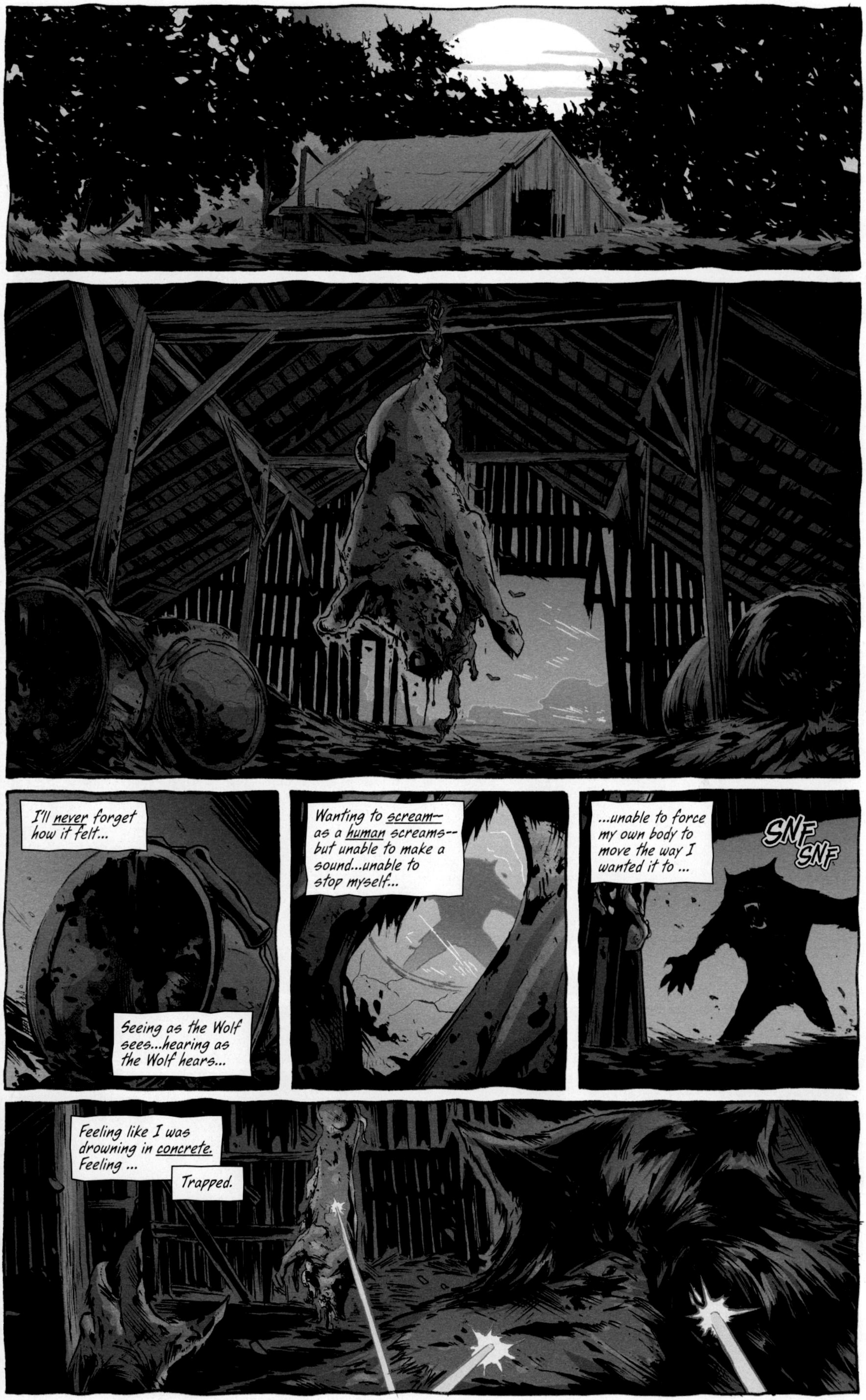
I'll never forget how it felt...
Seeing as the Wolf sees...hearing as the Wolf hears...
Wanting to scream— as a human screams-- but unable to make a sound...unable to stop myself...
...unable to force my own body to move the way I wanted it to ...
SNF SNF
Feeling like I was drowning in concrete. Feeling ...
Trapped.

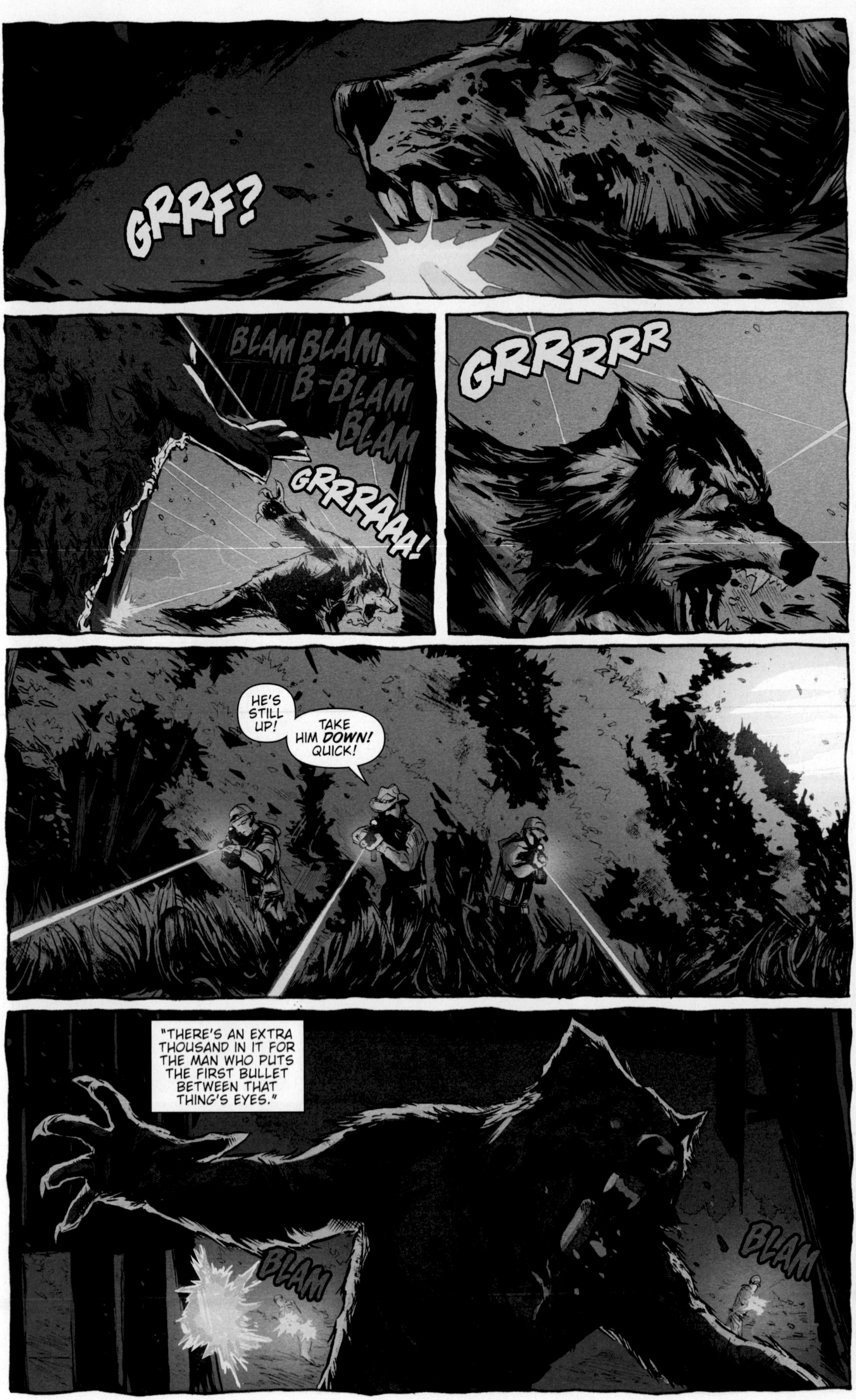
GRRF?
BLAM BLAM
B-BLAM
BLAM
GRRRAAA!
GRRRRR
HE'S STILL UP!
TAKE HIM DOWN! QUICK!
"THERE'S AN EXTRA THOUSAND IN IT FOR THE MAN WHO PUTS THE FIRST BULLET BETWEEN THAT THING'S EYES."
BLAM
BLAM

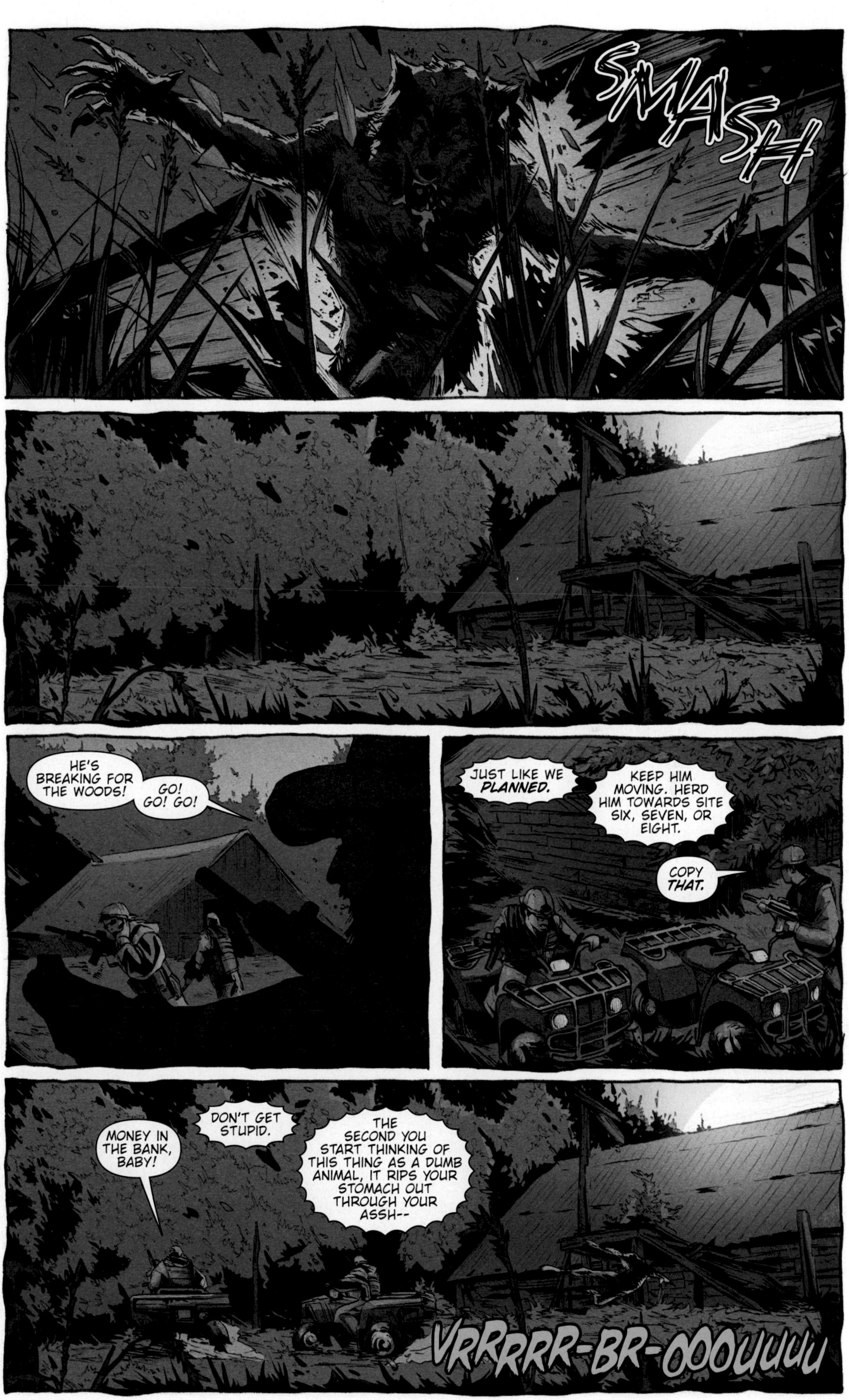
SMASH
HE'S BREAKING FOR THE WOODS!
GO! GO! GO!
JUST LIKE WE PLANNED.
KEEP HIM MOVING. HERD HIM TOWARDS SITE SIX, SEVEN, OR EIGHT.
COPY THAT.
MONEY IN THE BANK, BABY!
DON'T GET STUPID.
THE SECOND YOU START THINKING OF THIS THING AS A DUMB ANIMAL, IT RIPS YOUR STOMACH OUT THROUGH YOUR ASSH--
VRRRRR-BR-OOOuuuu

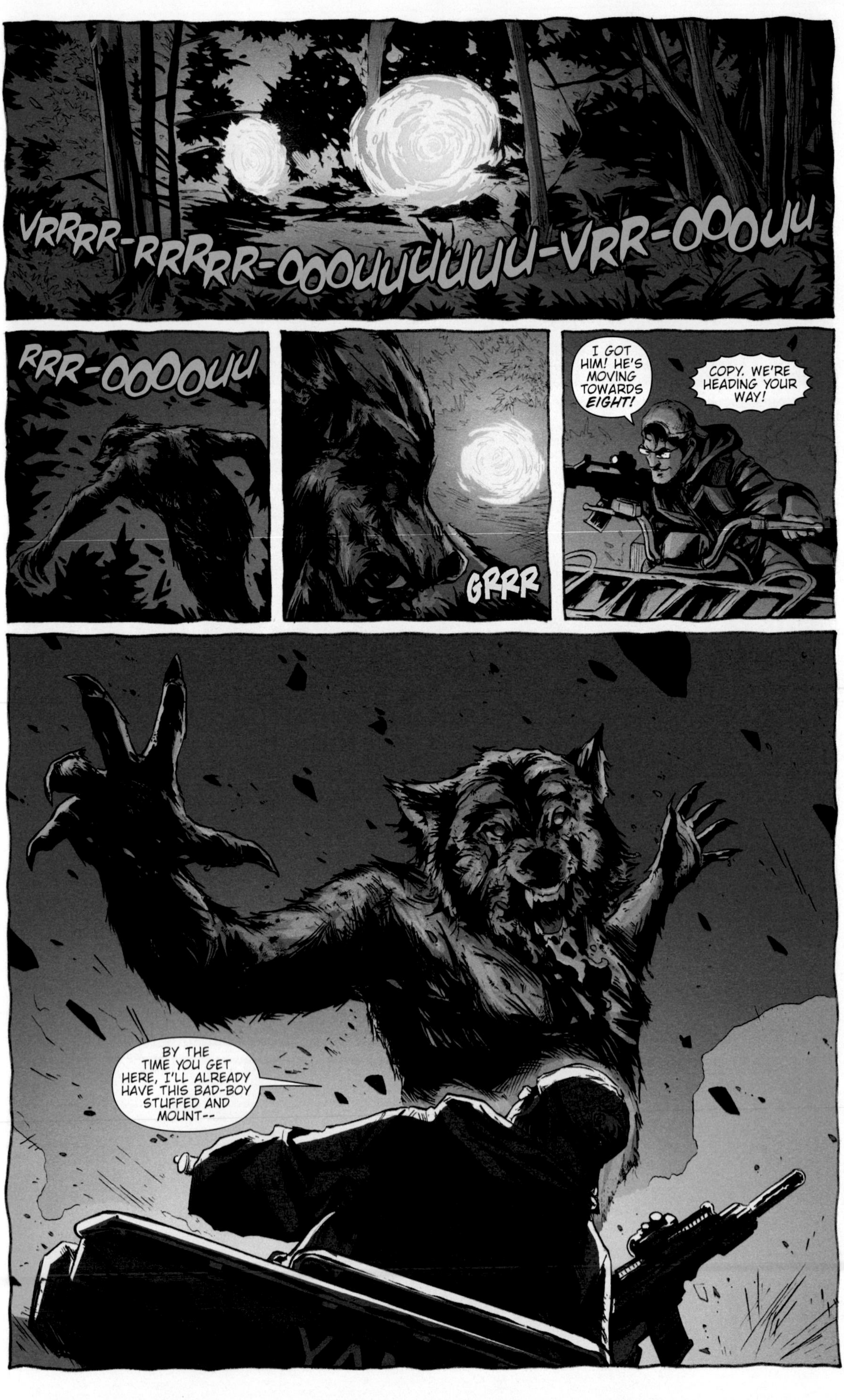
VRRRR-RRRRR-OOOUUUUUU-VRR-OOOUU
RRR-OOOOUU
GRRR
I GOT HIM! HE'S MOVING TOWARDS *EIGHT!*
COPY. WE'RE HEADING YOUR WAY!
BY THE TIME YOU GET HERE, I'LL ALREADY HAVE THIS BAD-BOY STUFFED AND MOUNT--

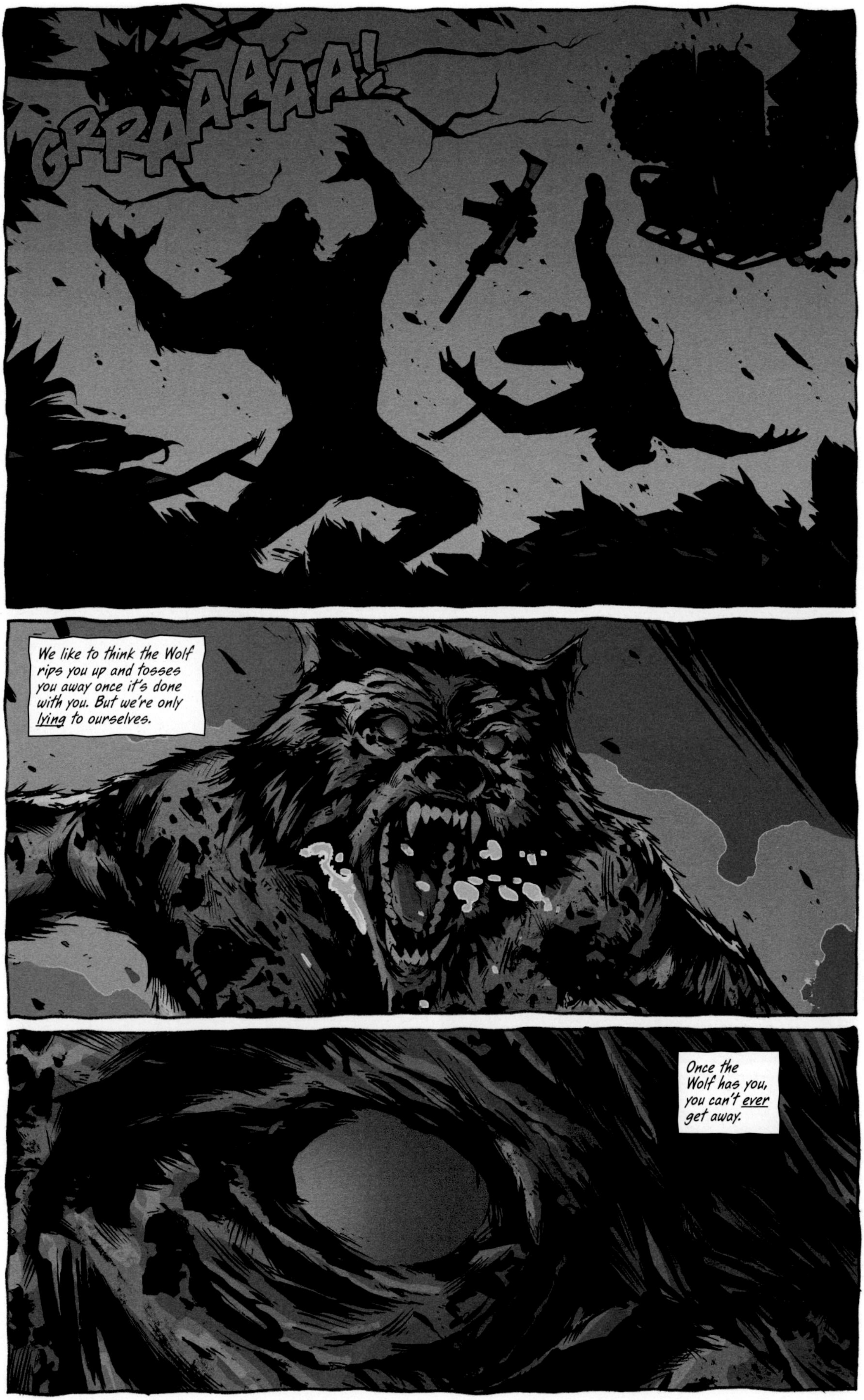
GRRAAAAAA!
We like to think the Wolf rips you up and tosses you away once it's done with you. But we're only lying to ourselves.
Once the Wolf has you, you can't ever get away.

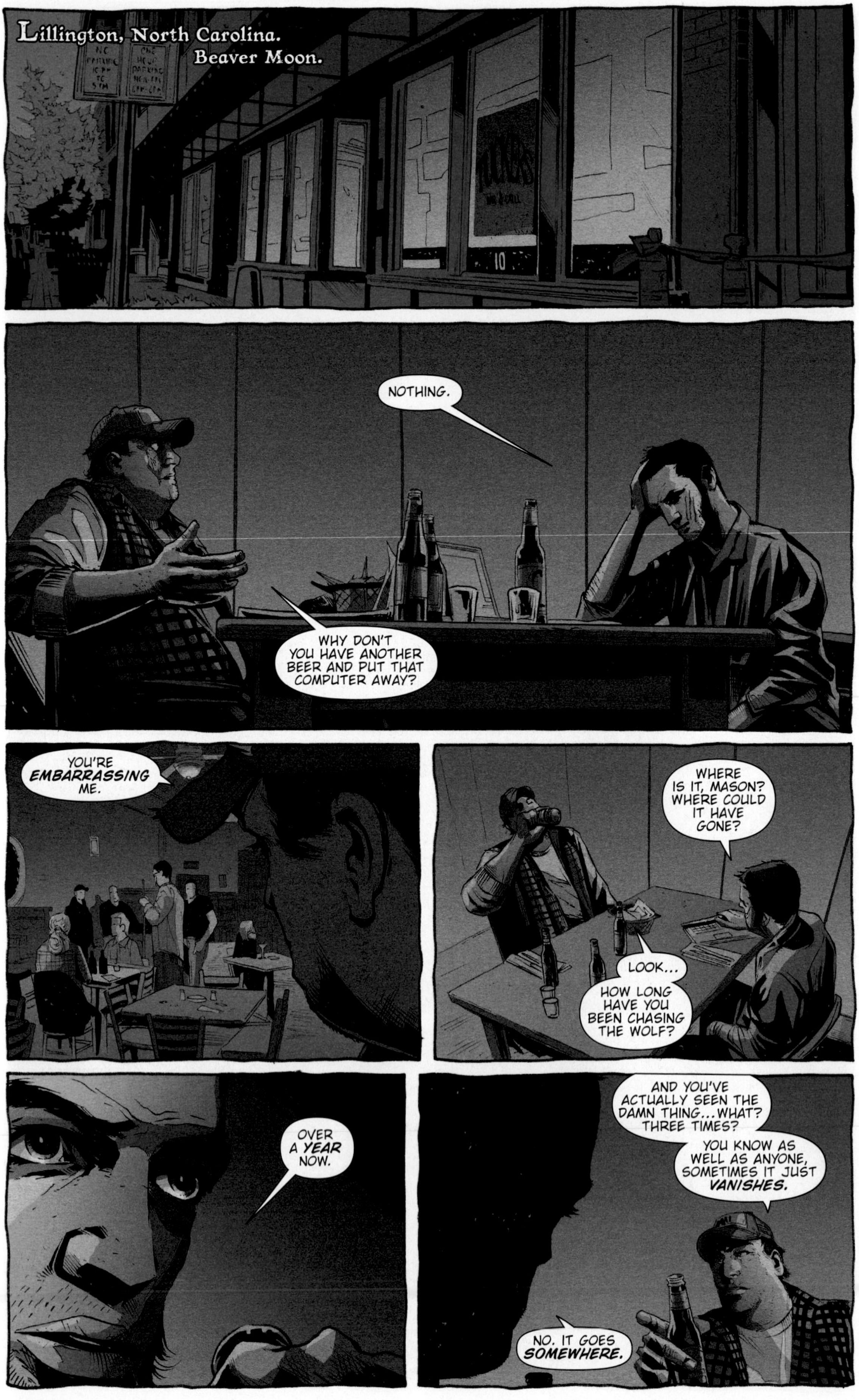
Lillington, North Carolina.
Beaver Moon.
NOTHING.
WHY DON'T YOU HAVE ANOTHER BEER AND PUT THAT COMPUTER AWAY?
YOU'RE EMBARRASSING ME.
WHERE IS IT, MASON? WHERE COULD IT HAVE GONE?
LOOK...
HOW LONG HAVE YOU BEEN CHASING THE WOLF?
OVER A YEAR NOW.
AND YOU'VE ACTUALLY SEEN THE DAMN THING...WHAT? THREE TIMES?
YOU KNOW AS WELL AS ANYONE, SOMETIMES IT JUST VANISHES.
NO. IT GOES SOMEWHERE.

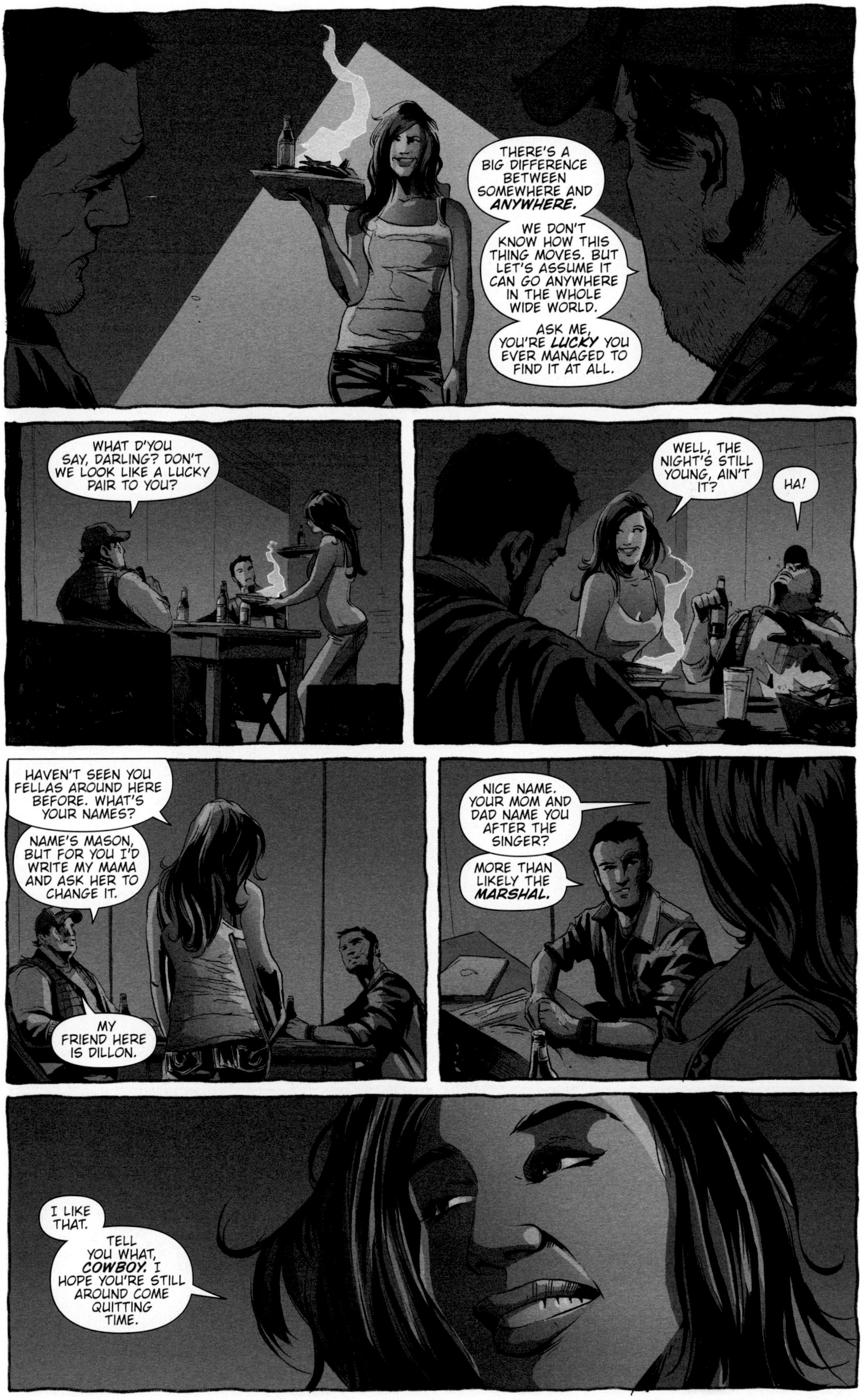

THERE'S A BIG DIFFERENCE BETWEEN SOMEWHERE AND ANYWHERE.
WE DON'T KNOW HOW THIS THING MOVES. BUT LET'S ASSUME IT CAN GO ANYWHERE IN THE WHOLE WIDE WORLD.
ASK ME, YOU'RE LUCKY YOU EVER MANAGED TO FIND IT AT ALL.
WHAT D'YOU SAY, DARLING? DON'T WE LOOK LIKE A LUCKY PAIR TO YOU?
WELL, THE NIGHT'S STILL YOUNG, AIN'T IT?
HA!
HAVEN'T SEEN YOU FELLAS AROUND HERE BEFORE. WHAT'S YOUR NAMES?
NAME'S MASON, BUT FOR YOU I'D WRITE MY MAMA AND ASK HER TO CHANGE IT.
MY FRIEND HERE IS DILLON.
NICE NAME. YOUR MOM AND DAD NAME YOU AFTER THE SINGER?
MORE THAN LIKELY THE MARSHAL.
I LIKE THAT.
TELL YOU WHAT, COWBOY. I HOPE YOU'RE STILL AROUND COME QUITTING TIME.

WHOO! YOU'D BEST LOOK LIVELY. THAT GIRL'S GOT HER EYES ON YOU.

SHE'S GOT HER EYES ON A BETTER TIP.

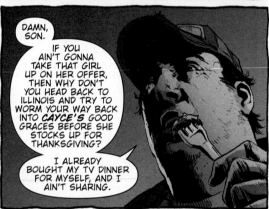

DAMN, SON. IF YOU AIN'T GONNA TAKE THAT GIRL UP ON HER OFFER, THEN WHY DON'T YOU HEAD BACK TO ILLINOIS AND TRY TO WORM YOUR WAY BACK INTO *CAYCE'S* GOOD GRACES BEFORE SHE STOCKS UP FOR THANKSGIVING?

I ALREADY BOUGHT MY TV DINNER FOR MYSELF, AND I AIN'T SHARING.

I TOLD YOU, I *CAN'T* GO BACK TO CAYCE.

I'M NO GOOD FOR HER. I'M A WRECK.

I TRY TO LIVE A *NORMAL* LIFE.

BUT I CAN'T EVEN EAT A "NORMAL" MEAL ANY MORE.

NO MATTER HOW MUCH THEY COOK THE MEAT, I CAN STILL TASTE THE *BLOOD.*

HERE'S THE THING.

WE KNOW THE WOLF JUMPS FROM PERSON TO PERSON WITH EVERY FULL MOON.

SAME CREATURE, AS NEAR AS WE CAN TELL, BUT A DIFFERENT PERSON EVERY MONTH. NEVER THE SAME PERSON TWICE.

WHAT IF WE'RE *WRONG* ABOUT THAT PART? WHAT IF I CHANGE AGAIN?

...

I'M NOT GOING TO RISK GETTING CLOSE TO ANYONE ELSE, NOT UNTIL THE WOLF IS DEAD, ONCE AND FOR ALL.

OKAY. I GET WHERE YOU'RE COMING FROM, BUT I CAN'T BE THE ONLY PERSON YOU INTERACT WITH. HELL! I DON'T EVEN LIKE MYSELF *THAT* MUCH!

YOU USED TO *HELP* PEOPLE... PEOPLE LIKE YOU...

PEOPLE LIKE *ME*.

GOTTA ADMIT, I NEVER EXPECTED TO HEAR THAT FROM YOU.

WASN'T IT *YOU* WHO SAID HELPING PEOPLE IS A WASTE OF TIME?

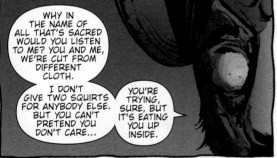

WHY IN THE NAME OF ALL THAT'S SACRED WOULD YOU LISTEN TO ME? YOU AND ME, WE'RE CUT FROM DIFFERENT CLOTH.

I DON'T GIVE TWO SQUIRTS FOR ANYBODY ELSE. BUT YOU CAN'T PRETEND YOU DON'T CARE...

YOU'RE TRYING, SURE, BUT IT'S EATING YOU UP INSIDE.

I'LL HAVE TO LIVE WITH THAT.

I HAD THE WOLF IN MY SIGHTS, MASON. I HAD MY FINGER ON THE TRIGGER. I WAS READY TO PUT ONE OF THE SILVER BULLETS YOU FORGED RIGHT IN ITS HEART.

AND I *HESITATED* BECAUSE I KNEW THERE WAS AN INNOCENT PERSON TRAPPED INSIDE IT.

WHAT AM I SUPPOSED TO DO? WAIT UNTIL AN *ASSHOLE* CHANGES?

WHY NOT? WORLD'S FULL OF 'EM. CAN'T IMAGINE YOU'D BE TWIDDLING YOUR THUMBS FOR LONG.

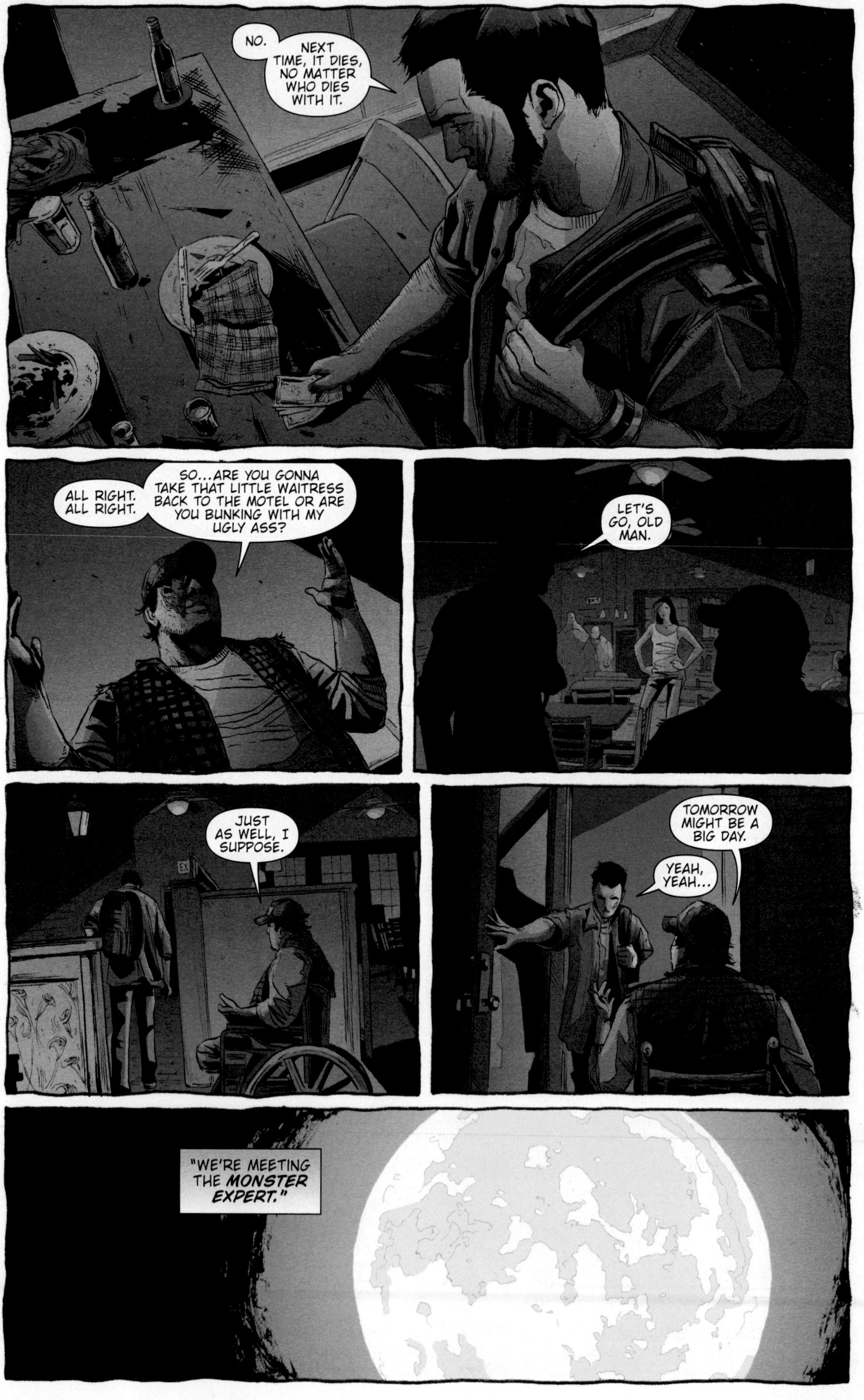
NO.
NEXT TIME, IT DIES, NO MATTER WHO DIES WITH IT.
ALL RIGHT. ALL RIGHT.
SO...ARE YOU GONNA TAKE THAT LITTLE WAITRESS BACK TO THE MOTEL OR ARE YOU BUNKING WITH MY UGLY ASS?
LET'S GO, OLD MAN.
JUST AS WELL, I SUPPOSE.
TOMORROW MIGHT BE A BIG DAY.
YEAH, YEAH...
"WE'RE MEETING THE *MONSTER EXPERT.*"

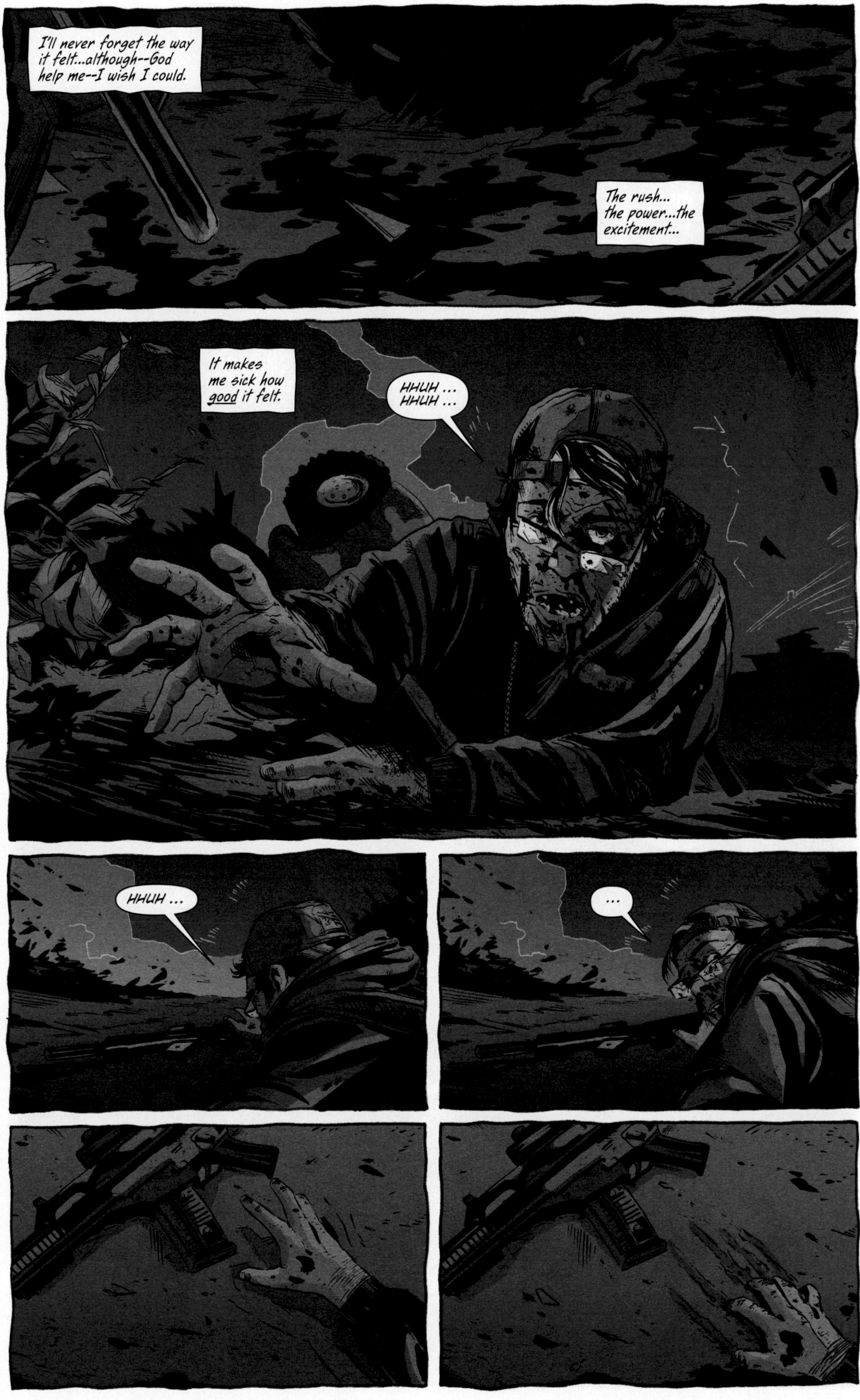
I'll never forget the way it felt...although--God help me--I wish I could.
The rush... the power...the excitement...
It makes me sick how good it felt.
HHUH ... HHUH ...
HHUH ...
...

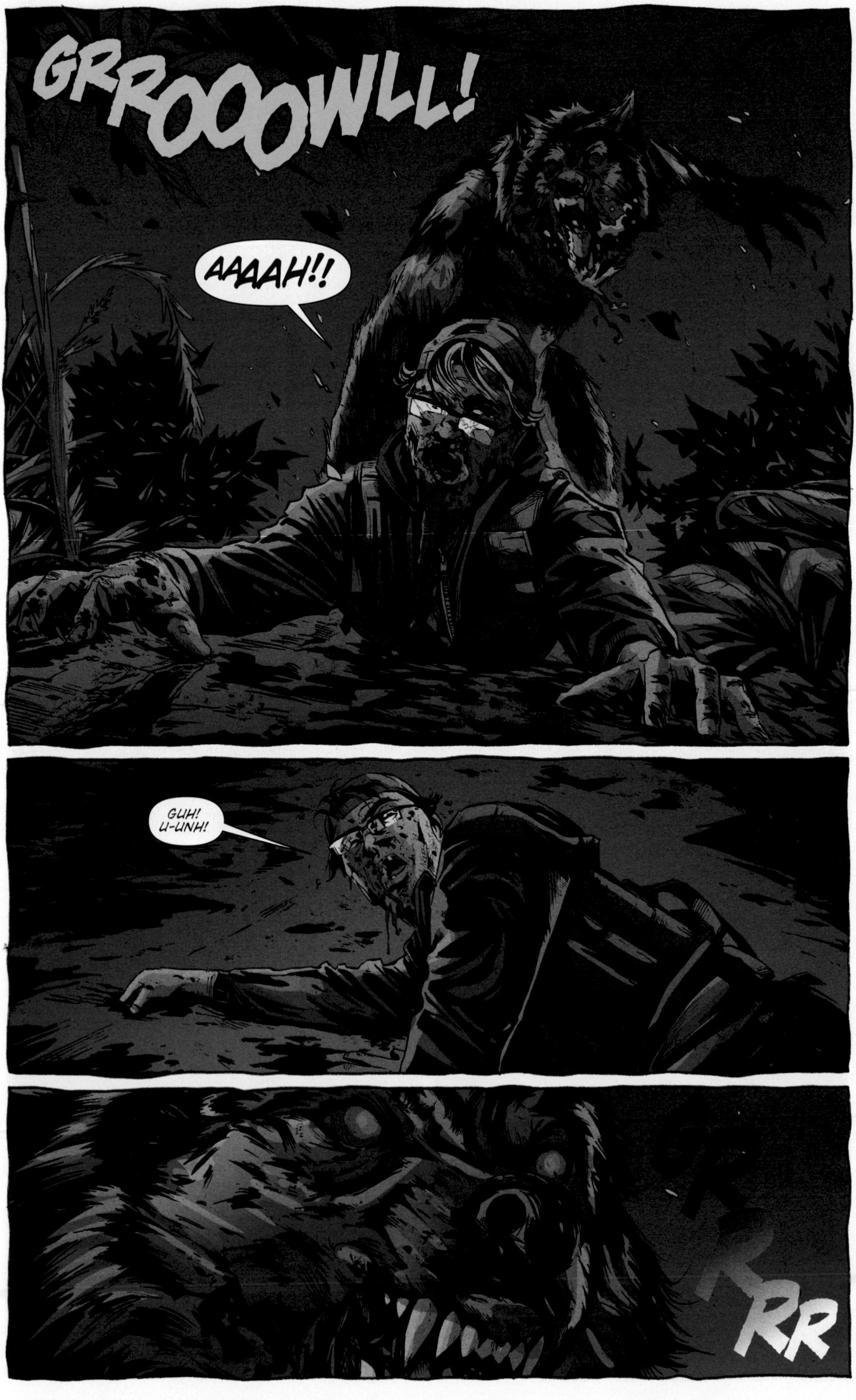
GRROOOWLL!
AAAAH!!
GUH! U-UNH!
RRRR

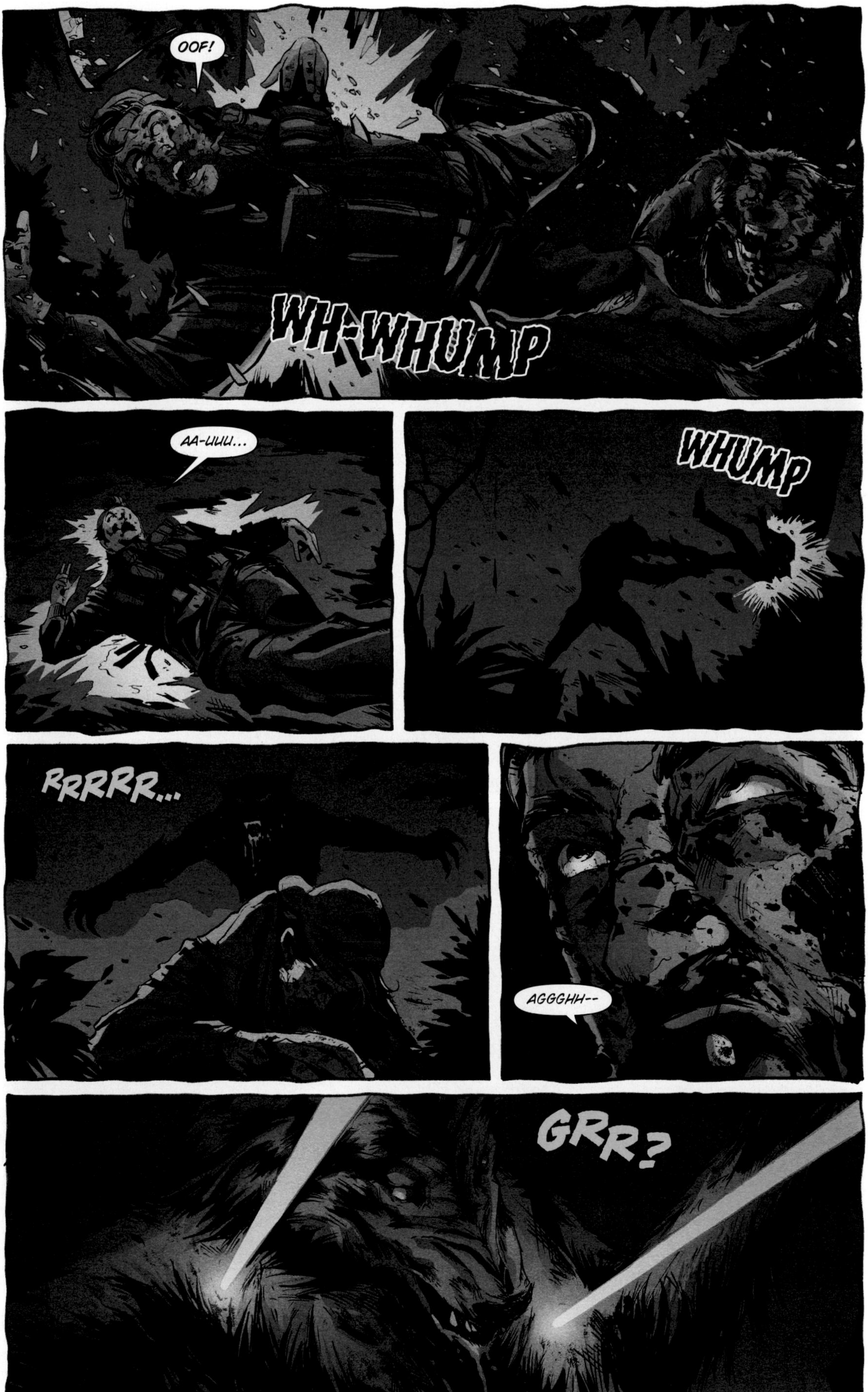
OOF!
WH-WHUMP
AA-UUU...
WHUMP
RRRRR...
AGGGHH--
GRR?

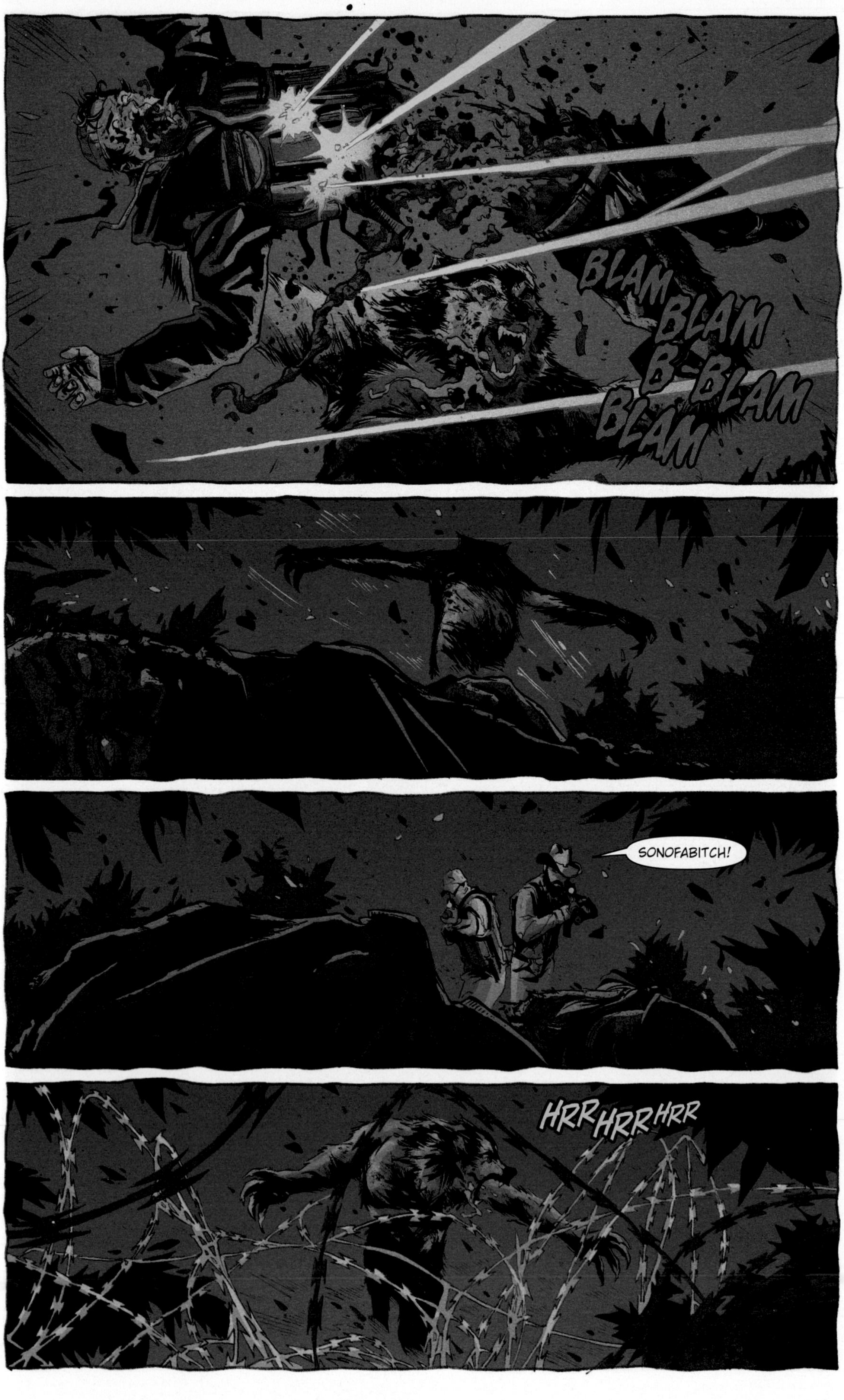
BLAM
BLAM
B-BLAM
BLAM
SONOFABITCH!
HRR HRR HRR

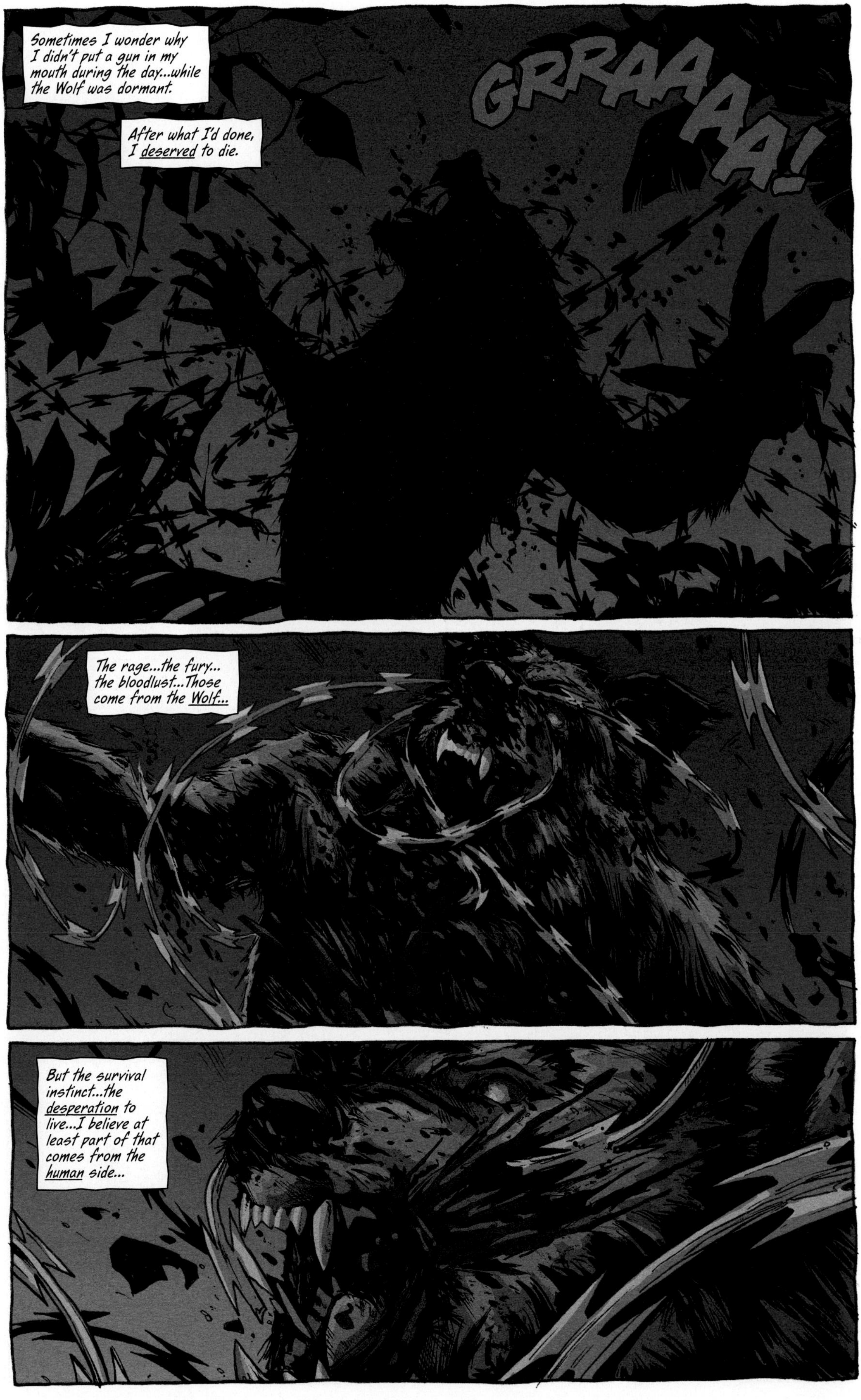
Sometimes I wonder why I didn't put a gun in my mouth during the day...while the Wolf was dormant.
After what I'd done, I deserved to die.
GRRAAAAA!
The rage...the fury... the bloodlust...Those come from the Wolf...
But the survival instinct...the desperation to live...I believe at least part of that comes from the human side...

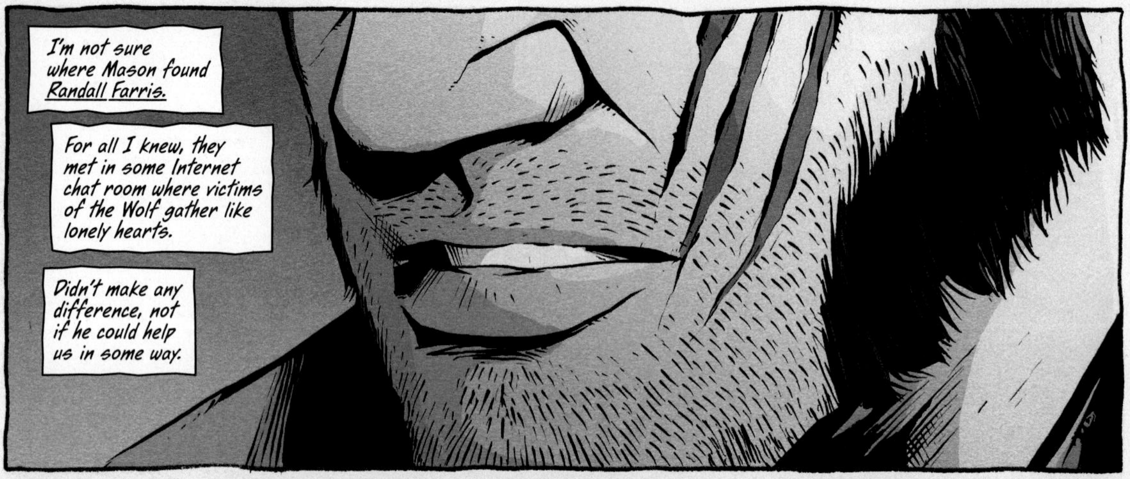
I'm not sure where Mason found Randall Farris.
For all I knew, they met in some Internet chat room where victims of the Wolf gather like lonely hearts.
Didn't make any difference, not if he could help us in some way.

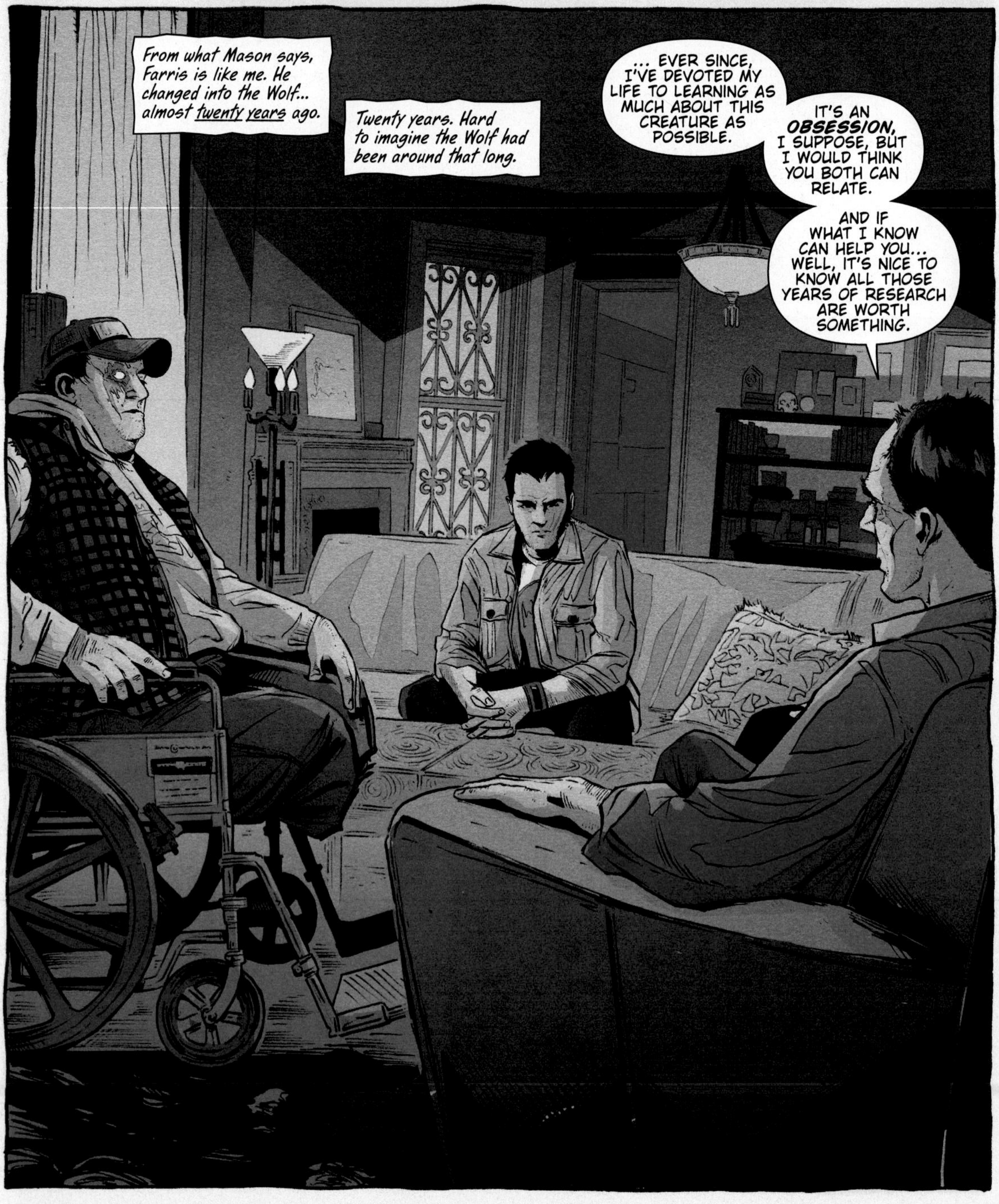
From what Mason says, Farris is like me. He changed into the Wolf... almost twenty years ago.
Twenty years. Hard to imagine the Wolf had been around that long.
... EVER SINCE, I'VE DEVOTED MY LIFE TO LEARNING AS MUCH ABOUT THIS CREATURE AS POSSIBLE.
IT'S AN OBSESSION, I SUPPOSE, BUT I WOULD THINK YOU BOTH CAN RELATE.
AND IF WHAT I KNOW CAN HELP YOU... WELL, IT'S NICE TO KNOW ALL THOSE YEARS OF RESEARCH ARE WORTH SOMETHING.

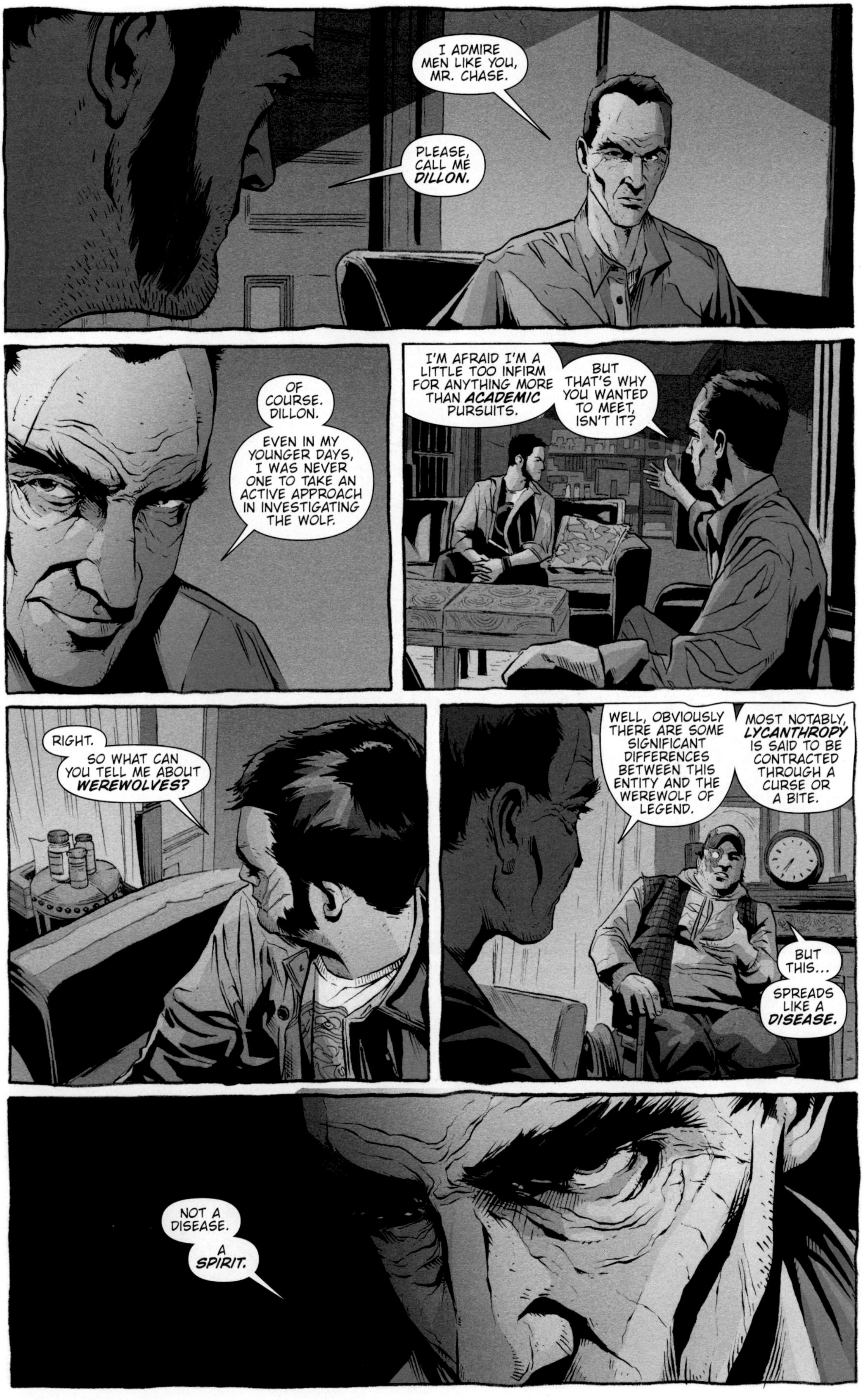
I ADMIRE MEN LIKE YOU, MR. CHASE.
PLEASE, CALL ME DILLON.
OF COURSE. DILLON.
EVEN IN MY YOUNGER DAYS, I WAS NEVER ONE TO TAKE AN ACTIVE APPROACH IN INVESTIGATING THE WOLF.
I'M AFRAID I'M A LITTLE TOO INFIRM FOR ANYTHING MORE THAN ACADEMIC PURSUITS.
BUT THAT'S WHY YOU WANTED TO MEET, ISN'T IT?
RIGHT.
SO WHAT CAN YOU TELL ME ABOUT WEREWOLVES?
WELL, OBVIOUSLY THERE ARE SOME SIGNIFICANT DIFFERENCES BETWEEN THIS ENTITY AND THE WEREWOLF OF LEGEND.
MOST NOTABLY, LYCANTHROPY IS SAID TO BE CONTRACTED THROUGH A CURSE OR A BITE.
BUT THIS...
SPREADS LIKE A DISEASE.
NOT A DISEASE.
A SPIRIT.

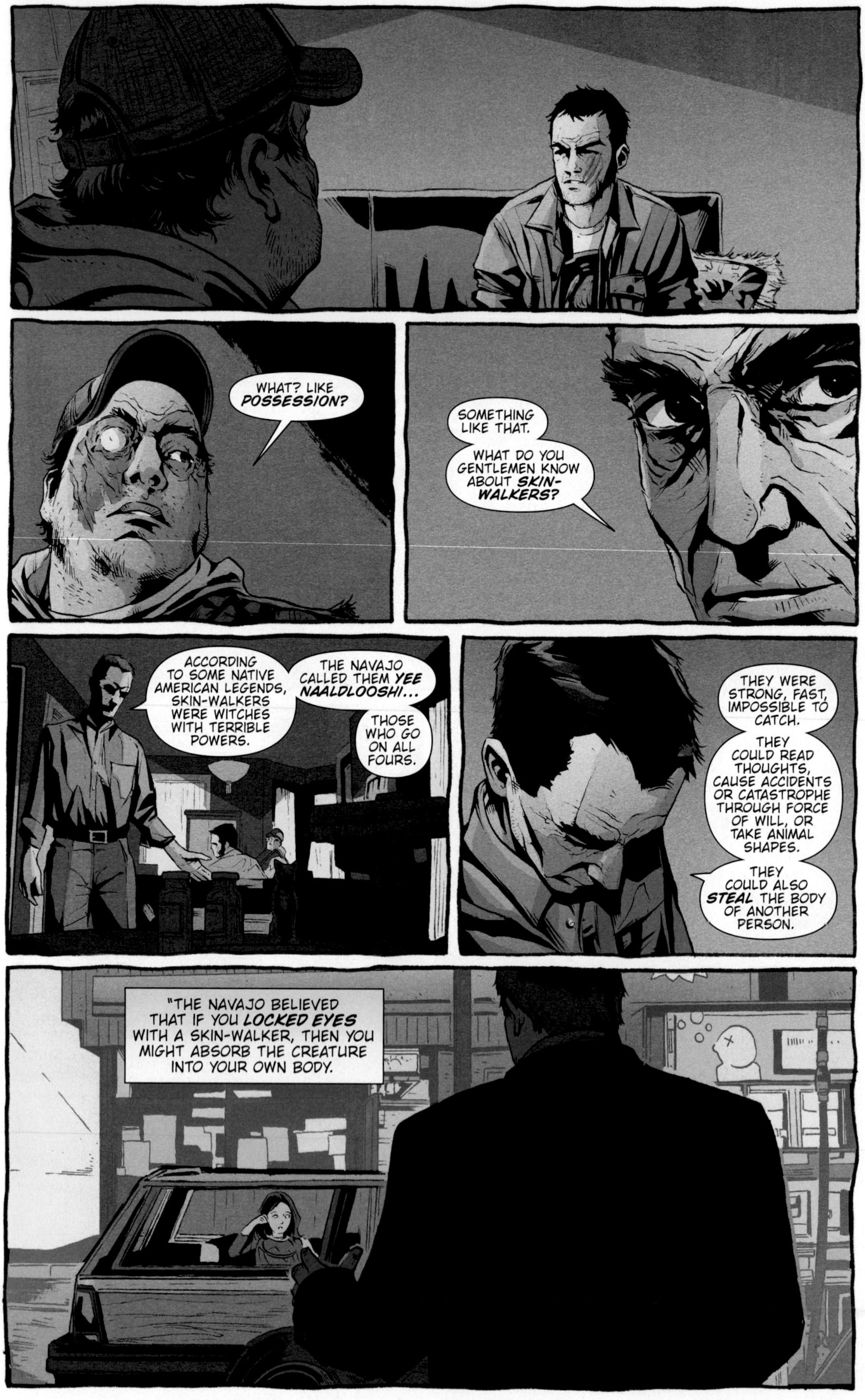
WHAT? LIKE POSSESSION?
SOMETHING LIKE THAT.
WHAT DO YOU GENTLEMEN KNOW ABOUT SKIN-WALKERS?
ACCORDING TO SOME NATIVE AMERICAN LEGENDS, SKIN-WALKERS WERE WITCHES WITH TERRIBLE POWERS.
THE NAVAJO CALLED THEM YEE NAALDLOOSHI...
THOSE WHO GO ON ALL FOURS.
THEY WERE STRONG, FAST, IMPOSSIBLE TO CATCH.
THEY COULD READ THOUGHTS, CAUSE ACCIDENTS OR CATASTROPHE THROUGH FORCE OF WILL, OR TAKE ANIMAL SHAPES.
THEY COULD ALSO STEAL THE BODY OF ANOTHER PERSON.
"THE NAVAJO BELIEVED THAT IF YOU LOCKED EYES WITH A SKIN-WALKER, THEN YOU MIGHT ABSORB THE CREATURE INTO YOUR OWN BODY.

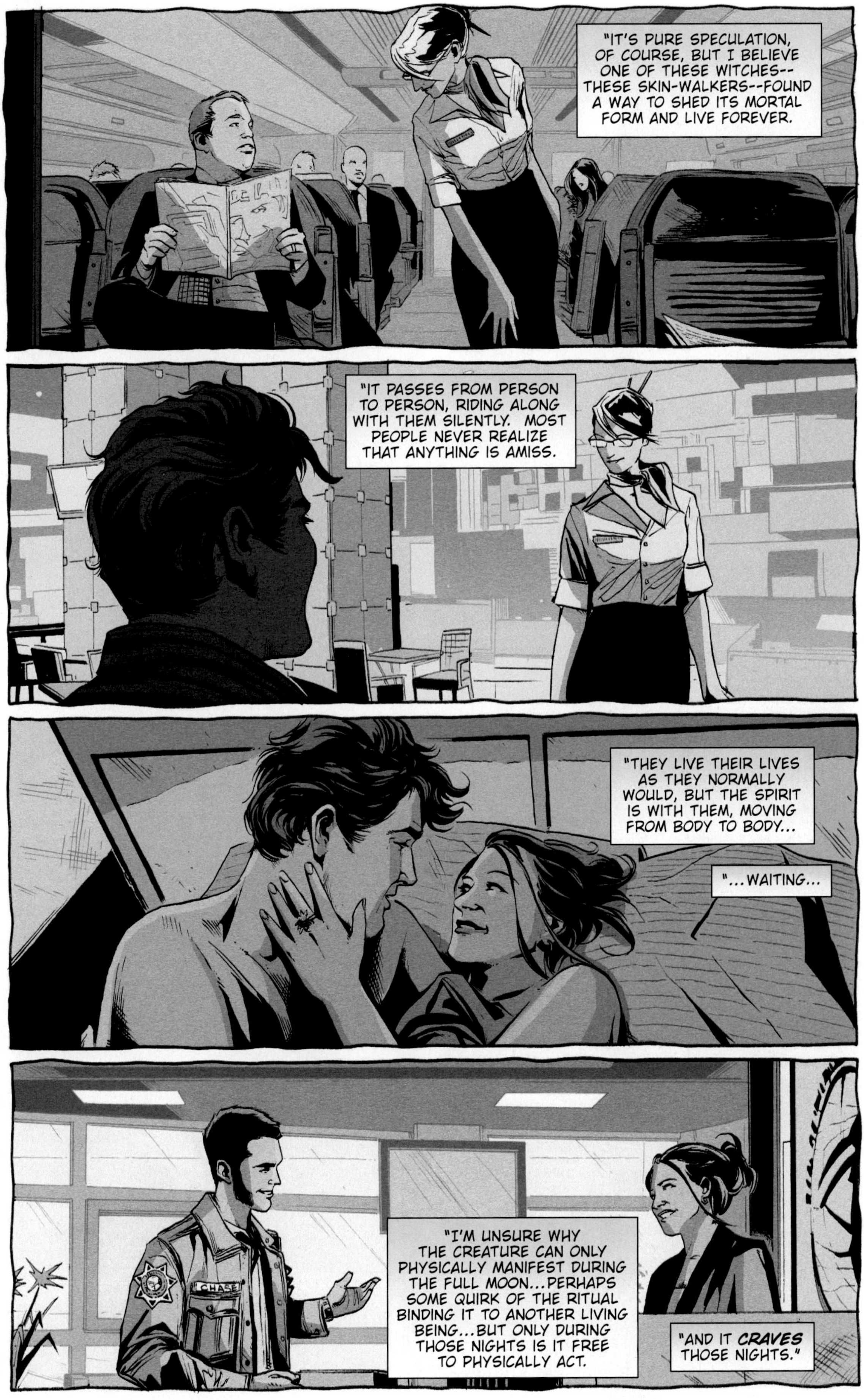
"IT'S PURE SPECULATION, OF COURSE, BUT I BELIEVE ONE OF THESE WITCHES-- THESE SKIN-WALKERS--FOUND A WAY TO SHED ITS MORTAL FORM AND LIVE FOREVER.
"IT PASSES FROM PERSON TO PERSON, RIDING ALONG WITH THEM SILENTLY. MOST PEOPLE NEVER REALIZE THAT ANYTHING IS AMISS.
"THEY LIVE THEIR LIVES AS THEY NORMALLY WOULD, BUT THE SPIRIT IS WITH THEM, MOVING FROM BODY TO BODY...
"...WAITING...
CHASE
"I'M UNSURE WHY THE CREATURE CAN ONLY PHYSICALLY MANIFEST DURING THE FULL MOON...PERHAPS SOME QUIRK OF THE RITUAL BINDING IT TO ANOTHER LIVING BEING...BUT ONLY DURING THOSE NIGHTS IS IT FREE TO PHYSICALLY ACT.
"AND IT *CRAVES* THOSE NIGHTS."

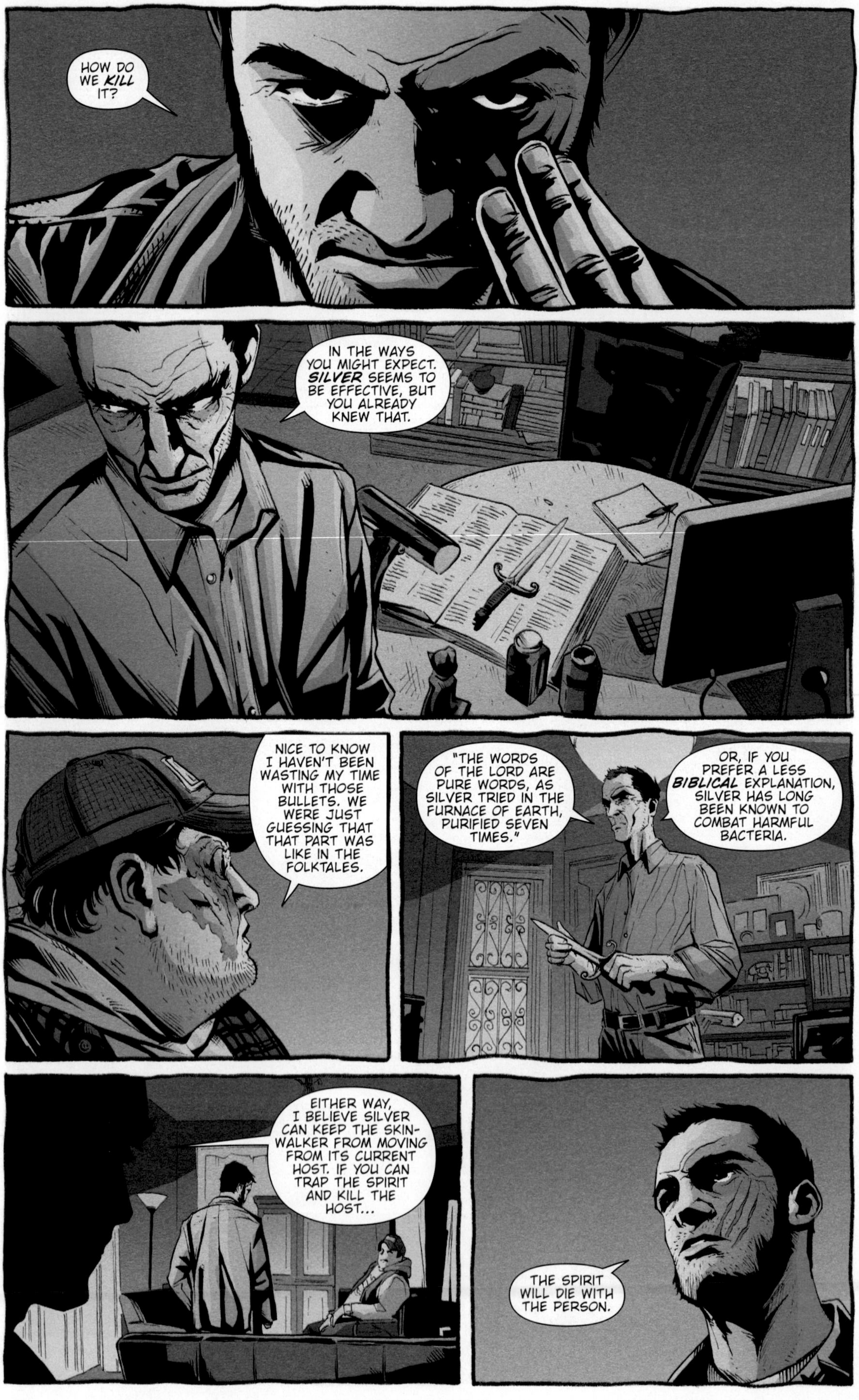
HOW DO WE KILL IT?
IN THE WAYS YOU MIGHT EXPECT. SILVER SEEMS TO BE EFFECTIVE, BUT YOU ALREADY KNEW THAT.
NICE TO KNOW I HAVEN'T BEEN WASTING MY TIME WITH THOSE BULLETS. WE WERE JUST GUESSING THAT THAT PART WAS LIKE IN THE FOLKTALES.
"THE WORDS OF THE LORD ARE PURE WORDS, AS SILVER TRIED IN THE FURNACE OF EARTH, PURIFIED SEVEN TIMES."
OR, IF YOU PREFER A LESS BIBLICAL EXPLANATION, SILVER HAS LONG BEEN KNOWN TO COMBAT HARMFUL BACTERIA.
EITHER WAY, I BELIEVE SILVER CAN KEEP THE SKIN-WALKER FROM MOVING FROM ITS CURRENT HOST. IF YOU CAN TRAP THE SPIRIT AND KILL THE HOST...
THE SPIRIT WILL DIE WITH THE PERSON.

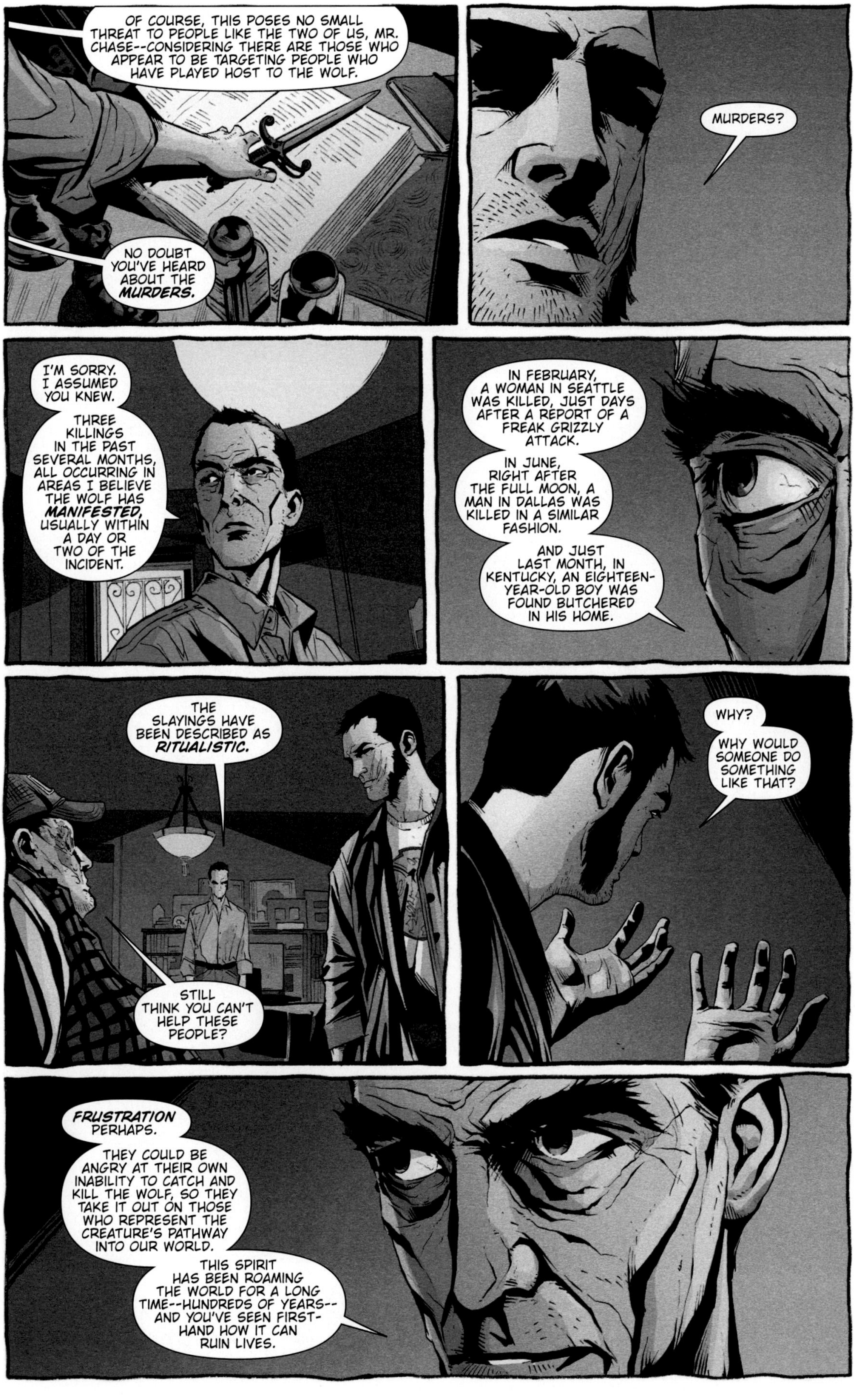
OF COURSE, THIS POSES NO SMALL THREAT TO PEOPLE LIKE THE TWO OF US, MR. CHASE--CONSIDERING THERE ARE THOSE WHO APPEAR TO BE TARGETING PEOPLE WHO HAVE PLAYED HOST TO THE WOLF.
NO DOUBT YOU'VE HEARD ABOUT THE ***MURDERS.***
MURDERS?
I'M SORRY. I ASSUMED YOU KNEW.
THREE KILLINGS IN THE PAST SEVERAL MONTHS, ALL OCCURRING IN AREAS I BELIEVE THE WOLF HAS ***MANIFESTED,*** USUALLY WITHIN A DAY OR TWO OF THE INCIDENT.
IN FEBRUARY, A WOMAN IN SEATTLE WAS KILLED, JUST DAYS AFTER A REPORT OF A FREAK GRIZZLY ATTACK.
IN JUNE, RIGHT AFTER THE FULL MOON, A MAN IN DALLAS WAS KILLED IN A SIMILAR FASHION.
AND JUST LAST MONTH, IN KENTUCKY, AN EIGHTEEN-YEAR-OLD BOY WAS FOUND BUTCHERED IN HIS HOME.
THE SLAYINGS HAVE BEEN DESCRIBED AS ***RITUALISTIC.***
STILL THINK YOU CAN'T HELP THESE PEOPLE?
WHY?
WHY WOULD SOMEONE DO SOMETHING LIKE THAT?
***FRUSTRATION*** PERHAPS.
THEY COULD BE ANGRY AT THEIR OWN INABILITY TO CATCH AND KILL THE WOLF, SO THEY TAKE IT OUT ON THOSE WHO REPRESENT THE CREATURE'S PATHWAY INTO OUR WORLD.
THIS SPIRIT HAS BEEN ROAMING THE WORLD FOR A LONG TIME--HUNDREDS OF YEARS--AND YOU'VE SEEN FIRST-HAND HOW IT CAN RUIN LIVES.

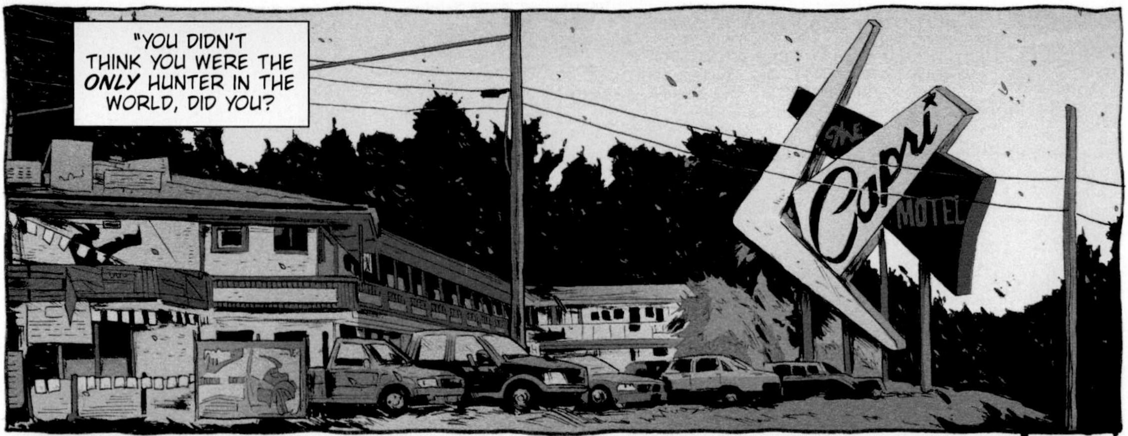
"YOU DIDN'T THINK YOU WERE THE ONLY HUNTER IN THE WORLD, DID YOU?
The Capri MOTEL

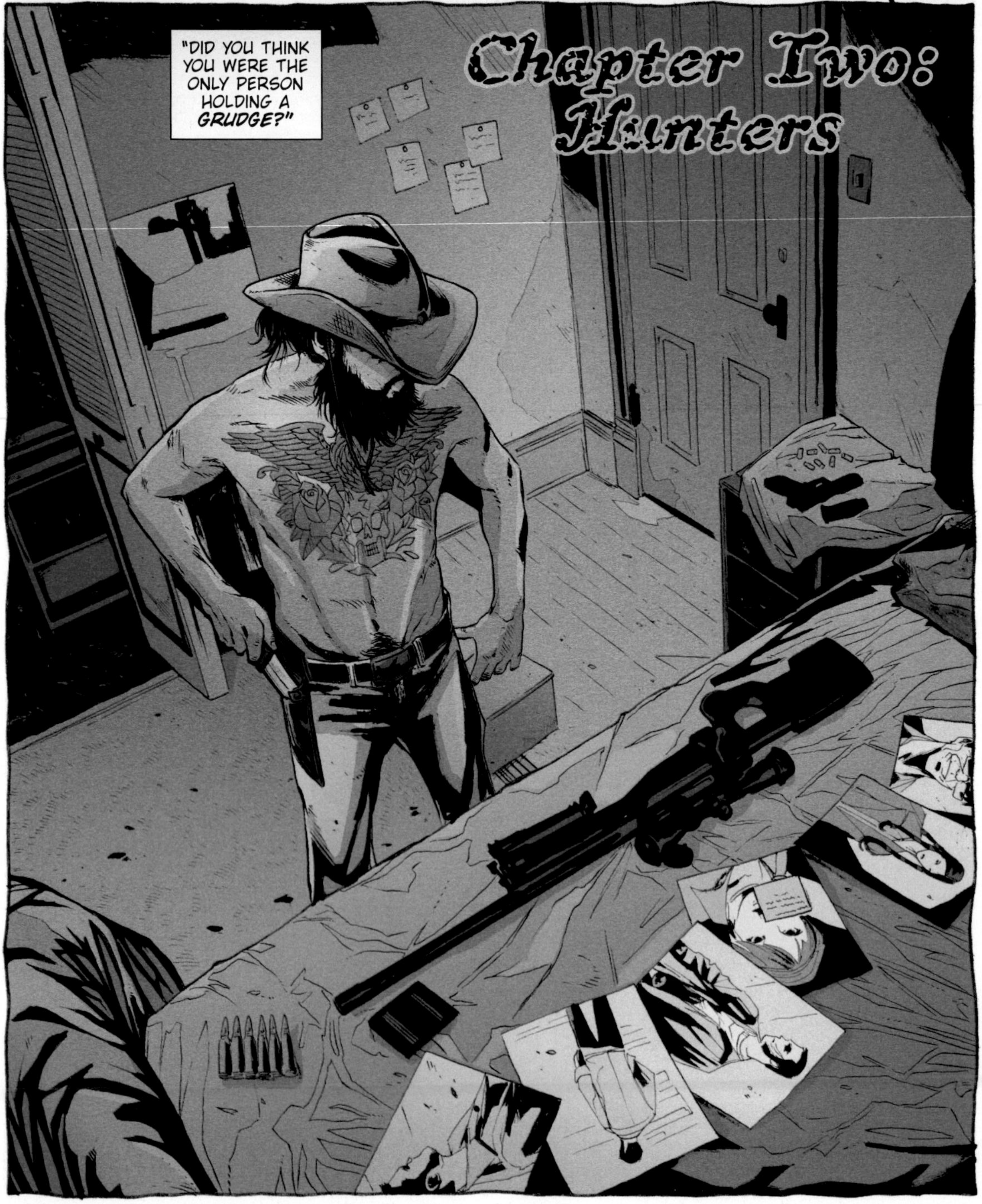
"DID YOU THINK YOU WERE THE ONLY PERSON HOLDING A GRUDGE?"
Chapter Two: Hunters

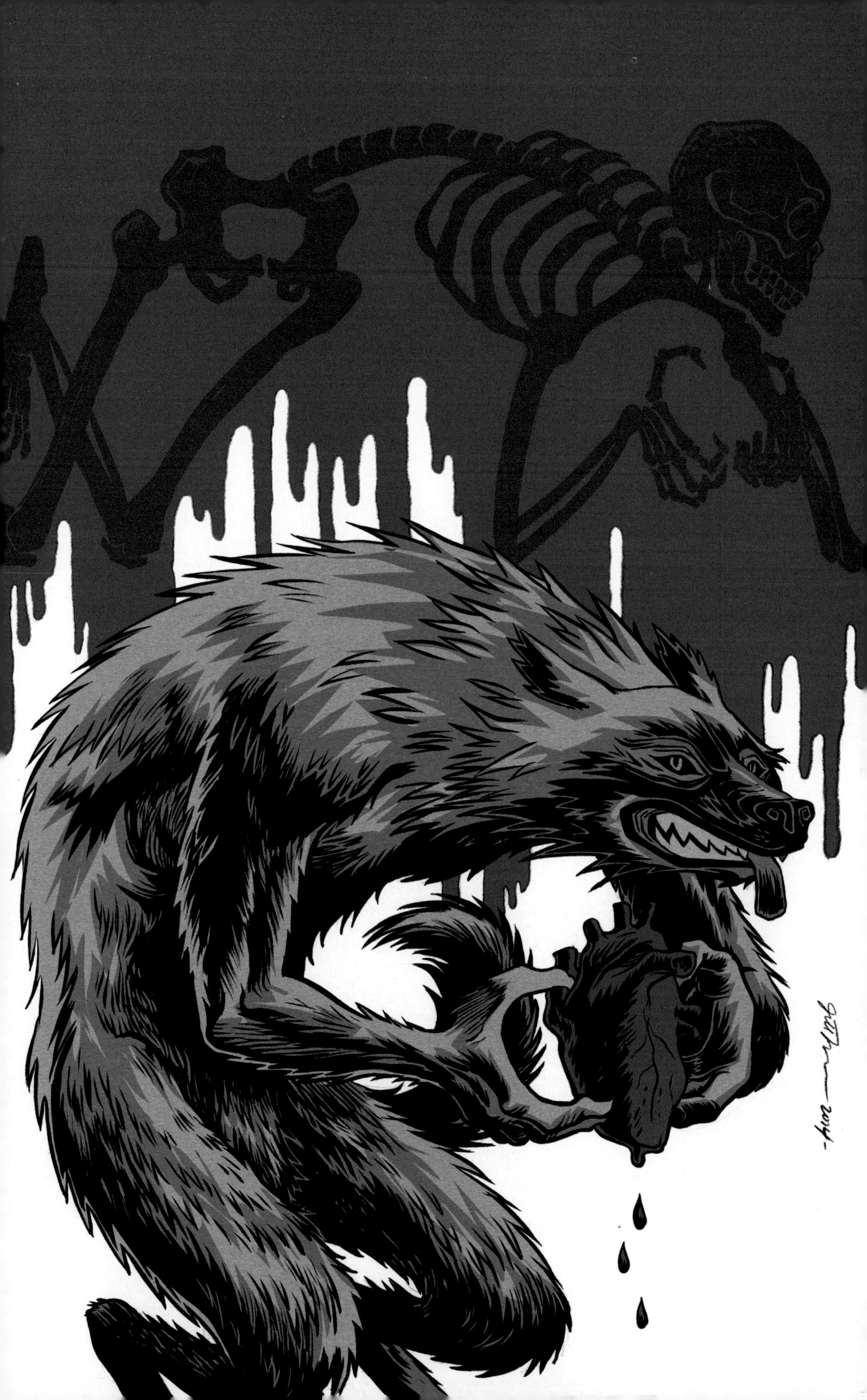

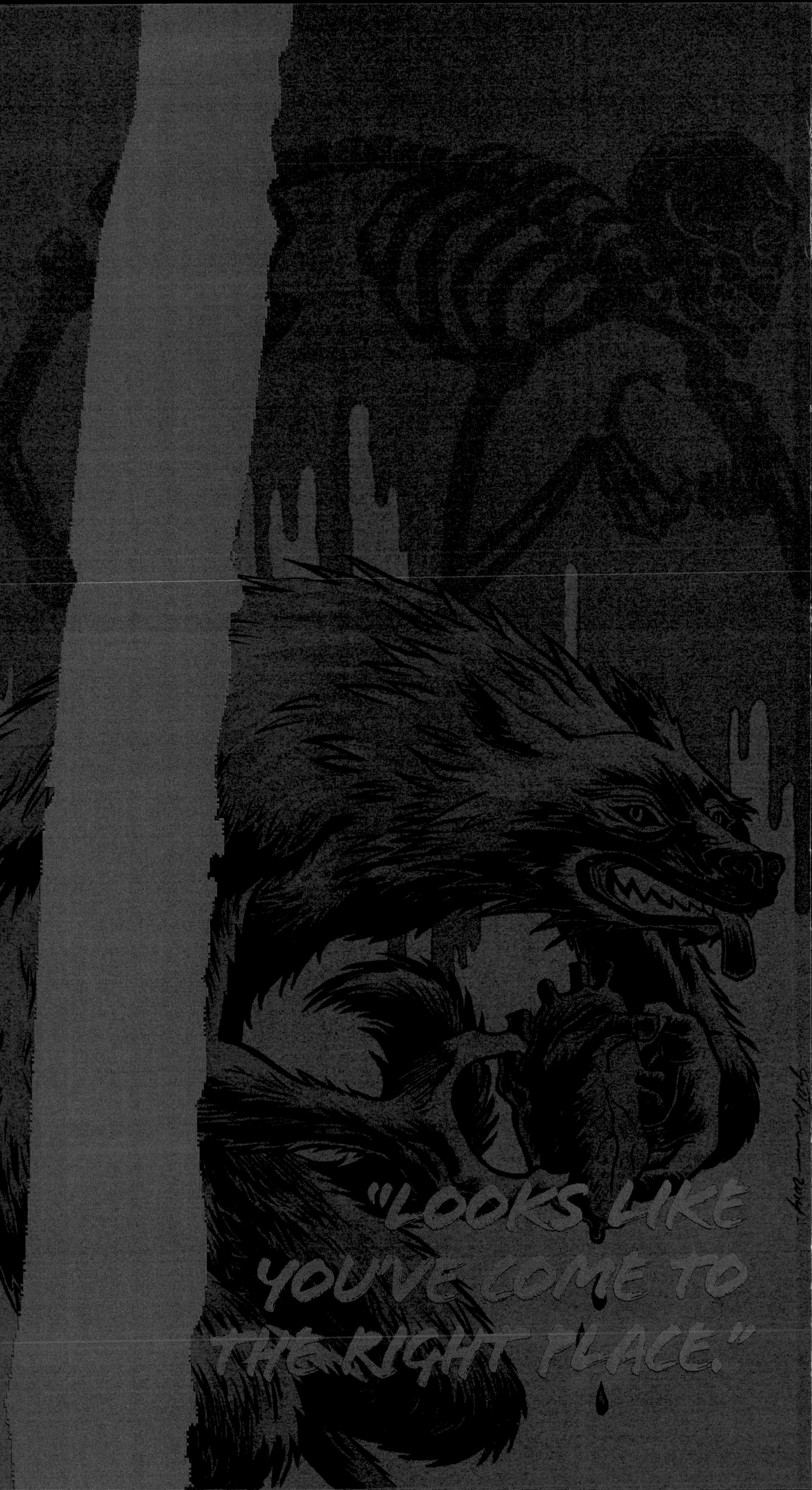
"LOOKS LIKE YOU'VE COME TO THE RIGHT PLACE."

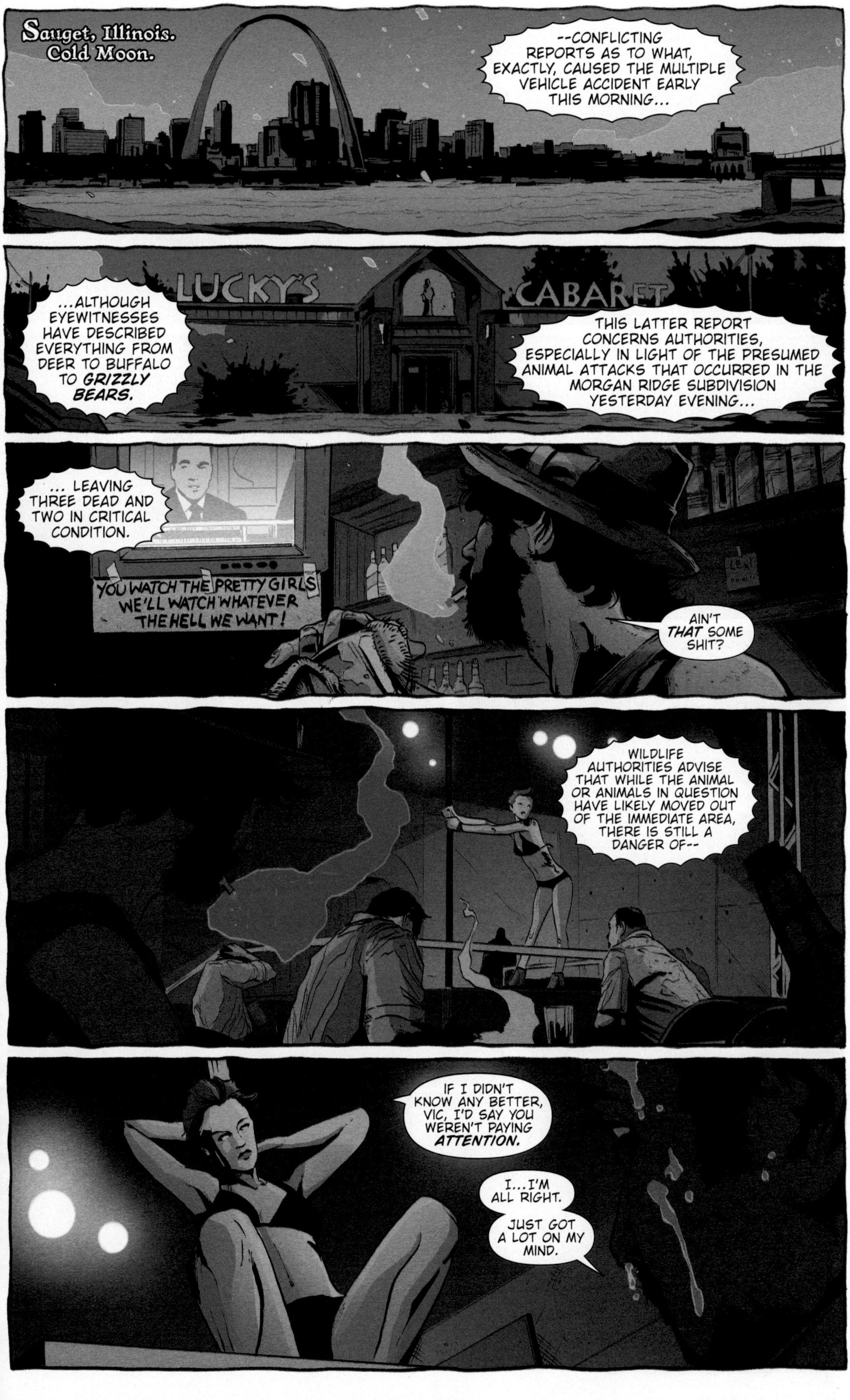
Sauget, Illinois. Cold Moon.
--CONFLICTING REPORTS AS TO WHAT, EXACTLY, CAUSED THE MULTIPLE VEHICLE ACCIDENT EARLY THIS MORNING...
LUCKY'S CABARET
...ALTHOUGH EYEWITNESSES HAVE DESCRIBED EVERYTHING FROM DEER TO BUFFALO TO GRIZZLY BEARS.
THIS LATTER REPORT CONCERNS AUTHORITIES, ESPECIALLY IN LIGHT OF THE PRESUMED ANIMAL ATTACKS THAT OCCURRED IN THE MORGAN RIDGE SUBDIVISION YESTERDAY EVENING...
... LEAVING THREE DEAD AND TWO IN CRITICAL CONDITION.
YOU WATCH THE PRETTY GIRLS WE'LL WATCH WHATEVER THE HELL WE WANT!
AIN'T THAT SOME SHIT?
WILDLIFE AUTHORITIES ADVISE THAT WHILE THE ANIMAL OR ANIMALS IN QUESTION HAVE LIKELY MOVED OUT OF THE IMMEDIATE AREA, THERE IS STILL A DANGER OF--
IF I DIDN'T KNOW ANY BETTER, VIC, I'D SAY YOU WEREN'T PAYING ATTENTION.
I...I'M ALL RIGHT.
JUST GOT A LOT ON MY MIND.

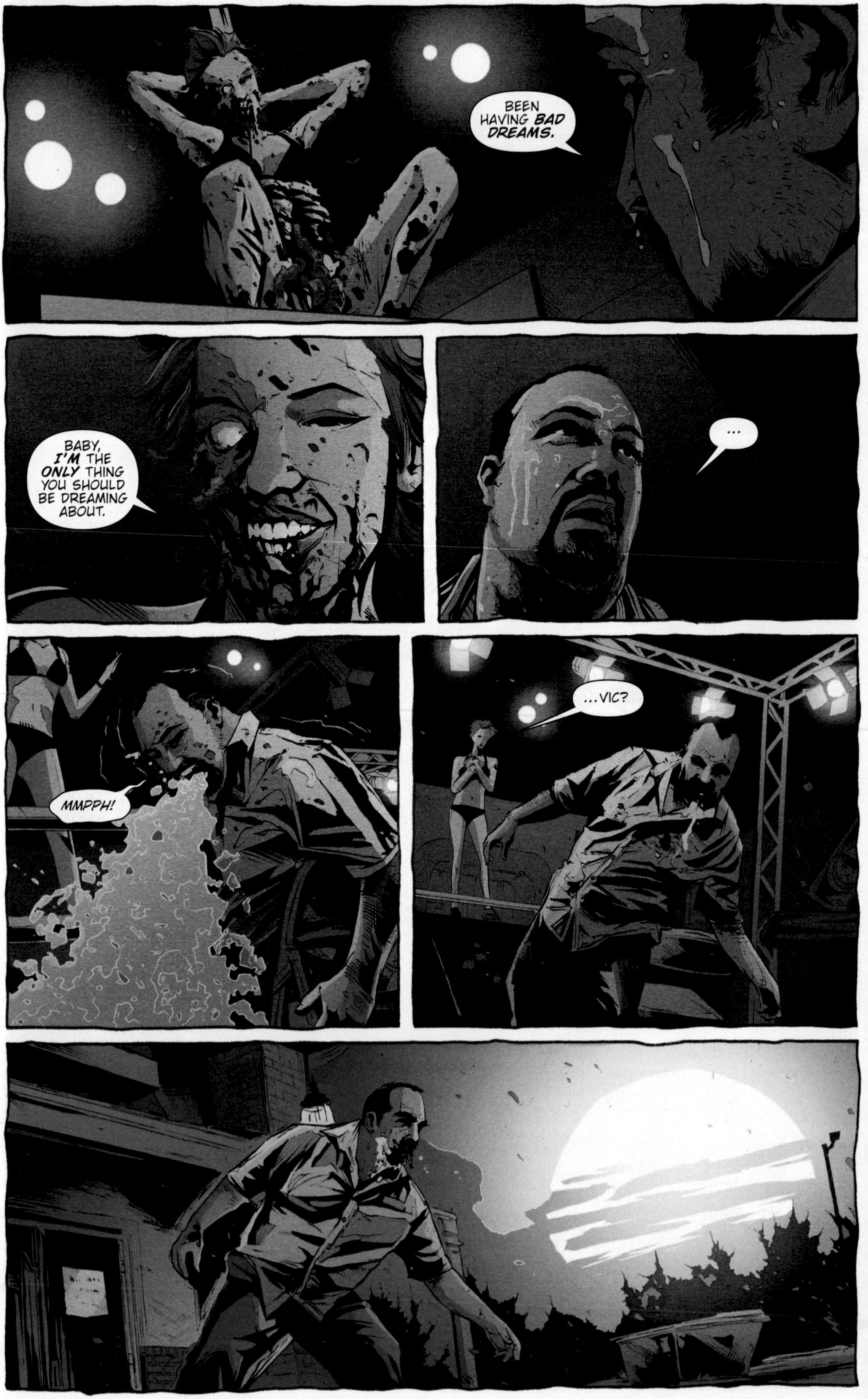
BEEN HAVING BAD DREAMS.
BABY, I'M THE ONLY THING YOU SHOULD BE DREAMING ABOUT.
...
MMPPH!
...VIC?

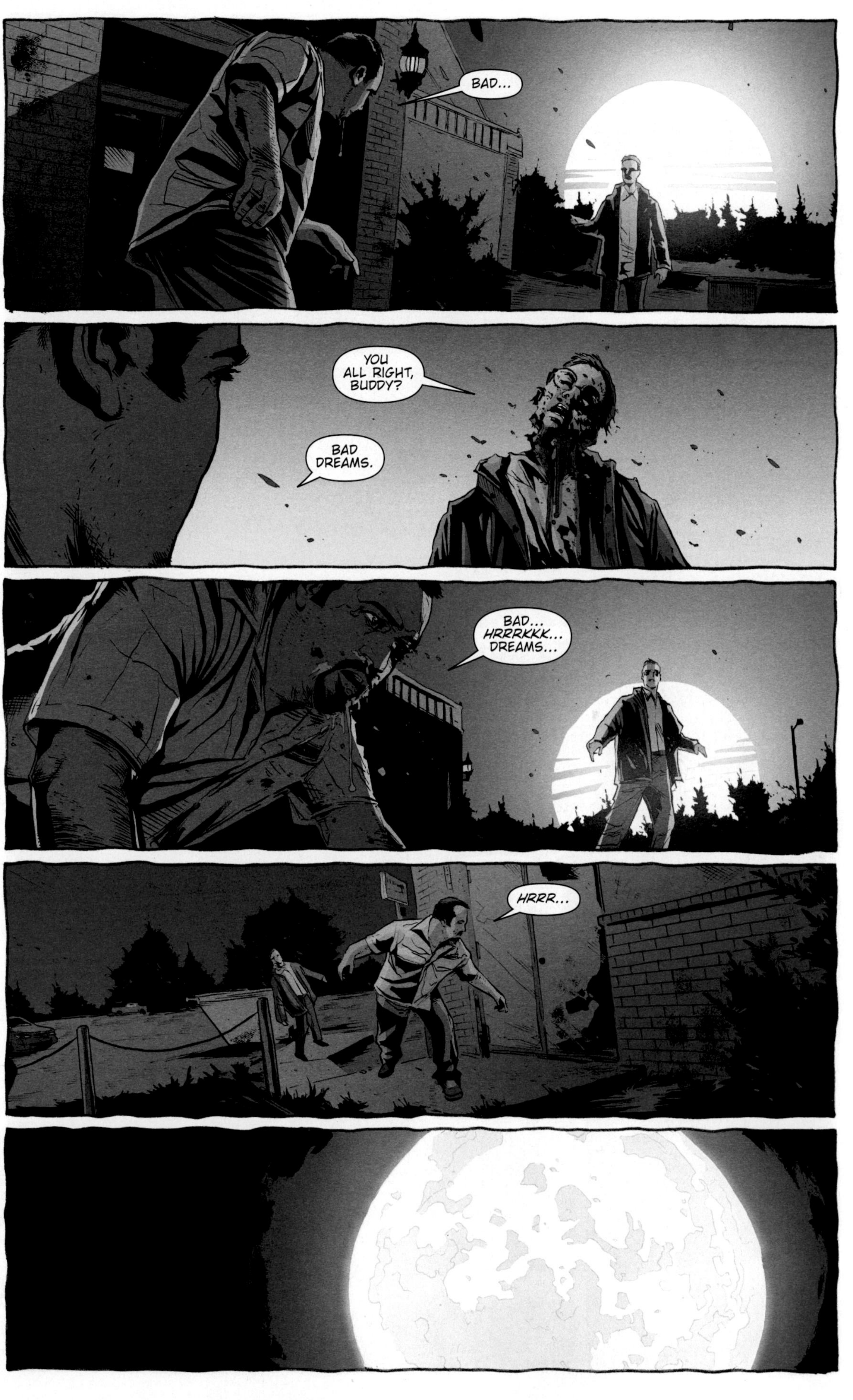
BAD...
YOU ALL RIGHT, BUDDY?
BAD DREAMS.
BAD... HRRRKKK... DREAMS...
HRRR...

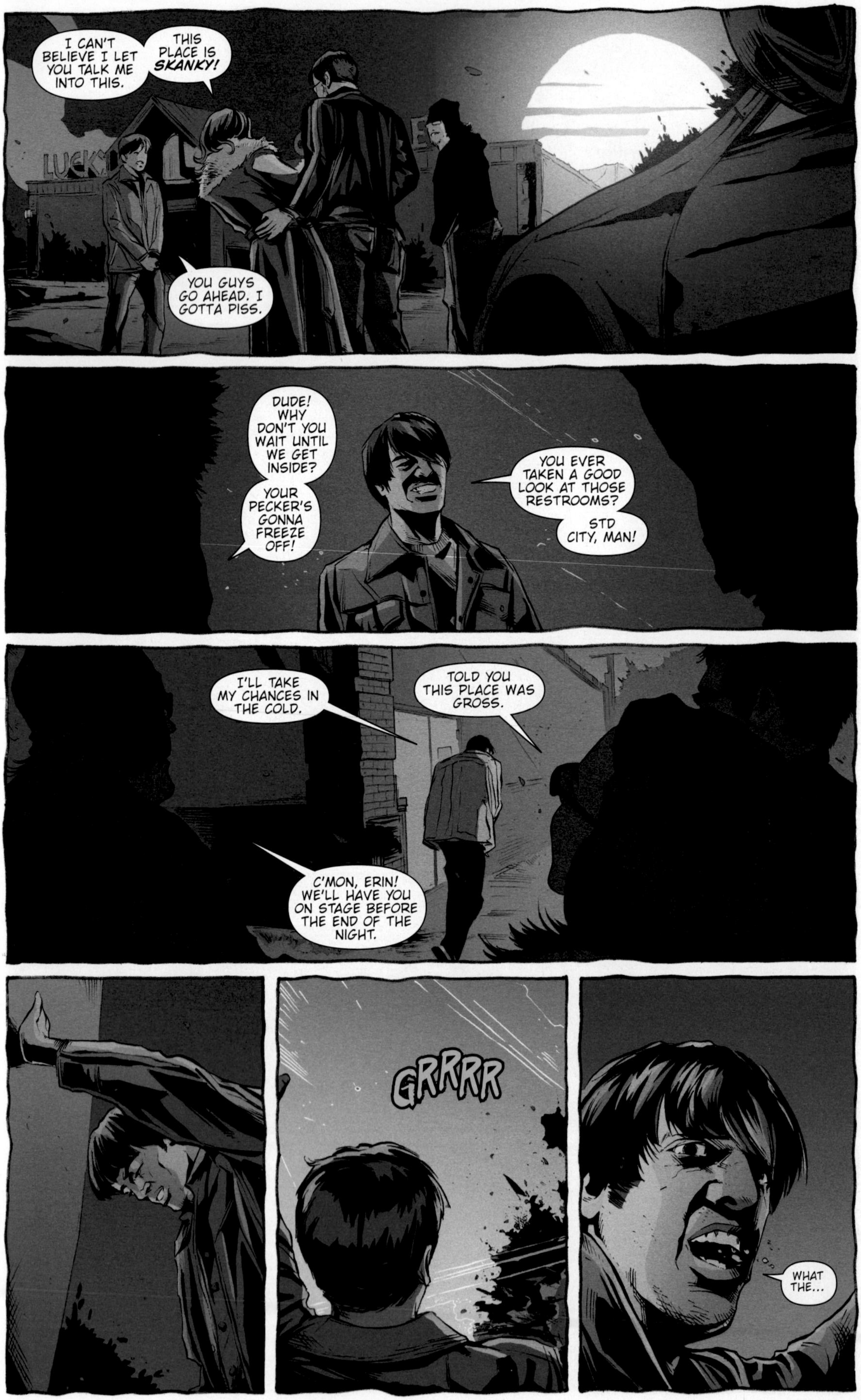
I CAN'T BELIEVE I LET YOU TALK ME INTO THIS.
THIS PLACE IS SKANKY!
YOU GUYS GO AHEAD. I GOTTA PISS.
DUDE! WHY DON'T YOU WAIT UNTIL WE GET INSIDE?
YOUR PECKER'S GONNA FREEZE OFF!
YOU EVER TAKEN A GOOD LOOK AT THOSE RESTROOMS?
STD CITY, MAN!
I'LL TAKE MY CHANCES IN THE COLD.
TOLD YOU THIS PLACE WAS GROSS.
C'MON, ERIN! WE'LL HAVE YOU ON STAGE BEFORE THE END OF THE NIGHT.
GRRRR
WHAT THE...

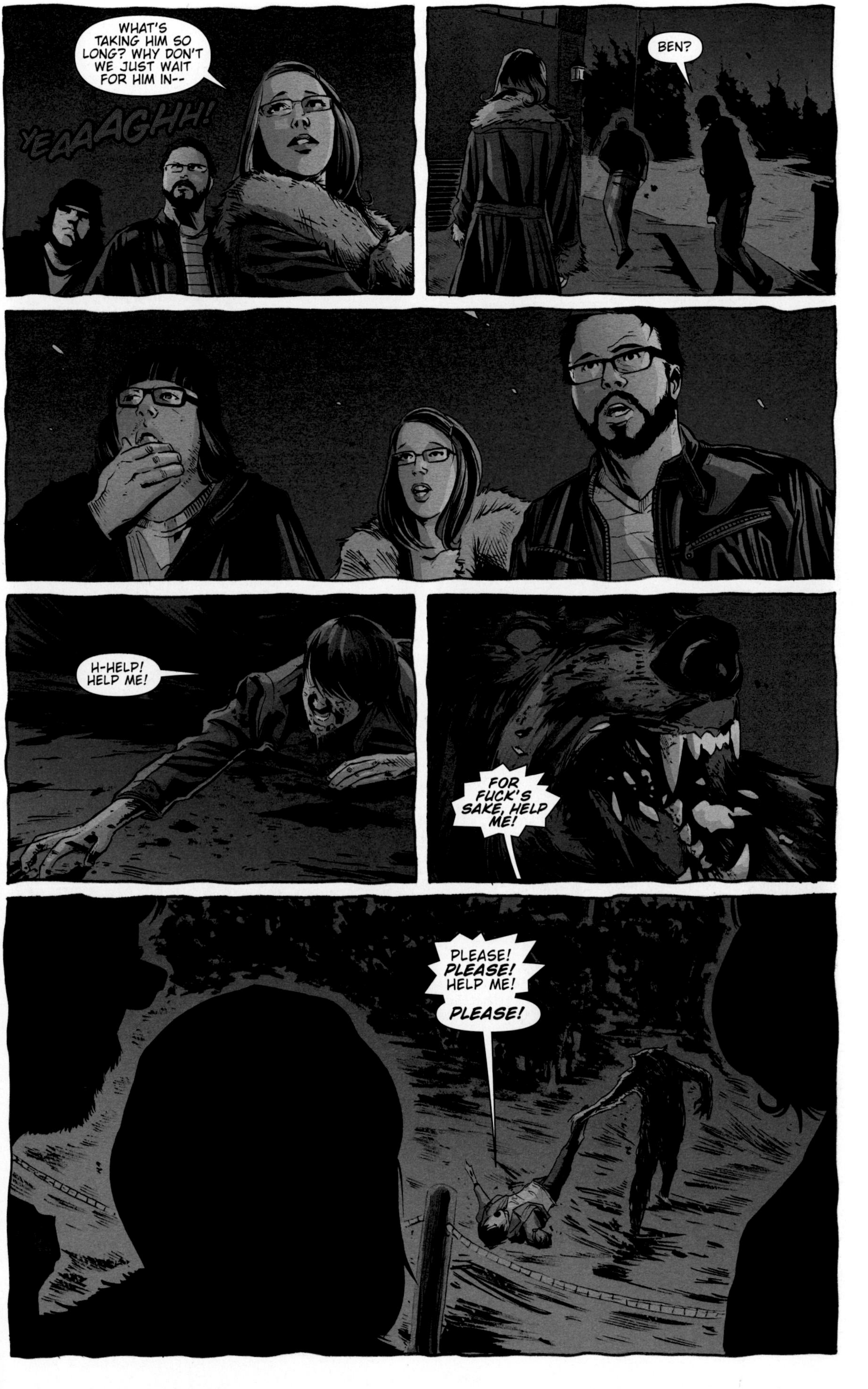
WHAT'S TAKING HIM SO LONG? WHY DON'T WE JUST WAIT FOR HIM IN--
YEAAAGHH!
BEN?
H-HELP! HELP ME!
FOR FUCK'S SAKE, HELP ME!
PLEASE! PLEASE! HELP ME! PLEASE!

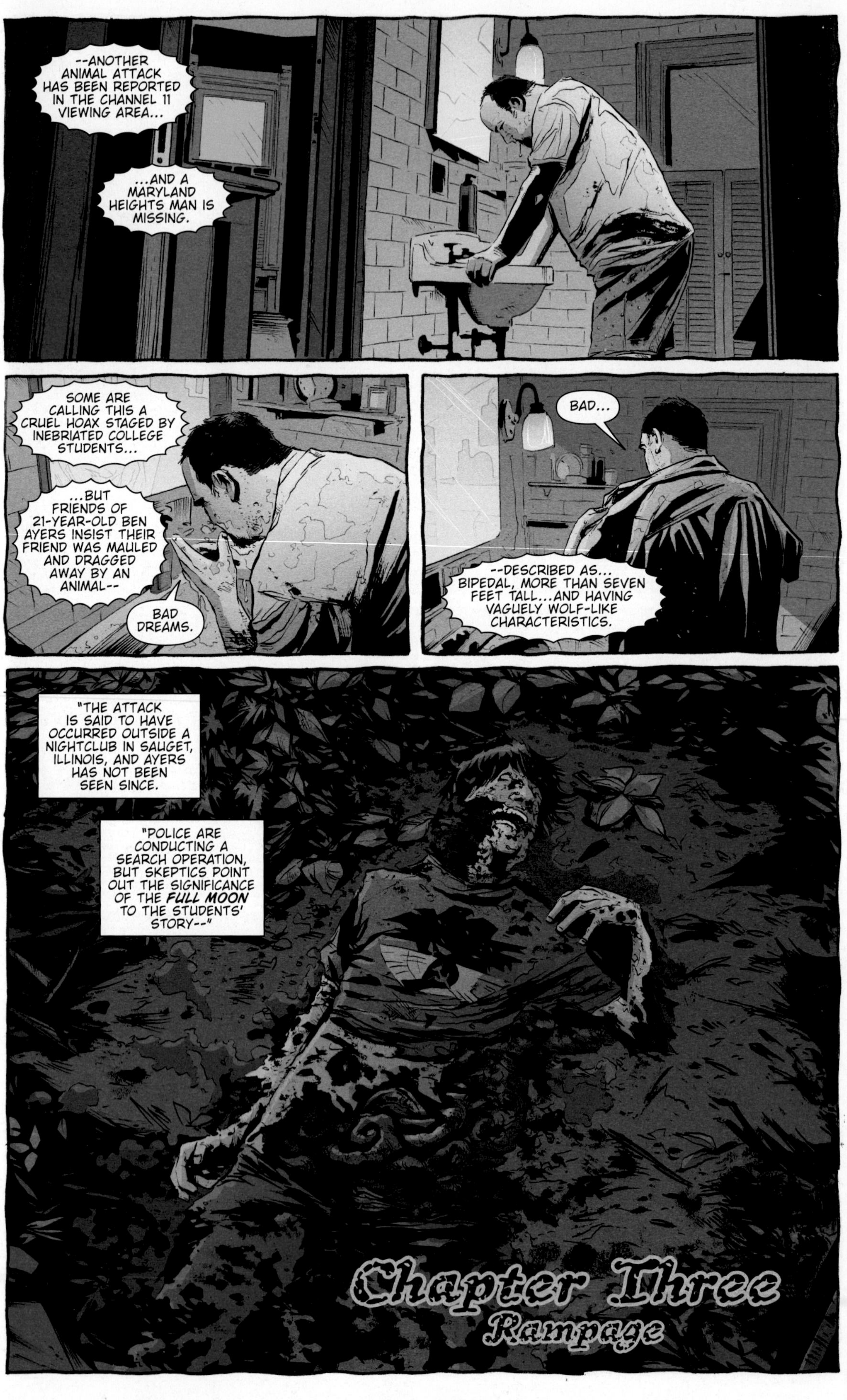
--ANOTHER ANIMAL ATTACK HAS BEEN REPORTED IN THE CHANNEL 11 VIEWING AREA...
...AND A MARYLAND HEIGHTS MAN IS MISSING.
SOME ARE CALLING THIS A CRUEL HOAX STAGED BY INEBRIATED COLLEGE STUDENTS...
...BUT FRIENDS OF 21-YEAR-OLD BEN AYERS INSIST THEIR FRIEND WAS MAULED AND DRAGGED AWAY BY AN ANIMAL--
BAD DREAMS.
BAD...
--DESCRIBED AS... BIPEDAL, MORE THAN SEVEN FEET TALL...AND HAVING VAGUELY WOLF-LIKE CHARACTERISTICS.
"THE ATTACK IS SAID TO HAVE OCCURRED OUTSIDE A NIGHTCLUB IN SAUGET, ILLINOIS, AND AYERS HAS NOT BEEN SEEN SINCE.
"POLICE ARE CONDUCTING A SEARCH OPERATION, BUT SKEPTICS POINT OUT THE SIGNIFICANCE OF THE *FULL MOON* TO THE STUDENTS' STORY--"
Chapter Three
Rampage

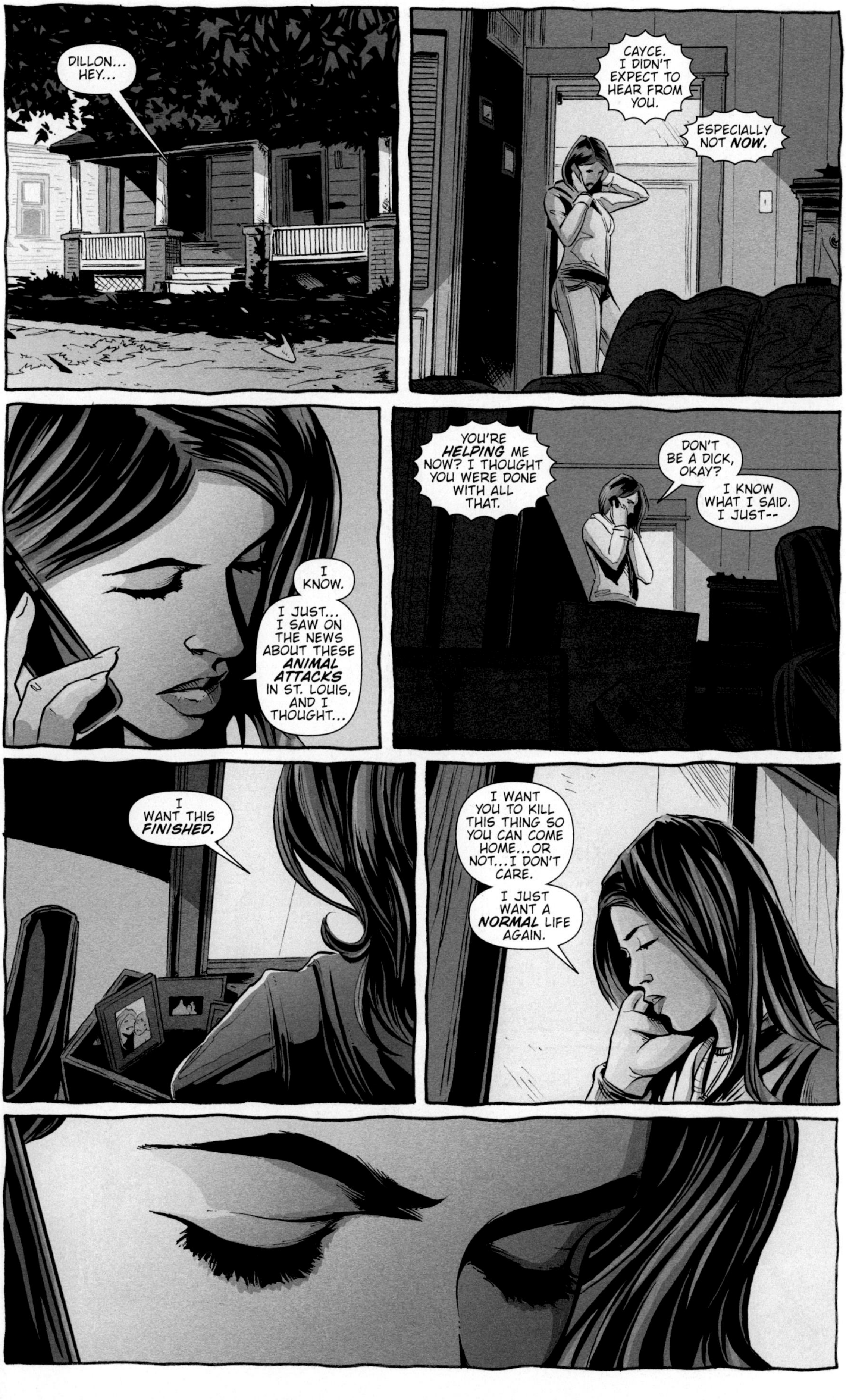
DILLON... HEY...
CAYCE. I DIDN'T EXPECT TO HEAR FROM YOU.
ESPECIALLY NOT NOW.
I KNOW.
I JUST... I SAW ON THE NEWS ABOUT THESE ANIMAL ATTACKS IN ST. LOUIS, AND I THOUGHT...
YOU'RE HELPING ME NOW? I THOUGHT YOU WERE DONE WITH ALL THAT.
DON'T BE A DICK, OKAY?
I KNOW WHAT I SAID. I JUST--
I WANT THIS FINISHED.
I WANT YOU TO KILL THIS THING SO YOU CAN COME HOME...OR NOT...I DON'T CARE.
I JUST WANT A NORMAL LIFE AGAIN.

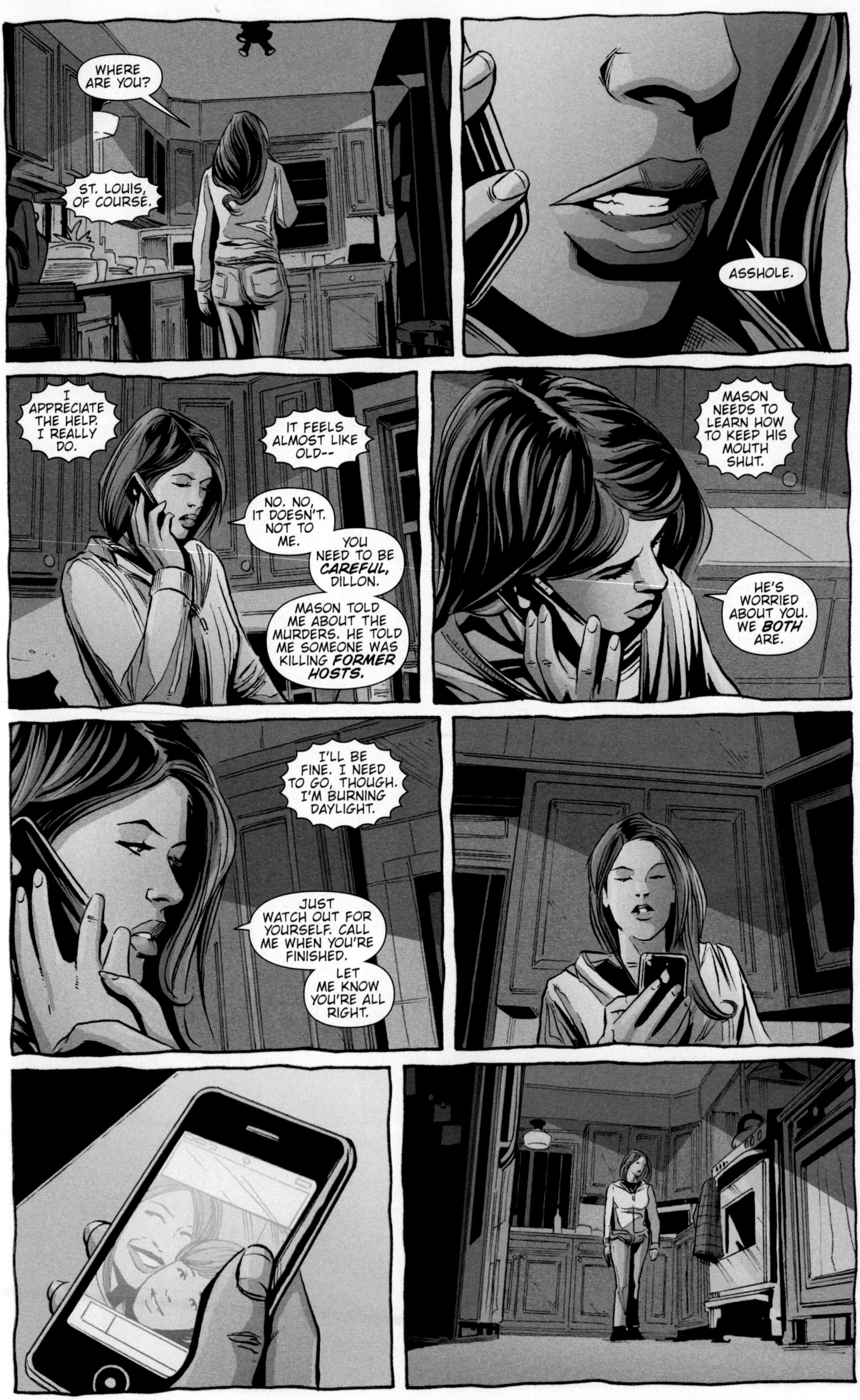
WHERE ARE YOU?
ST. LOUIS, OF COURSE.
ASSHOLE.
I APPRECIATE THE HELP. I REALLY DO.
IT FEELS ALMOST LIKE OLD--
NO. NO, IT DOESN'T. NOT TO ME.
YOU NEED TO BE CAREFUL, DILLON.
MASON TOLD ME ABOUT THE MURDERS. HE TOLD ME SOMEONE WAS KILLING FORMER HOSTS.
MASON NEEDS TO LEARN HOW TO KEEP HIS MOUTH SHUT.
HE'S WORRIED ABOUT YOU. WE BOTH ARE.
I'LL BE FINE. I NEED TO GO, THOUGH. I'M BURNING DAYLIGHT.
JUST WATCH OUT FOR YOURSELF. CALL ME WHEN YOU'RE FINISHED.
LET ME KNOW YOU'RE ALL RIGHT.

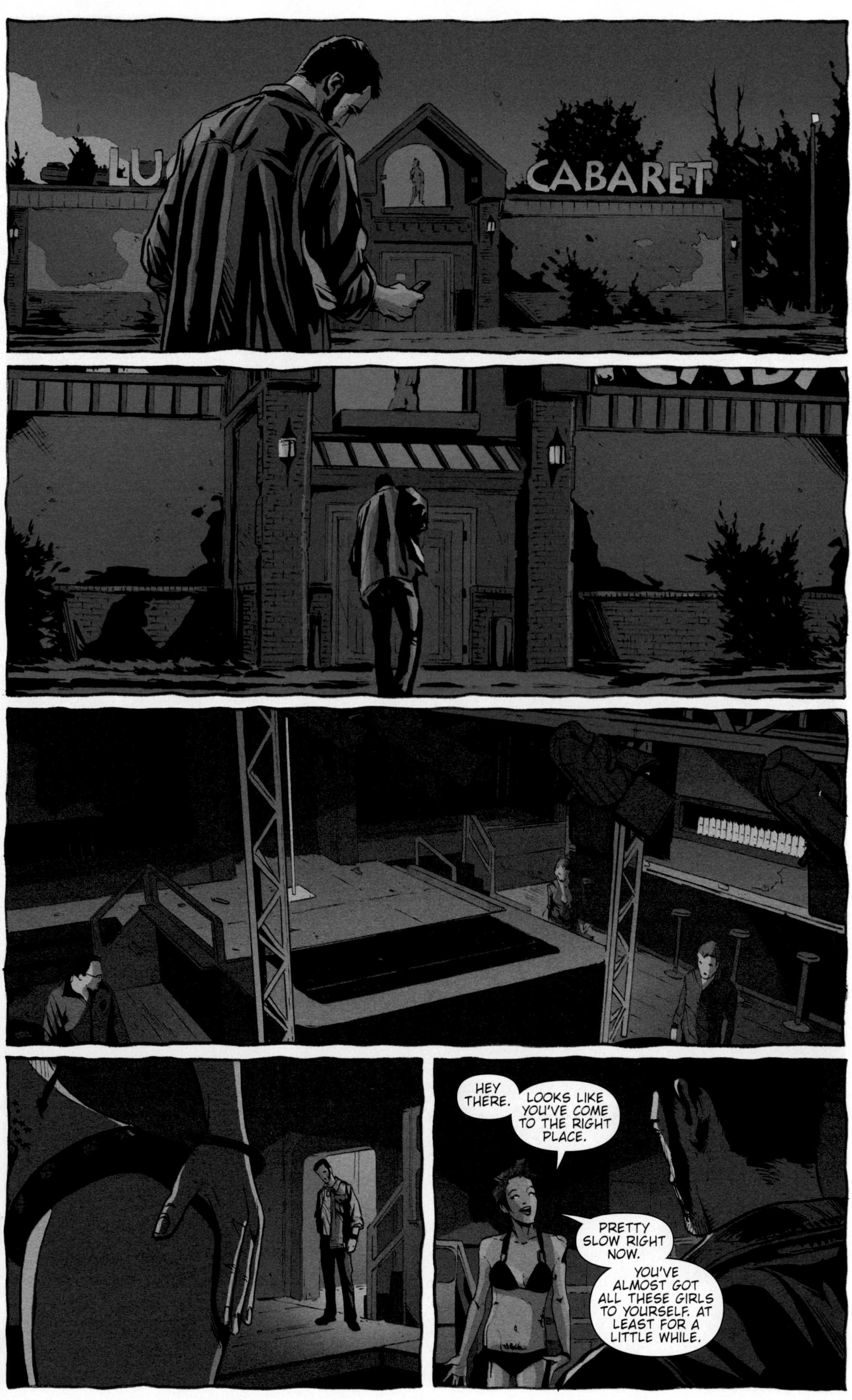
LU
CABARET
HEY THERE.
LOOKS LIKE YOU'VE COME TO THE RIGHT PLACE.
PRETTY SLOW RIGHT NOW.
YOU'VE ALMOST GOT ALL THESE GIRLS TO YOURSELF. AT LEAST FOR A LITTLE WHILE.

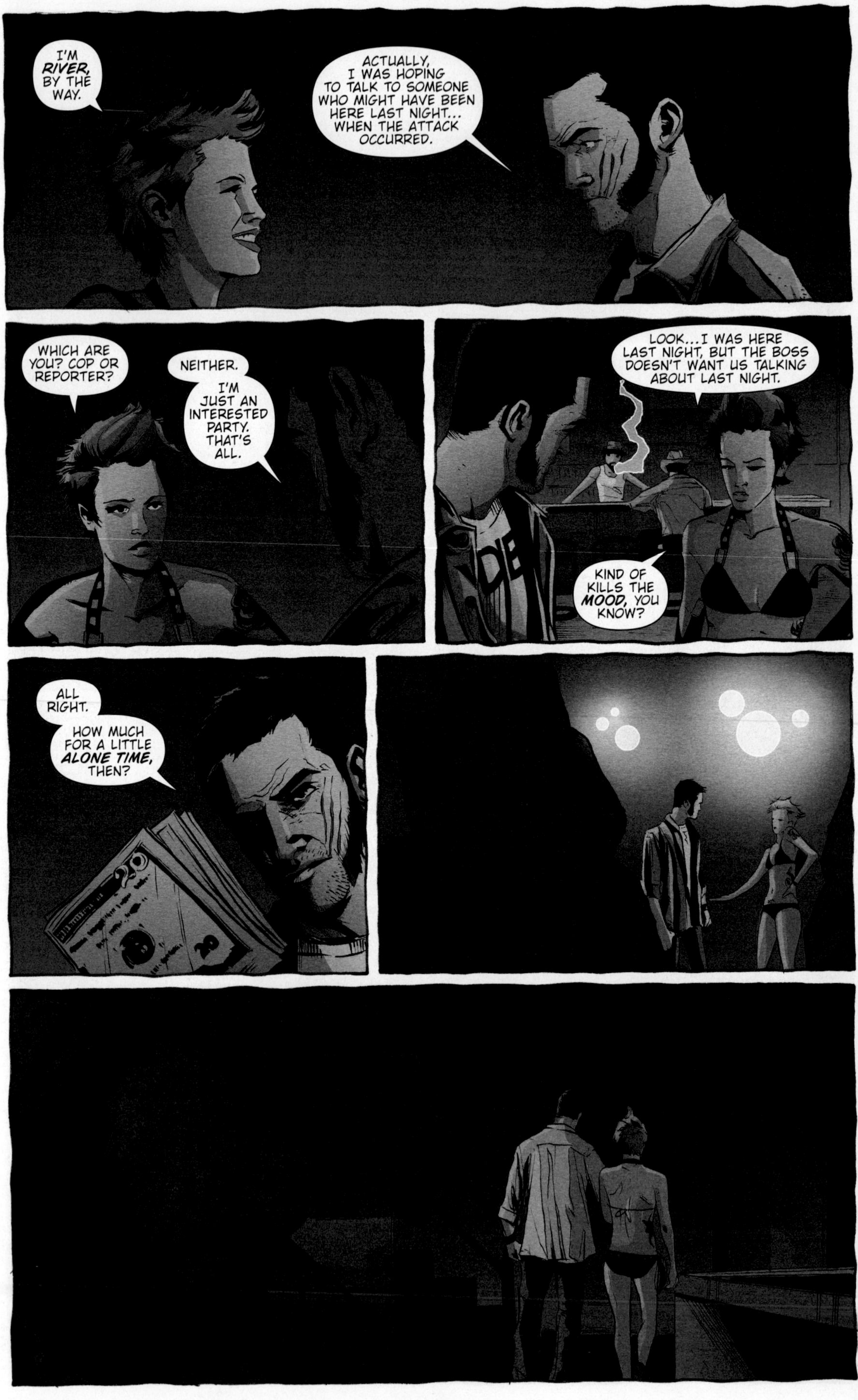
I'M **RIVER,** BY THE WAY.
ACTUALLY, I WAS HOPING TO TALK TO SOMEONE WHO MIGHT HAVE BEEN HERE LAST NIGHT... WHEN THE ATTACK OCCURRED.
WHICH ARE YOU? COP OR REPORTER?
NEITHER.
I'M JUST AN INTERESTED PARTY. THAT'S ALL.
LOOK...I WAS HERE LAST NIGHT, BUT THE BOSS DOESN'T WANT US TALKING ABOUT LAST NIGHT.
KIND OF KILLS THE **MOOD,** YOU KNOW?
ALL RIGHT.
HOW MUCH FOR A LITTLE **ALONE TIME,** THEN?

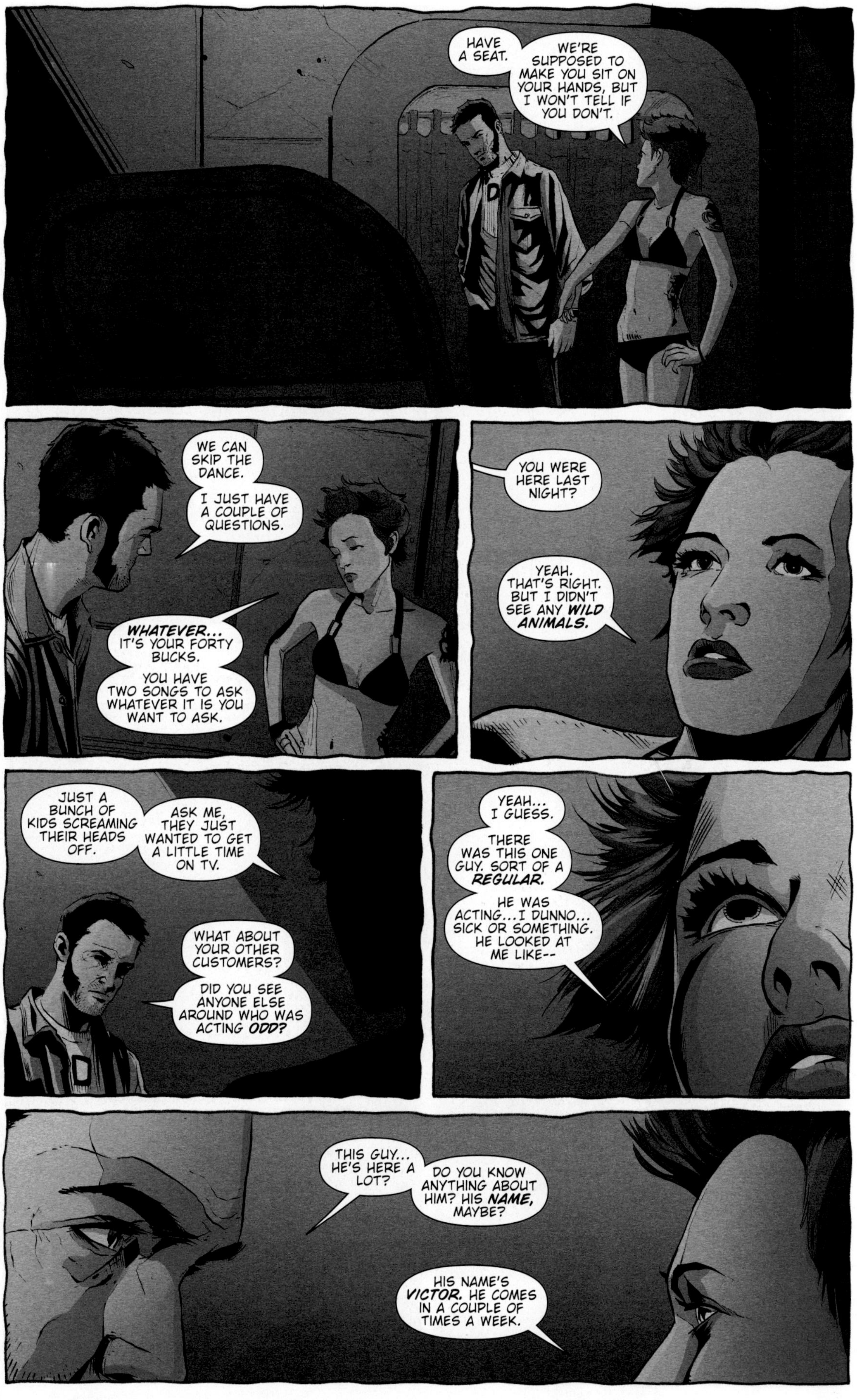
HAVE A SEAT.
WE'RE SUPPOSED TO MAKE YOU SIT ON YOUR HANDS, BUT I WON'T TELL IF YOU DON'T.
WE CAN SKIP THE DANCE.
I JUST HAVE A COUPLE OF QUESTIONS.
WHATEVER... IT'S YOUR FORTY BUCKS.
YOU HAVE TWO SONGS TO ASK WHATEVER IT IS YOU WANT TO ASK.
YOU WERE HERE LAST NIGHT?
YEAH. THAT'S RIGHT. BUT I DIDN'T SEE ANY WILD ANIMALS.
JUST A BUNCH OF KIDS SCREAMING THEIR HEADS OFF.
ASK ME, THEY JUST WANTED TO GET A LITTLE TIME ON TV.
WHAT ABOUT YOUR OTHER CUSTOMERS?
DID YOU SEE ANYONE ELSE AROUND WHO WAS ACTING ODD?
YEAH... I GUESS.
THERE WAS THIS ONE GUY. SORT OF A REGULAR.
HE WAS ACTING...I DUNNO... SICK OR SOMETHING. HE LOOKED AT ME LIKE--
THIS GUY... HE'S HERE A LOT?
DO YOU KNOW ANYTHING ABOUT HIM? HIS NAME, MAYBE?
HIS NAME'S VICTOR. HE COMES IN A COUPLE OF TIMES A WEEK.

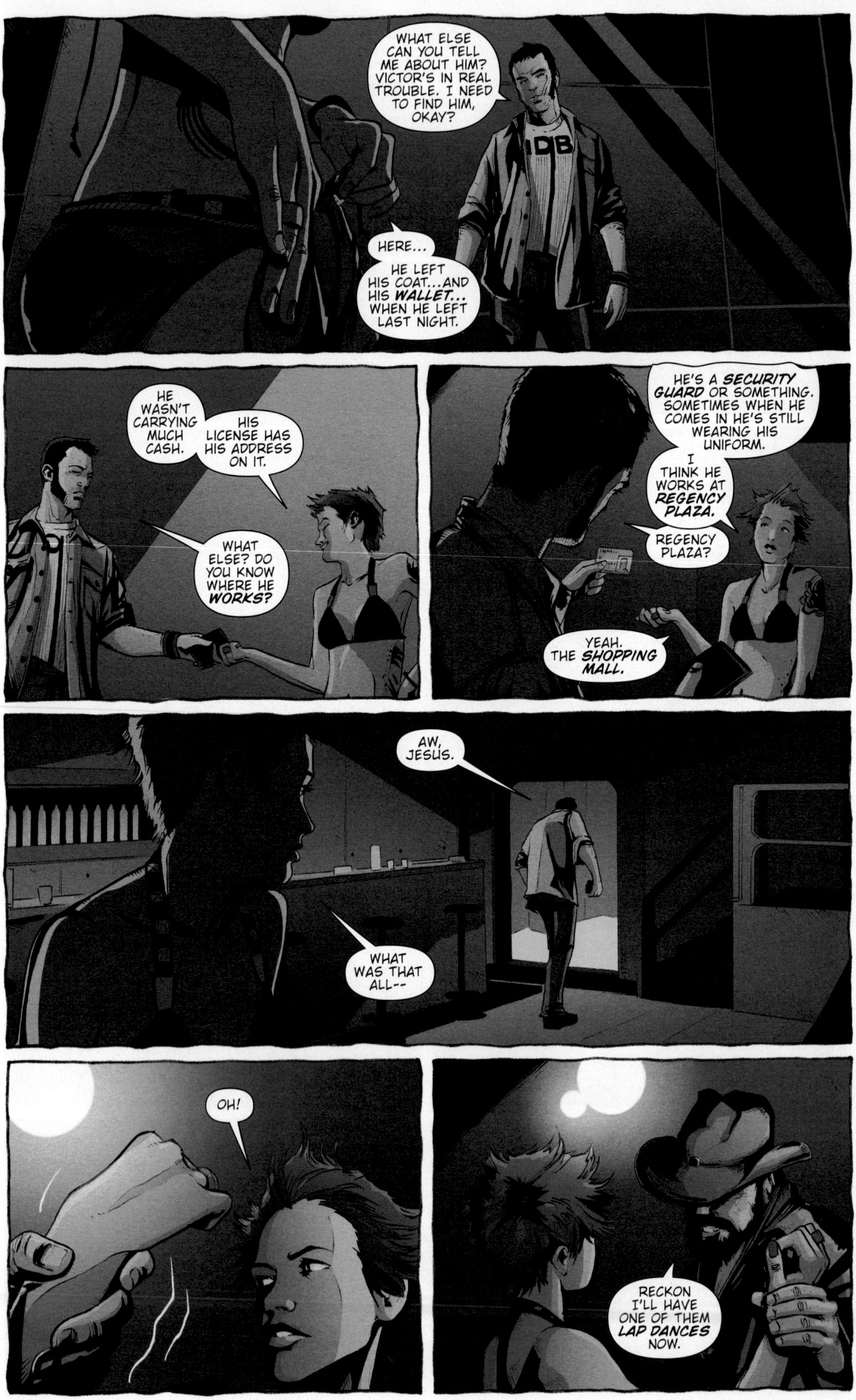
WHAT ELSE CAN YOU TELL ME ABOUT HIM? VICTOR'S IN REAL TROUBLE. I NEED TO FIND HIM, OKAY?
HERE...
HE LEFT HIS COAT...AND HIS ***WALLET...*** WHEN HE LEFT LAST NIGHT.
HE WASN'T CARRYING MUCH CASH.
HIS LICENSE HAS HIS ADDRESS ON IT.
WHAT ELSE? DO YOU KNOW WHERE HE ***WORKS?***
HE'S A ***SECURITY GUARD*** OR SOMETHING. SOMETIMES WHEN HE COMES IN HE'S STILL WEARING HIS UNIFORM.
I THINK HE WORKS AT ***REGENCY PLAZA.***
REGENCY PLAZA?
YEAH. THE ***SHOPPING MALL.***
AW, JESUS.
WHAT WAS THAT ALL--
OH!
RECKON I'LL HAVE ONE OF THEM ***LAP DANCES*** NOW.

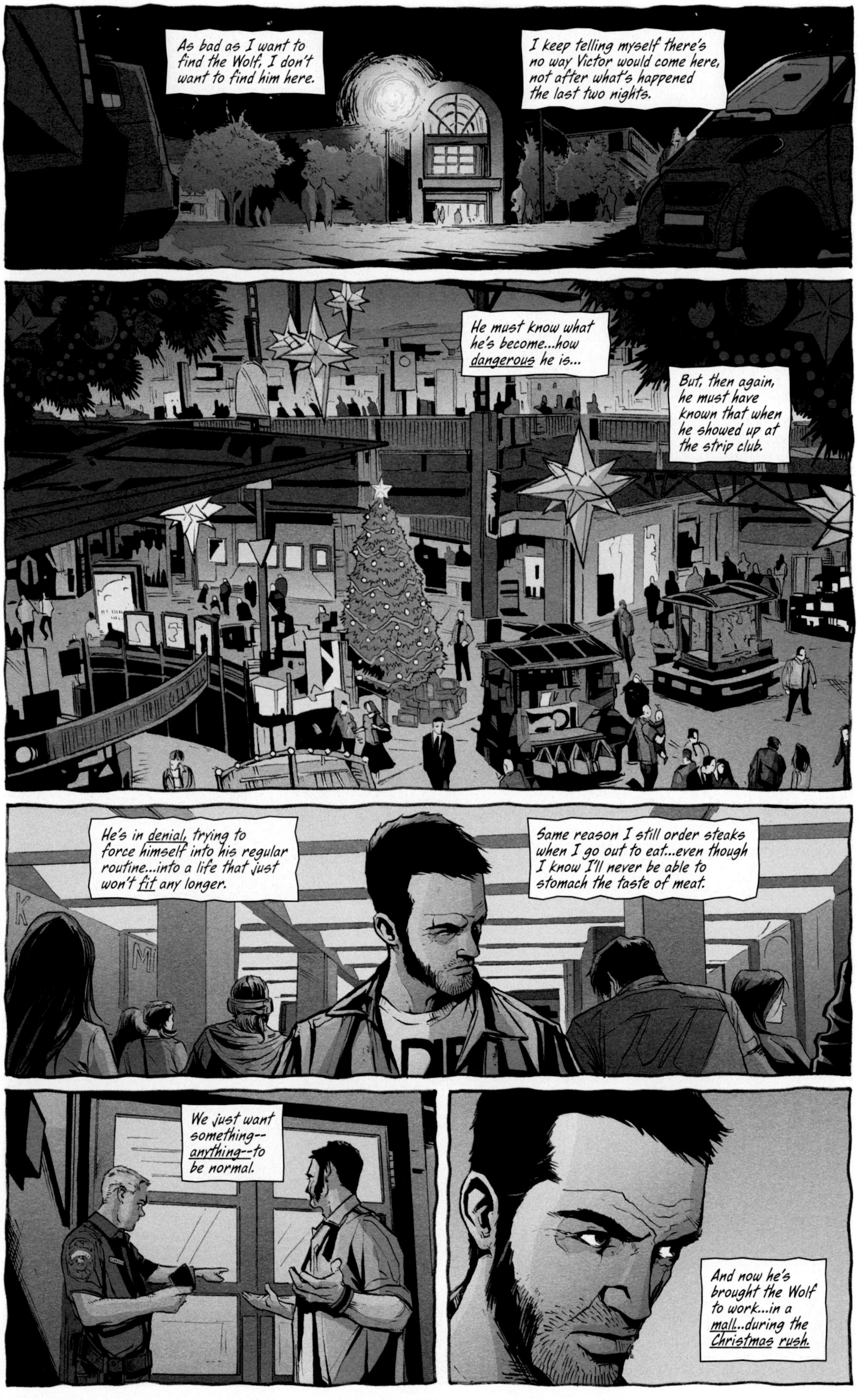

As bad as I want to find the Wolf, I don't want to find him here.
I keep telling myself there's no way Victor would come here, not after what's happened the last two nights.
He must know what he's become...how dangerous he is...
But, then again, he must have known that when he showed up at the strip club.
He's in denial, trying to force himself into his regular routine...into a life that just won't fit any longer.
Same reason I still order steaks when I go out to eat...even though I know I'll never be able to stomach the taste of meat.
We just want something--anything--to be normal.
And now he's brought the Wolf to work...in a mall...during the Christmas rush.

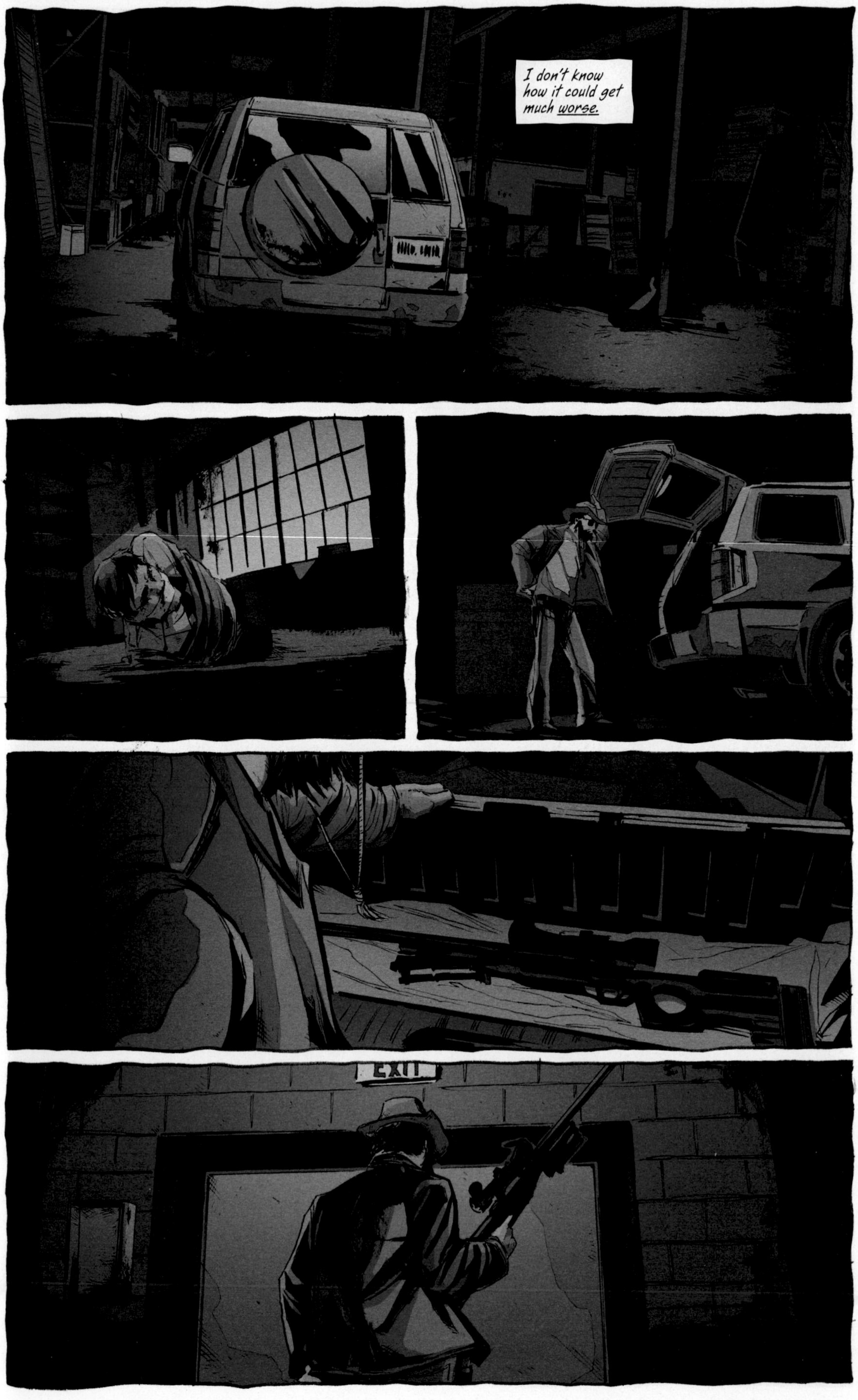
I don't know how it could get much worse.

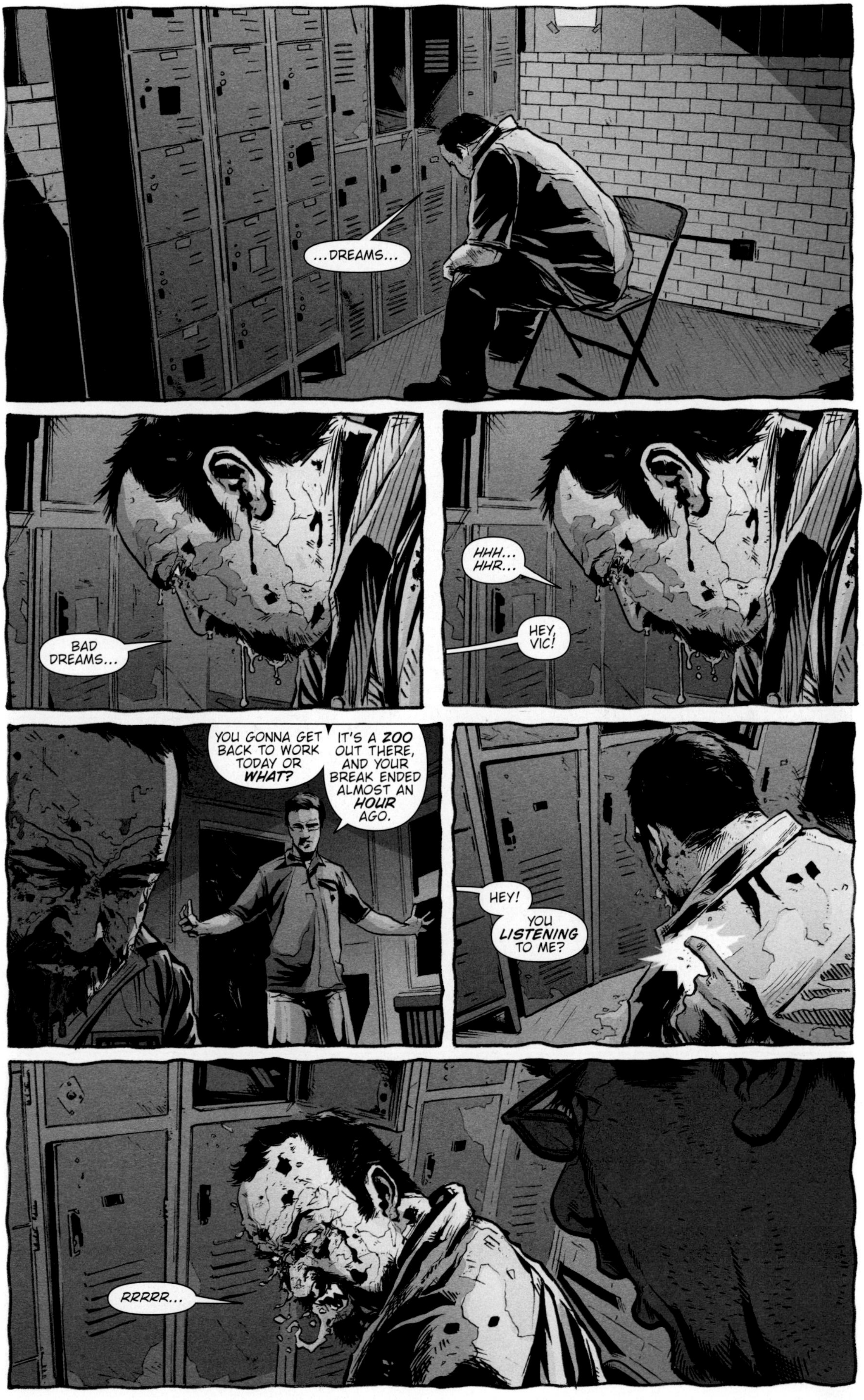
...DREAMS...
BAD DREAMS...
HHH... HHR...
HEY, VIC!
YOU GONNA GET BACK TO WORK TODAY OR WHAT?
IT'S A ZOO OUT THERE, AND YOUR BREAK ENDED ALMOST AN HOUR AGO.
HEY!
YOU LISTENING TO ME?
RRRRR...

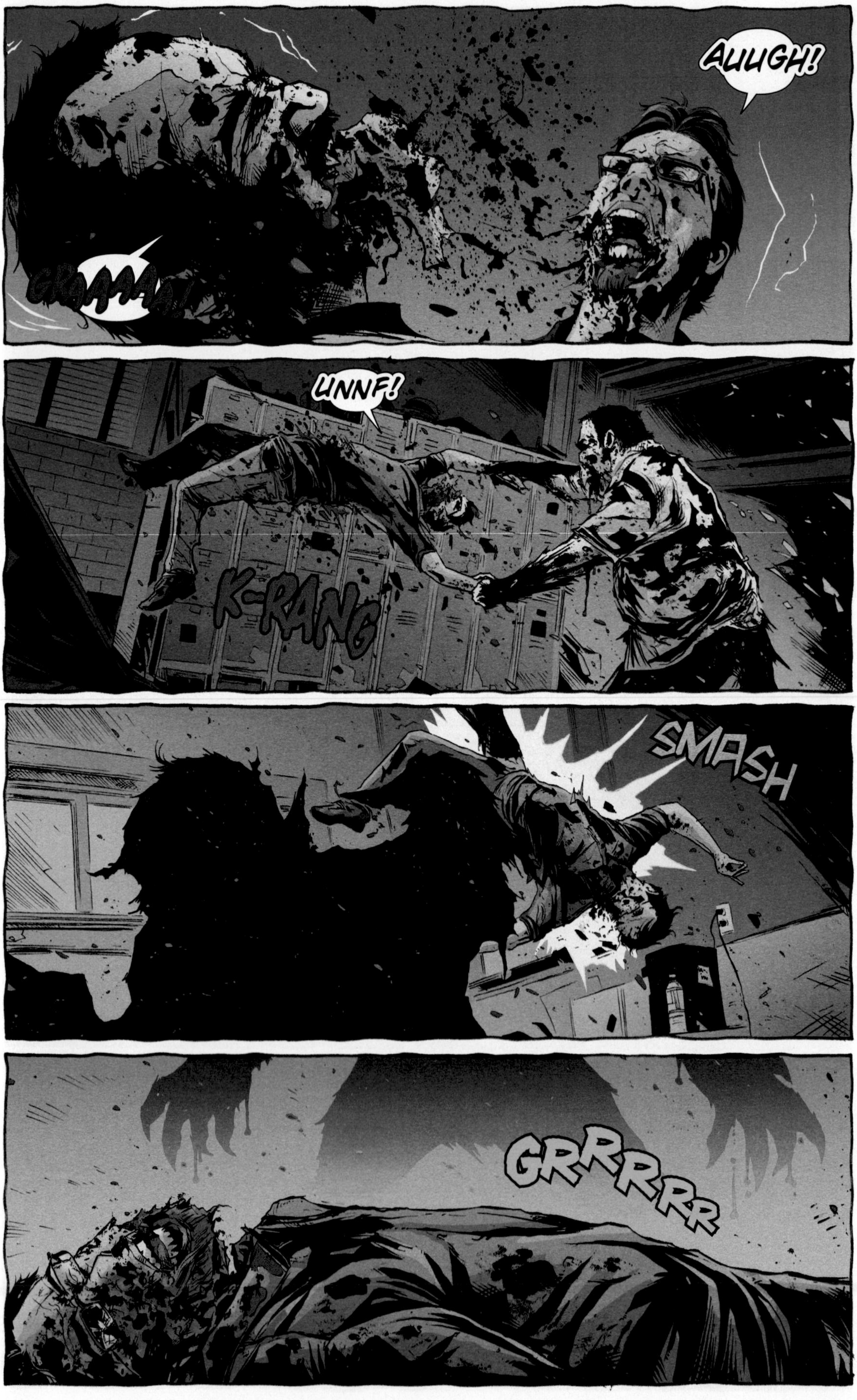
AUUGH!
UNNF!
K-RANG
SMASH
GRRRRRR

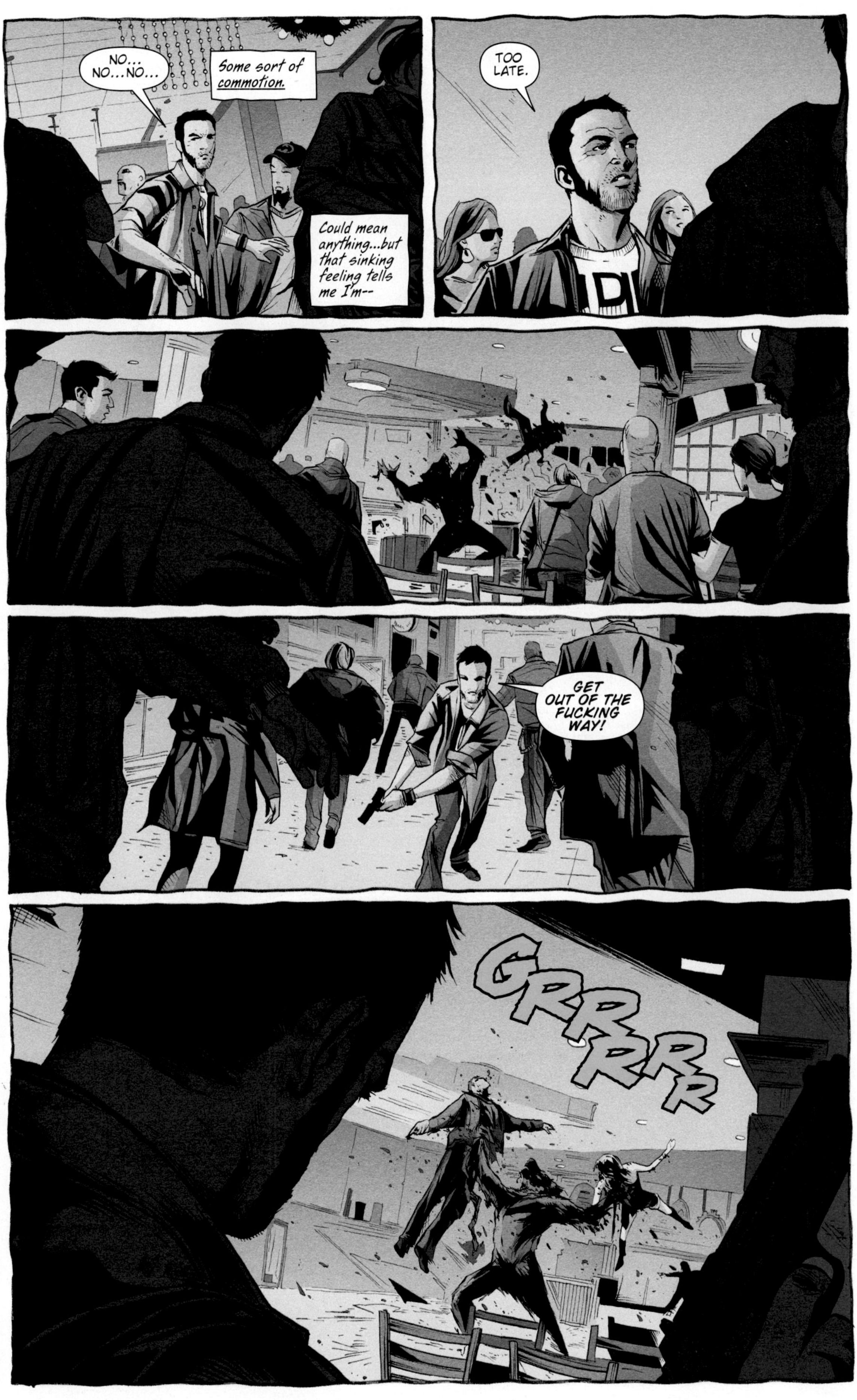
NO... NO...NO...
Some sort of commotion.
Could mean anything...but that sinking feeling tells me I'm--
TOO LATE.
GET OUT OF THE FUCKING WAY!
GRRRRR

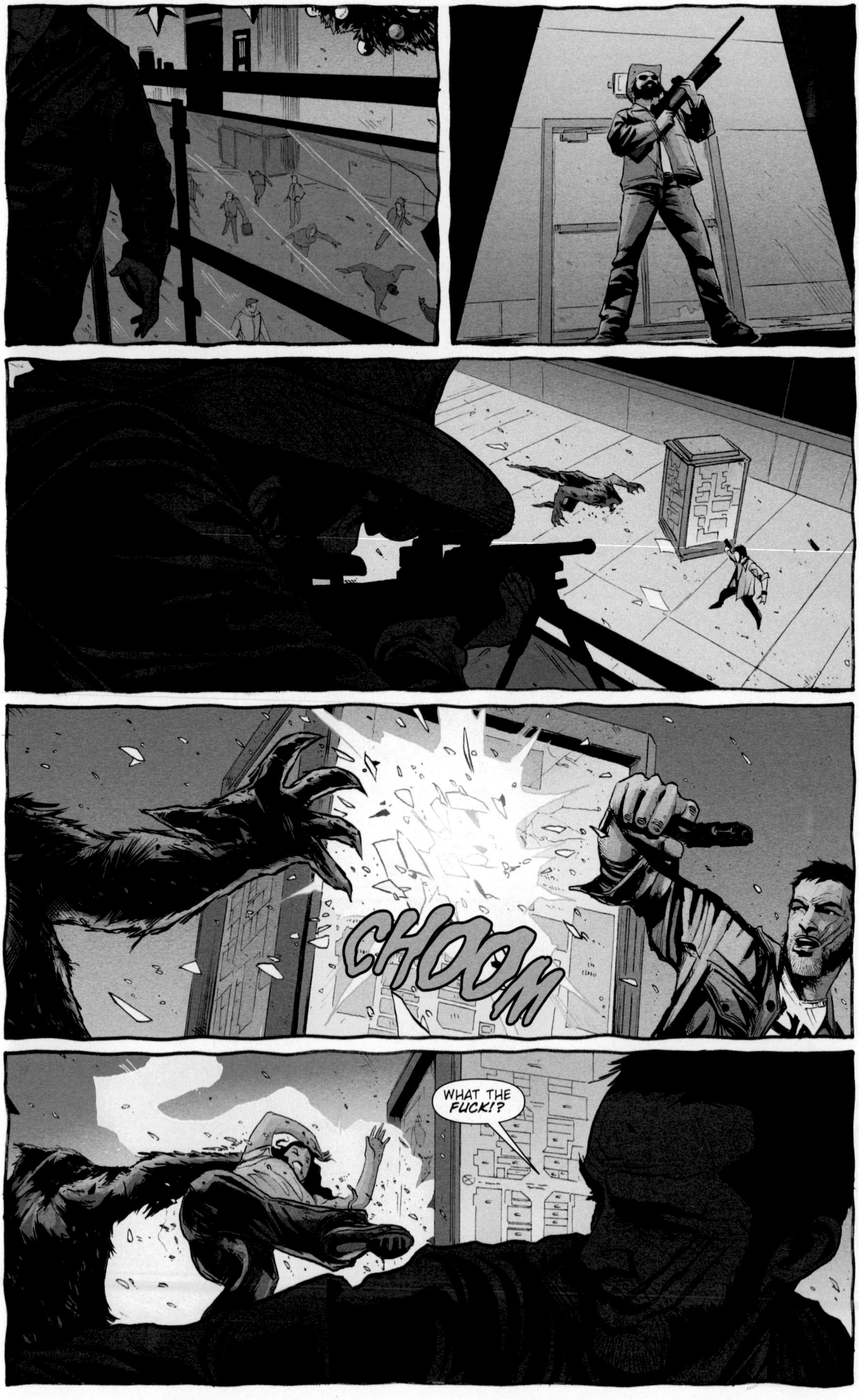
CHOOM
WHAT THE FUCK!?

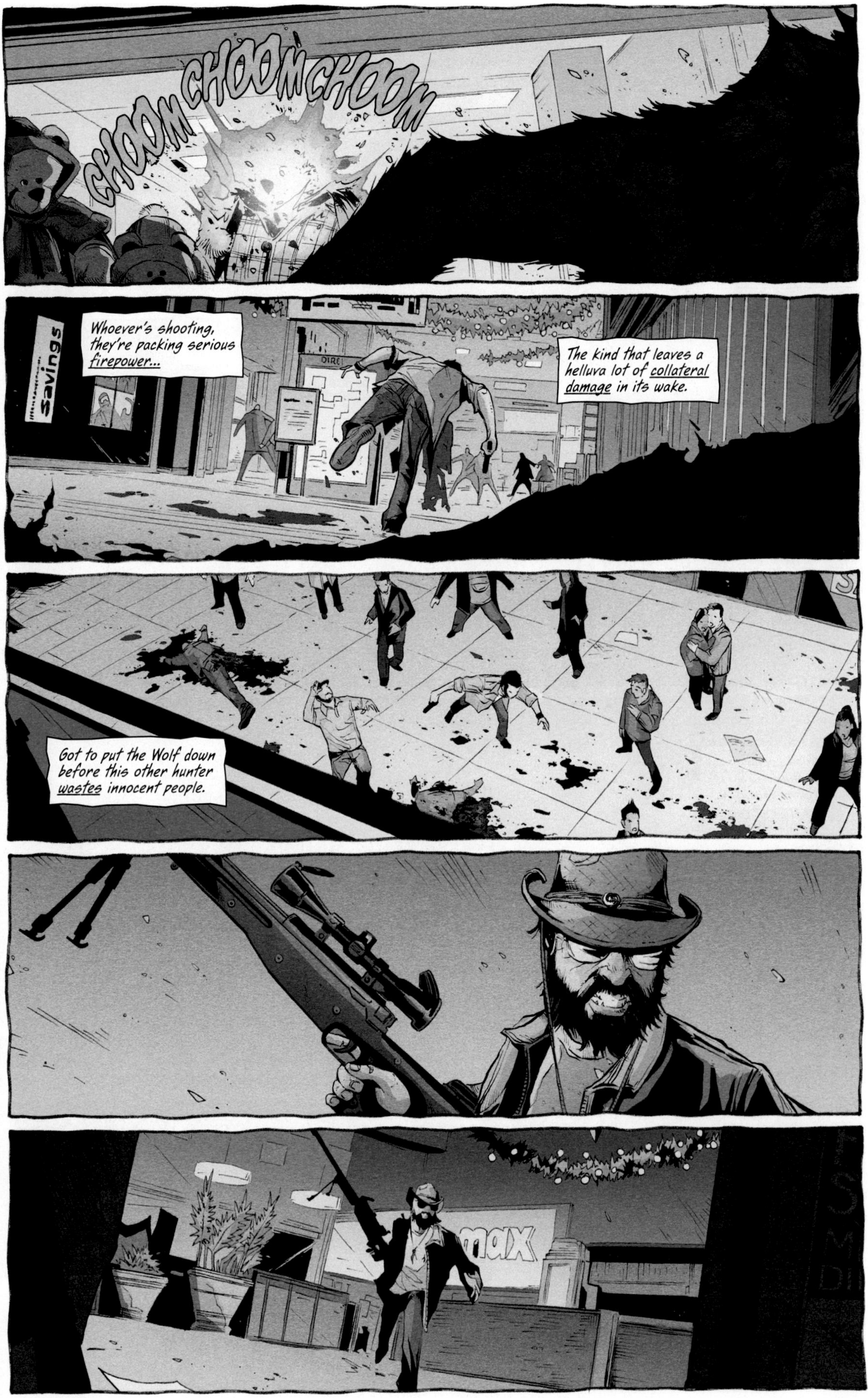
CHOOM CHOOM CHOOM CHOOM
Savings
Whoever's shooting, they're packing serious firepower...
The kind that leaves a helluva lot of collateral damage in its wake.
Got to put the Wolf down before this other hunter wastes innocent people.
max

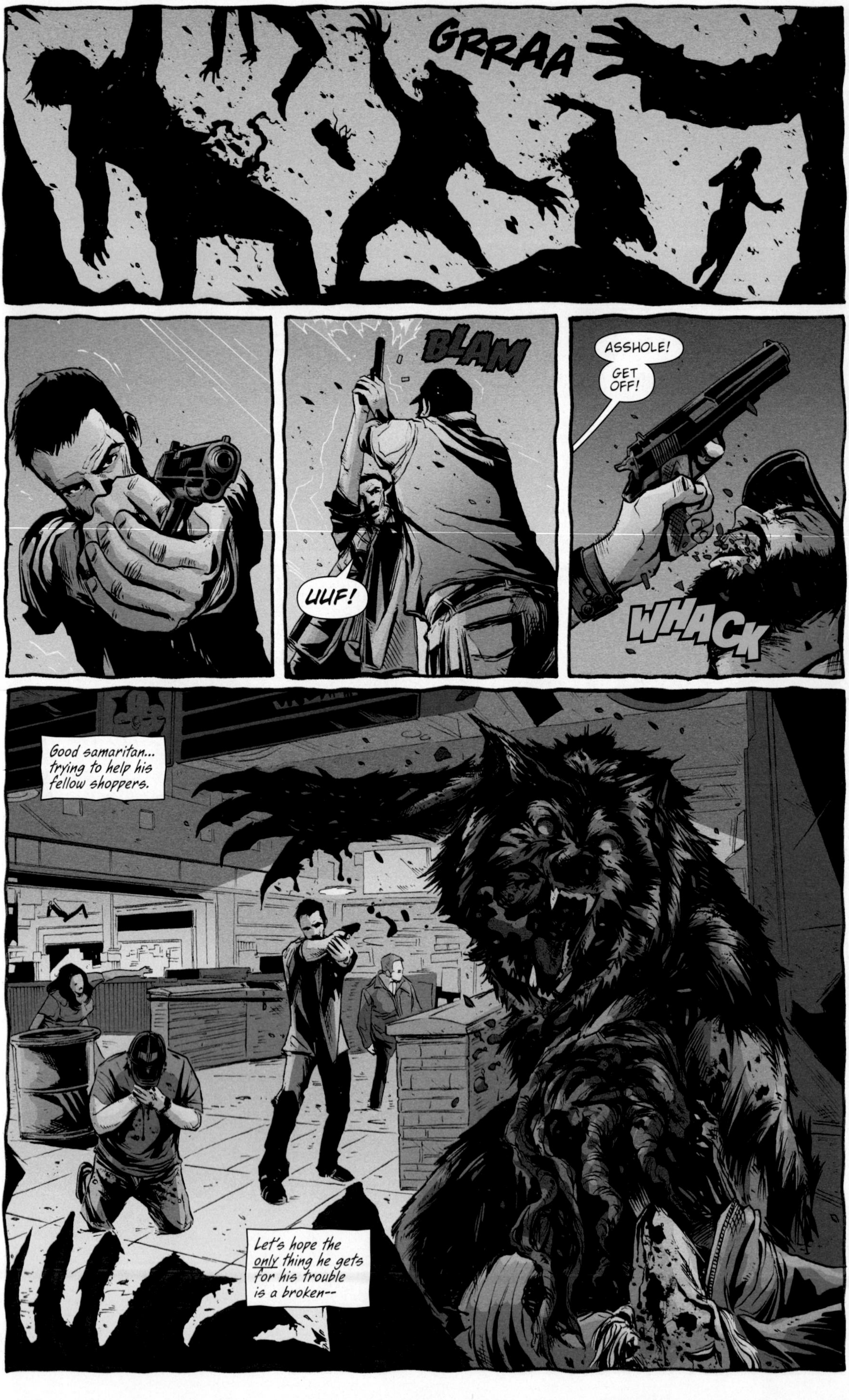
GRRAA
BLAM
UUF!
ASSHOLE!
GET OFF!
WHACK
Good samaritan... trying to help his fellow shoppers.
Let's hope the only thing he gets for his trouble is a broken--

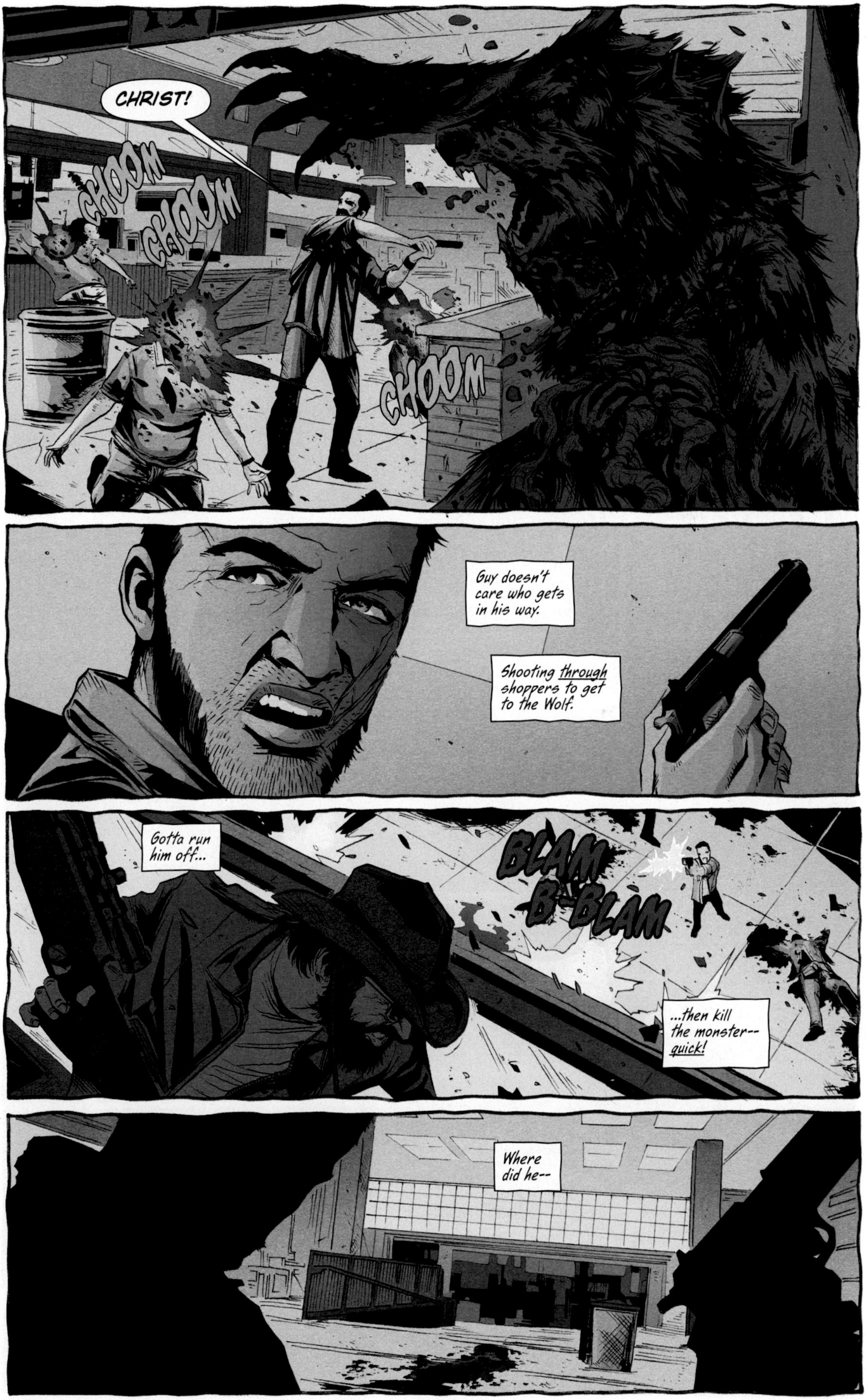
CHRIST!
CHOOM
CHOOM
CHOOM
Guy doesn't care who gets in his way.
Shooting through shoppers to get to the Wolf.
Gotta run him off...
BLAM
B-BLAM
...then kill the monster--quick!
Where did he--

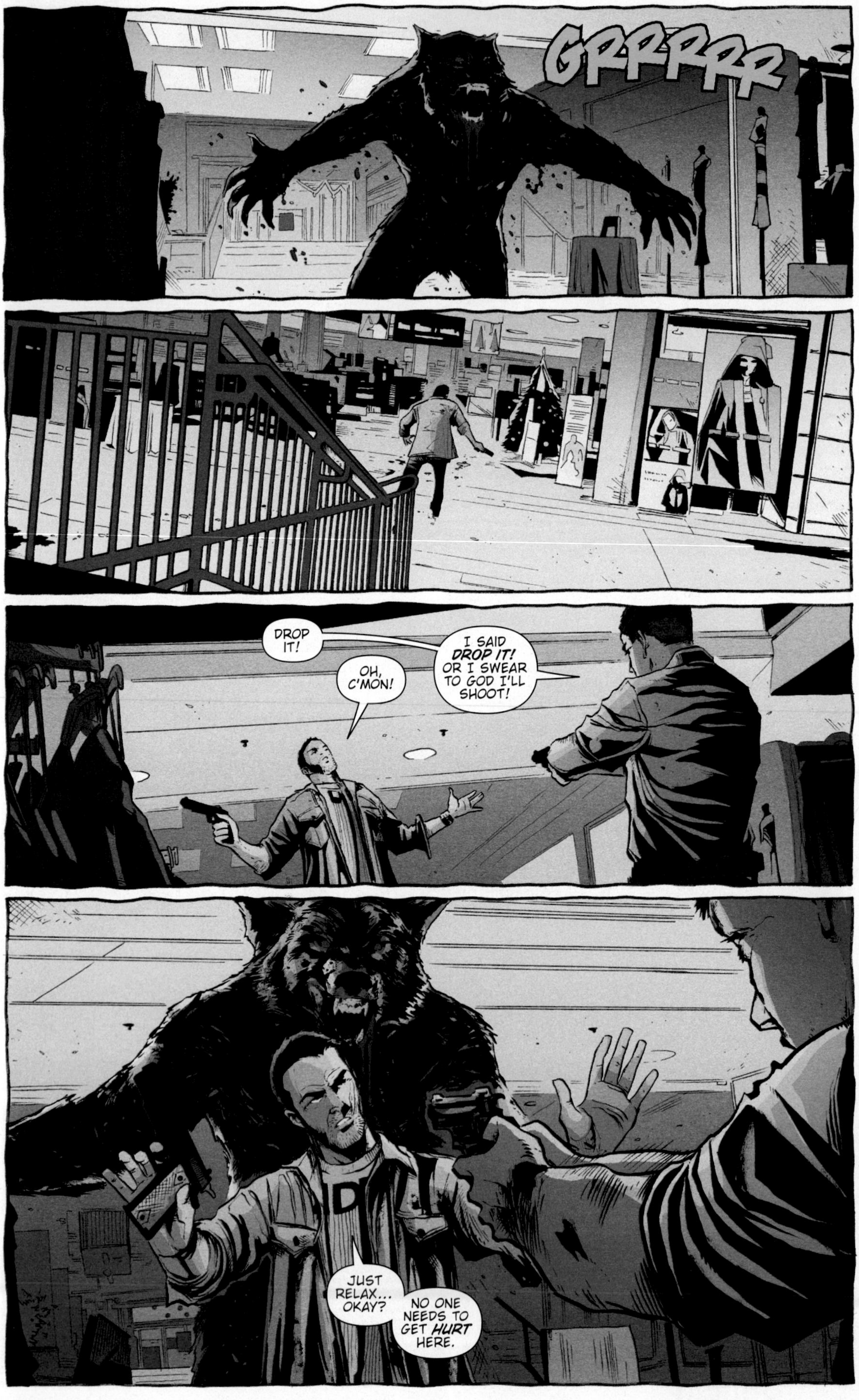
GRRRRR
DROP IT!
I SAID DROP IT! OR I SWEAR TO GOD I'LL SHOOT!
OH, C'MON!
JUST RELAX... OKAY?
NO ONE NEEDS TO GET HURT HERE.

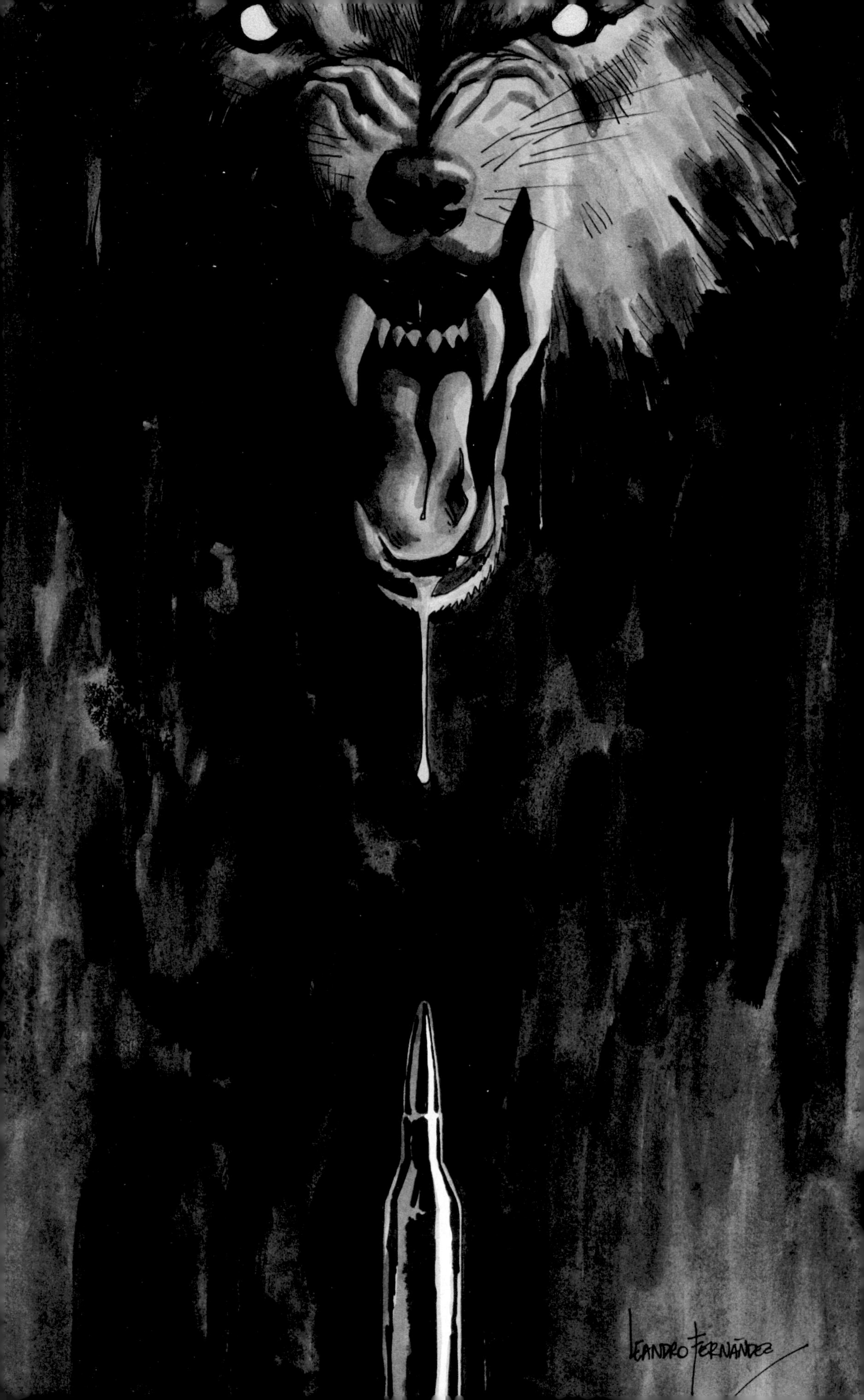
LEANDRO FERNÁNDEZ

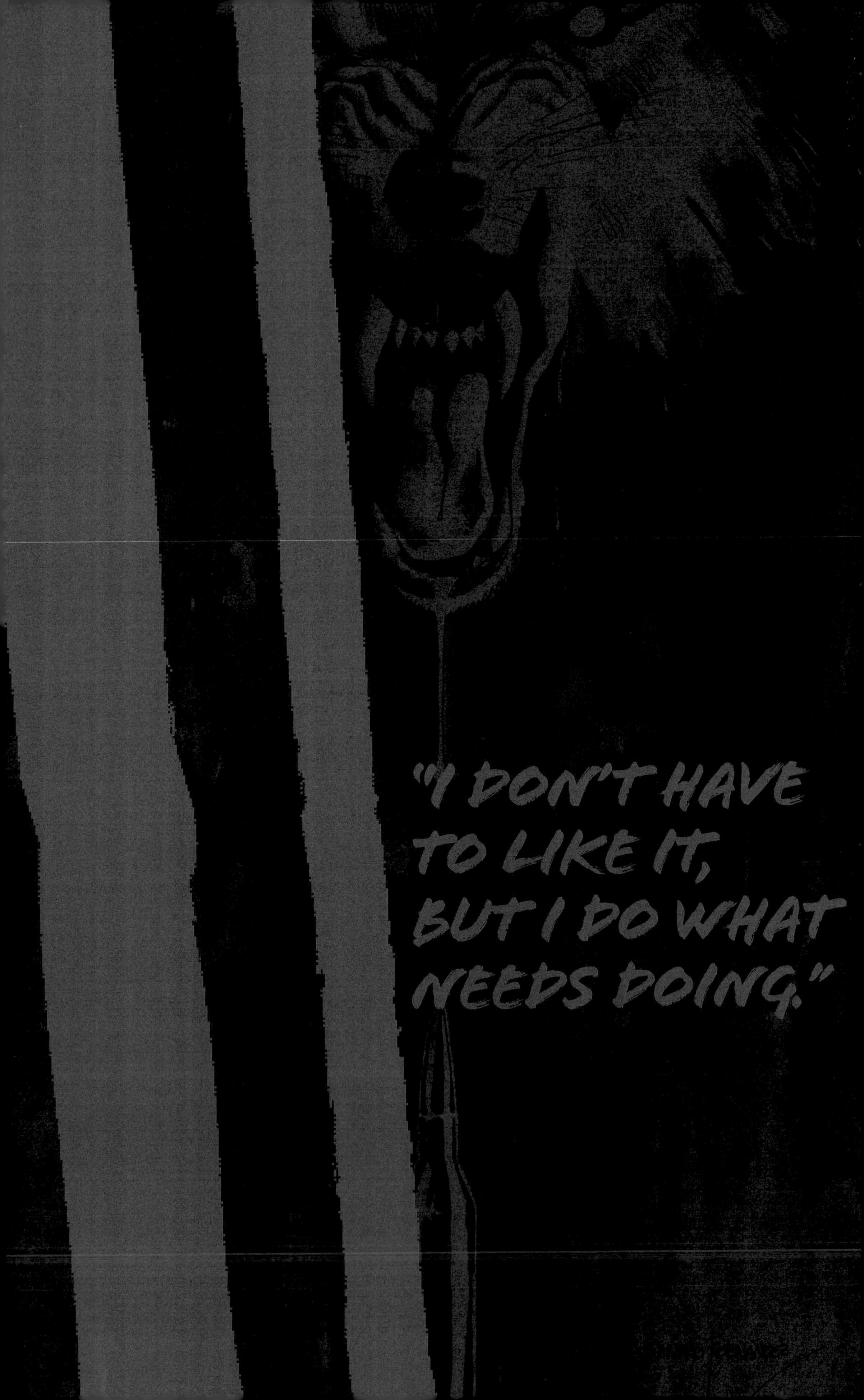
"I DON'T HAVE
TO LIKE IT,
BUT I DO WHAT
NEEDS DOING."

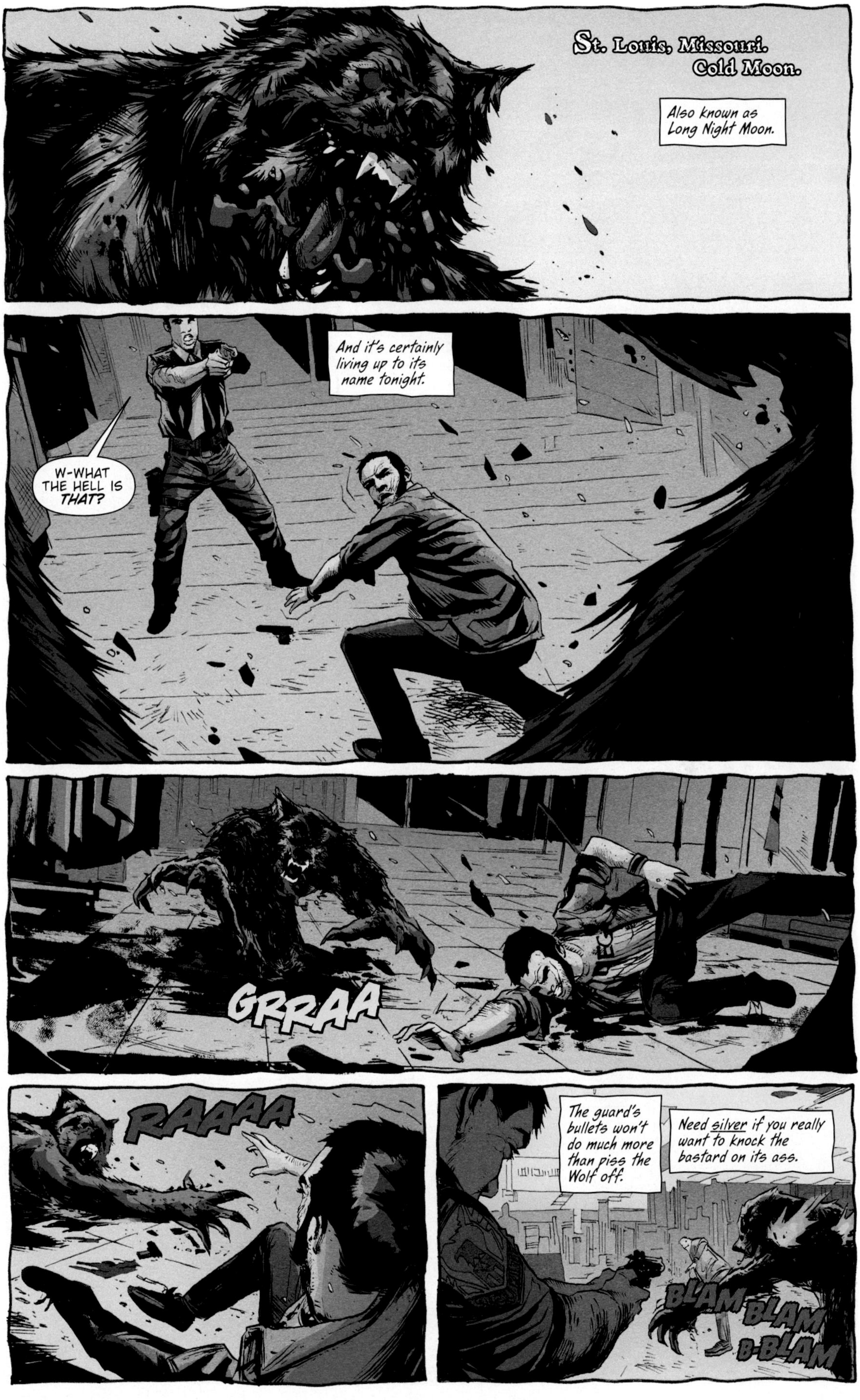
St. Louis, Missouri.
Cold Moon.
Also known as Long Night Moon.
And it's certainly living up to its name tonight.
W-WHAT THE HELL IS THAT?
GRRAA
RAAAA
The guard's bullets won't do much more than piss the Wolf off.
Need silver if you really want to knock the bastard on its ass.
BLAM
BLAM
B-BLAM

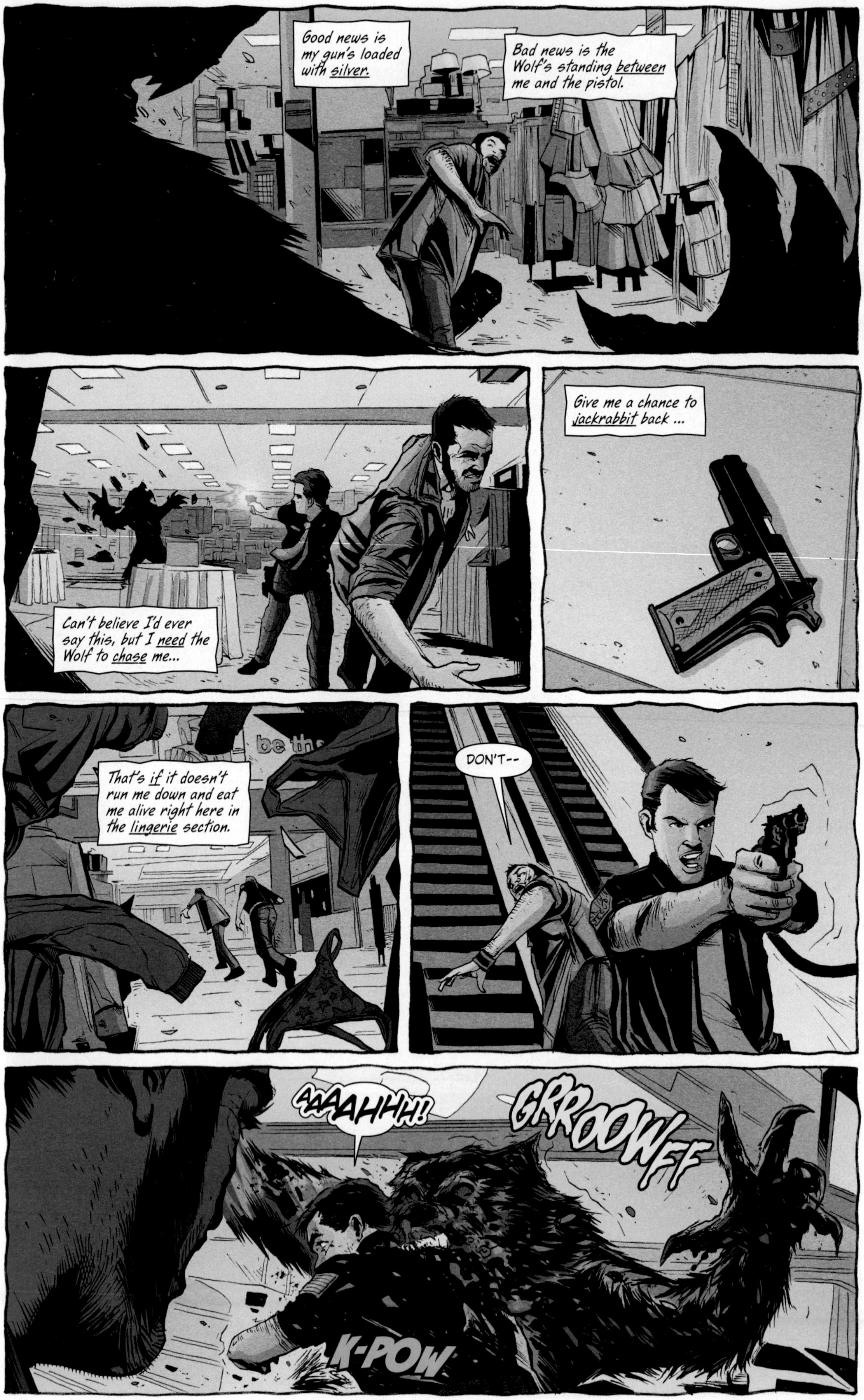
Good news is my gun's loaded with silver.
Bad news is the Wolf's standing between me and the pistol.
Can't believe I'd ever say this, but I need the Wolf to chase me...
Give me a chance to jackrabbit back ...
That's if it doesn't run me down and eat me alive right here in the lingerie section.
DON'T--
AAAAHHH!
GRROOWFF
K-POW

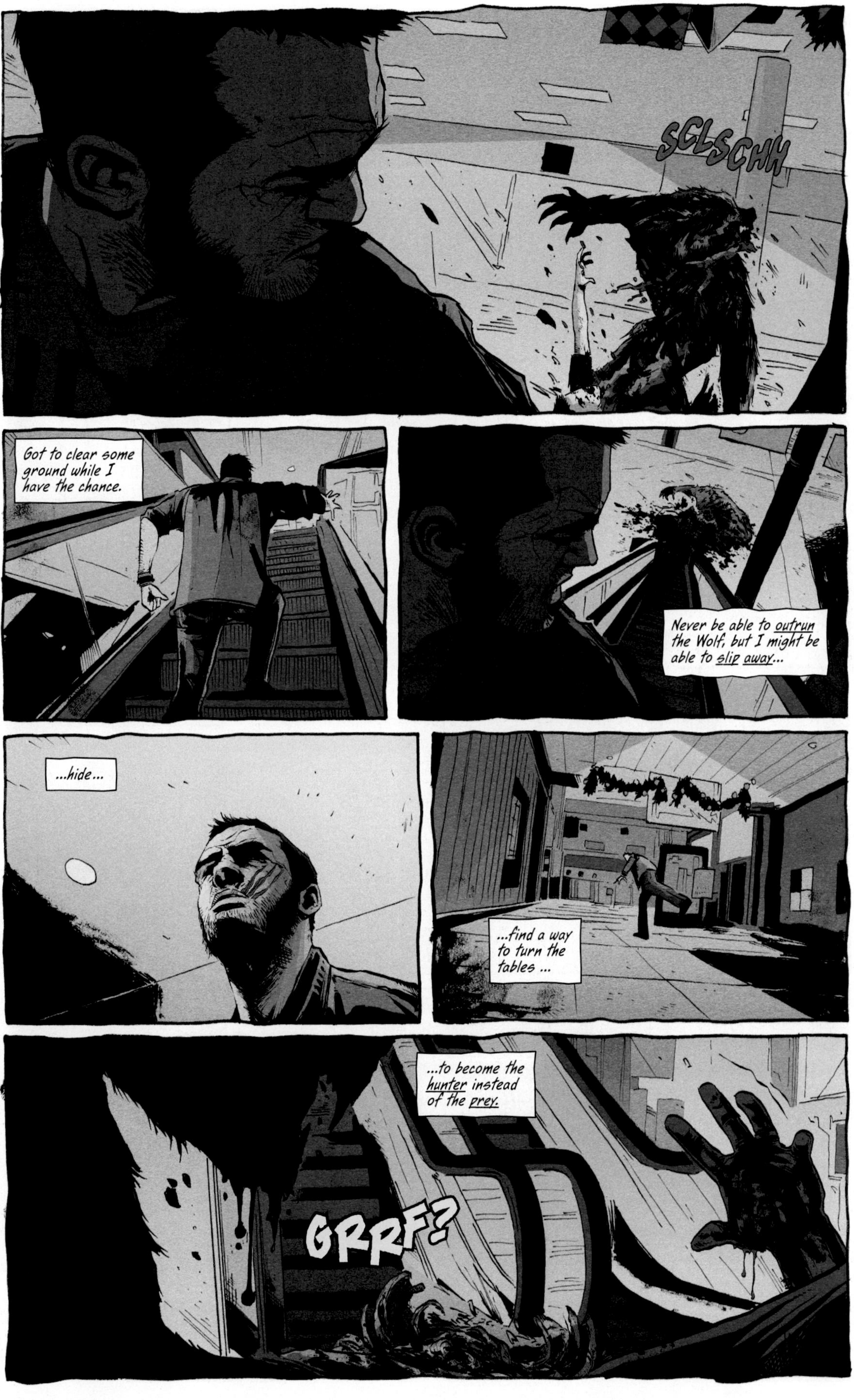
SCLSCHH
Got to clear some ground while I have the chance.
Never be able to outrun the Wolf, but I might be able to slip away...
...hide...
...find a way to turn the tables ...
...to become the hunter instead of the prey.
GRRF?

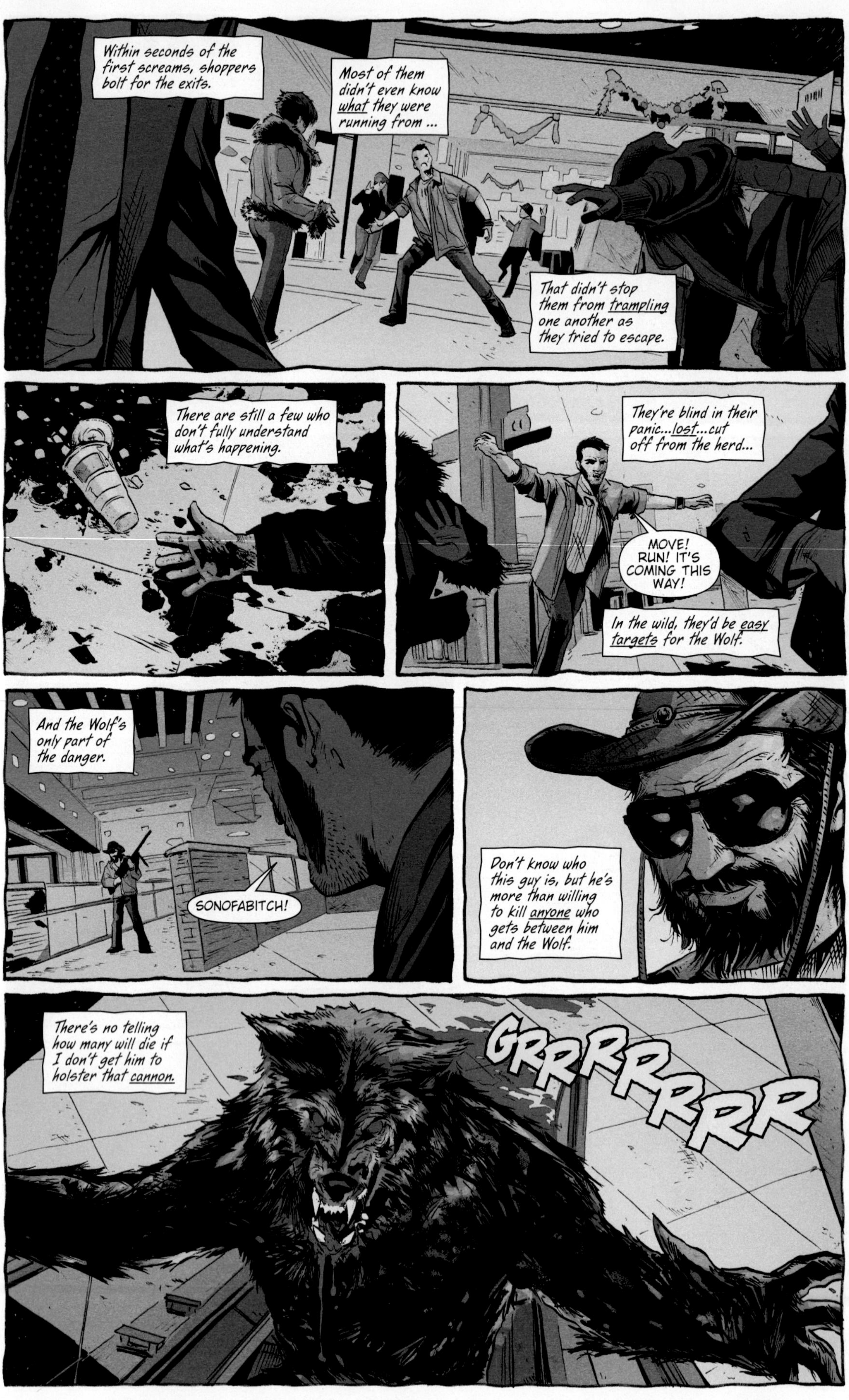
Within seconds of the first screams, shoppers bolt for the exits.
Most of them didn't even know what they were running from ...
That didn't stop them from trampling one another as they tried to escape.
There are still a few who don't fully understand what's happening.
They're blind in their panic...lost...cut off from the herd...
MOVE! RUN! IT'S COMING THIS WAY!
In the wild, they'd be easy targets for the Wolf.
And the Wolf's only part of the danger.
SONOFABITCH!
Don't know who this guy is, but he's more than willing to kill anyone who gets between him and the Wolf.
There's no telling how many will die if I don't get him to holster that cannon.
GRRRRRRR

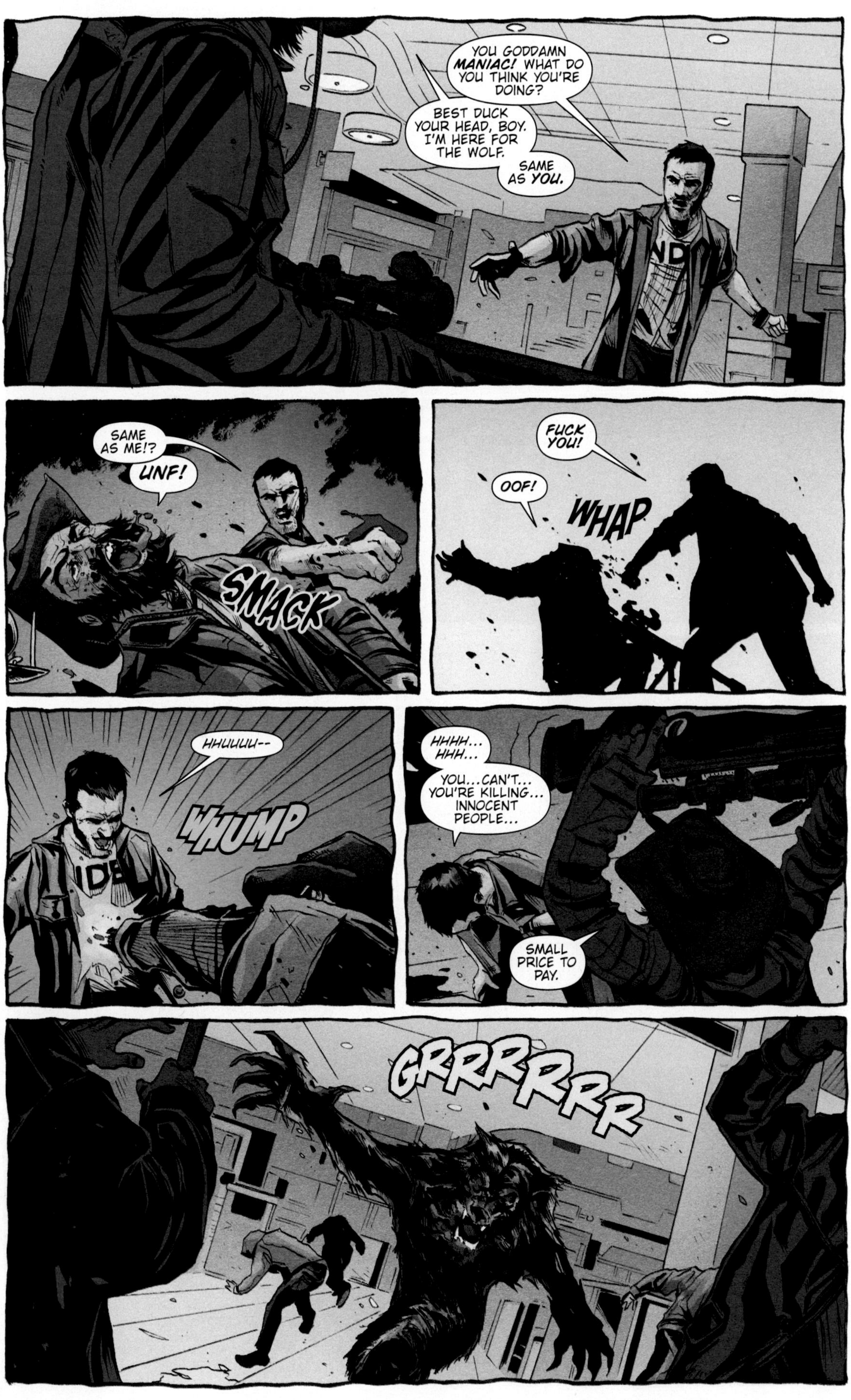
YOU GODDAMN MANIAC! WHAT DO YOU THINK YOU'RE DOING?
BEST DUCK YOUR HEAD, BOY. I'M HERE FOR THE WOLF.
SAME AS YOU.
SAME AS ME!?
UNF!
SMACK
FUCK YOU!
OOF!
WHAP
HHUUUU--
WHUMP
HHHH... HHH...
YOU...CAN'T... YOU'RE KILLING... INNOCENT PEOPLE...
SMALL PRICE TO PAY.
GRRRRRRR

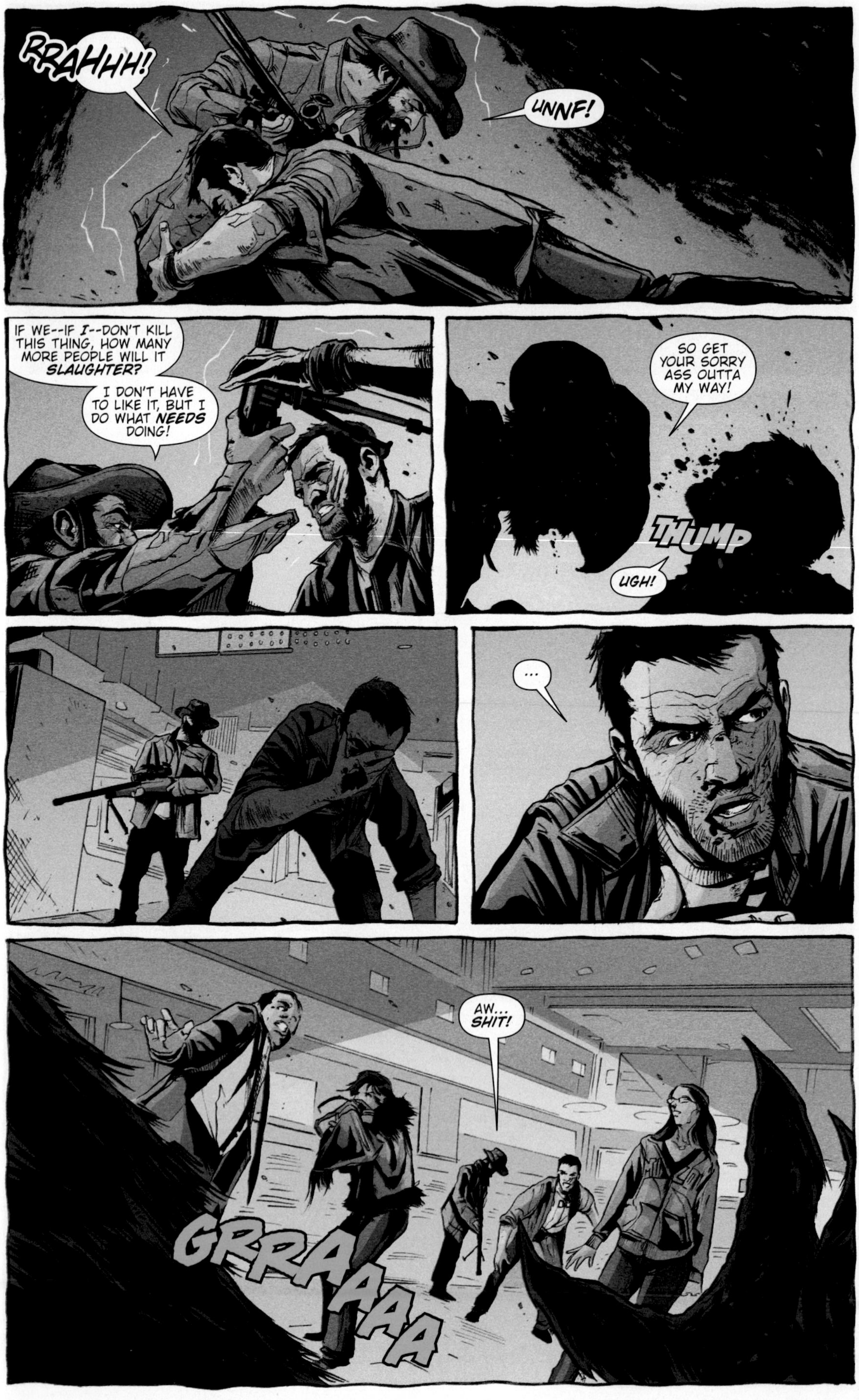
RRAHHH!
UNNF!
IF WE--IF I--DON'T KILL THIS THING, HOW MANY MORE PEOPLE WILL IT SLAUGHTER?
I DON'T HAVE TO LIKE IT, BUT I DO WHAT NEEDS DOING!
SO GET YOUR SORRY ASS OUTTA MY WAY!
THUMP
UGH!
...
AW... SHIT!
GRRAAAAA

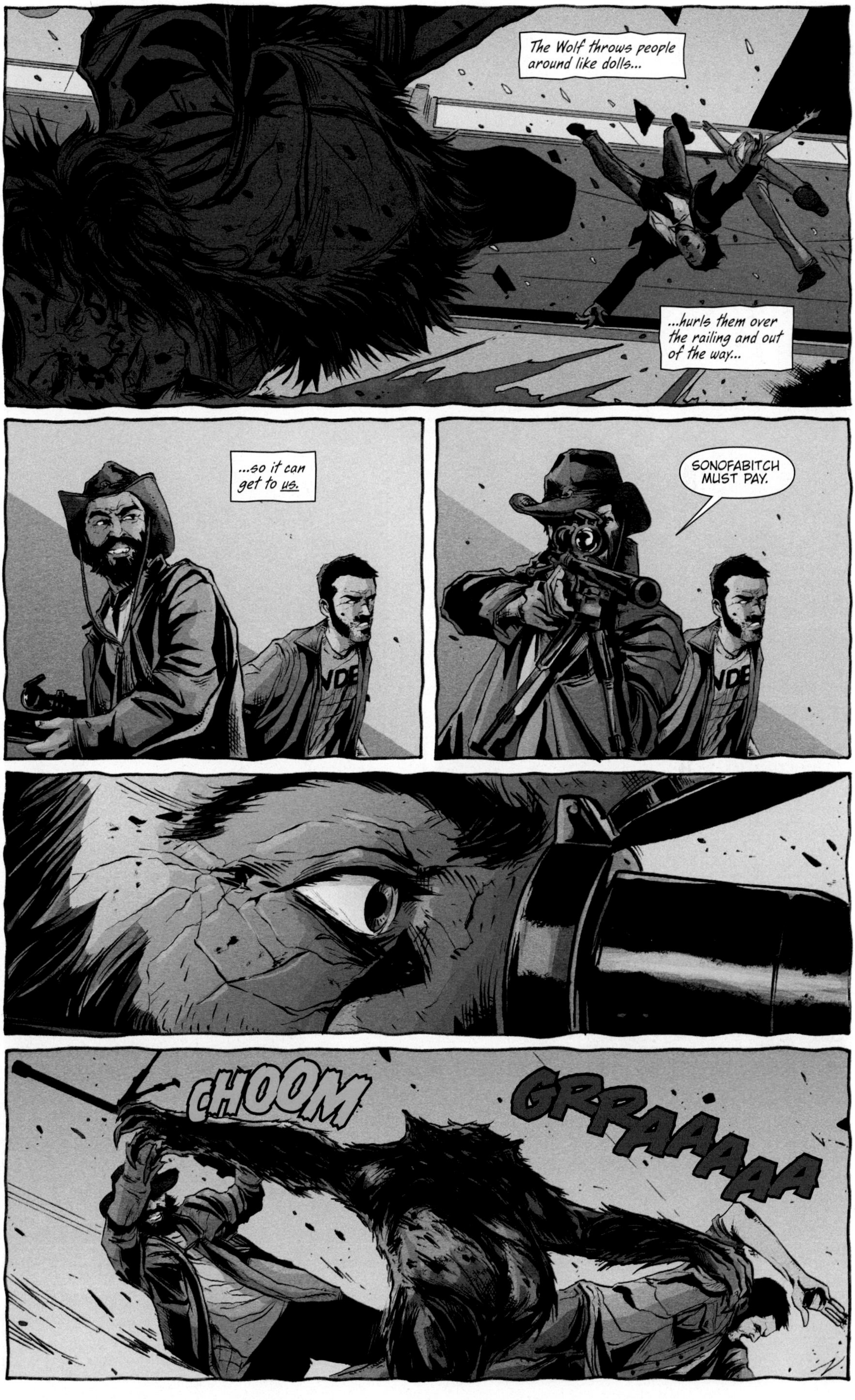
The Wolf throws people around like dolls...
...hurls them over the railing and out of the way...
...so it can get to us.
SONOFABITCH MUST PAY.
CHOOM
GRRAAAAAA

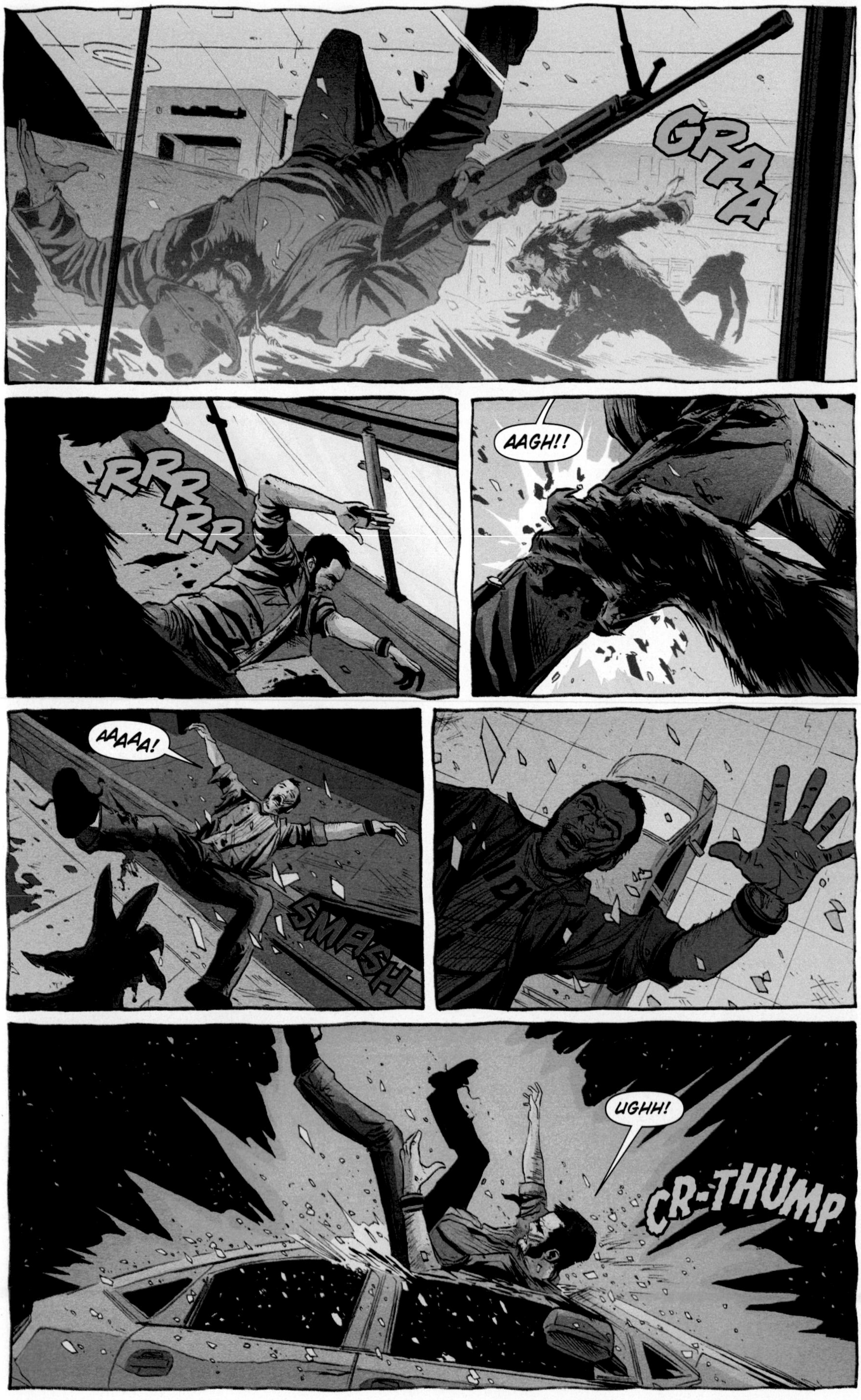
GRAA
RRRRRR
AAGH!!
AAAAA!
SMASH
UGHH!
CR-THUMP

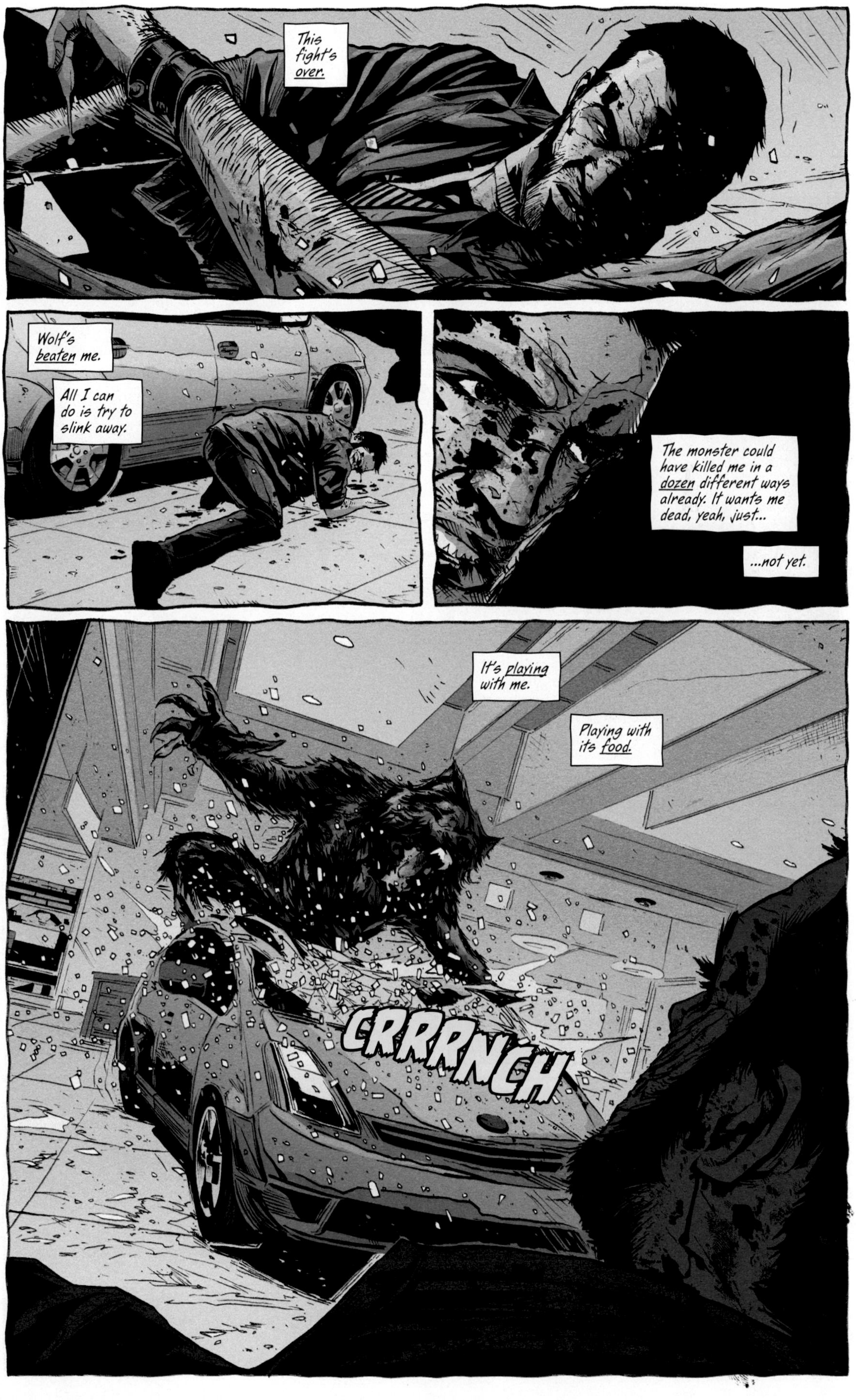
This fight's over.
Wolf's beaten me.
All I can do is try to slink away.
The monster could have killed me in a dozen different ways already. It wants me dead, yeah, just...
...not yet.
It's playing with me.
Playing with its food.
CRRRNCH

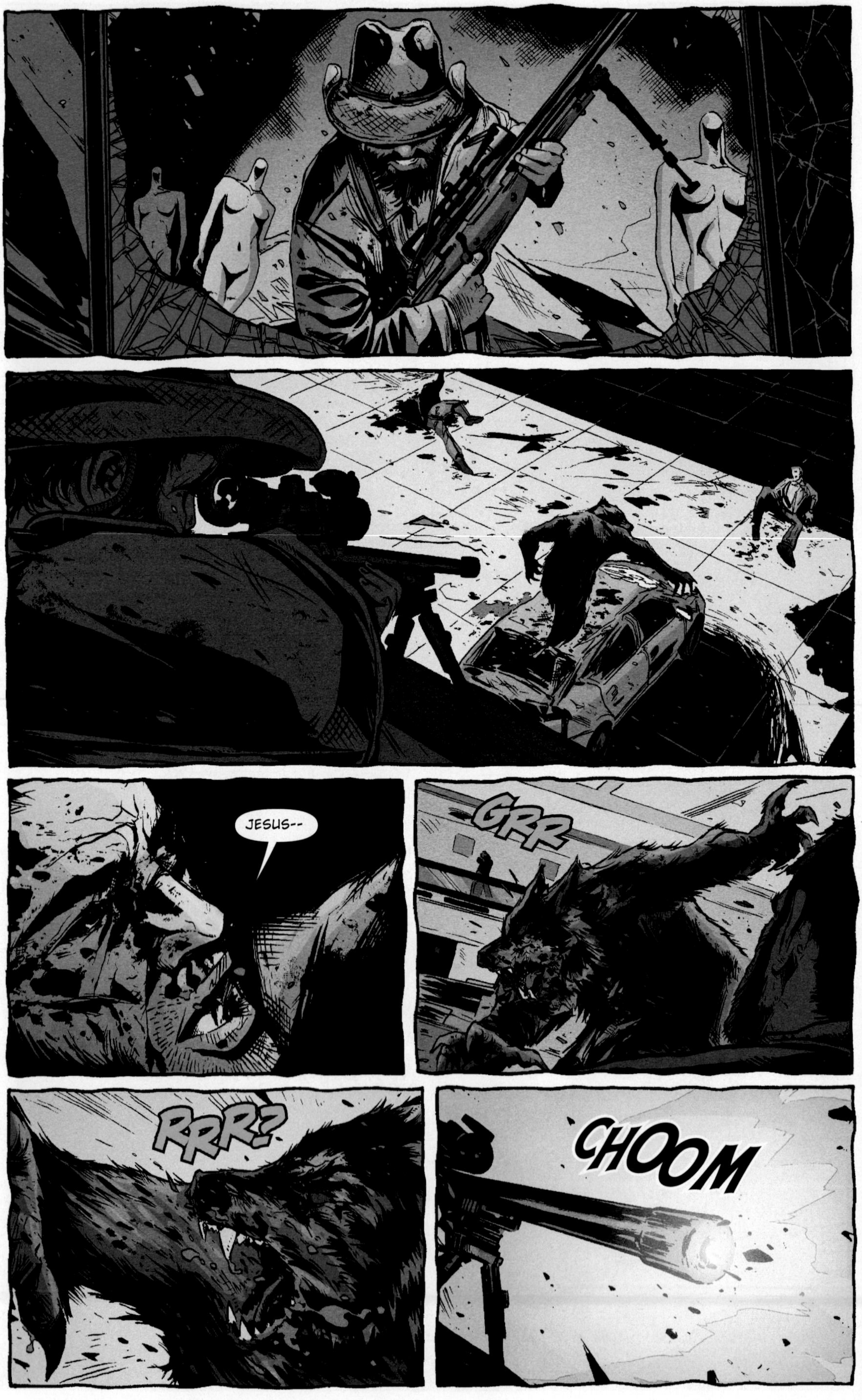
JESUS--
GRR
RRR?
CHOOM

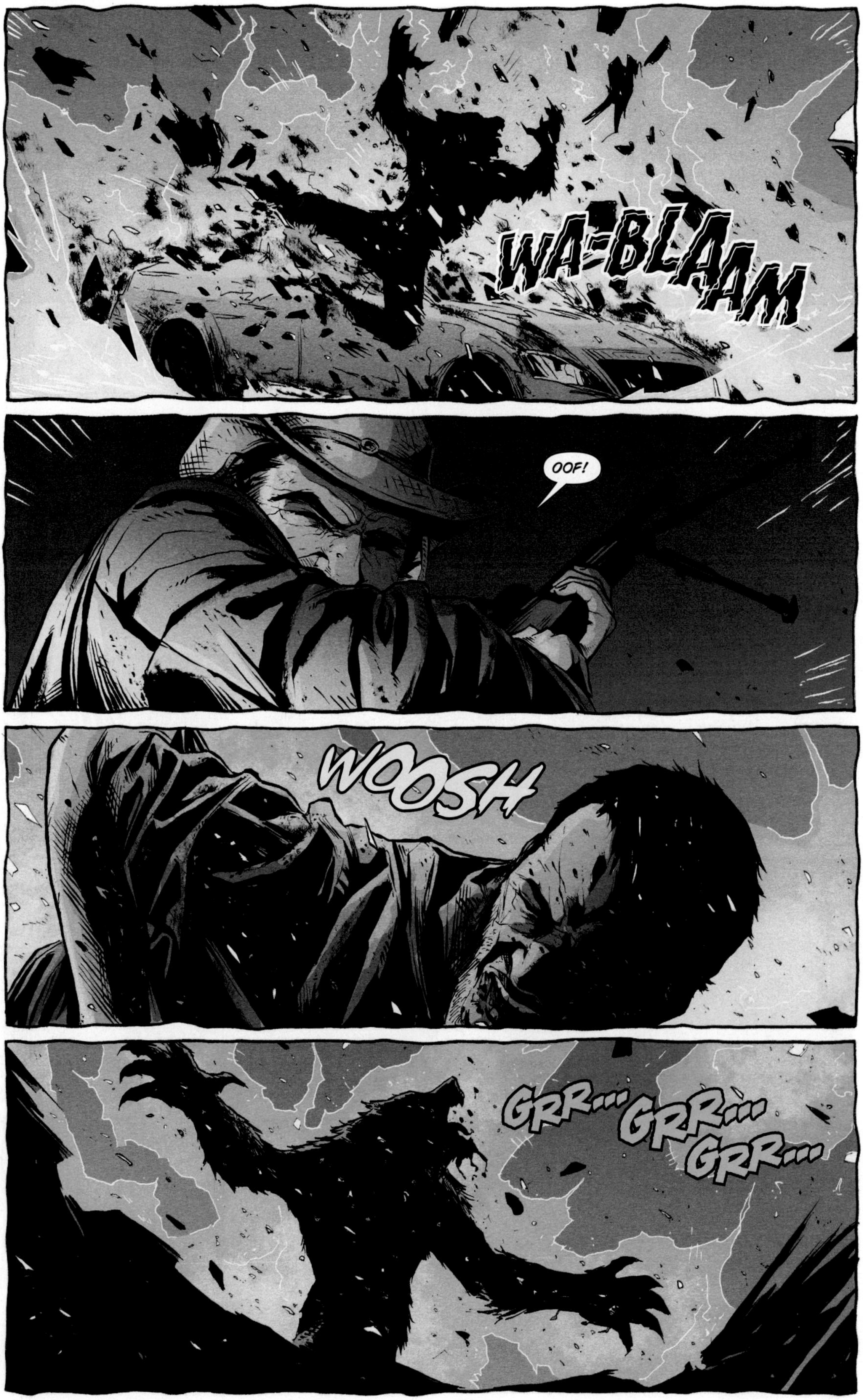
WA-BLAAM
OOF!
WOOSH
GRR... GRR... GRR...

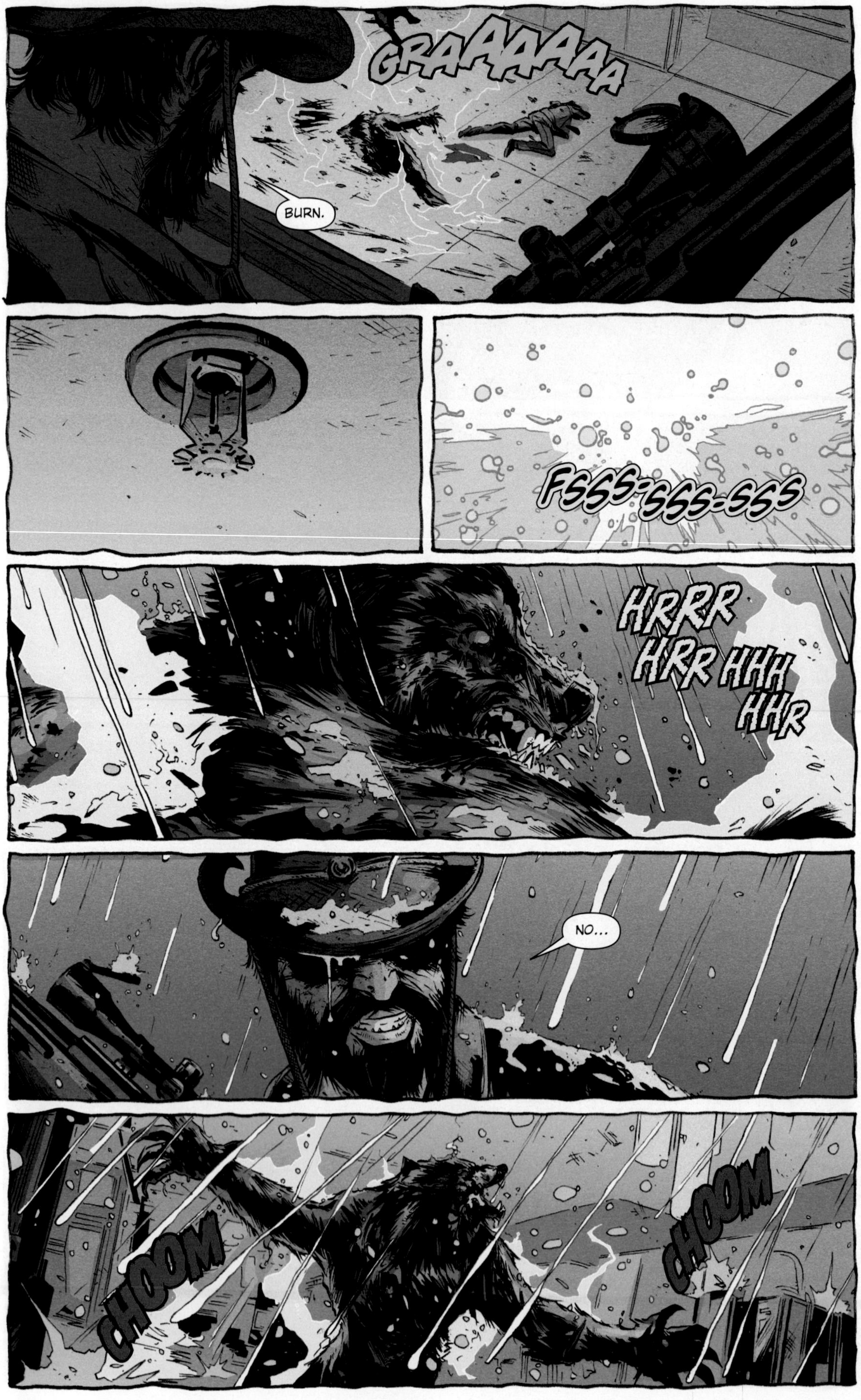
GRAAAAAA
BURN.
FSSS-SSS-SSS
HRRR HRR HHH HHR
NO...
CHOOM
CHOOM

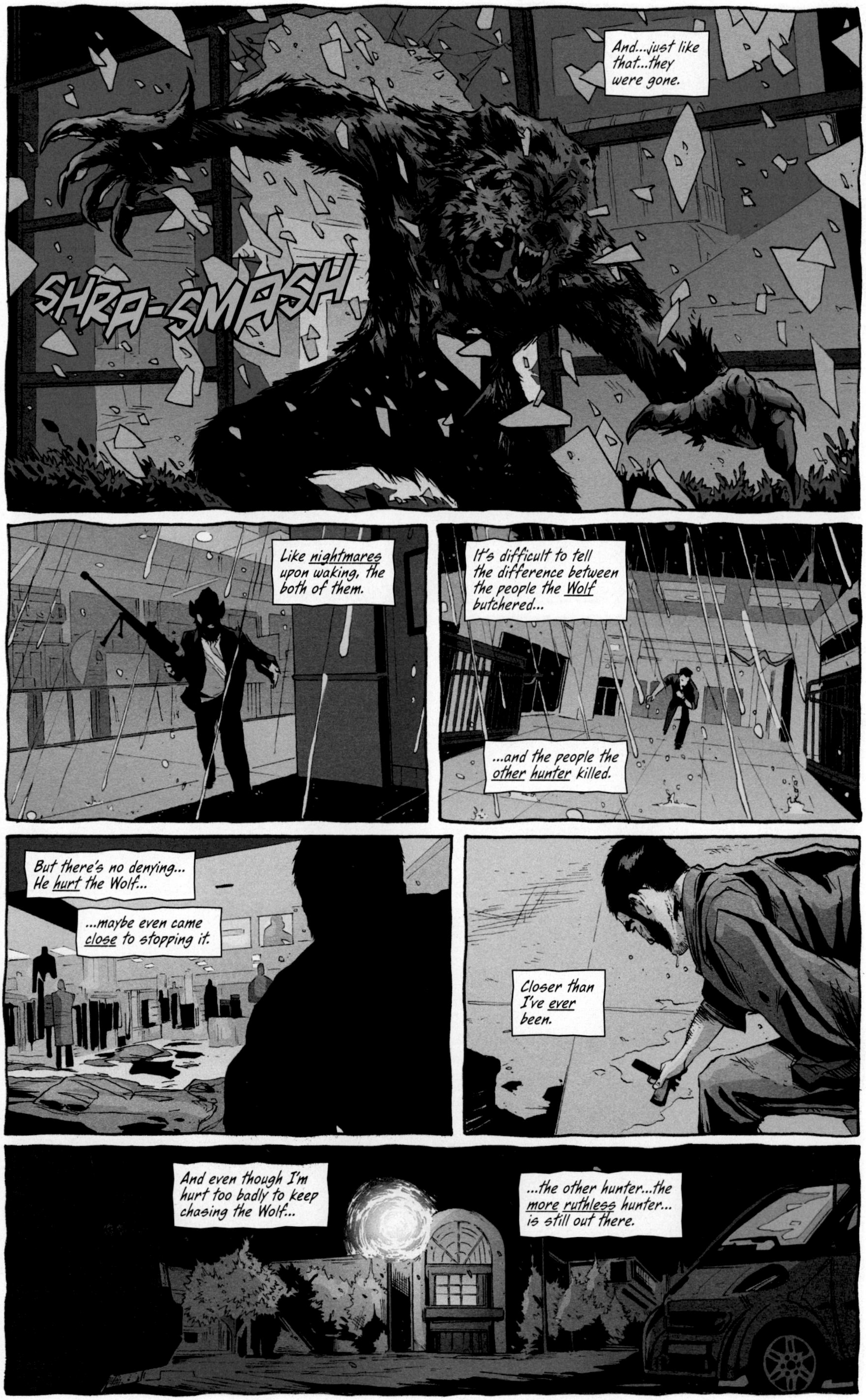
And...just like that...they were gone.
SHRA-SMASH
Like nightmares upon waking, the both of them.
It's difficult to tell the difference between the people the Wolf butchered...
...and the people the other hunter killed.
But there's no denying... He hurt the Wolf...
...maybe even came close to stopping it.
Closer than I've ever been.
And even though I'm hurt too badly to keep chasing the Wolf...
...the other hunter...the more ruthless hunter... is still out there.

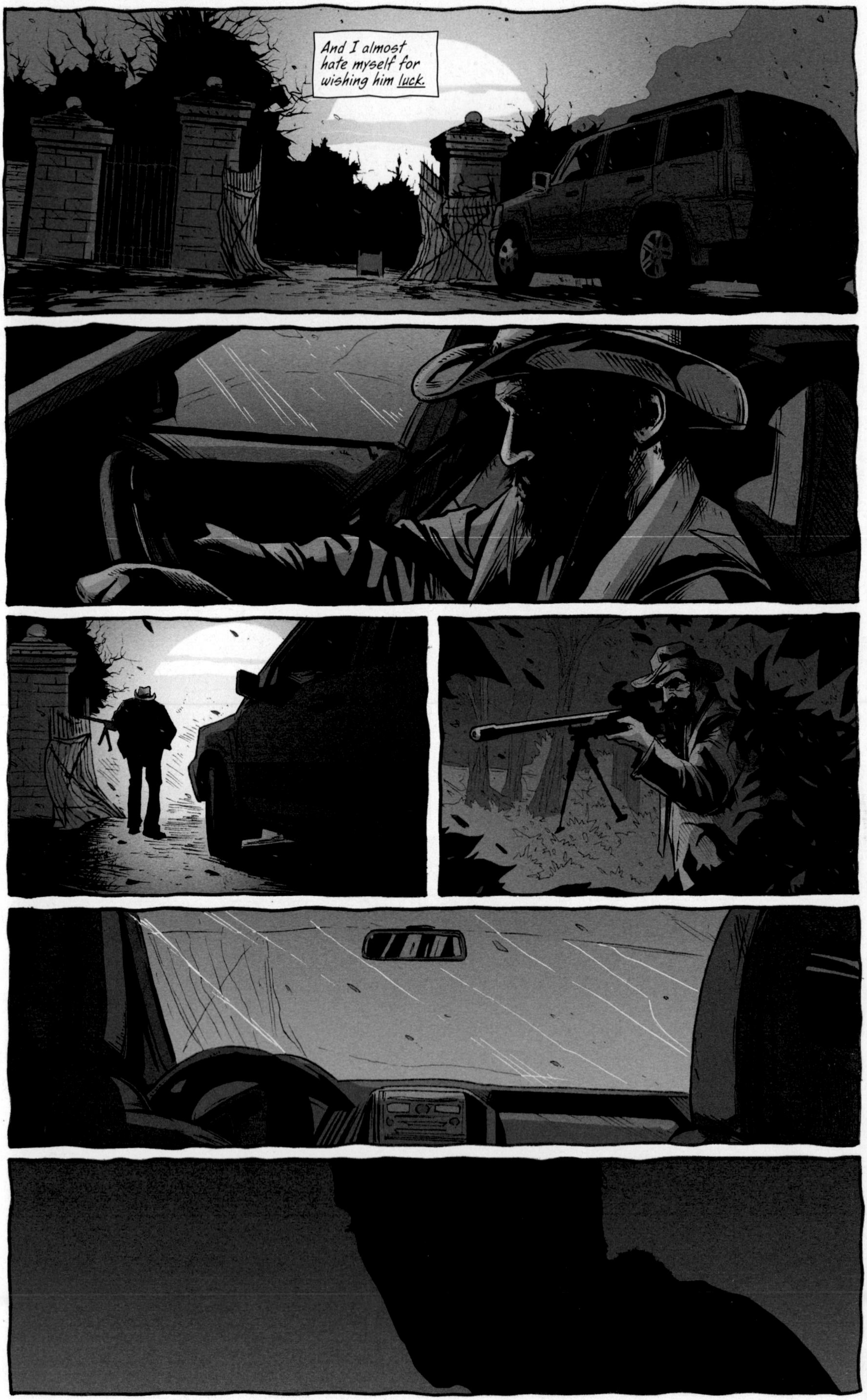
And I almost hate myself for wishing him luck.

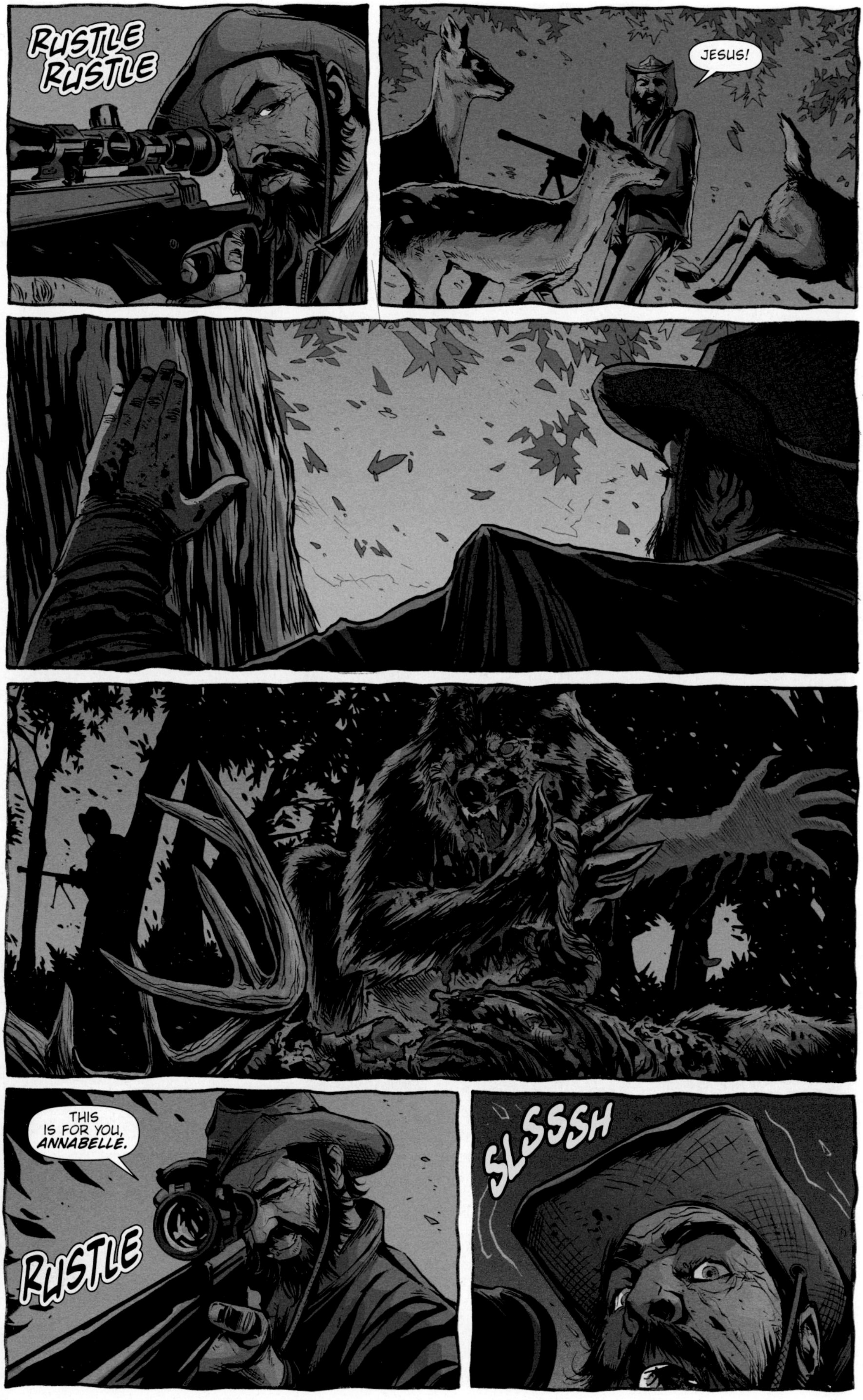
RUSTLE RUSTLE
JESUS!
THIS IS FOR YOU, ANNABELLE.
RUSTLE
SLSSSH

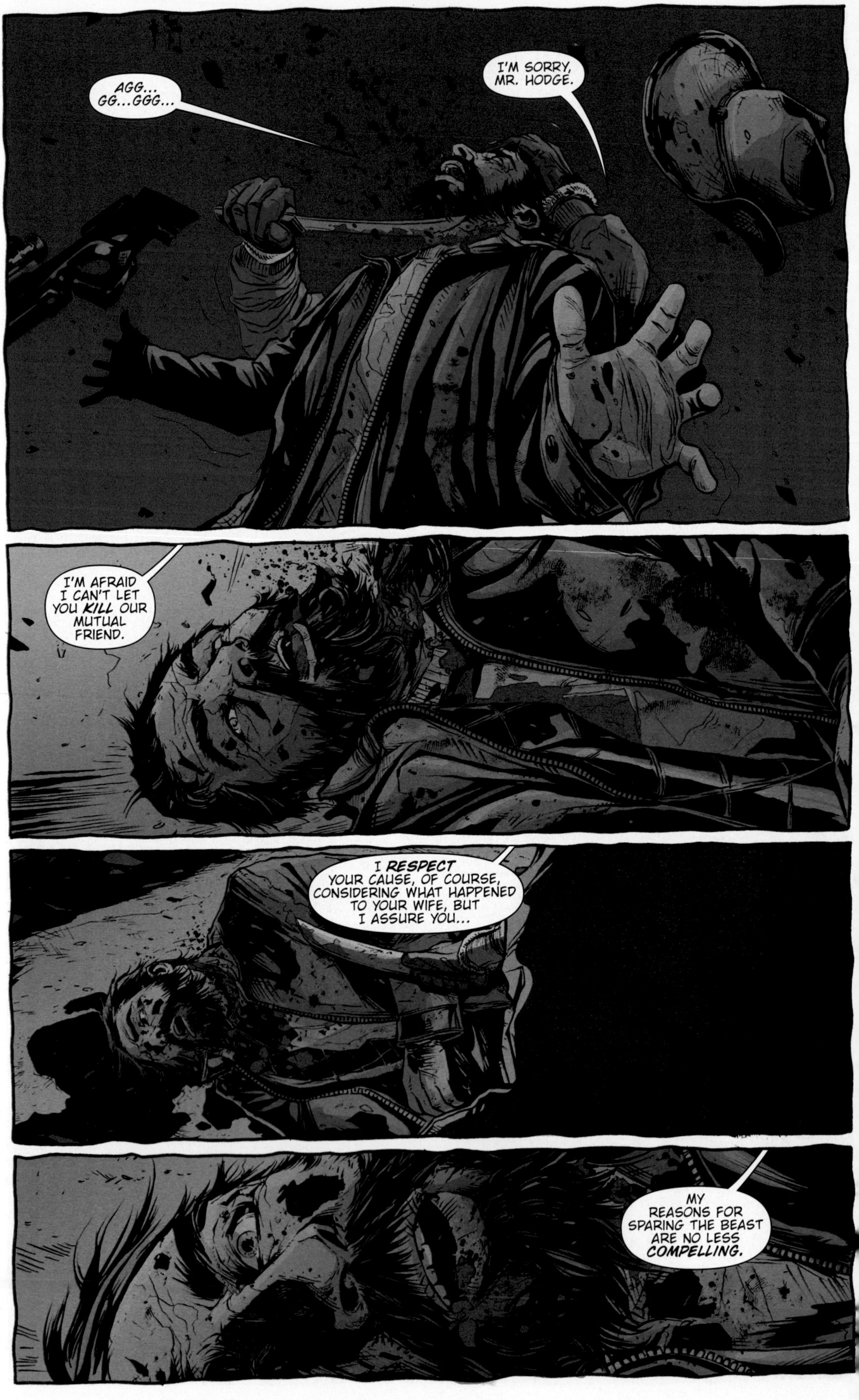
AGG...
GG...GGG...
I'M SORRY, MR. HODGE.
I'M AFRAID I CAN'T LET YOU KILL OUR MUTUAL FRIEND.
I RESPECT YOUR CAUSE, OF COURSE, CONSIDERING WHAT HAPPENED TO YOUR WIFE, BUT I ASSURE YOU...
MY REASONS FOR SPARING THE BEAST ARE NO LESS COMPELLING.

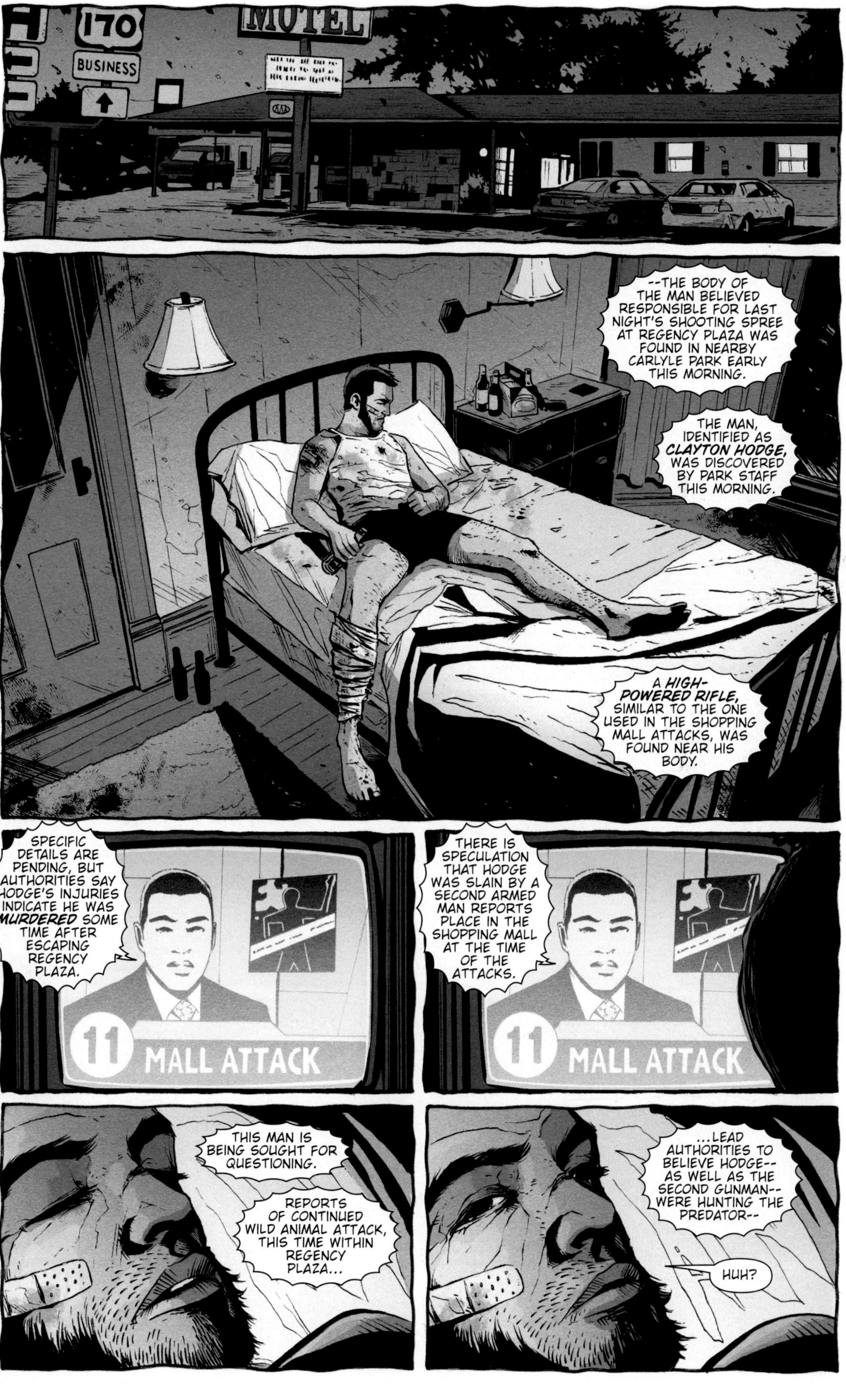
170
BUSINESS
MOTEL
--THE BODY OF THE MAN BELIEVED RESPONSIBLE FOR LAST NIGHT'S SHOOTING SPREE AT REGENCY PLAZA WAS FOUND IN NEARBY CARLYLE PARK EARLY THIS MORNING.
THE MAN, IDENTIFIED AS CLAYTON HODGE, WAS DISCOVERED BY PARK STAFF THIS MORNING.
A HIGH-POWERED RIFLE, SIMILAR TO THE ONE USED IN THE SHOPPING MALL ATTACKS, WAS FOUND NEAR HIS BODY.
SPECIFIC DETAILS ARE PENDING, BUT AUTHORITIES SAY HODGE'S INJURIES INDICATE HE WAS MURDERED SOME TIME AFTER ESCAPING REGENCY PLAZA.
11
MALL ATTACK
THERE IS SPECULATION THAT HODGE WAS SLAIN BY A SECOND ARMED MAN REPORTS PLACE IN THE SHOPPING MALL AT THE TIME OF THE ATTACKS.
11
MALL ATTACK
THIS MAN IS BEING SOUGHT FOR QUESTIONING.
REPORTS OF CONTINUED WILD ANIMAL ATTACK, THIS TIME WITHIN REGENCY PLAZA...
...LEAD AUTHORITIES TO BELIEVE HODGE--AS WELL AS THE SECOND GUNMAN--WERE HUNTING THE PREDATOR--
HUH?

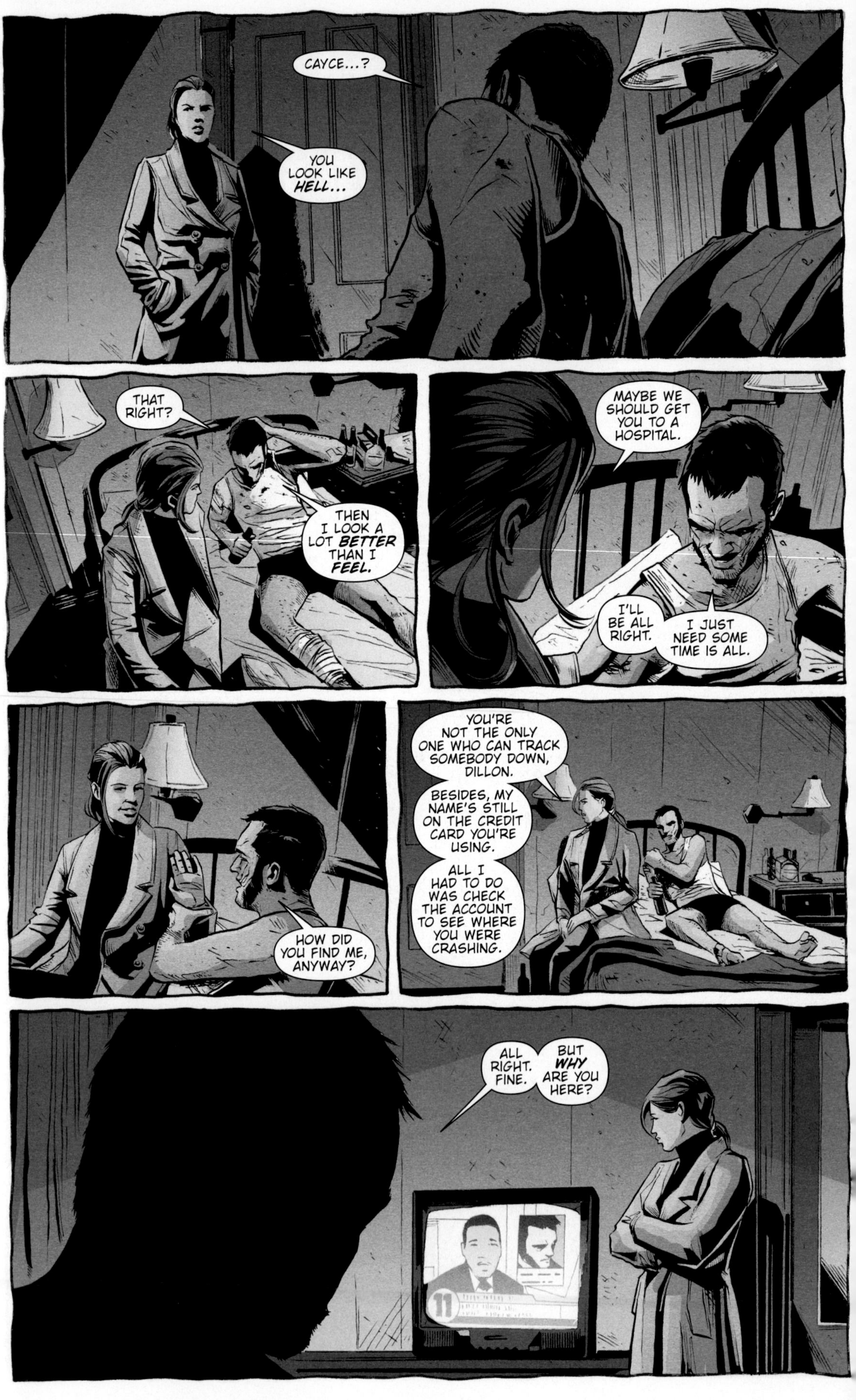
CAYCE...?
YOU LOOK LIKE HELL...
THAT RIGHT?
THEN I LOOK A LOT BETTER THAN I FEEL.
MAYBE WE SHOULD GET YOU TO A HOSPITAL.
I'LL BE ALL RIGHT.
I JUST NEED SOME TIME IS ALL.
HOW DID YOU FIND ME, ANYWAY?
YOU'RE NOT THE ONLY ONE WHO CAN TRACK SOMEBODY DOWN, DILLON.
BESIDES, MY NAME'S STILL ON THE CREDIT CARD YOU'RE USING.
ALL I HAD TO DO WAS CHECK THE ACCOUNT TO SEE WHERE YOU WERE CRASHING.
ALL RIGHT. FINE.
BUT WHY ARE YOU HERE?
11

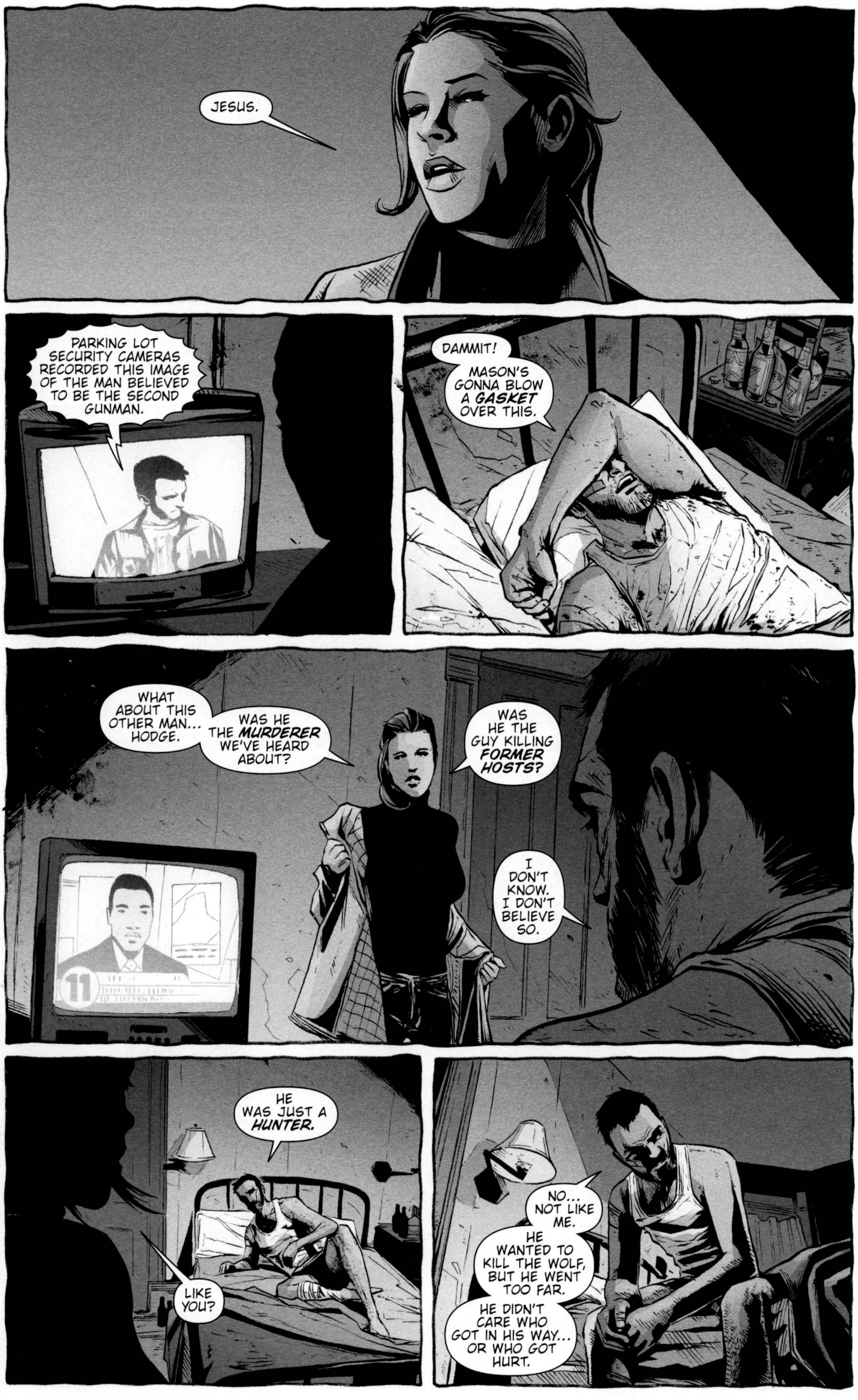
JESUS.
PARKING LOT SECURITY CAMERAS RECORDED THIS IMAGE OF THE MAN BELIEVED TO BE THE SECOND GUNMAN.
DAMMIT!
MASON'S GONNA BLOW A **GASKET** OVER THIS.
WHAT ABOUT THIS OTHER MAN... HODGE.
WAS HE THE **MURDERER** WE'VE HEARD ABOUT?
WAS HE THE GUY KILLING **FORMER HOSTS?**
11
I DON'T KNOW. I DON'T BELIEVE SO.
HE WAS JUST A **HUNTER.**
LIKE YOU?
NO... NOT LIKE ME.
HE WANTED TO KILL THE WOLF, BUT HE WENT TOO FAR.
HE DIDN'T CARE WHO GOT IN HIS WAY... OR WHO GOT HURT.

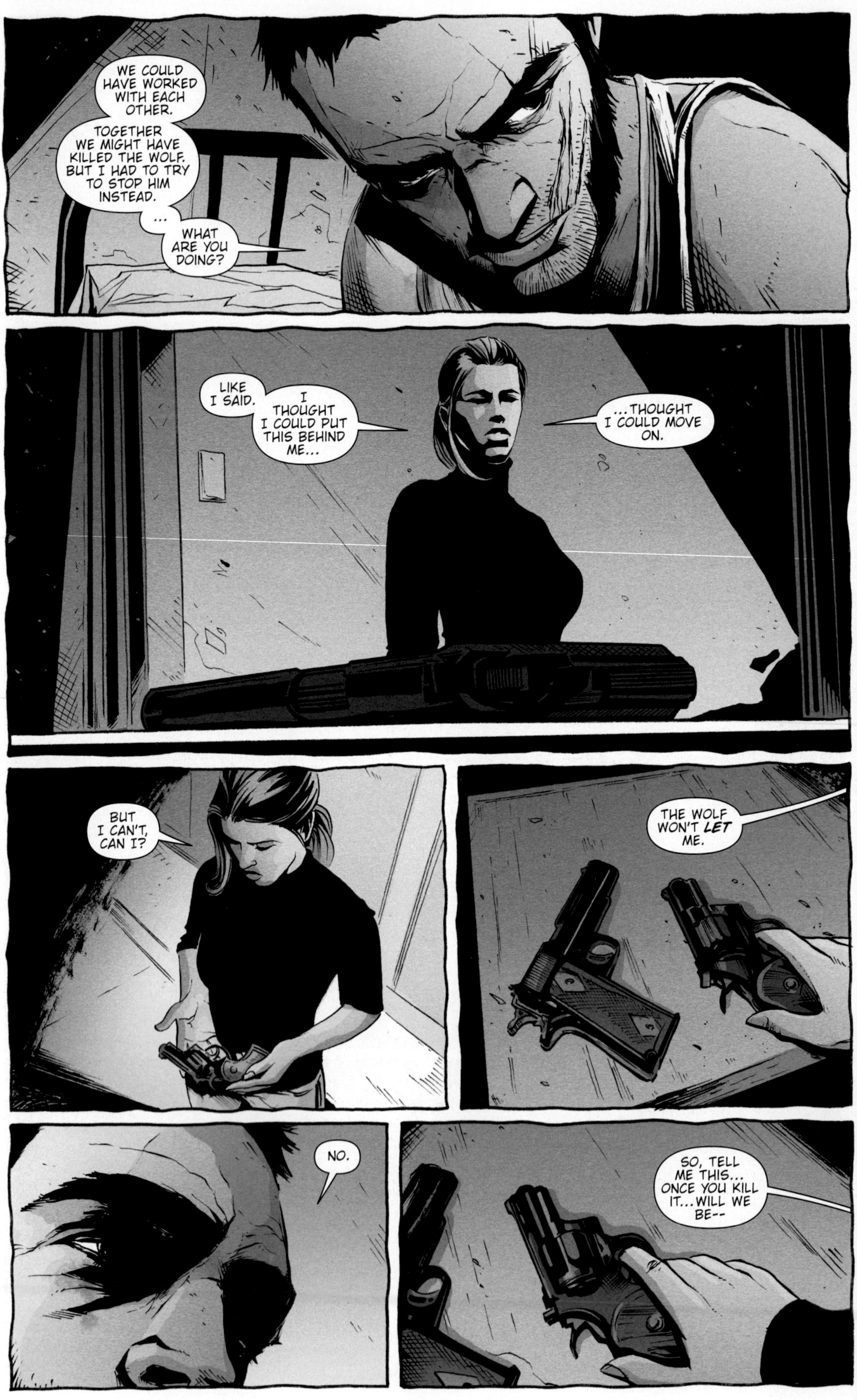
WE COULD HAVE WORKED WITH EACH OTHER.
TOGETHER WE MIGHT HAVE KILLED THE WOLF. BUT I HAD TO TRY TO STOP HIM INSTEAD.
...
WHAT ARE YOU DOING?
LIKE I SAID.
I THOUGHT I COULD PUT THIS BEHIND ME...
...THOUGHT I COULD MOVE ON.
BUT I CAN'T, CAN I?
THE WOLF WON'T *LET* ME.
NO.
SO, TELL ME THIS... ONCE YOU KILL IT... WILL WE BE--

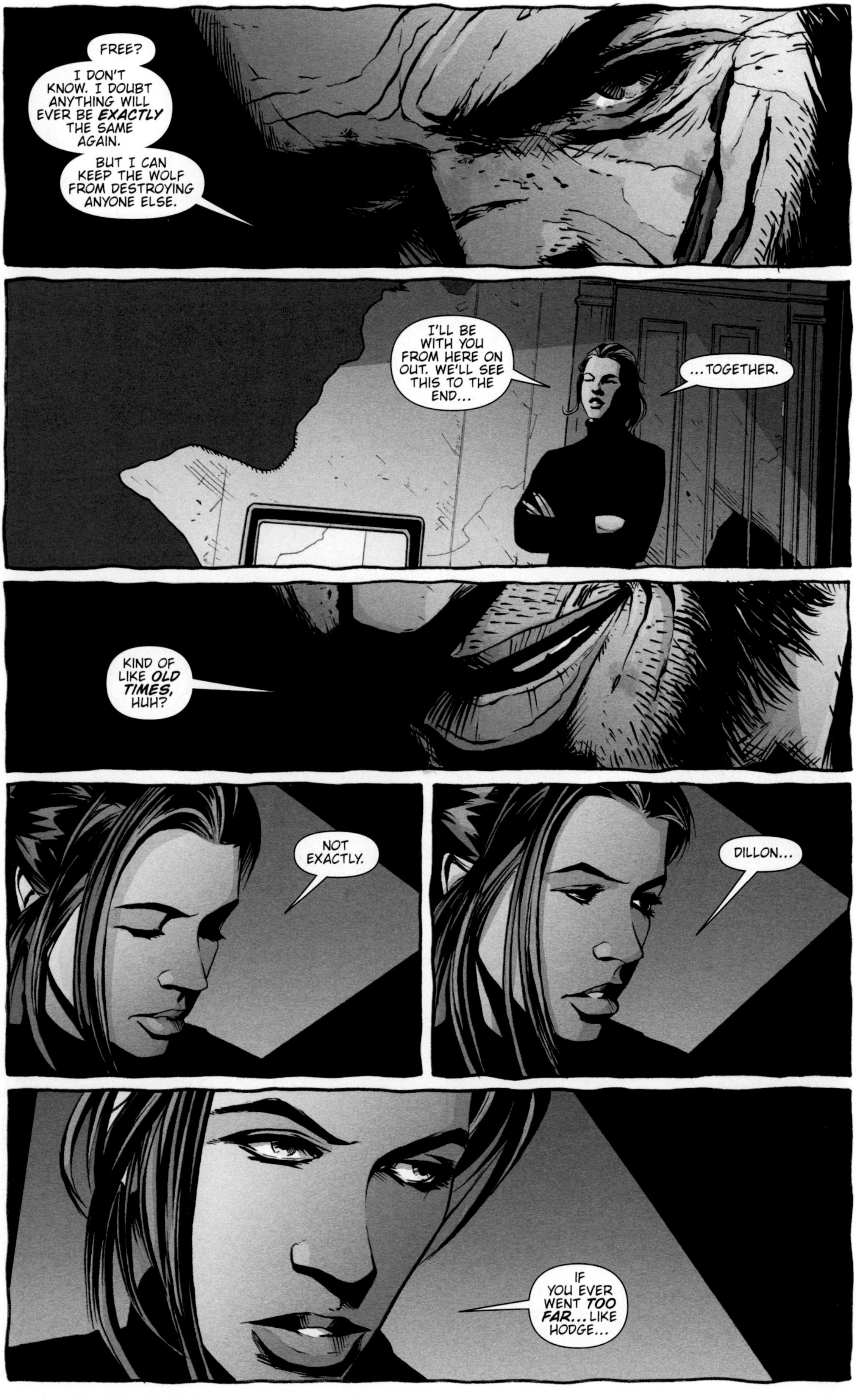
FREE?
I DON'T KNOW. I DOUBT ANYTHING WILL EVER BE EXACTLY THE SAME AGAIN.
BUT I CAN KEEP THE WOLF FROM DESTROYING ANYONE ELSE.
I'LL BE WITH YOU FROM HERE ON OUT. WE'LL SEE THIS TO THE END...
...TOGETHER.
KIND OF LIKE OLD TIMES, HUH?
NOT EXACTLY.
DILLON...
IF YOU EVER WENT TOO FAR... LIKE HODGE...

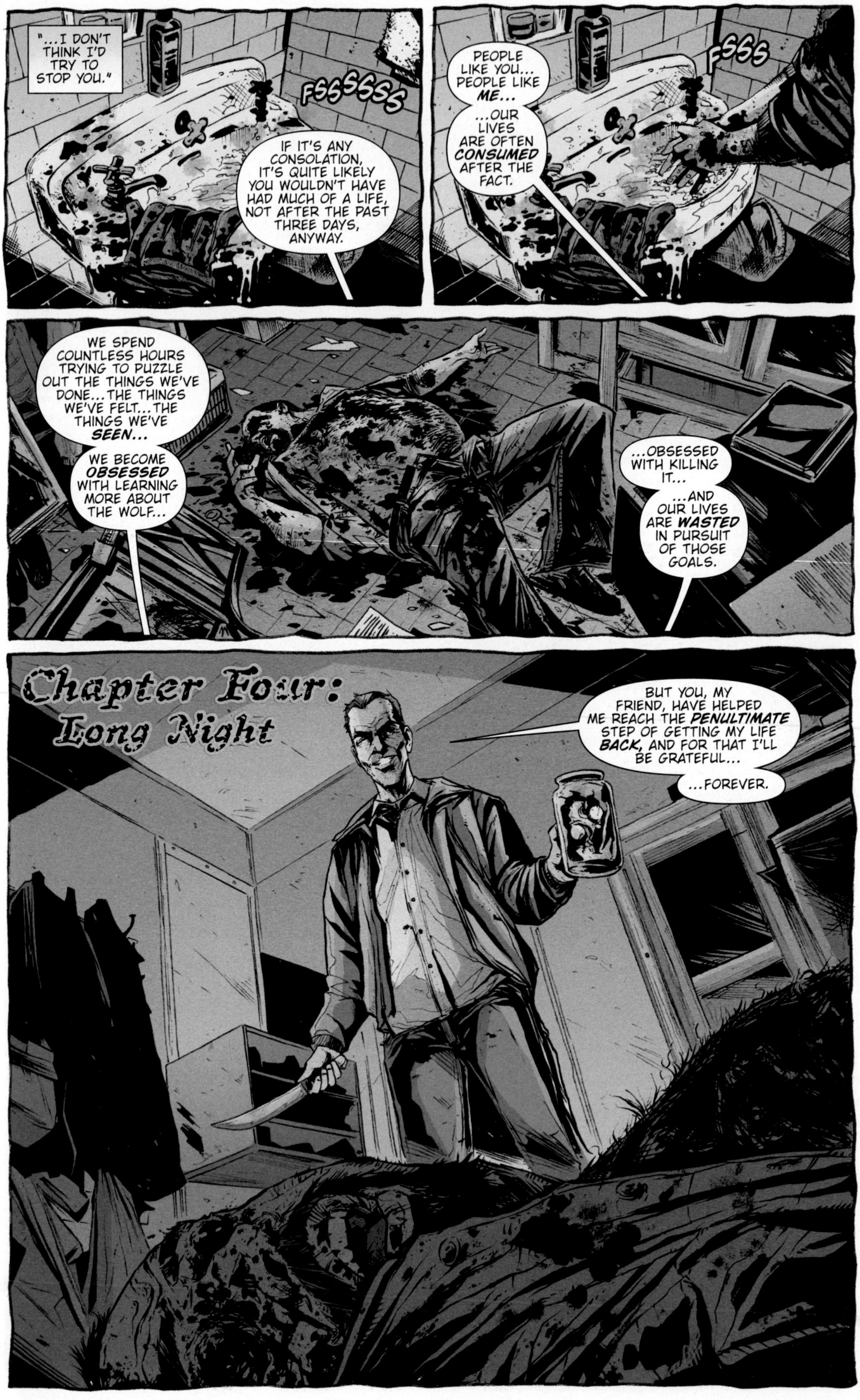
"...I DON'T THINK I'D TRY TO STOP YOU."
FSSSSSS
IF IT'S ANY CONSOLATION, IT'S QUITE LIKELY YOU WOULDN'T HAVE HAD MUCH OF A LIFE, NOT AFTER THE PAST THREE DAYS, ANYWAY.
FSSS
PEOPLE LIKE YOU... PEOPLE LIKE ME...
...OUR LIVES ARE OFTEN CONSUMED AFTER THE FACT.
WE SPEND COUNTLESS HOURS TRYING TO PUZZLE OUT THE THINGS WE'VE DONE...THE THINGS WE'VE FELT...THE THINGS WE'VE SEEN...
WE BECOME OBSESSED WITH LEARNING MORE ABOUT THE WOLF...
...OBSESSED WITH KILLING IT...
...AND OUR LIVES ARE WASTED IN PURSUIT OF THOSE GOALS.
Chapter Four: Long Night
BUT YOU, MY FRIEND, HAVE HELPED ME REACH THE PENULTIMATE STEP OF GETTING MY LIFE BACK, AND FOR THAT I'LL BE GRATEFUL...
...FOREVER.

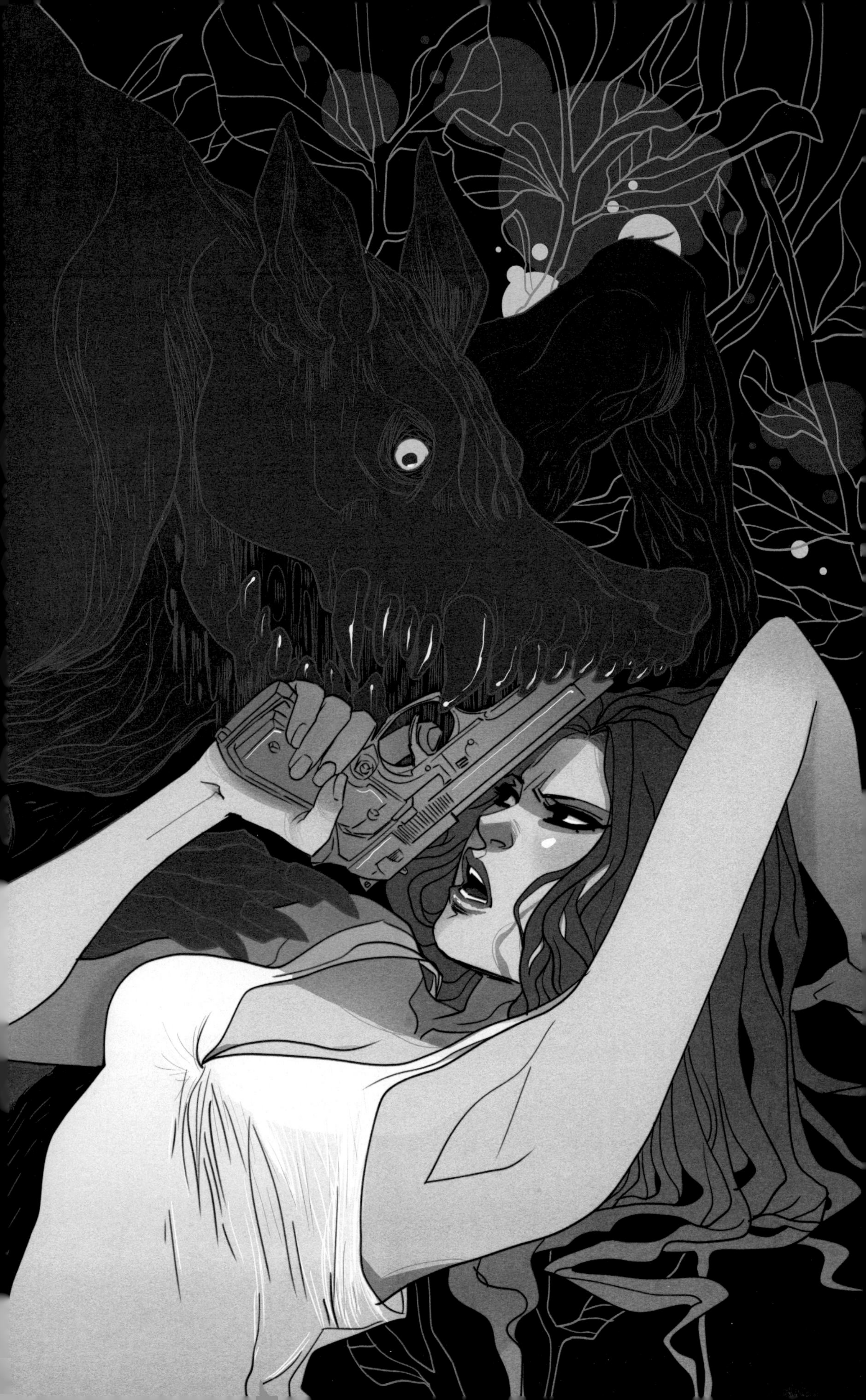

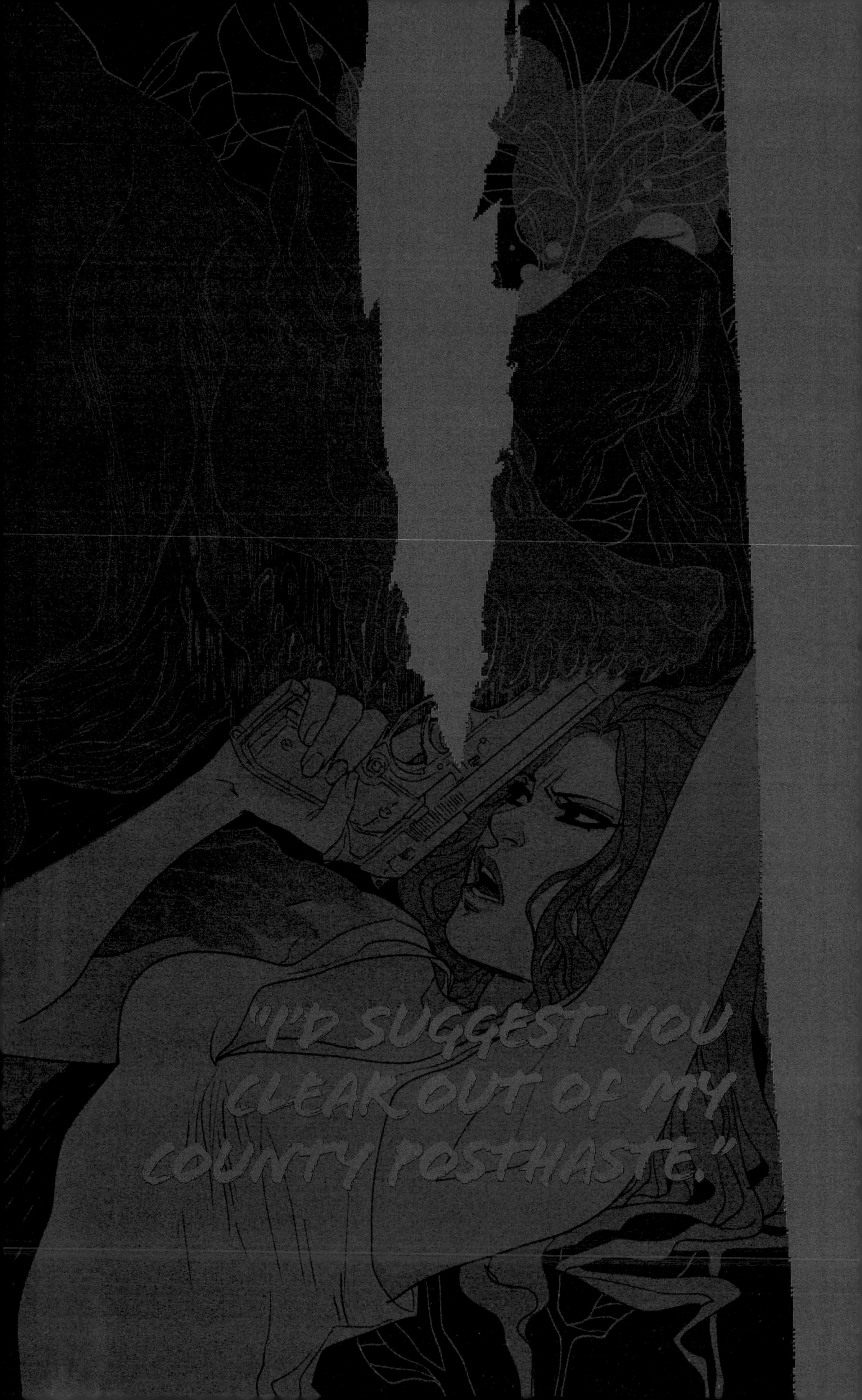
"I'D SUGGEST YOU CLEAR OUT OF MY COUNTY POSTHASTE."

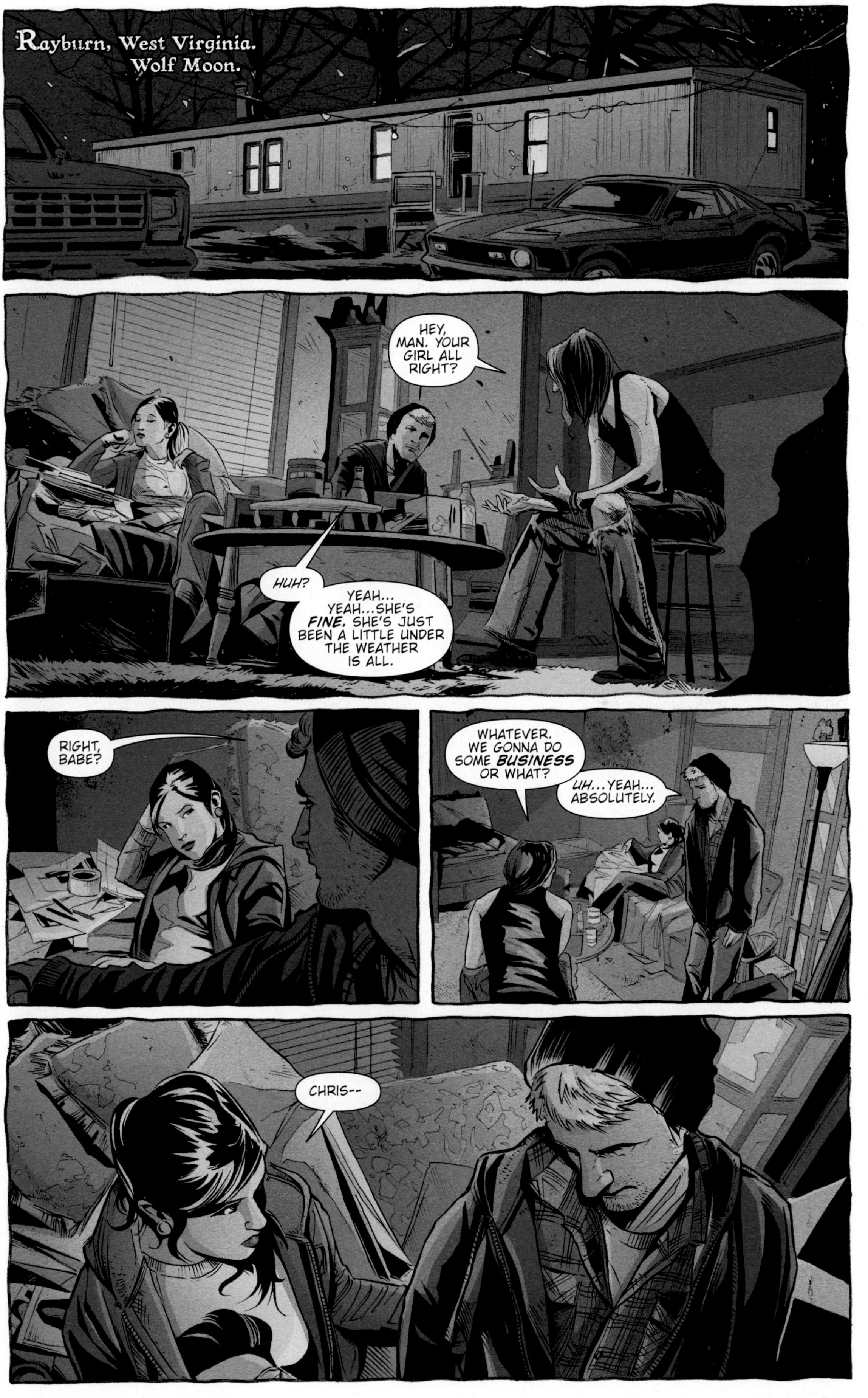
Rayburn, West Virginia.
Wolf Moon.
HEY, MAN. YOUR GIRL ALL RIGHT?
HUH?
YEAH... YEAH...SHE'S FINE. SHE'S JUST BEEN A LITTLE UNDER THE WEATHER IS ALL.
RIGHT, BABE?
WHATEVER. WE GONNA DO SOME BUSINESS OR WHAT?
UH...YEAH... ABSOLUTELY.
CHRIS--

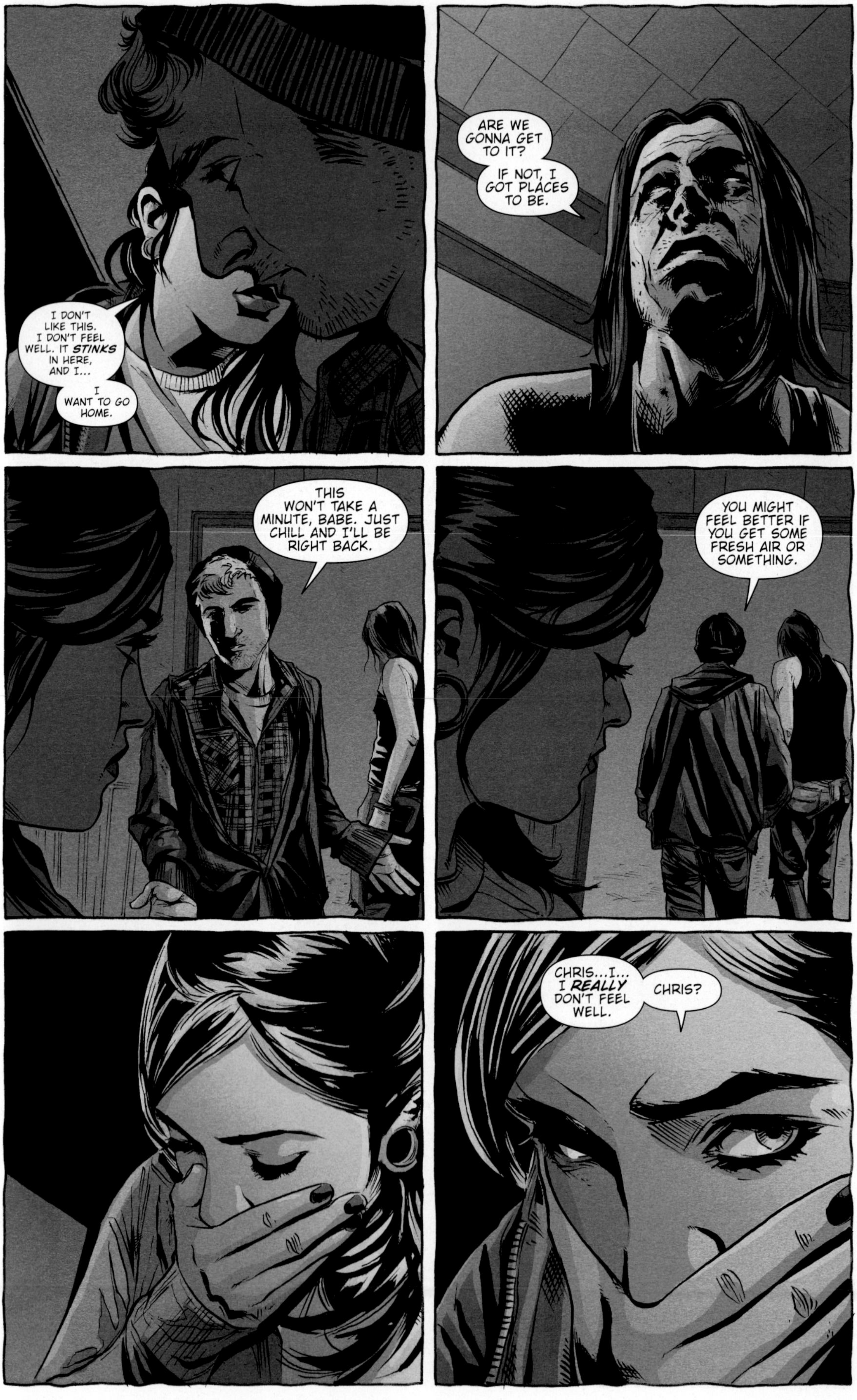
I DON'T LIKE THIS. I DON'T FEEL WELL. IT **STINKS** IN HERE, AND I...
I WANT TO GO HOME.
ARE WE GONNA GET TO IT?
IF NOT, I GOT PLACES TO BE.
THIS WON'T TAKE A MINUTE, BABE. JUST CHILL AND I'LL BE RIGHT BACK.
YOU MIGHT FEEL BETTER IF YOU GET SOME FRESH AIR OR SOMETHING.
CHRIS...I... I **REALLY** DON'T FEEL WELL.
CHRIS?

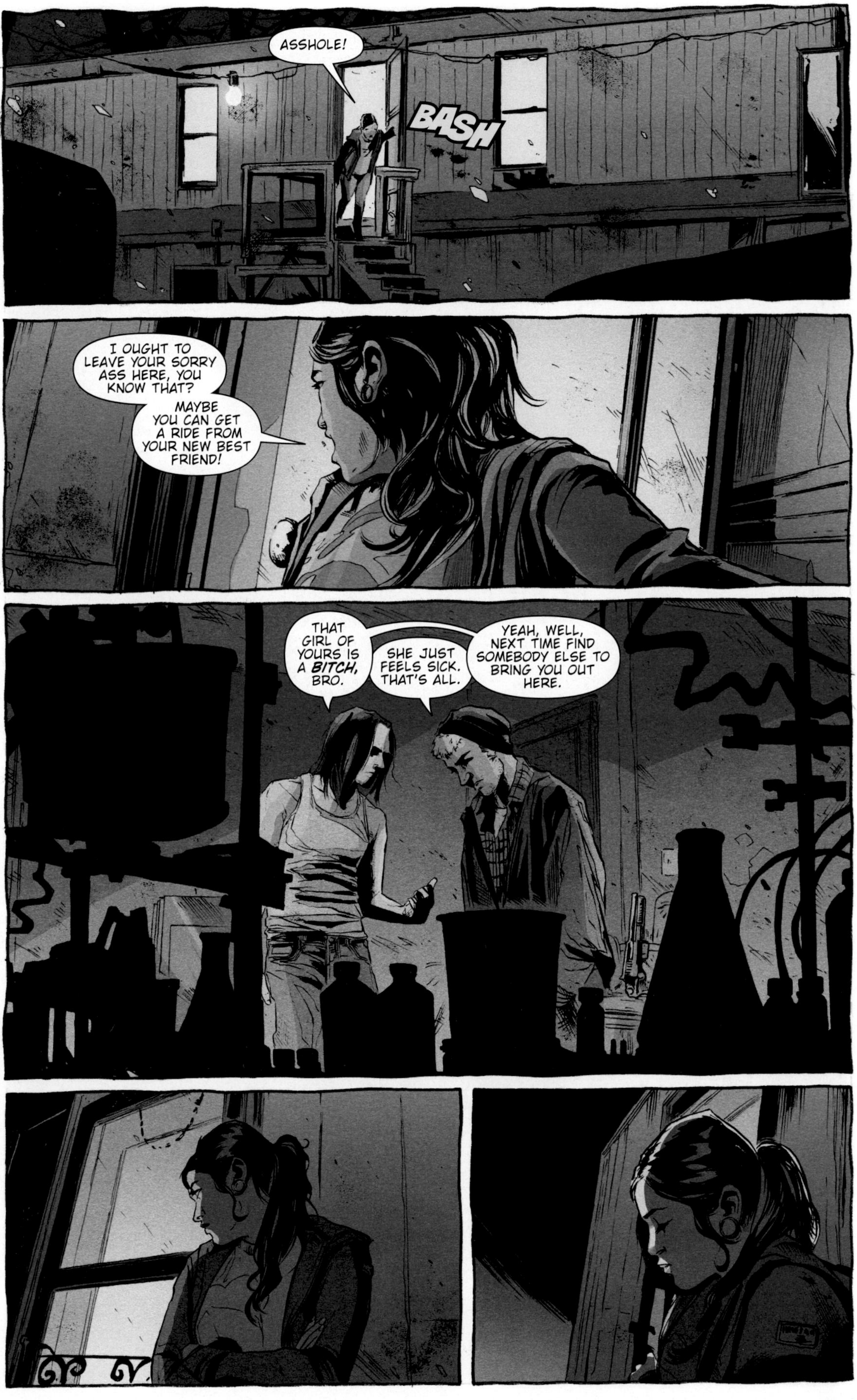
ASSHOLE!
BASH
I OUGHT TO LEAVE YOUR SORRY ASS HERE, YOU KNOW THAT?
MAYBE YOU CAN GET A RIDE FROM YOUR NEW BEST FRIEND!
THAT GIRL OF YOURS IS A *BITCH*, BRO.
SHE JUST FEELS SICK. THAT'S ALL.
YEAH, WELL, NEXT TIME FIND SOMEBODY ELSE TO BRING YOU OUT HERE.

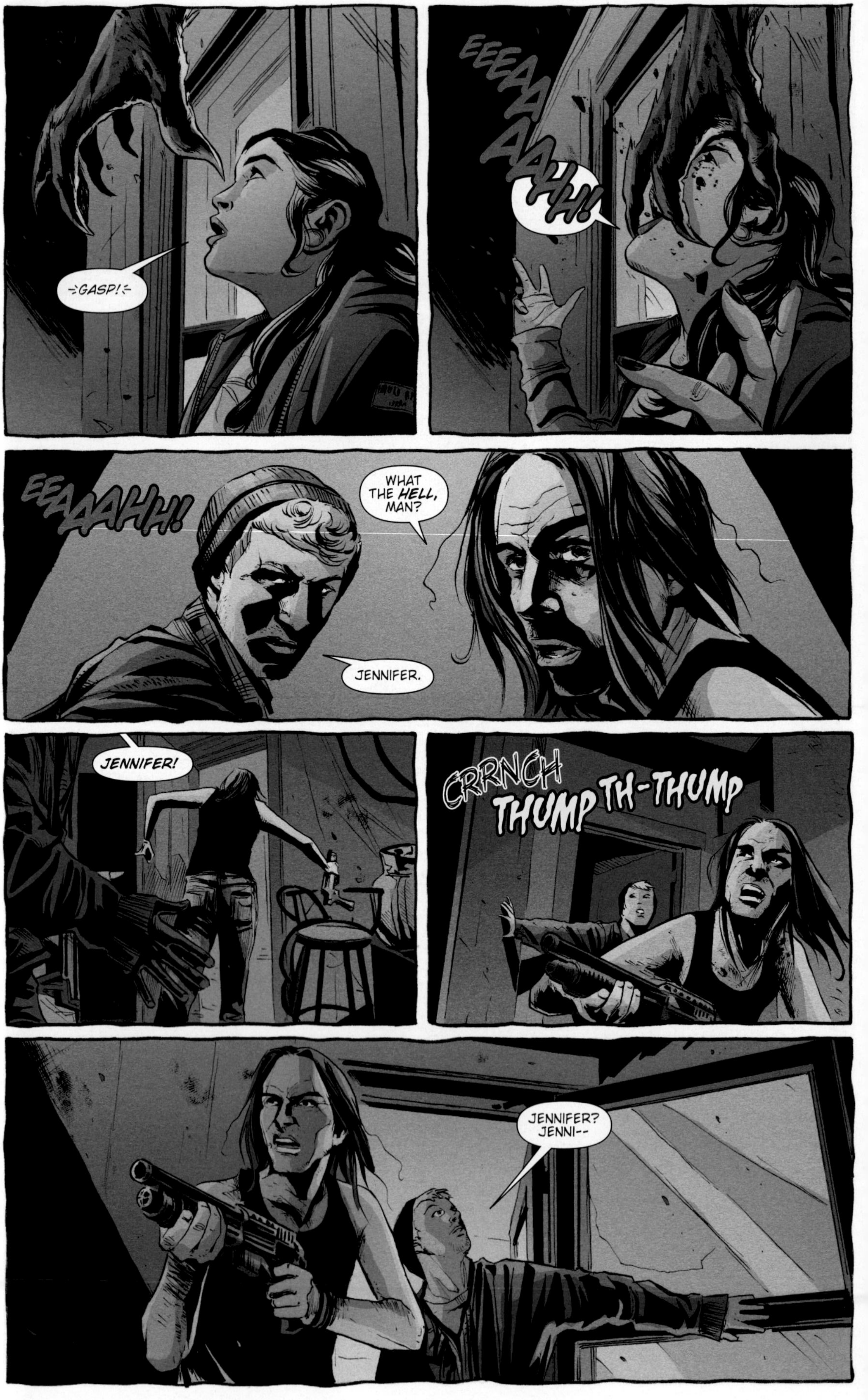

~GASP!~
EEEAAAAAHH!
EEAAAHH!
WHAT THE HELL, MAN?
JENNIFER.
JENNIFER!
CRRNCH
THUMP TH-THUMP
JENNIFER? JENNI--

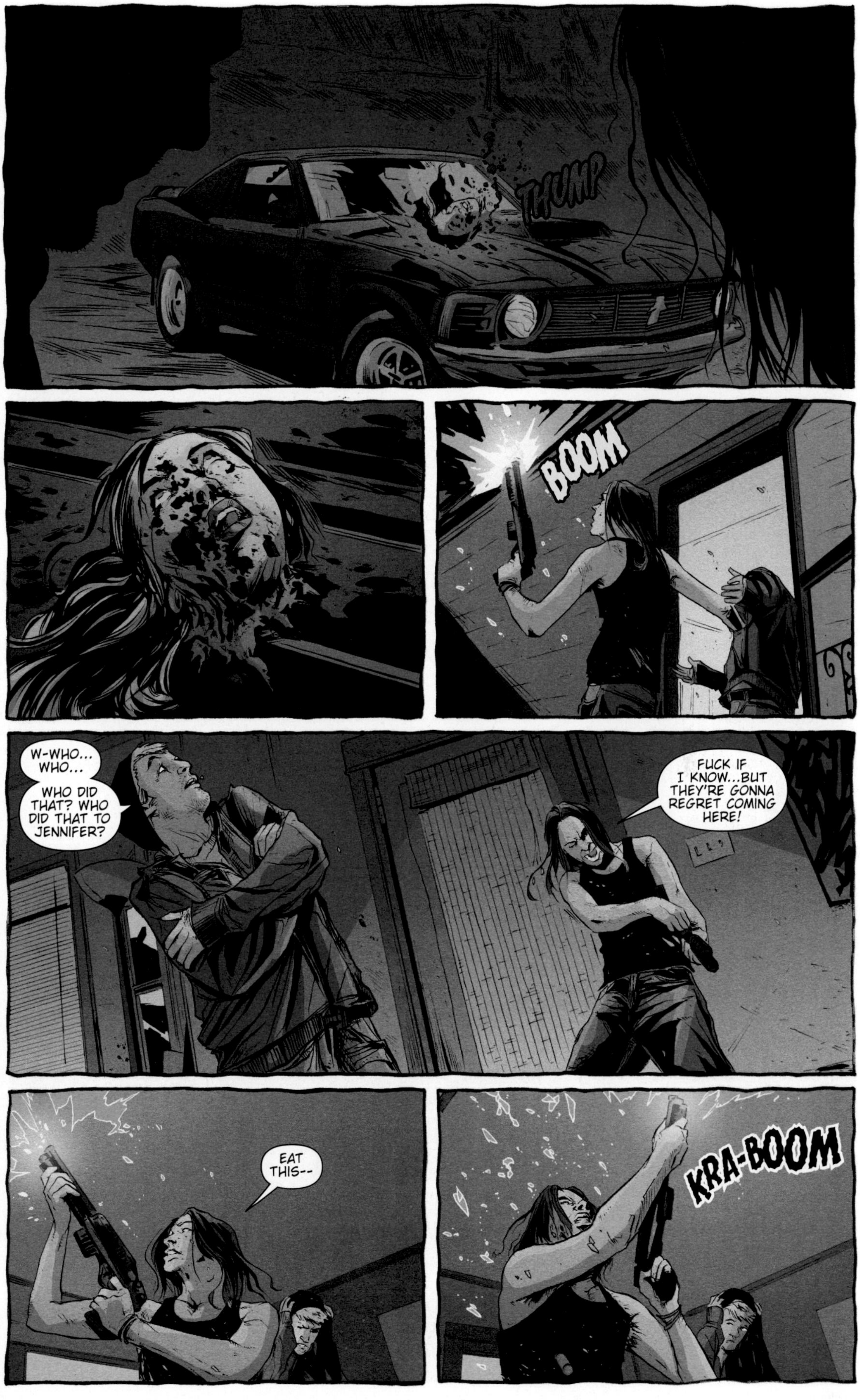
THUMP
BOOM
W-WHO... WHO...
WHO DID THAT? WHO DID THAT TO JENNIFER?
FUCK IF I KNOW...BUT THEY'RE GONNA REGRET COMING HERE!
EAT THIS--
KRA-BOOM

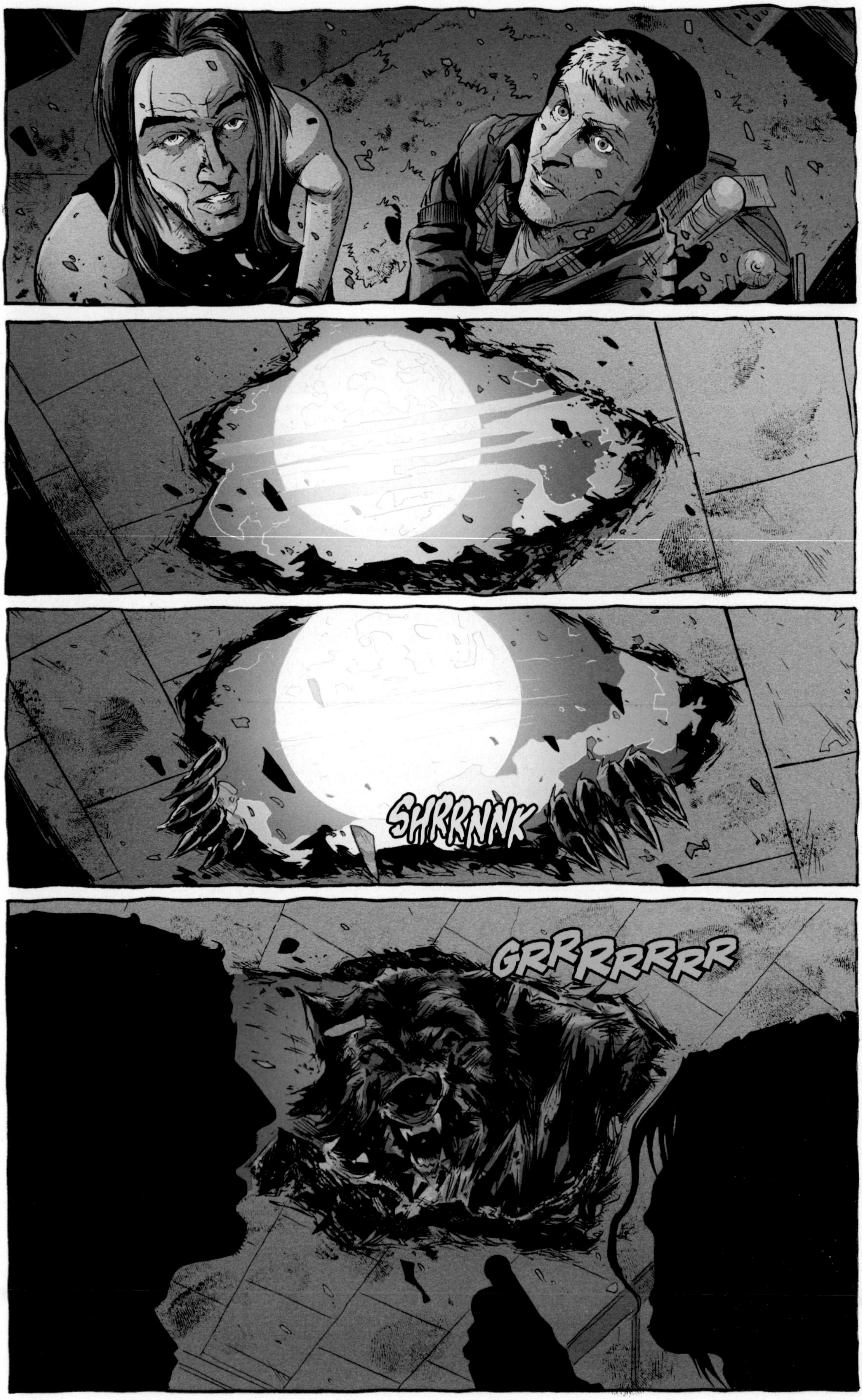
SHRRNNK
GRRRRRRR

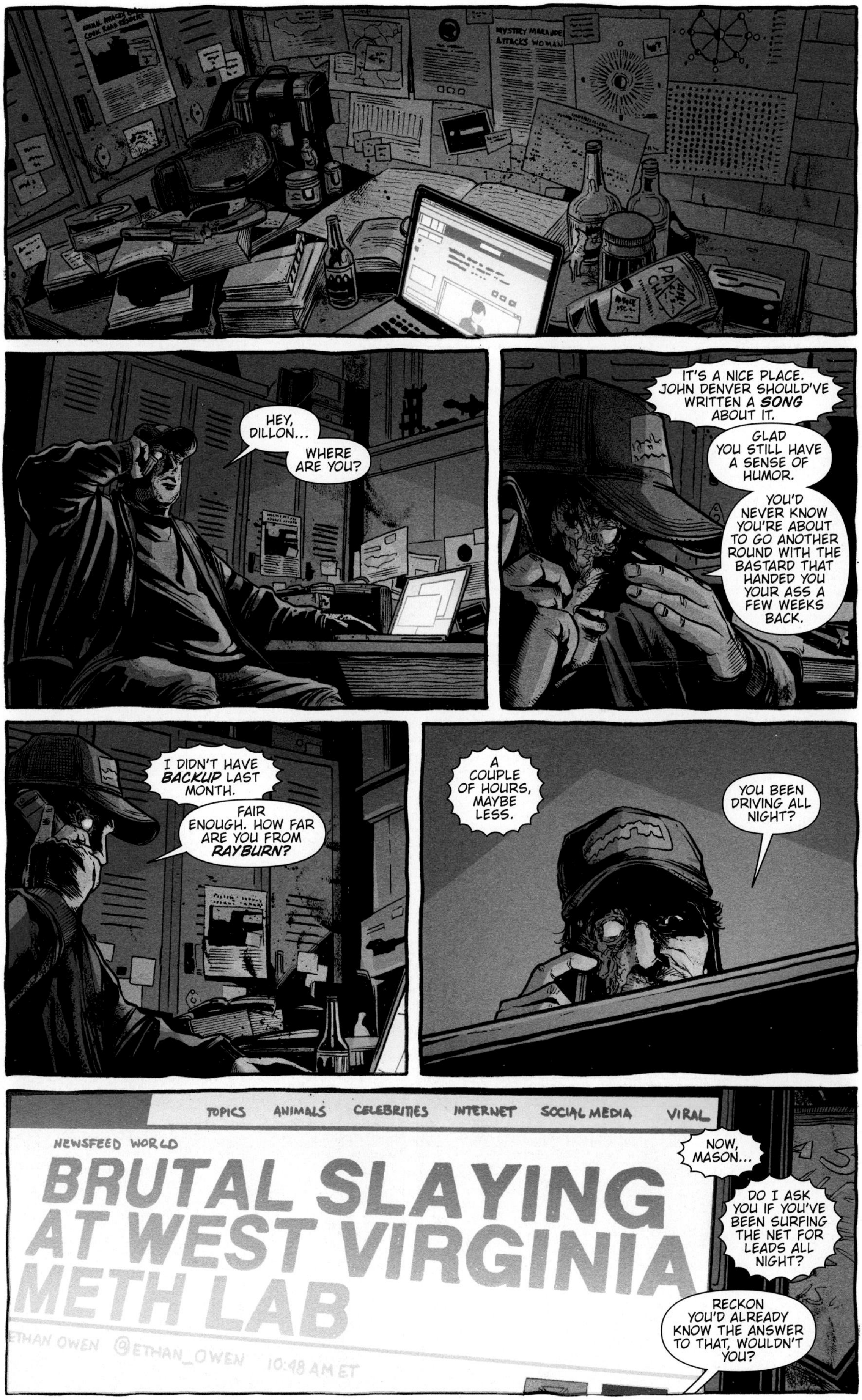
HEY, DILLON...
WHERE ARE YOU?
IT'S A NICE PLACE. JOHN DENVER SHOULD'VE WRITTEN A SONG ABOUT IT.
GLAD YOU STILL HAVE A SENSE OF HUMOR.
YOU'D NEVER KNOW YOU'RE ABOUT TO GO ANOTHER ROUND WITH THE BASTARD THAT HANDED YOU YOUR ASS A FEW WEEKS BACK.
I DIDN'T HAVE BACKUP LAST MONTH.
FAIR ENOUGH. HOW FAR ARE YOU FROM RAYBURN?
A COUPLE OF HOURS, MAYBE LESS.
YOU BEEN DRIVING ALL NIGHT?
TOPICS ANIMALS CELEBRITIES INTERNET SOCIAL MEDIA VIRAL
NEWSFEED WORLD
BRUTAL SLAYING AT WEST VIRGINIA METH LAB
ETHAN OWEN @ETHAN_OWEN 10:48 AM ET
NOW, MASON...
DO I ASK YOU IF YOU'VE BEEN SURFING THE NET FOR LEADS ALL NIGHT?
RECKON YOU'D ALREADY KNOW THE ANSWER TO THAT, WOULDN'T YOU?

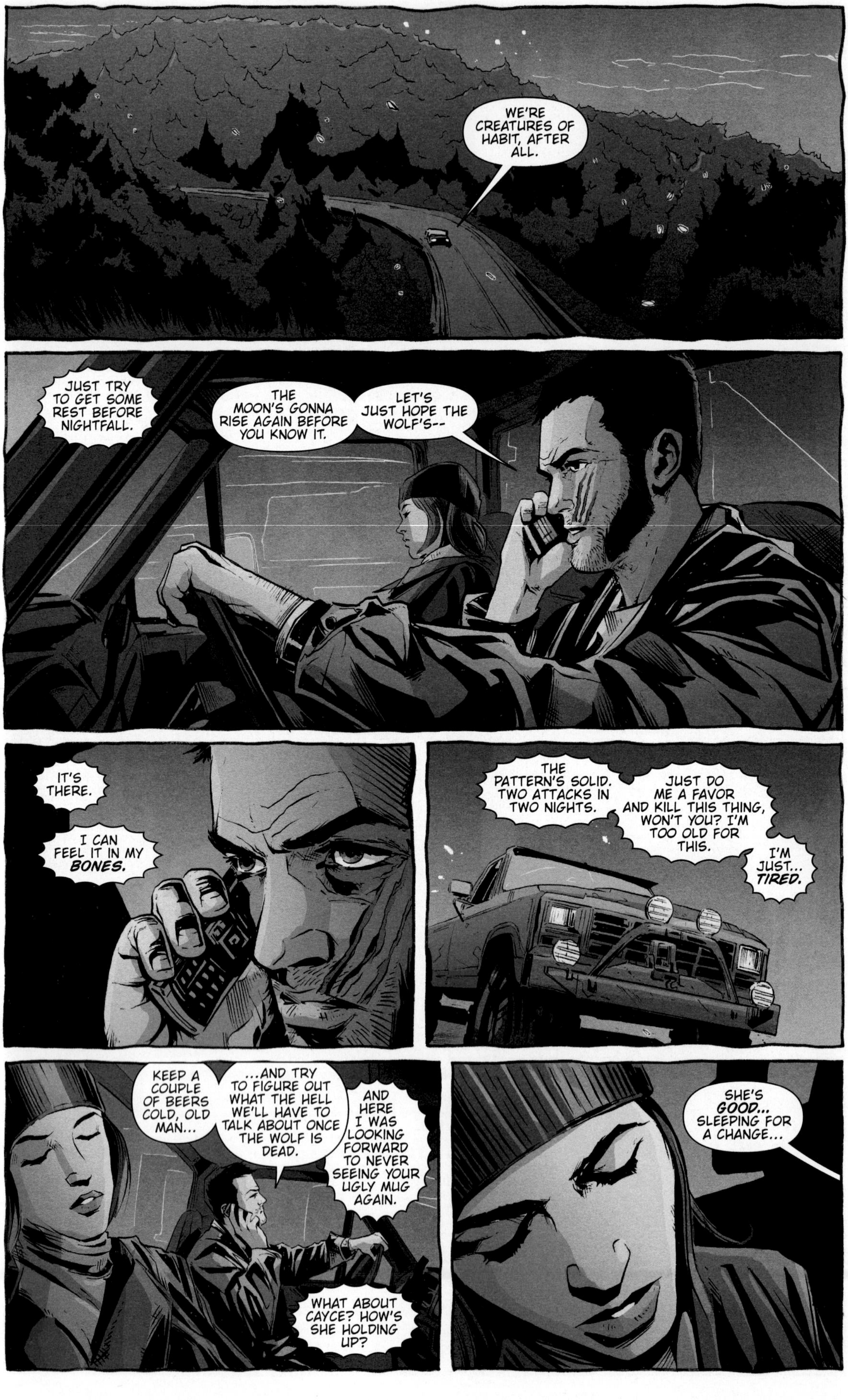
WE'RE CREATURES OF HABIT, AFTER ALL.
JUST TRY TO GET SOME REST BEFORE NIGHTFALL.
THE MOON'S GONNA RISE AGAIN BEFORE YOU KNOW IT.
LET'S JUST HOPE THE WOLF'S--
IT'S THERE.
I CAN FEEL IT IN MY **BONES.**
THE PATTERN'S SOLID. TWO ATTACKS IN TWO NIGHTS.
JUST DO ME A FAVOR AND KILL THIS THING, WON'T YOU? I'M TOO OLD FOR THIS.
I'M JUST... **TIRED.**
KEEP A COUPLE OF BEERS COLD, OLD MAN...
...AND TRY TO FIGURE OUT WHAT THE HELL WE'LL HAVE TO TALK ABOUT ONCE THE WOLF IS DEAD.
AND HERE I WAS LOOKING FORWARD TO NEVER SEEING YOUR UGLY MUG AGAIN.
WHAT ABOUT CAYCE? HOW'S SHE HOLDING UP?
SHE'S **GOOD...** SLEEPING FOR A CHANGE...

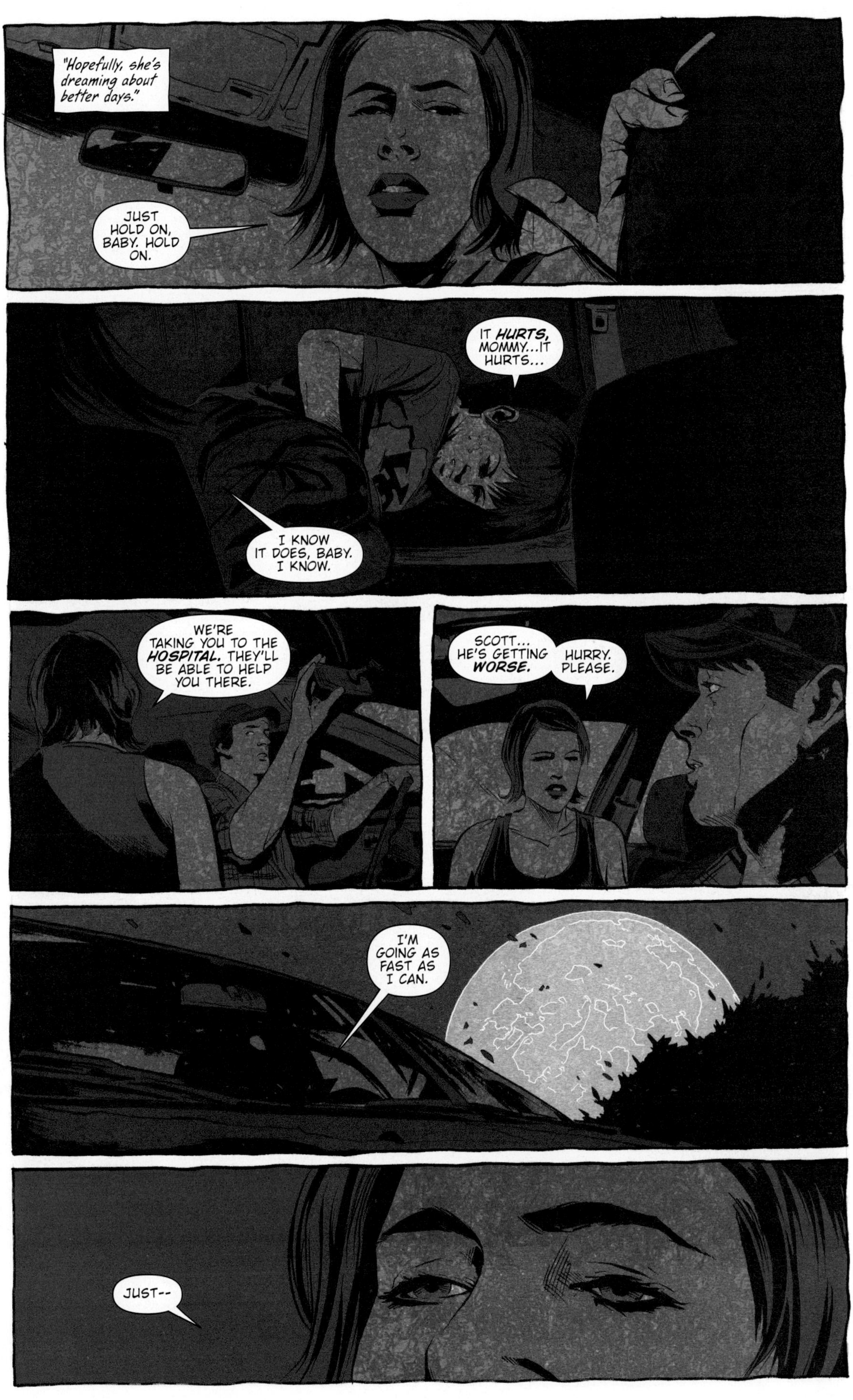
"Hopefully, she's dreaming about better days."
JUST HOLD ON, BABY. HOLD ON.
IT **HURTS,** MOMMY...IT HURTS...
I KNOW IT DOES, BABY. I KNOW.
WE'RE TAKING YOU TO THE **HOSPITAL.** THEY'LL BE ABLE TO HELP YOU THERE.
SCOTT... HE'S GETTING **WORSE.**
HURRY. PLEASE.
I'M GOING AS FAST AS I CAN.
JUST--

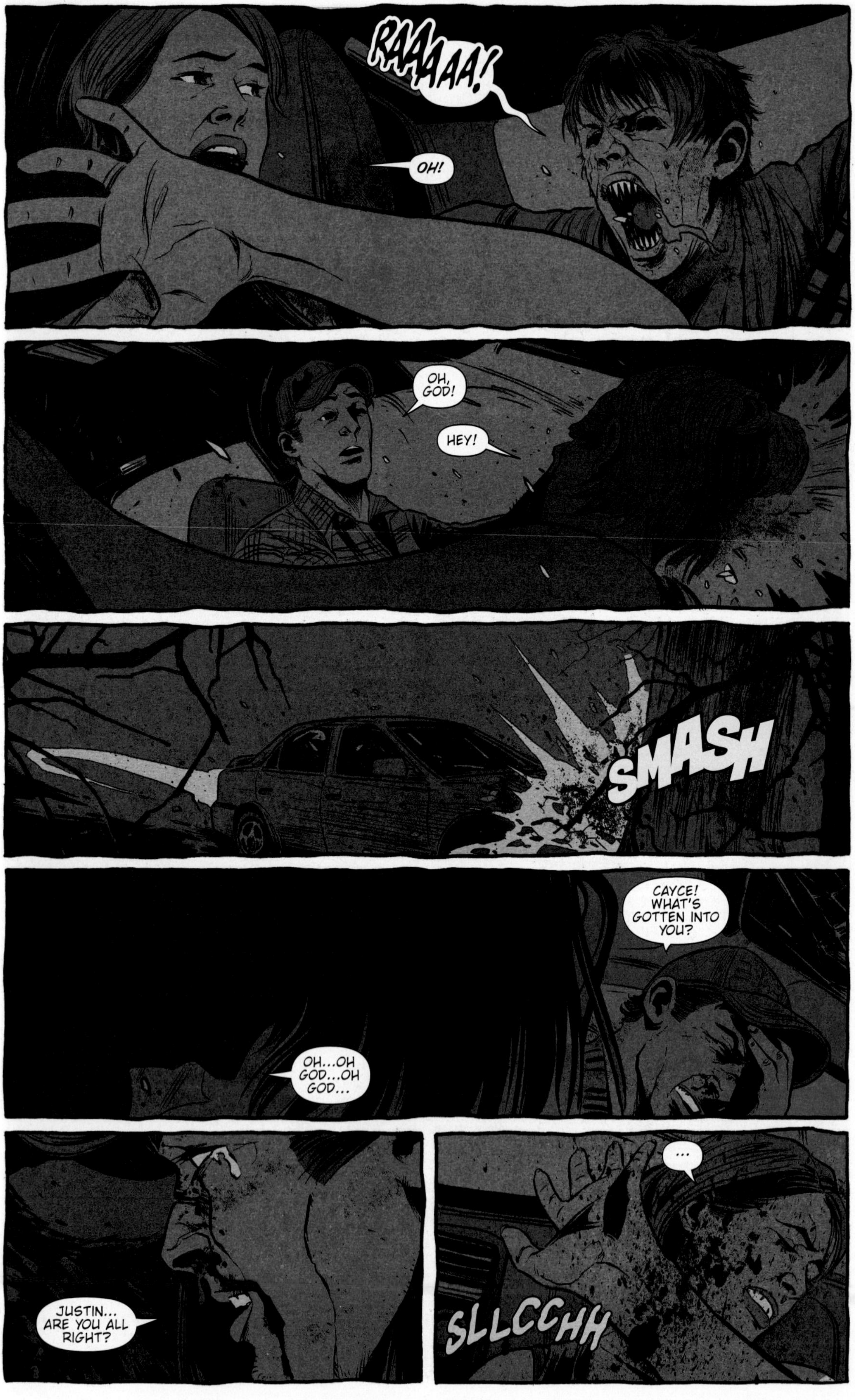
RAAAAAA!
OH!
OH, GOD!
HEY!
SMASH
CAYCE! WHAT'S GOTTEN INTO YOU?
OH...OH GOD...OH GOD...
JUSTIN... ARE YOU ALL RIGHT?
...
SLLCCHH

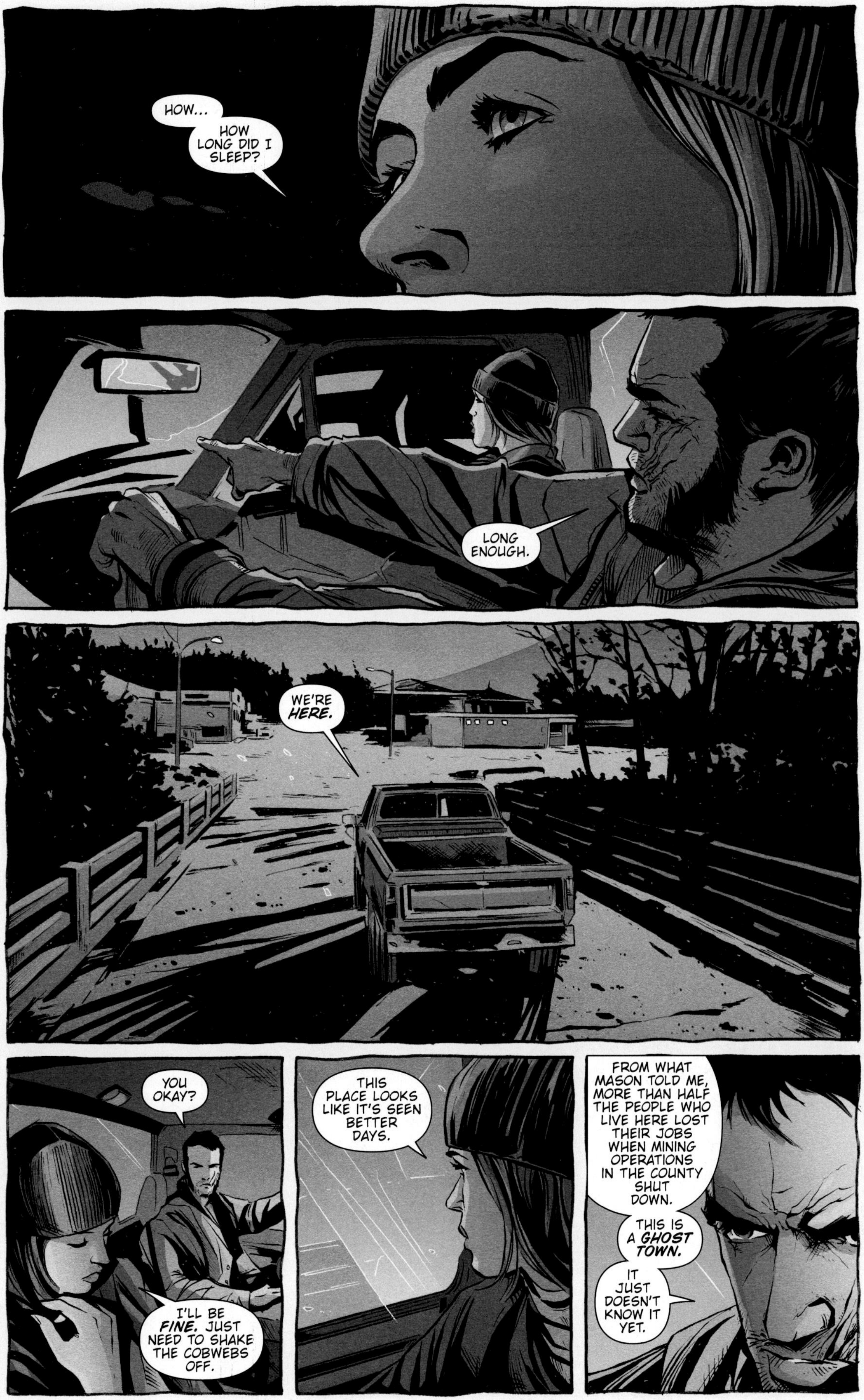
HOW...
HOW LONG DID I SLEEP?
LONG ENOUGH.
WE'RE HERE.
YOU OKAY?
I'LL BE FINE. JUST NEED TO SHAKE THE COBWEBS OFF.
THIS PLACE LOOKS LIKE IT'S SEEN BETTER DAYS.
FROM WHAT MASON TOLD ME, MORE THAN HALF THE PEOPLE WHO LIVE HERE LOST THEIR JOBS WHEN MINING OPERATIONS IN THE COUNTY SHUT DOWN.
THIS IS A GHOST TOWN.
IT JUST DOESN'T KNOW IT YET.

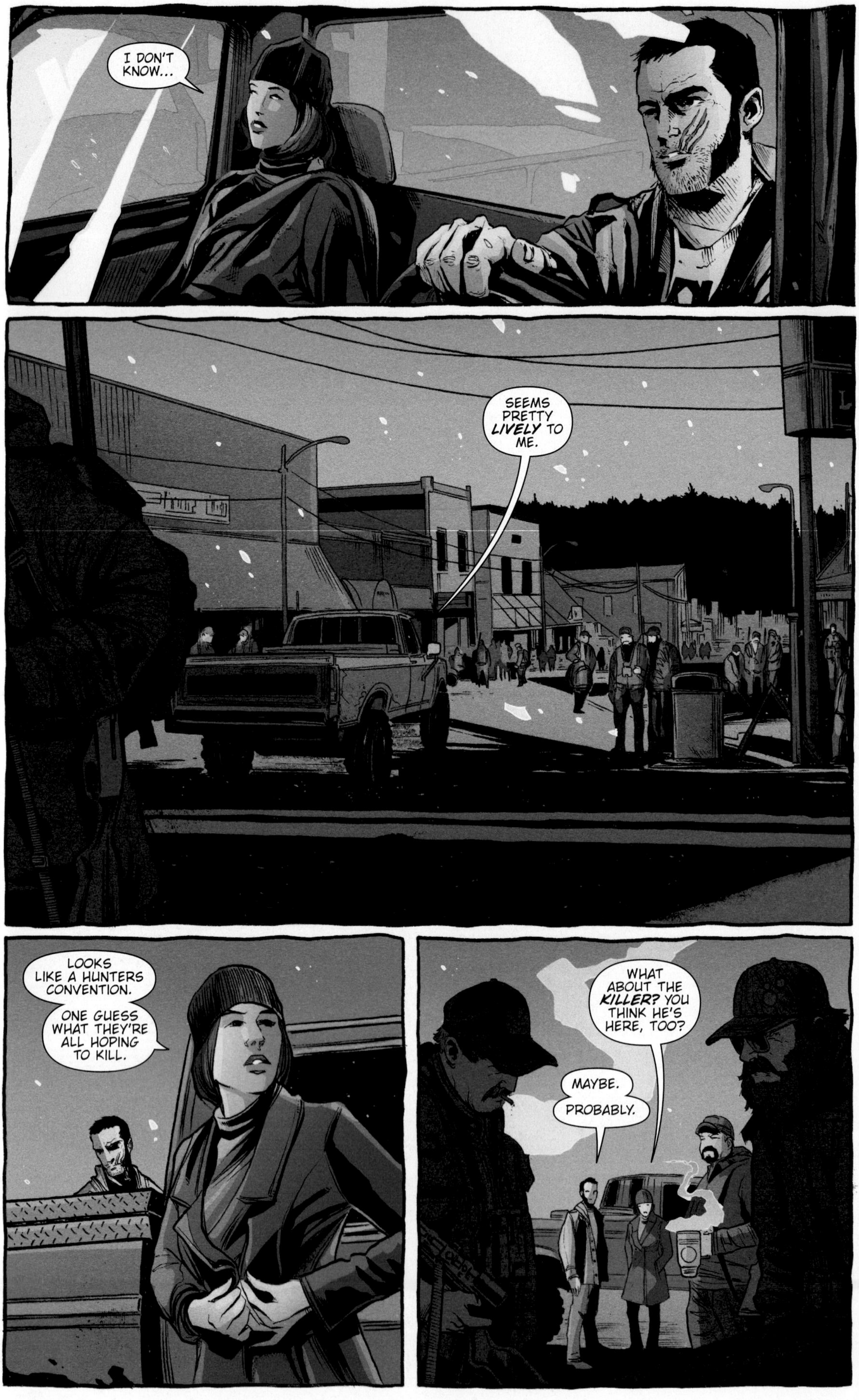
I DON'T KNOW...
SEEMS PRETTY LIVELY TO ME.
LOOKS LIKE A HUNTERS CONVENTION.
ONE GUESS WHAT THEY'RE ALL HOPING TO KILL.
WHAT ABOUT THE KILLER? YOU THINK HE'S HERE, TOO?
MAYBE.
PROBABLY.

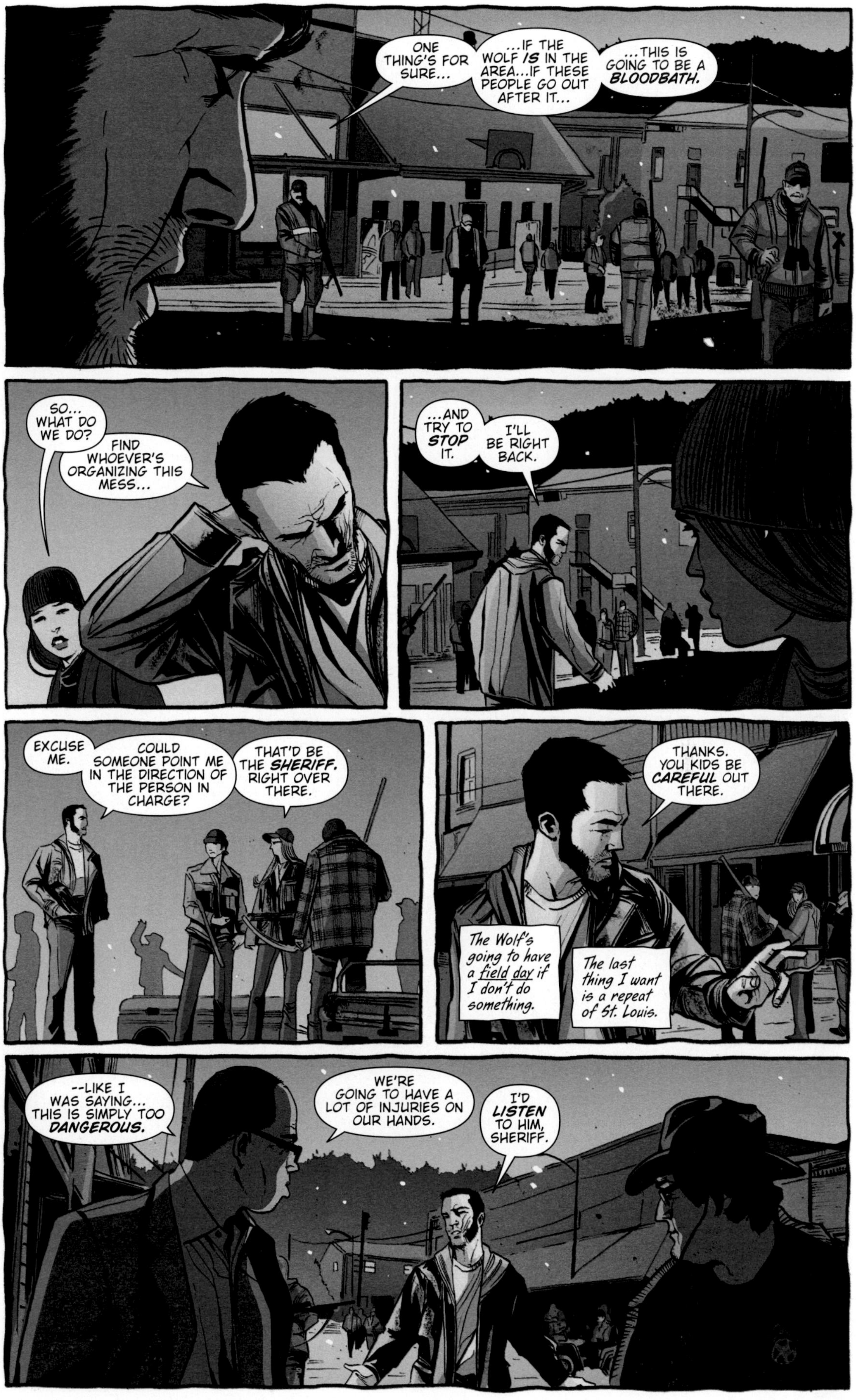
ONE THING'S FOR SURE...
...IF THE WOLF IS IN THE AREA...IF THESE PEOPLE GO OUT AFTER IT...
...THIS IS GOING TO BE A BLOODBATH.
SO... WHAT DO WE DO?
FIND WHOEVER'S ORGANIZING THIS MESS...
...AND TRY TO STOP IT.
I'LL BE RIGHT BACK.
EXCUSE ME.
COULD SOMEONE POINT ME IN THE DIRECTION OF THE PERSON IN CHARGE?
THAT'D BE THE SHERIFF. RIGHT OVER THERE.
THANKS. YOU KIDS BE CAREFUL OUT THERE.
The Wolf's going to have a field day if I don't do something.
The last thing I want is a repeat of St. Louis.
--LIKE I WAS SAYING... THIS IS SIMPLY TOO DANGEROUS.
WE'RE GOING TO HAVE A LOT OF INJURIES ON OUR HANDS.
I'D LISTEN TO HIM, SHERIFF.

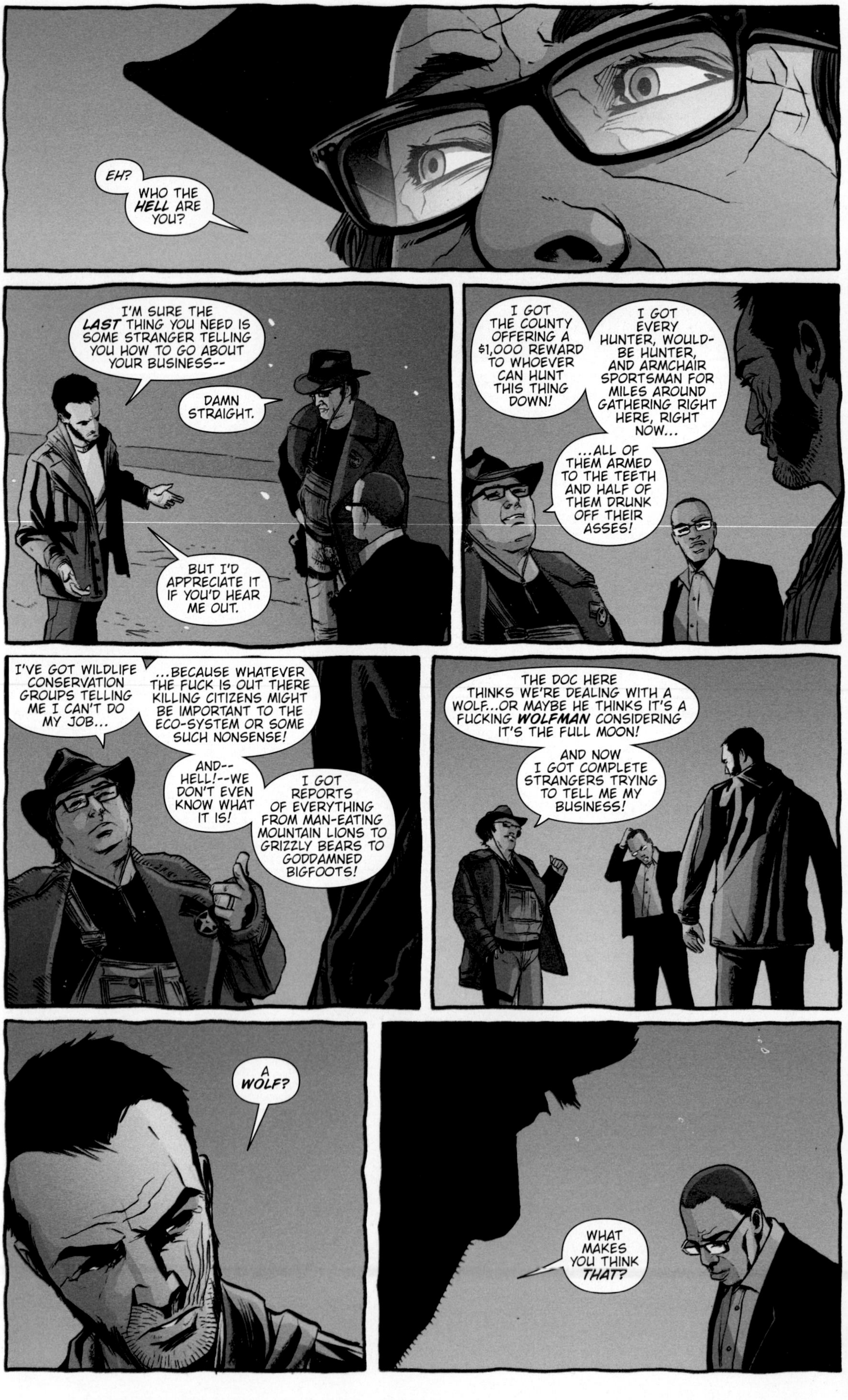
EH?
WHO THE HELL ARE YOU?
I'M SURE THE LAST THING YOU NEED IS SOME STRANGER TELLING YOU HOW TO GO ABOUT YOUR BUSINESS--
DAMN STRAIGHT.
BUT I'D APPRECIATE IT IF YOU'D HEAR ME OUT.
I GOT THE COUNTY OFFERING A $1,000 REWARD TO WHOEVER CAN HUNT THIS THING DOWN!
I GOT EVERY HUNTER, WOULD-BE HUNTER, AND ARMCHAIR SPORTSMAN FOR MILES AROUND GATHERING RIGHT HERE, RIGHT NOW...
...ALL OF THEM ARMED TO THE TEETH AND HALF OF THEM DRUNK OFF THEIR ASSES!
I'VE GOT WILDLIFE CONSERVATION GROUPS TELLING ME I CAN'T DO MY JOB...
...BECAUSE WHATEVER THE FUCK IS OUT THERE KILLING CITIZENS MIGHT BE IMPORTANT TO THE ECO-SYSTEM OR SOME SUCH NONSENSE!
AND--HELL!--WE DON'T EVEN KNOW WHAT IT IS!
I GOT REPORTS OF EVERYTHING FROM MAN-EATING MOUNTAIN LIONS TO GRIZZLY BEARS TO GODDAMNED BIGFOOTS!
THE DOC HERE THINKS WE'RE DEALING WITH A WOLF...OR MAYBE HE THINKS IT'S A FUCKING WOLFMAN CONSIDERING IT'S THE FULL MOON!
AND NOW I GOT COMPLETE STRANGERS TRYING TO TELL ME MY BUSINESS!
A WOLF?
WHAT MAKES YOU THINK THAT?

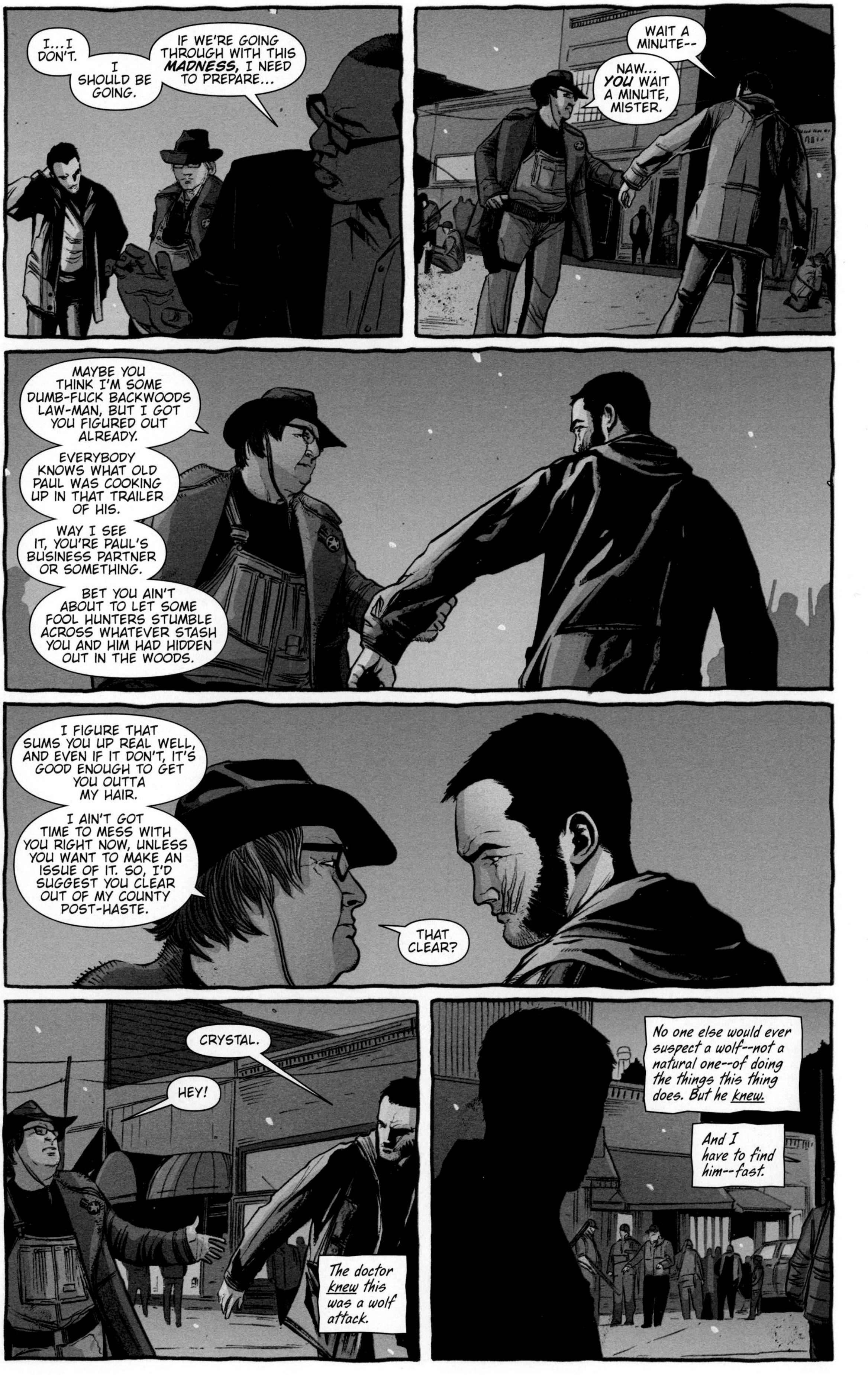
I...I DON'T.
I SHOULD BE GOING.
IF WE'RE GOING THROUGH WITH THIS MADNESS, I NEED TO PREPARE...
WAIT A MINUTE--
NAW... YOU WAIT A MINUTE, MISTER.
MAYBE YOU THINK I'M SOME DUMB-FUCK BACKWOODS LAW-MAN, BUT I GOT YOU FIGURED OUT ALREADY.
EVERYBODY KNOWS WHAT OLD PAUL WAS COOKING UP IN THAT TRAILER OF HIS.
WAY I SEE IT, YOU'RE PAUL'S BUSINESS PARTNER OR SOMETHING.
BET YOU AIN'T ABOUT TO LET SOME FOOL HUNTERS STUMBLE ACROSS WHATEVER STASH YOU AND HIM HAD HIDDEN OUT IN THE WOODS.
I FIGURE THAT SUMS YOU UP REAL WELL, AND EVEN IF IT DON'T, IT'S GOOD ENOUGH TO GET YOU OUTTA MY HAIR.
I AIN'T GOT TIME TO MESS WITH YOU RIGHT NOW, UNLESS YOU WANT TO MAKE AN ISSUE OF IT. SO, I'D SUGGEST YOU CLEAR OUT OF MY COUNTY POST-HASTE.
THAT CLEAR?
CRYSTAL.
HEY!
The doctor knew this was a wolf attack.
No one else would ever suspect a wolf--not a natural one--of doing the things this thing does. But he knew.
And I have to find him--fast.

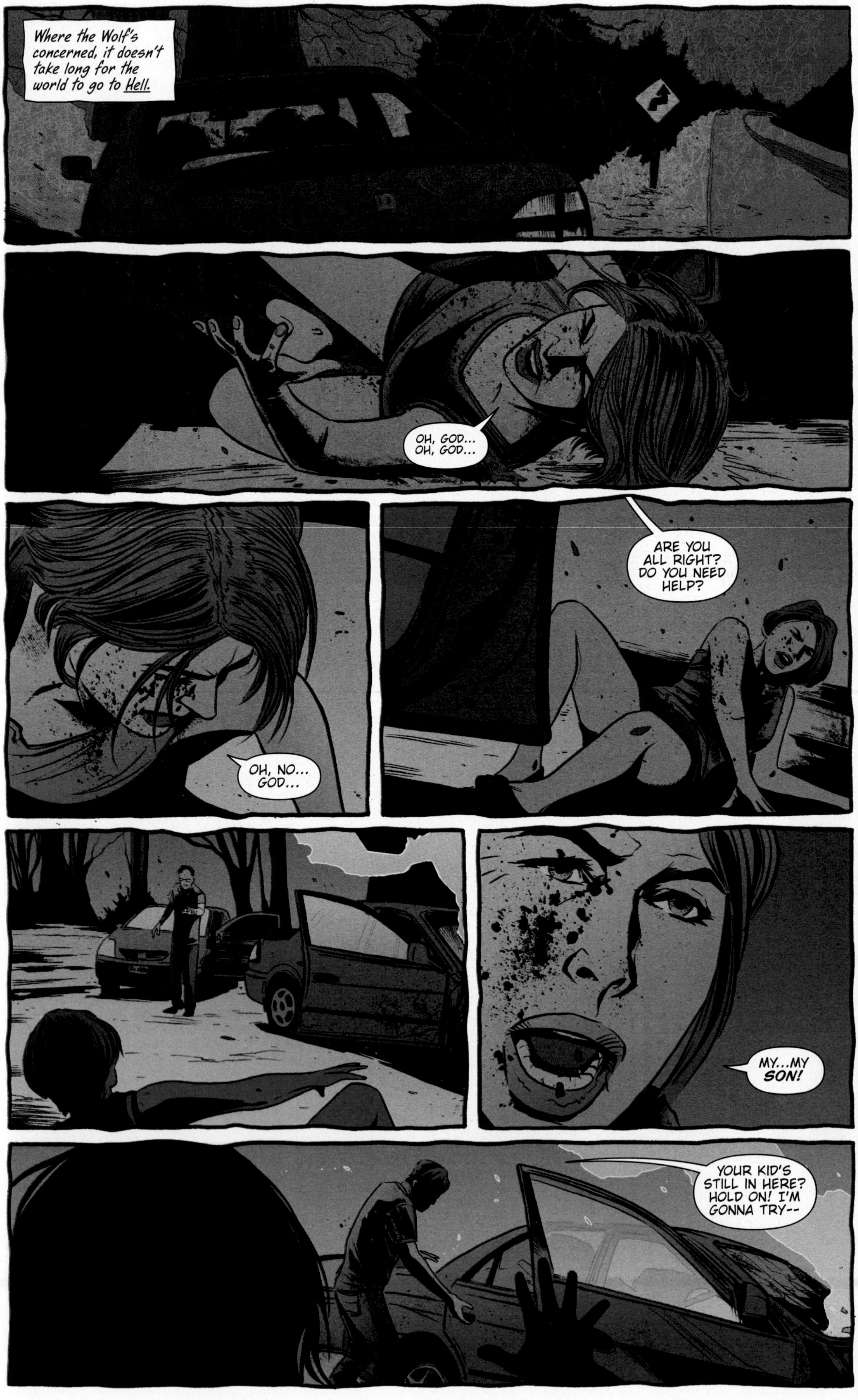
Where the Wolf's concerned, it doesn't take long for the world to go to Hell.
OH, GOD... OH, GOD...
OH, NO... GOD...
ARE YOU ALL RIGHT? DO YOU NEED HELP?
MY...MY SON!
YOUR KID'S STILL IN HERE? HOLD ON! I'M GONNA TRY--

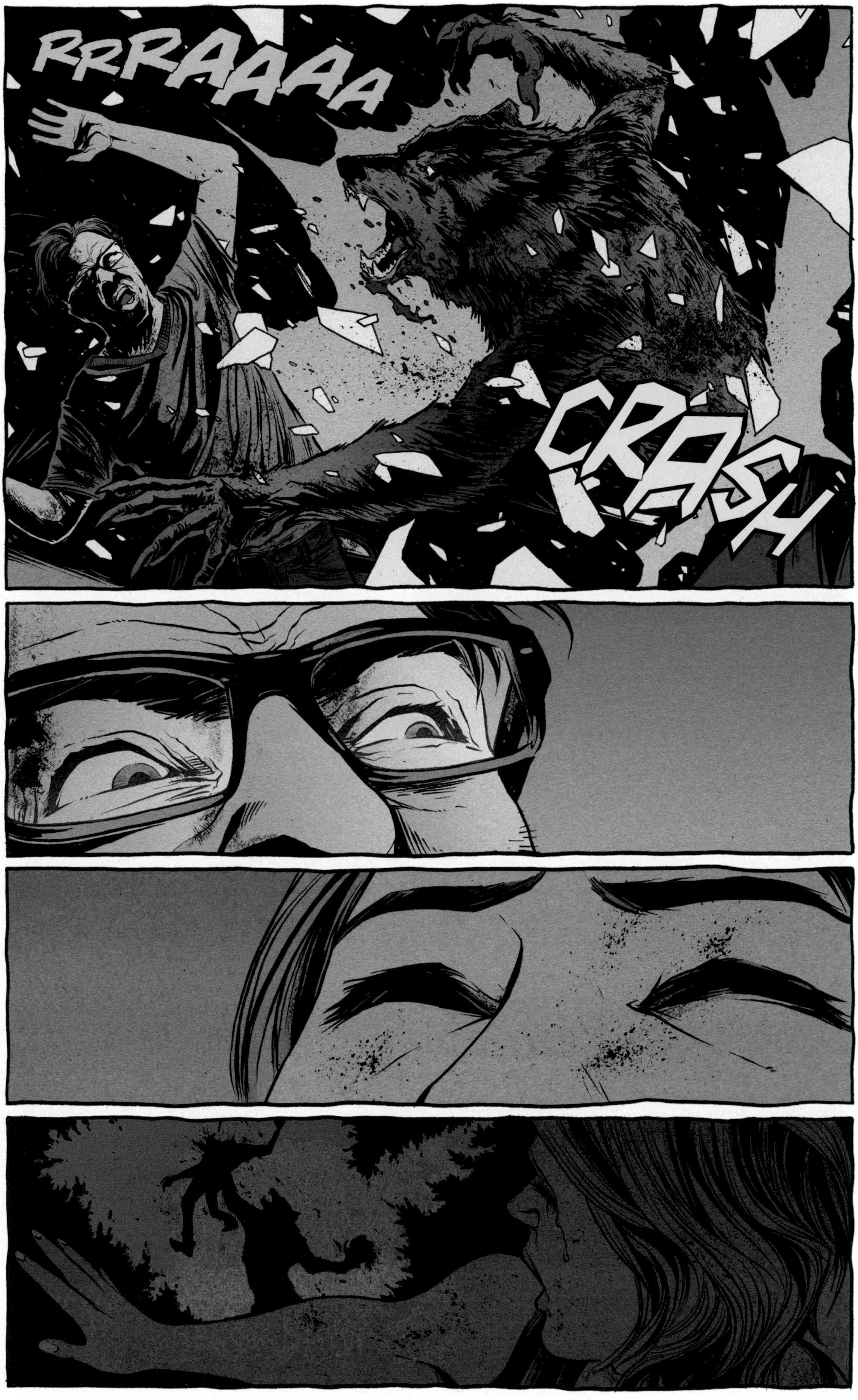
RRRAAAAA
CRASH

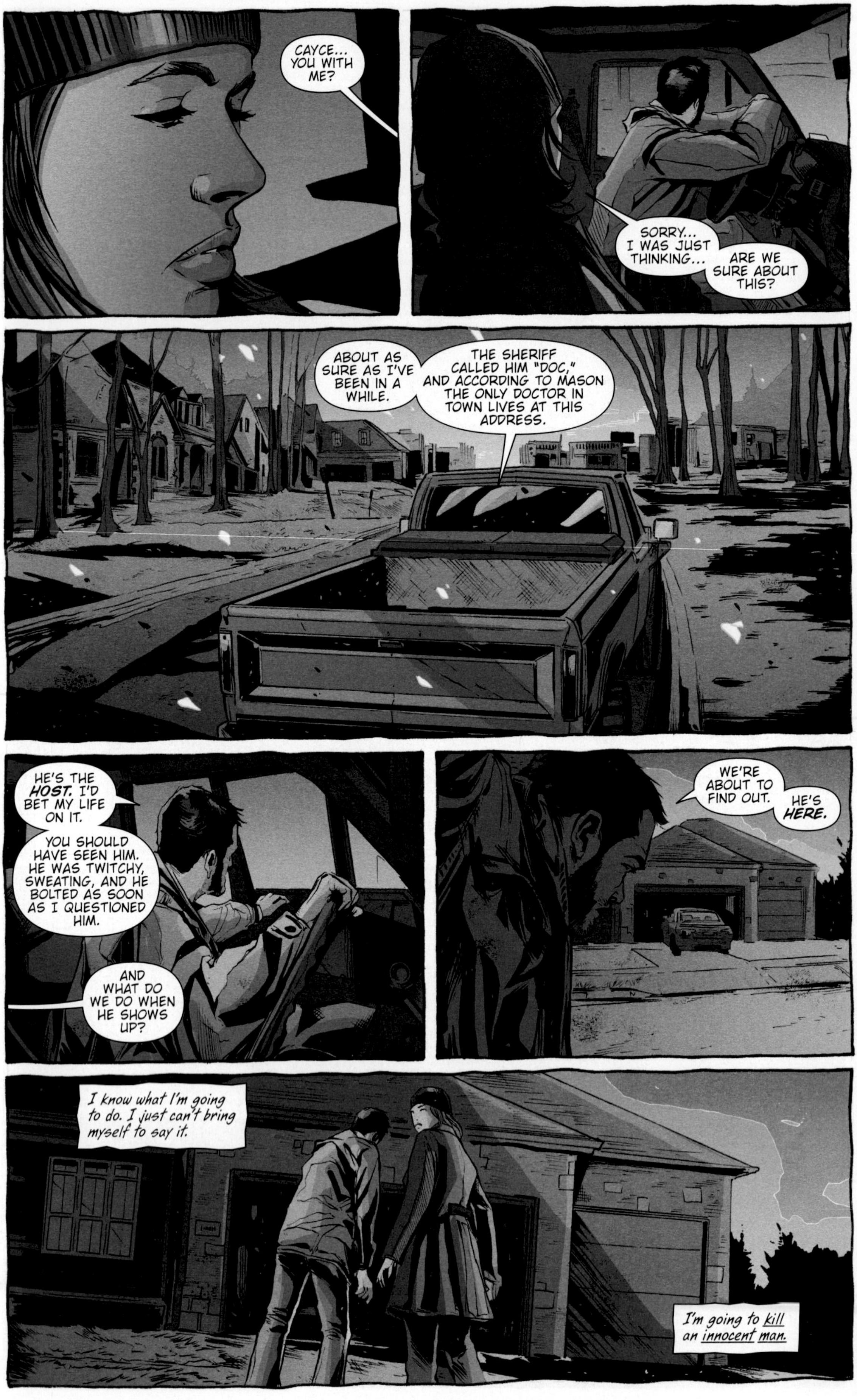

CAYCE... YOU WITH ME?
SORRY... I WAS JUST THINKING...
ARE WE SURE ABOUT THIS?
ABOUT AS SURE AS I'VE BEEN IN A WHILE.
THE SHERIFF CALLED HIM "DOC," AND ACCORDING TO MASON THE ONLY DOCTOR IN TOWN LIVES AT THIS ADDRESS.
HE'S THE HOST. I'D BET MY LIFE ON IT.
YOU SHOULD HAVE SEEN HIM. HE WAS TWITCHY, SWEATING, AND HE BOLTED AS SOON AS I QUESTIONED HIM.
AND WHAT DO WE DO WHEN HE SHOWS UP?
WE'RE ABOUT TO FIND OUT.
HE'S HERE.
I know what I'm going to do. I just can't bring myself to say it.
I'm going to kill an innocent man.

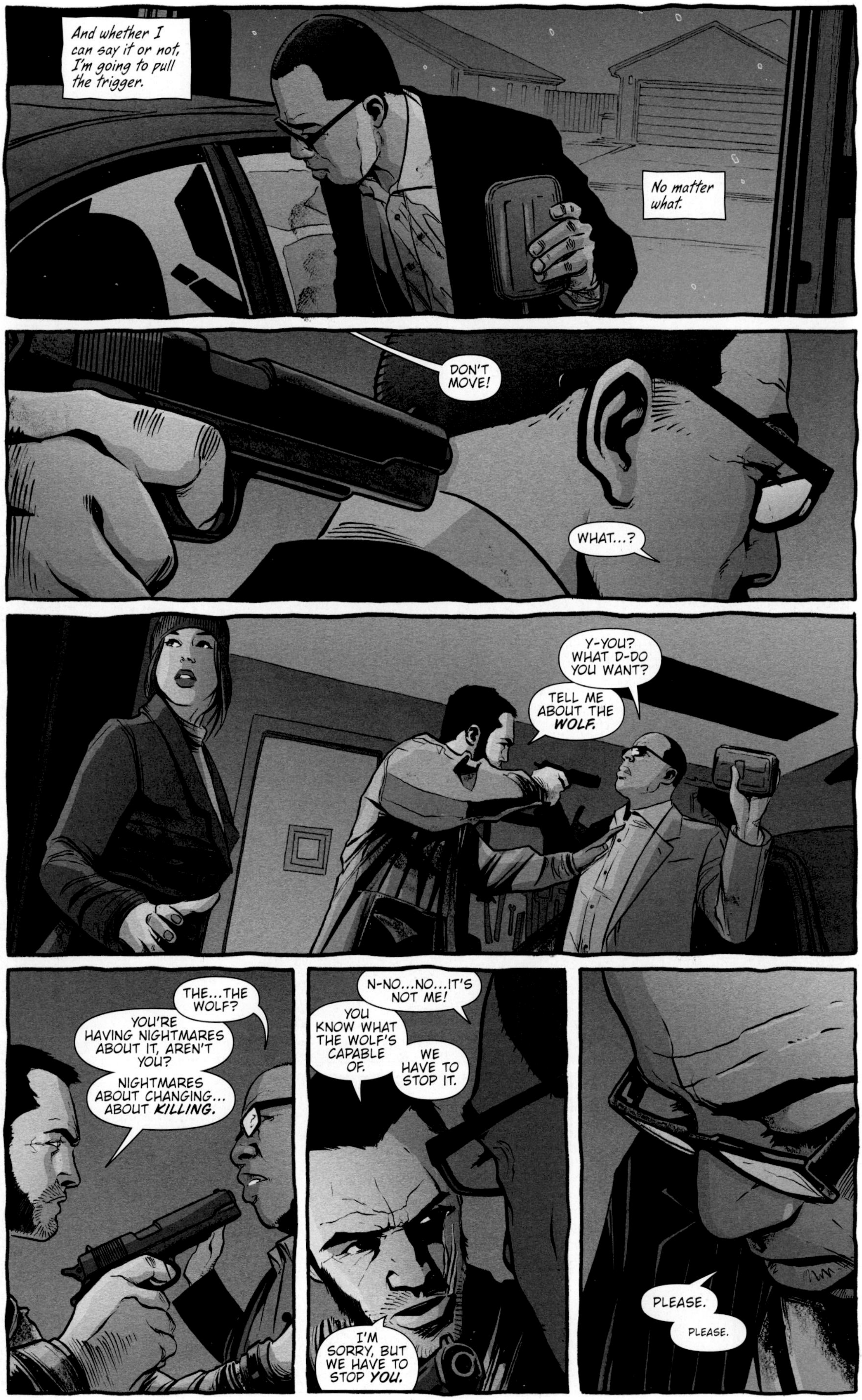
And whether I can say it or not, I'm going to pull the trigger.
No matter what.
DON'T MOVE!
WHAT...?
Y-YOU? WHAT D-DO YOU WANT?
TELL ME ABOUT THE WOLF.
THE...THE WOLF?
YOU'RE HAVING NIGHTMARES ABOUT IT, AREN'T YOU?
NIGHTMARES ABOUT CHANGING... ABOUT KILLING.
N-NO...NO...IT'S NOT ME!
YOU KNOW WHAT THE WOLF'S CAPABLE OF.
WE HAVE TO STOP IT.
I'M SORRY, BUT WE HAVE TO STOP YOU.
PLEASE.
PLEASE.

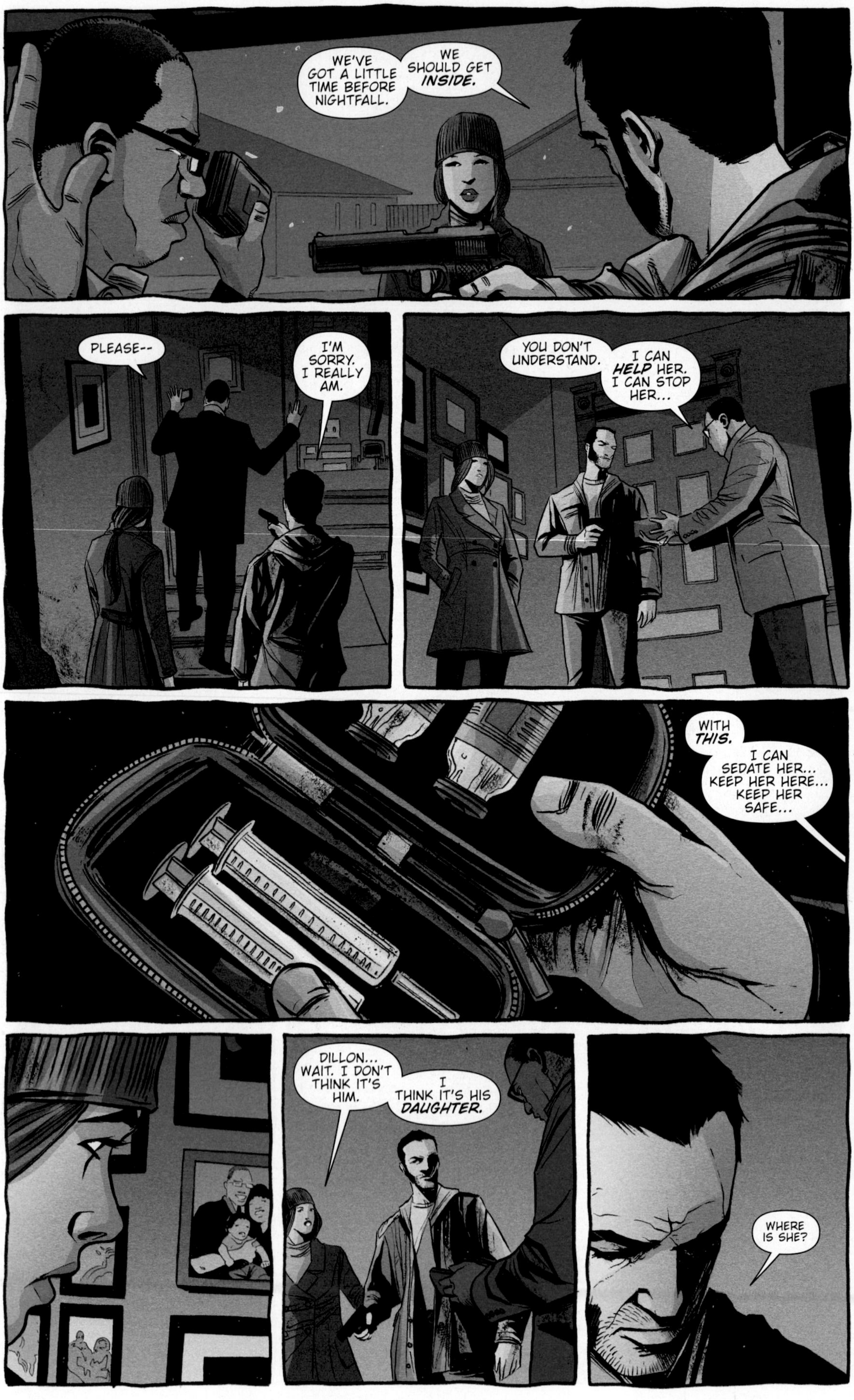
WE'VE GOT A LITTLE TIME BEFORE NIGHTFALL.
WE SHOULD GET *INSIDE.*
PLEASE--
I'M SORRY. I REALLY AM.
YOU DON'T UNDERSTAND.
I CAN *HELP* HER. I CAN STOP HER...
WITH *THIS.*
I CAN SEDATE HER... KEEP HER HERE... KEEP HER SAFE...
DILLON... WAIT. I DON'T THINK IT'S HIM.
I THINK IT'S HIS *DAUGHTER.*
WHERE IS SHE?

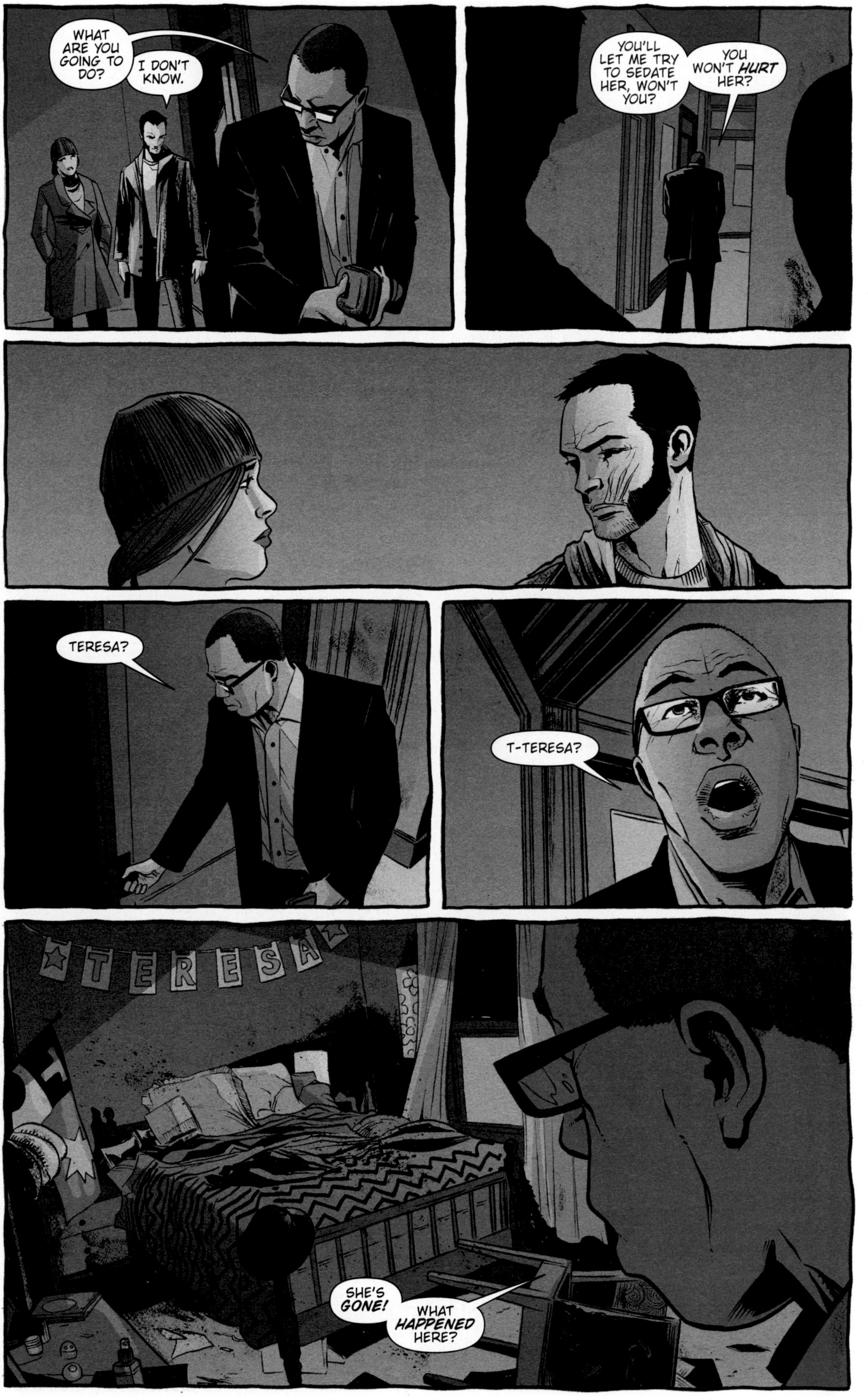
WHAT ARE YOU GOING TO DO?
I DON'T KNOW.
YOU'LL LET ME TRY TO SEDATE HER, WON'T YOU?
YOU WON'T *HURT* HER?
TERESA?
T-TERESA?
TERESA
SHE'S *GONE!*
WHAT *HAPPENED* HERE?

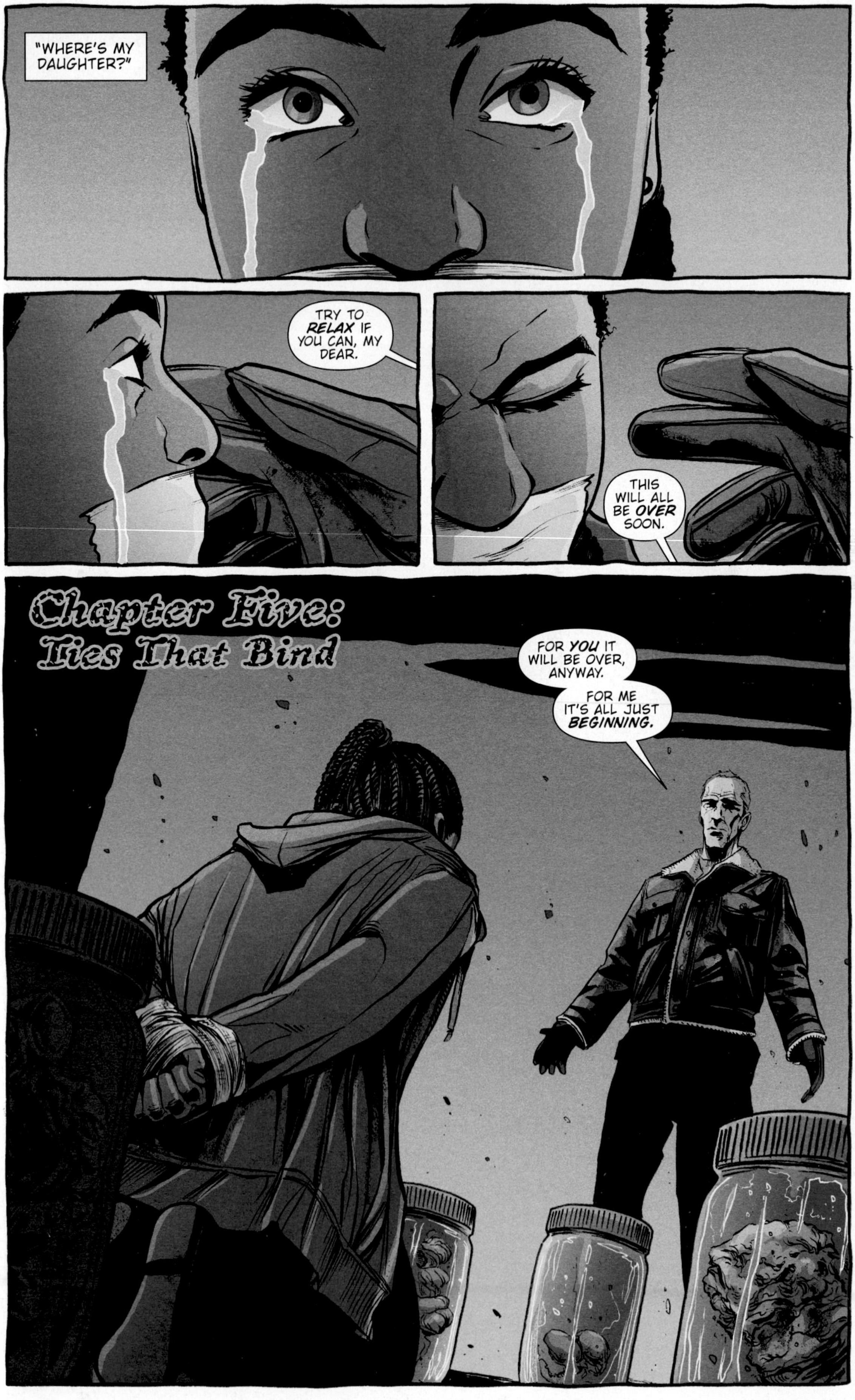
"WHERE'S MY DAUGHTER?"
TRY TO RELAX IF YOU CAN, MY DEAR.
THIS WILL ALL BE OVER SOON.
Chapter Five: Ties That Bind
FOR YOU IT WILL BE OVER, ANYWAY.
FOR ME IT'S ALL JUST BEGINNING.

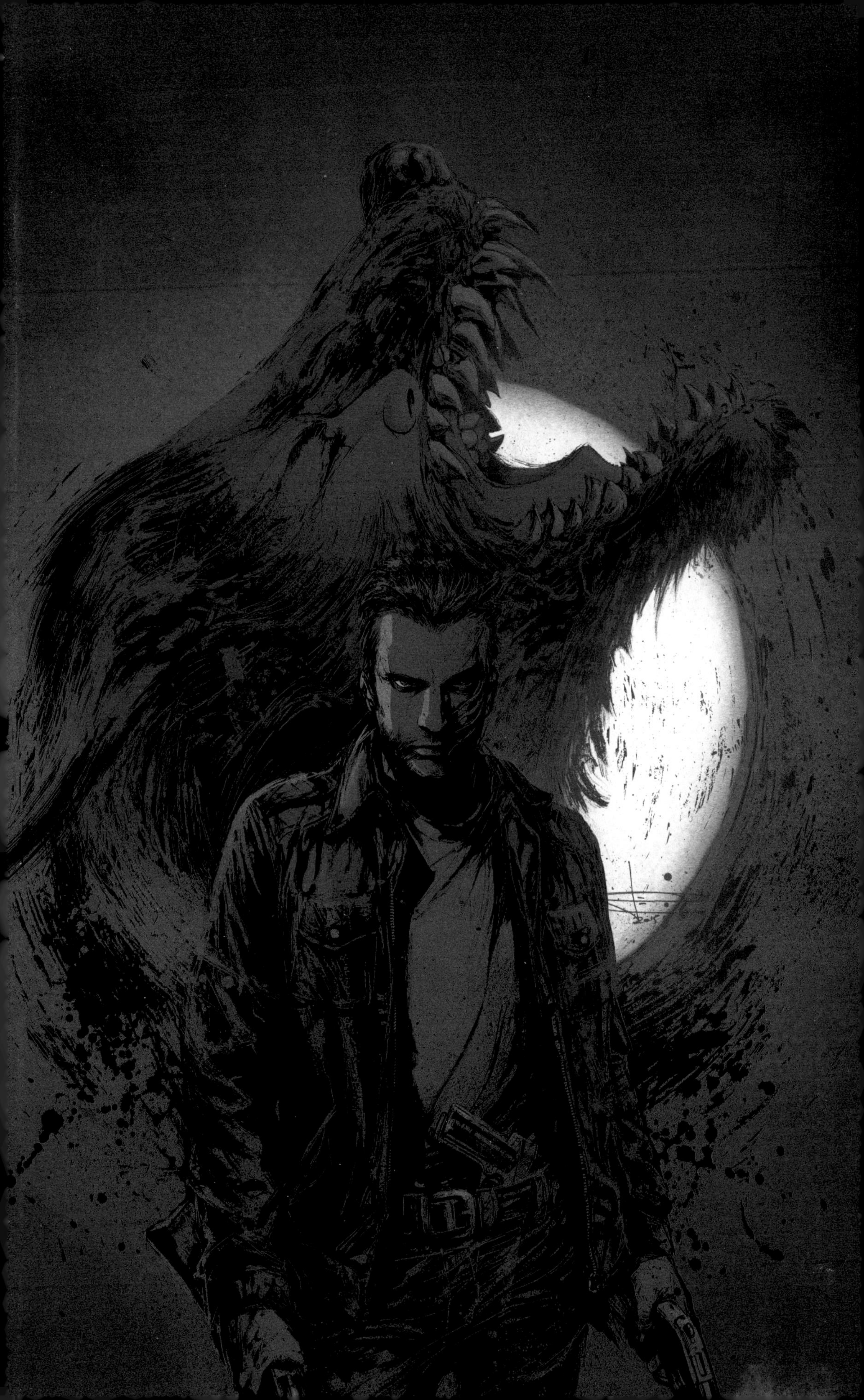

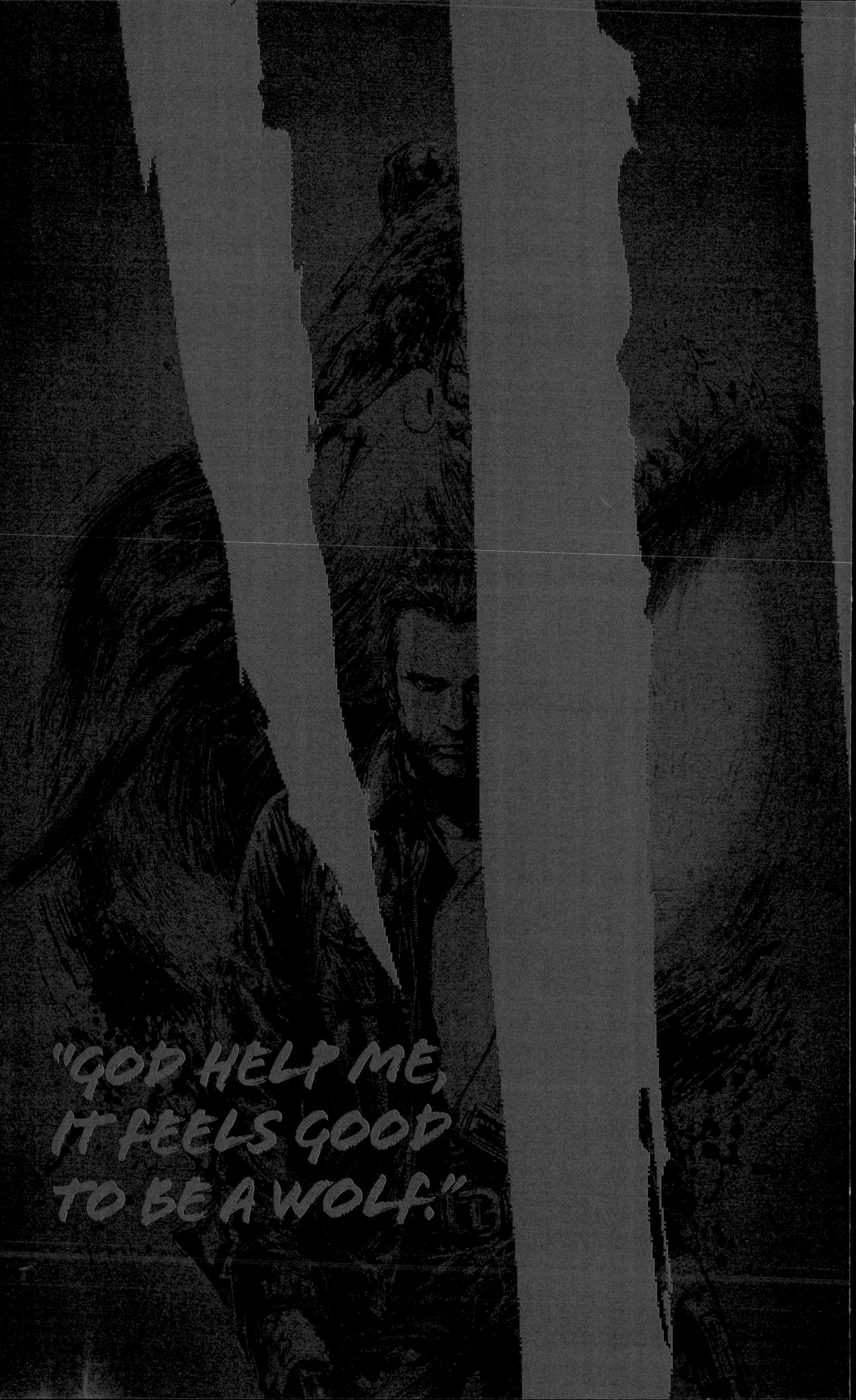
"GOD HELP ME,
IT FEELS GOOD
TO BE A WOLF."

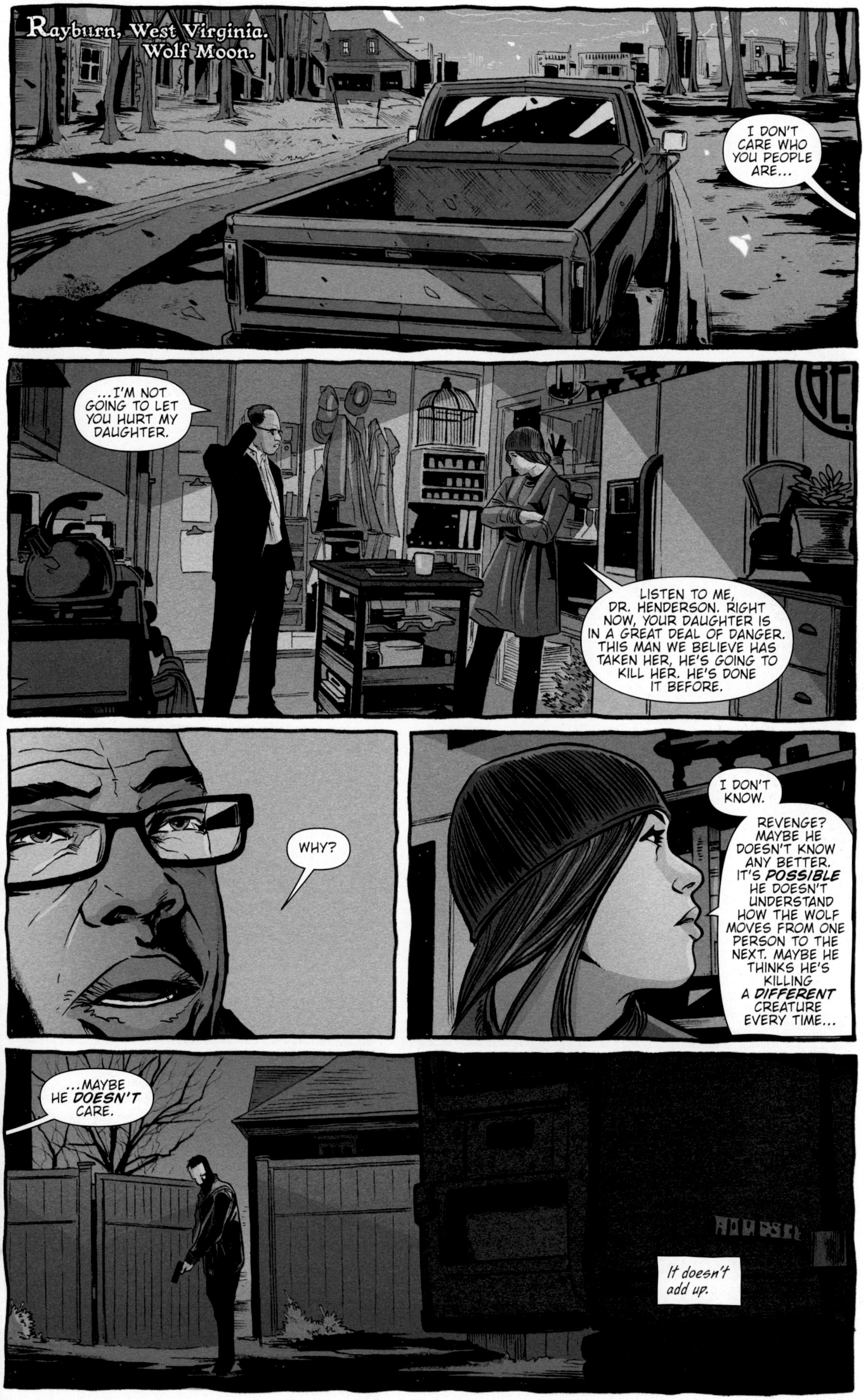
Rayburn, West Virginia. Wolf Moon.
I DON'T CARE WHO YOU PEOPLE ARE...
...I'M NOT GOING TO LET YOU HURT MY DAUGHTER.
LISTEN TO ME, DR. HENDERSON. RIGHT NOW, YOUR DAUGHTER IS IN A GREAT DEAL OF DANGER. THIS MAN WE BELIEVE HAS TAKEN HER, HE'S GOING TO KILL HER. HE'S DONE IT BEFORE.
WHY?
I DON'T KNOW.
REVENGE? MAYBE HE DOESN'T KNOW ANY BETTER. IT'S POSSIBLE HE DOESN'T UNDERSTAND HOW THE WOLF MOVES FROM ONE PERSON TO THE NEXT. MAYBE HE THINKS HE'S KILLING A DIFFERENT CREATURE EVERY TIME...
...MAYBE HE DOESN'T CARE.
It doesn't add up.

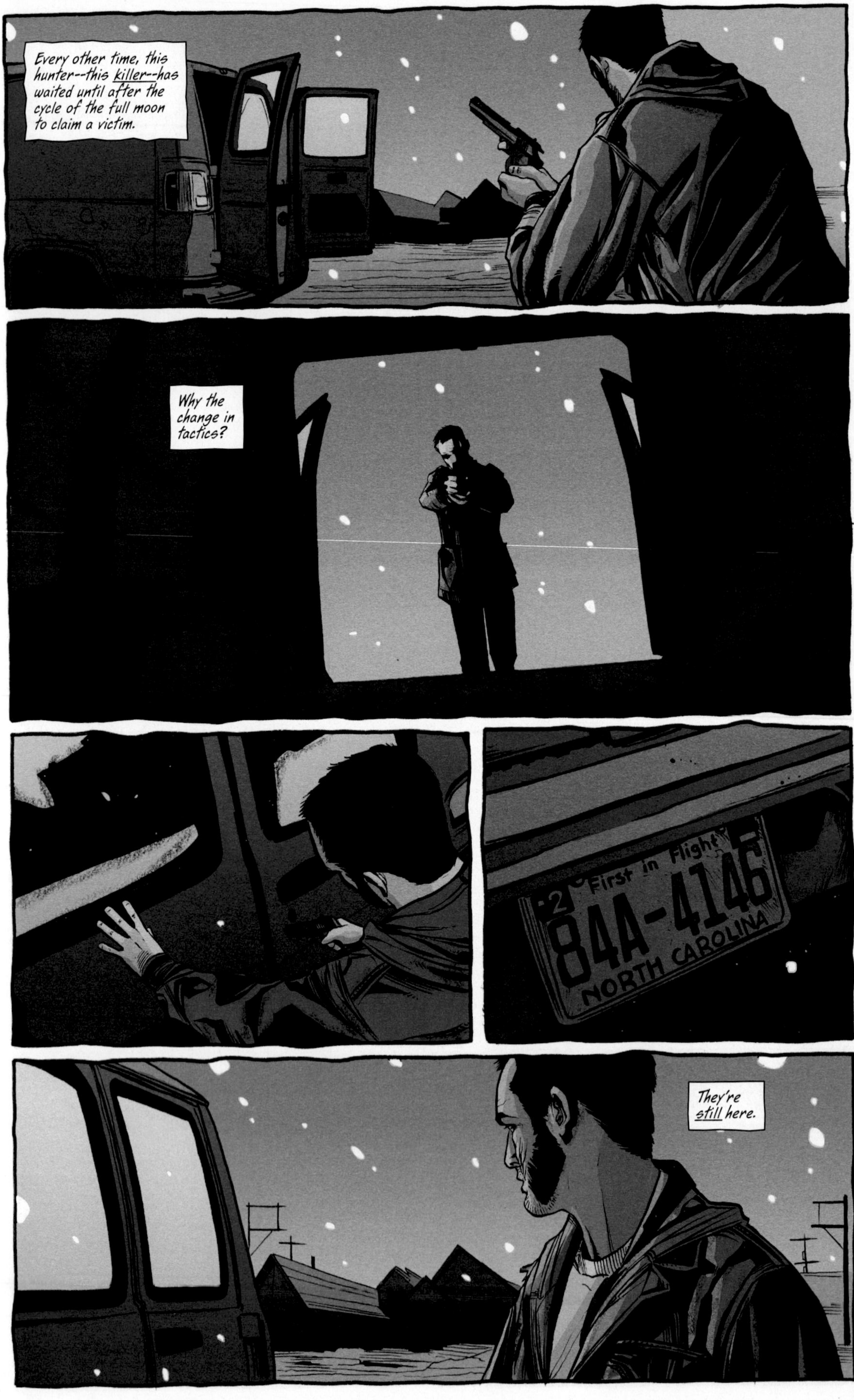
Every other time, this hunter--this killer--has waited until after the cycle of the full moon to claim a victim.
Why the change in tactics?
First in Flight
84A-4146
NORTH CAROLINA
They're still here.

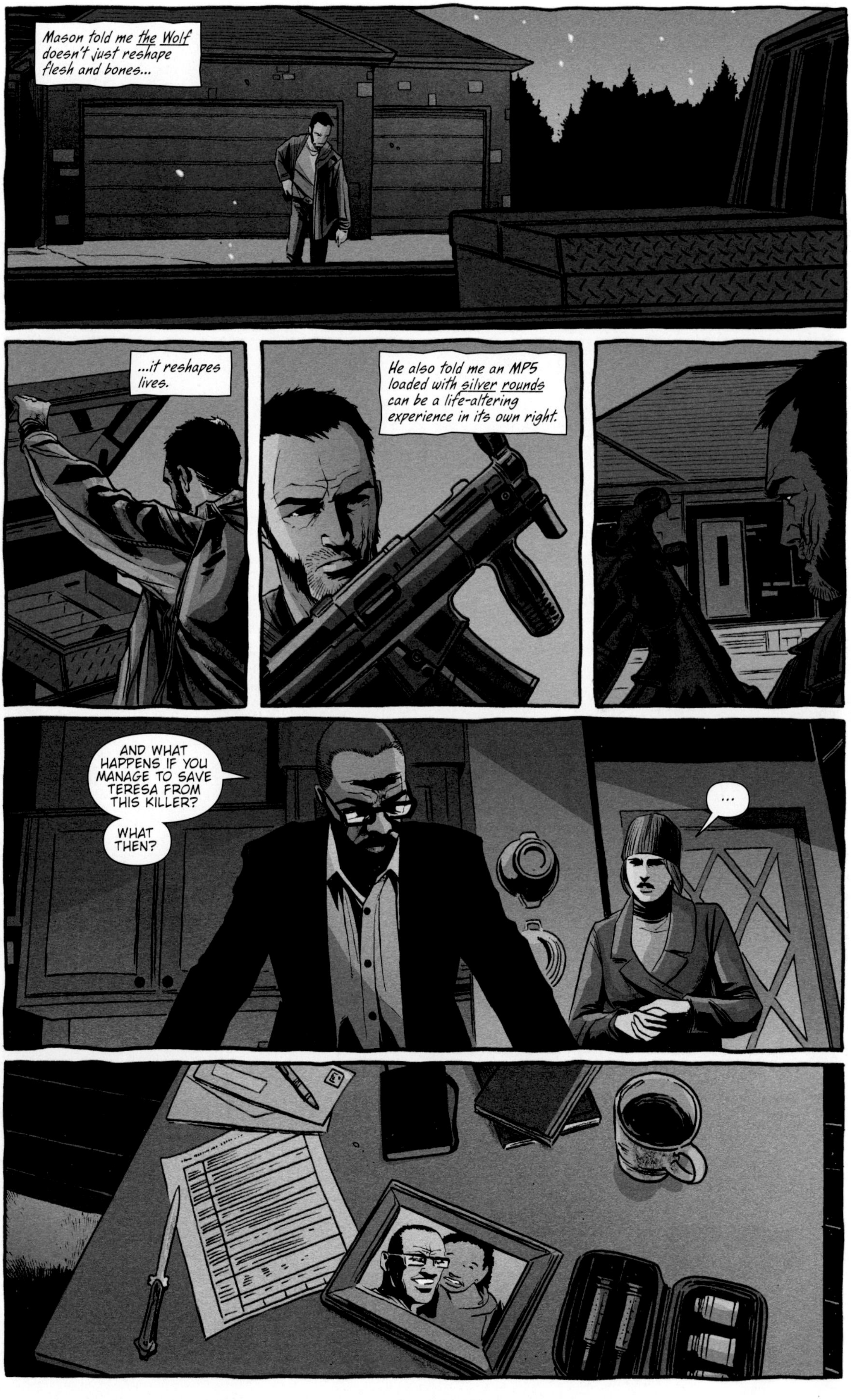
Mason told me the Wolf doesn't just reshape flesh and bones...
...it reshapes lives.
He also told me an MP5 loaded with silver rounds can be a life-altering experience in its own right.
AND WHAT HAPPENS IF YOU MANAGE TO SAVE TERESA FROM THIS KILLER?
WHAT THEN?
...

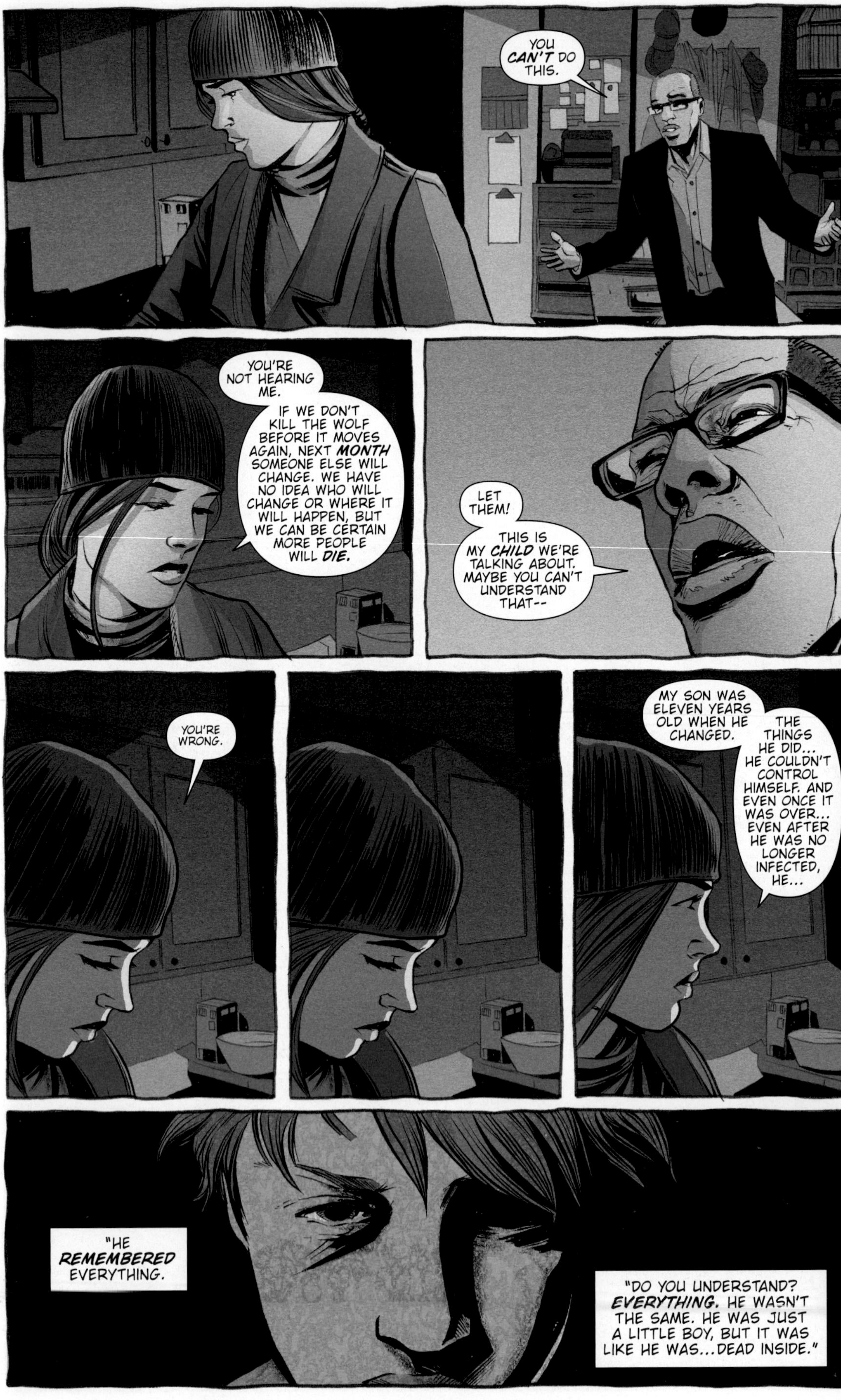
YOU *CAN'T* DO THIS.
YOU'RE NOT HEARING ME.
IF WE DON'T KILL THE WOLF BEFORE IT MOVES AGAIN, NEXT *MONTH* SOMEONE ELSE WILL CHANGE. WE HAVE NO IDEA WHO WILL CHANGE OR WHERE IT WILL HAPPEN, BUT WE CAN BE CERTAIN MORE PEOPLE WILL *DIE.*
LET THEM!
THIS IS MY *CHILD* WE'RE TALKING ABOUT. MAYBE YOU CAN'T UNDERSTAND THAT--
YOU'RE WRONG.
MY SON WAS ELEVEN YEARS OLD WHEN HE CHANGED.
THE THINGS HE DID... HE COULDN'T CONTROL HIMSELF. AND EVEN ONCE IT WAS OVER... EVEN AFTER HE WAS NO LONGER INFECTED, HE...
"HE *REMEMBERED* EVERYTHING.
"DO YOU UNDERSTAND? *EVERYTHING.* HE WASN'T THE SAME. HE WAS JUST A LITTLE BOY, BUT IT WAS LIKE HE WAS...DEAD INSIDE."

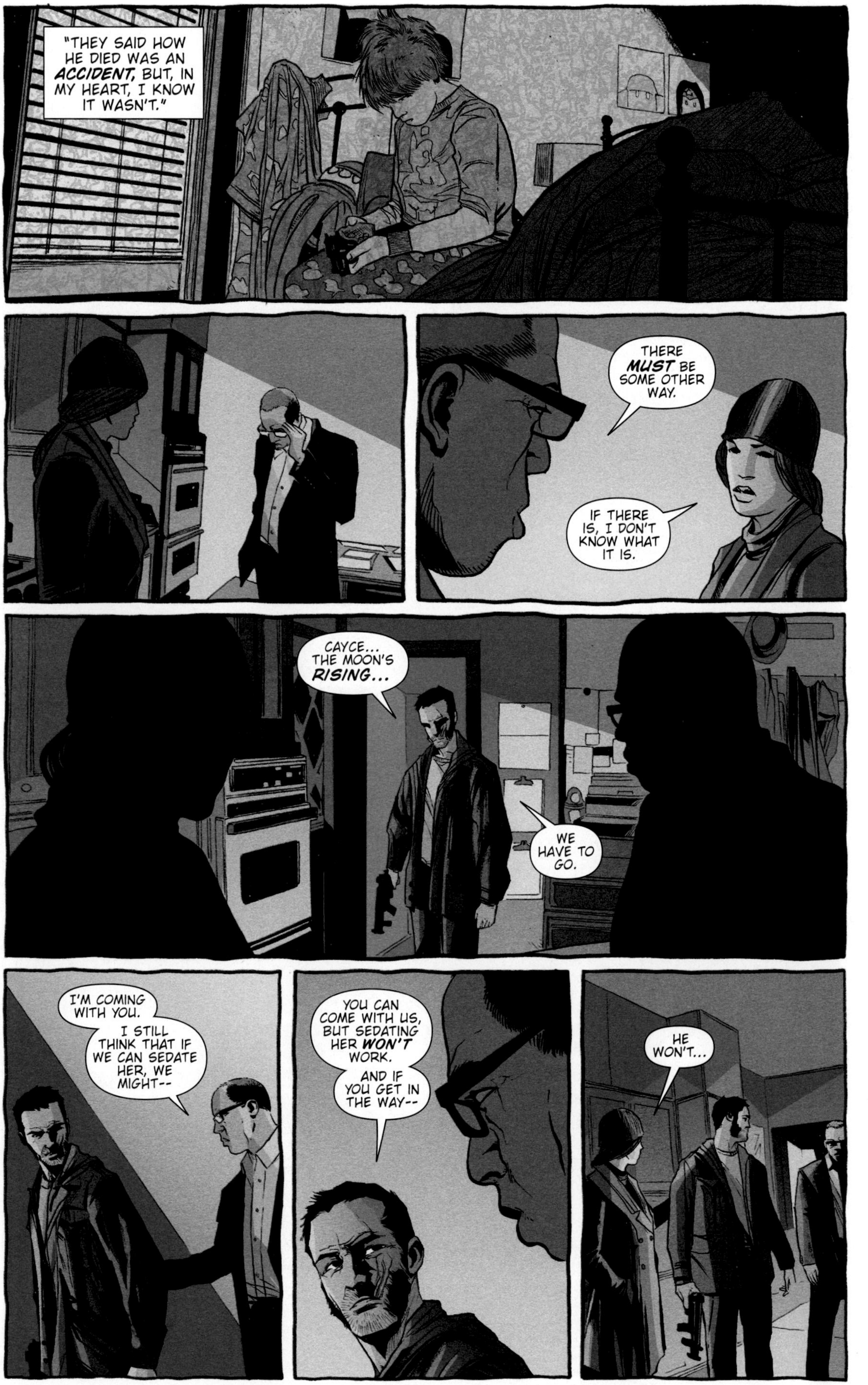
"THEY SAID HOW HE DIED WAS AN ACCIDENT, BUT, IN MY HEART, I KNOW IT WASN'T."
THERE MUST BE SOME OTHER WAY.
IF THERE IS, I DON'T KNOW WHAT IT IS.
CAYCE... THE MOON'S RISING...
WE HAVE TO GO.
I'M COMING WITH YOU.
I STILL THINK THAT IF WE CAN SEDATE HER, WE MIGHT--
YOU CAN COME WITH US, BUT SEDATING HER WON'T WORK.
AND IF YOU GET IN THE WAY--
HE WON'T...

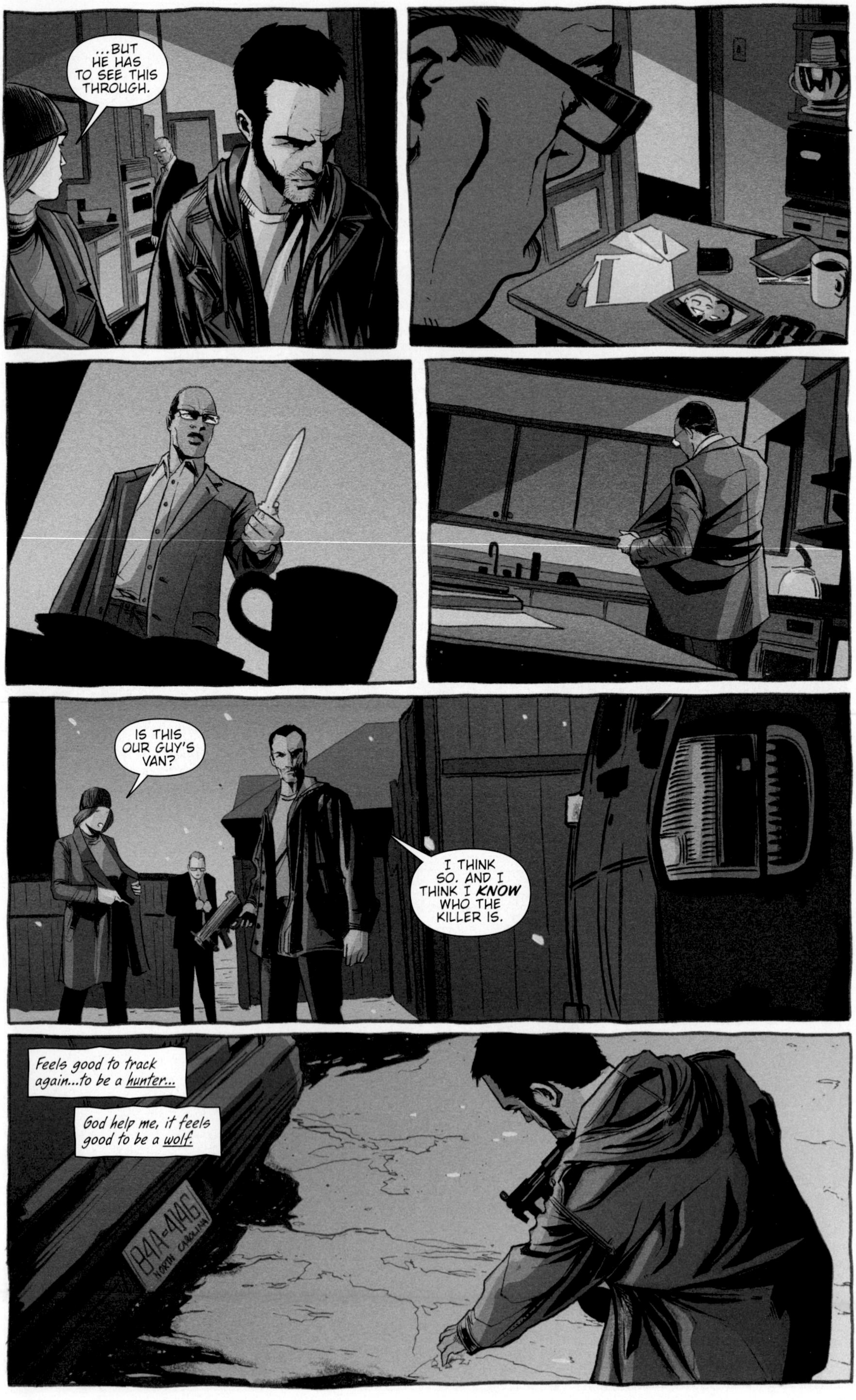
...BUT HE HAS TO SEE THIS THROUGH.
IS THIS OUR GUY'S VAN?
I THINK SO. AND I THINK I KNOW WHO THE KILLER IS.
Feels good to track again...to be a hunter...
God help me, it feels good to be a wolf.
B4A-4146
NORTH CAROLINA

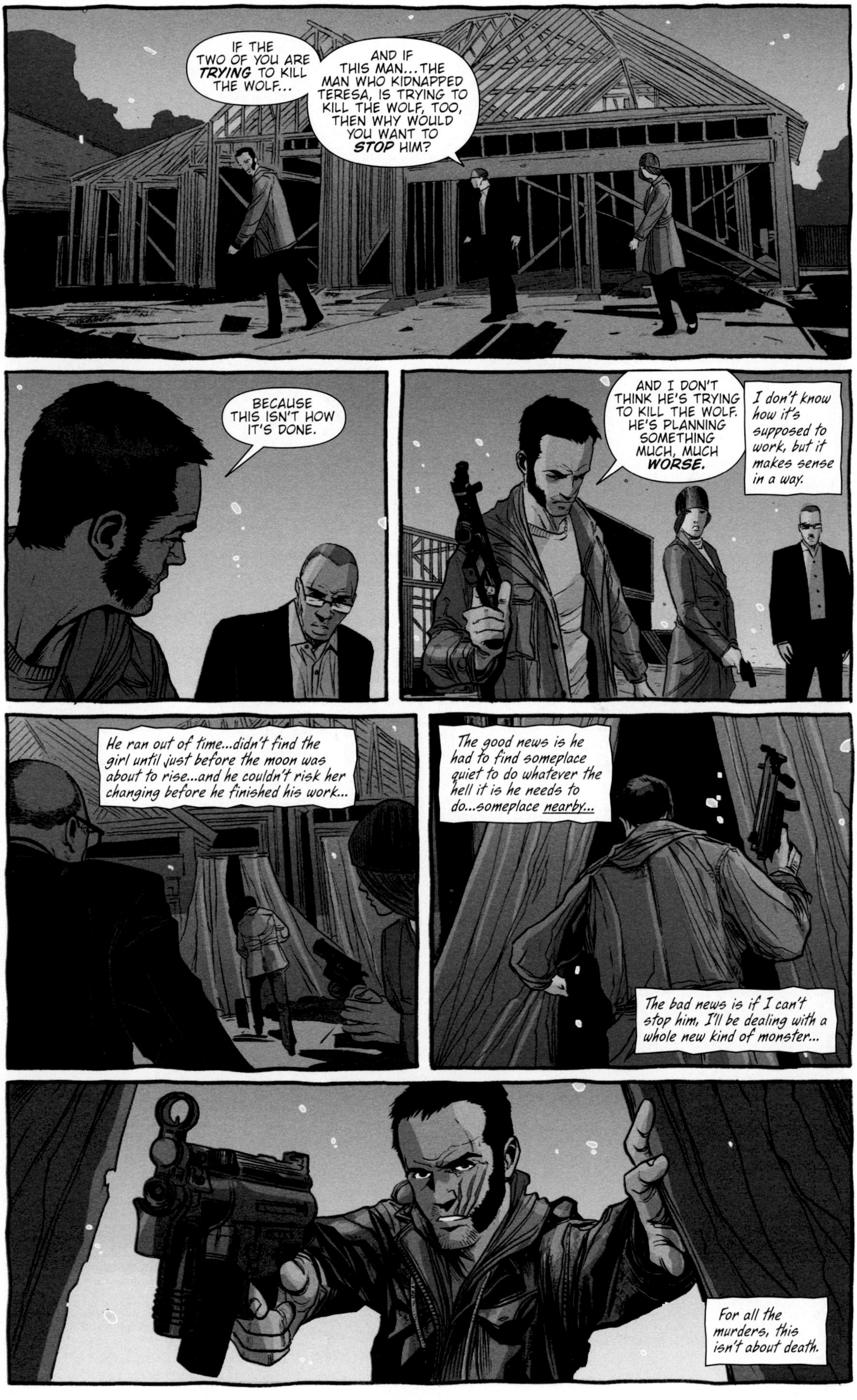
IF THE TWO OF YOU ARE TRYING TO KILL THE WOLF...
AND IF THIS MAN...THE MAN WHO KIDNAPPED TERESA, IS TRYING TO KILL THE WOLF, TOO, THEN WHY WOULD YOU WANT TO STOP HIM?
BECAUSE THIS ISN'T HOW IT'S DONE.
AND I DON'T THINK HE'S TRYING TO KILL THE WOLF. HE'S PLANNING SOMETHING MUCH, MUCH WORSE.
I don't know how it's supposed to work, but it makes sense in a way.
He ran out of time...didn't find the girl until just before the moon was about to rise...and he couldn't risk her changing before he finished his work...
The good news is he had to find someplace quiet to do whatever the hell it is he needs to do...someplace nearby...
The bad news is if I can't stop him, I'll be dealing with a whole new kind of monster...
For all the murders, this isn't about death.

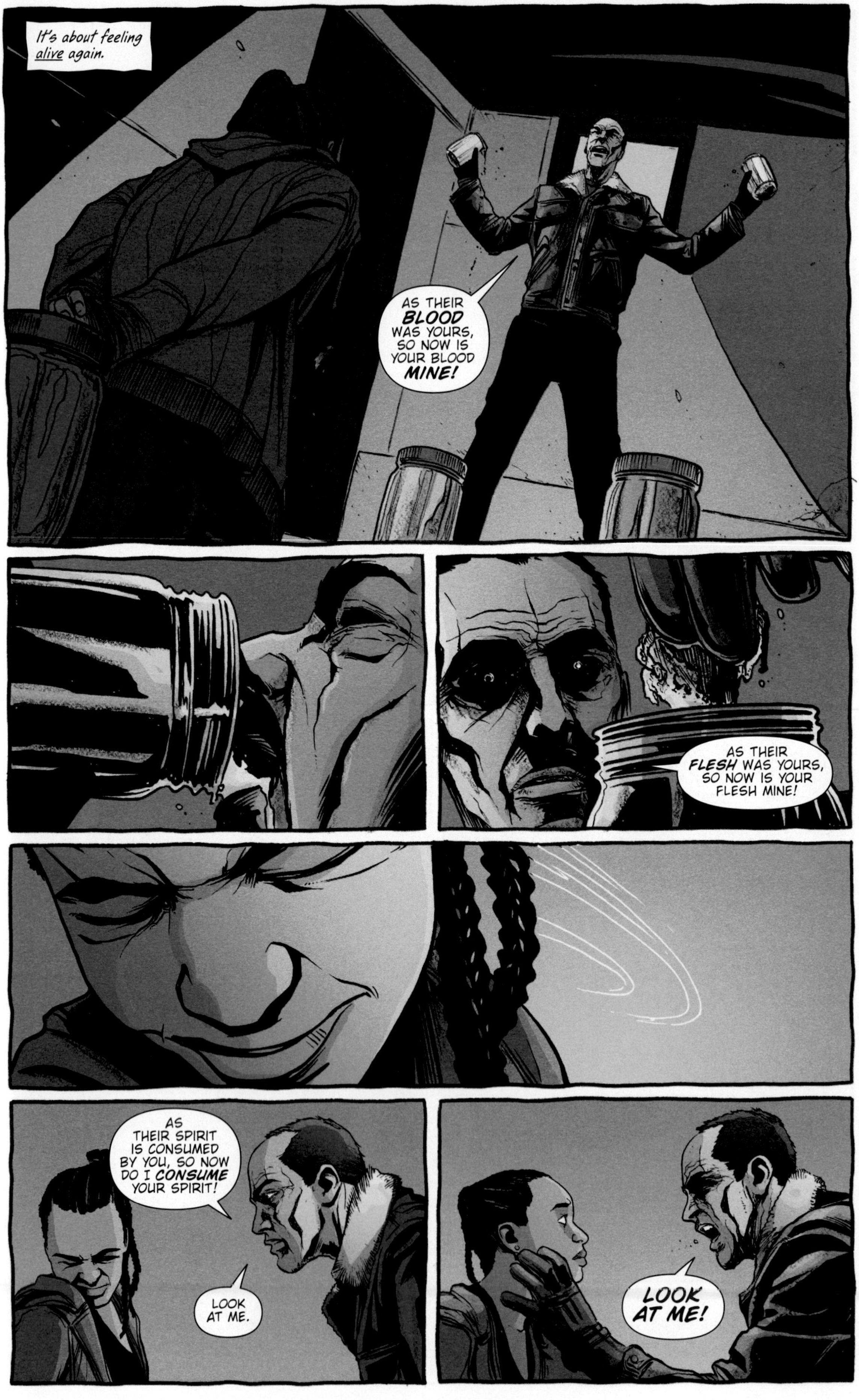
It's about feeling alive again.
AS THEIR BLOOD WAS YOURS, SO NOW IS YOUR BLOOD MINE!
AS THEIR FLESH WAS YOURS, SO NOW IS YOUR FLESH MINE!
AS THEIR SPIRIT IS CONSUMED BY YOU, SO NOW DO I CONSUME YOUR SPIRIT!
LOOK AT ME.
LOOK AT ME!

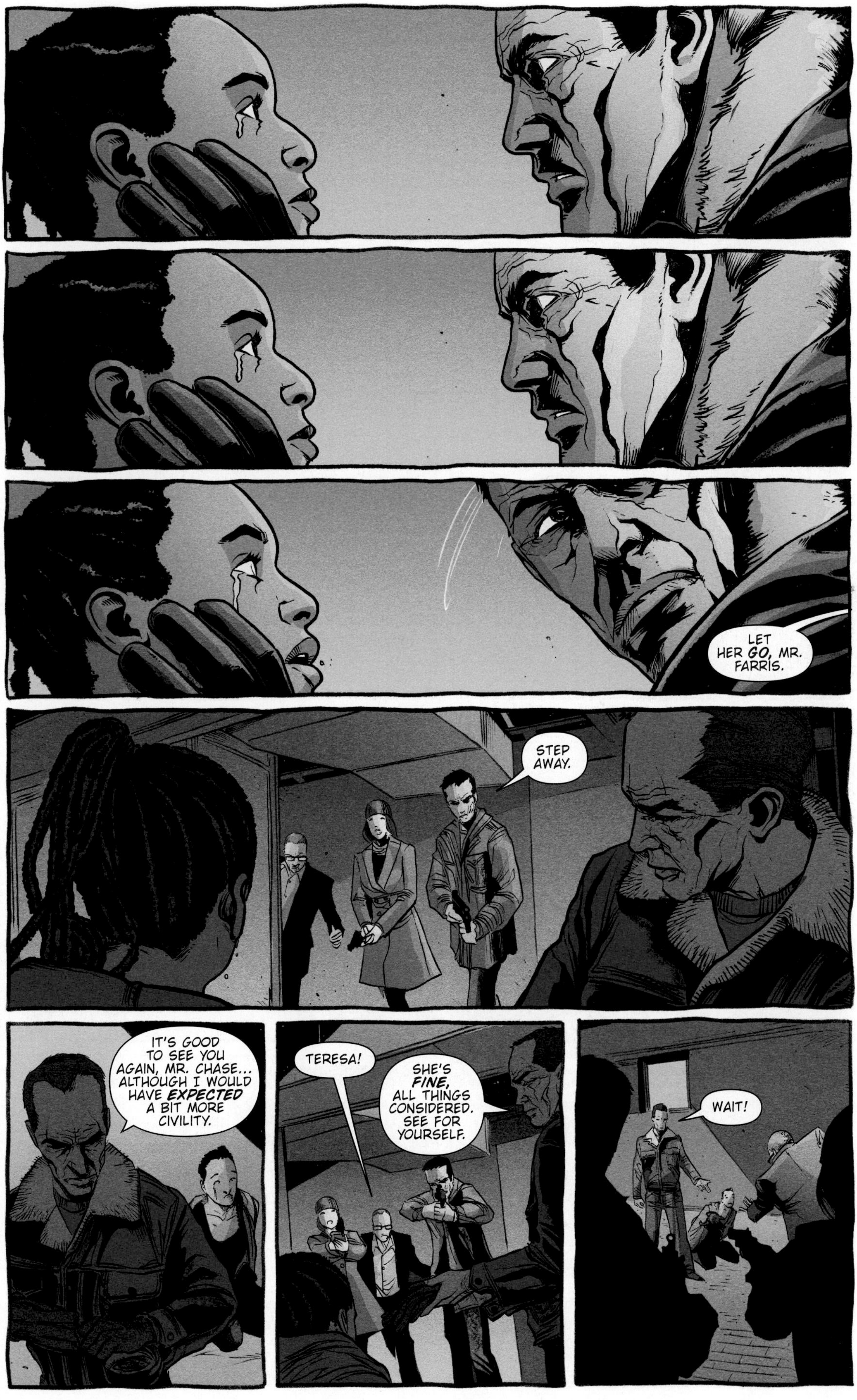
LET HER GO, MR. FARRIS.
STEP AWAY.
IT'S GOOD TO SEE YOU AGAIN, MR. CHASE... ALTHOUGH I WOULD HAVE *EXPECTED* A BIT MORE CIVILITY.
TERESA!
SHE'S *FINE*, ALL THINGS CONSIDERED. SEE FOR YOURSELF.
WAIT!

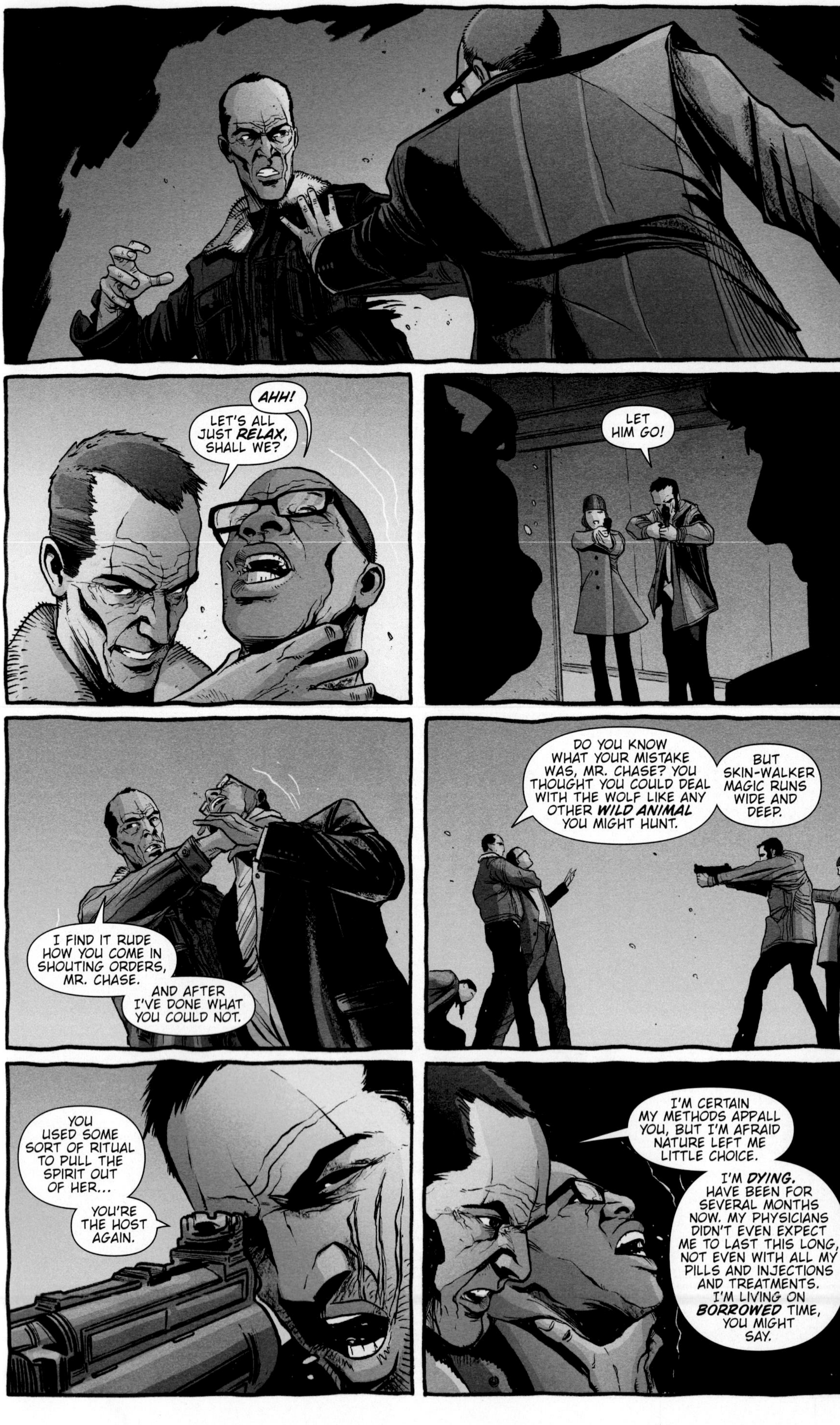
AHH!
LET'S ALL JUST RELAX, SHALL WE?
LET HIM GO!
I FIND IT RUDE HOW YOU COME IN SHOUTING ORDERS, MR. CHASE.
AND AFTER I'VE DONE WHAT YOU COULD NOT.
DO YOU KNOW WHAT YOUR MISTAKE WAS, MR. CHASE? YOU THOUGHT YOU COULD DEAL WITH THE WOLF LIKE ANY OTHER WILD ANIMAL YOU MIGHT HUNT.
BUT SKIN-WALKER MAGIC RUNS WIDE AND DEEP.
YOU USED SOME SORT OF RITUAL TO PULL THE SPIRIT OUT OF HER...
YOU'RE THE HOST AGAIN.
I'M CERTAIN MY METHODS APPALL YOU, BUT I'M AFRAID NATURE LEFT ME LITTLE CHOICE.
I'M DYING. HAVE BEEN FOR SEVERAL MONTHS NOW. MY PHYSICIANS DIDN'T EVEN EXPECT ME TO LAST THIS LONG, NOT EVEN WITH ALL MY PILLS AND INJECTIONS AND TREATMENTS. I'M LIVING ON BORROWED TIME, YOU MIGHT SAY.

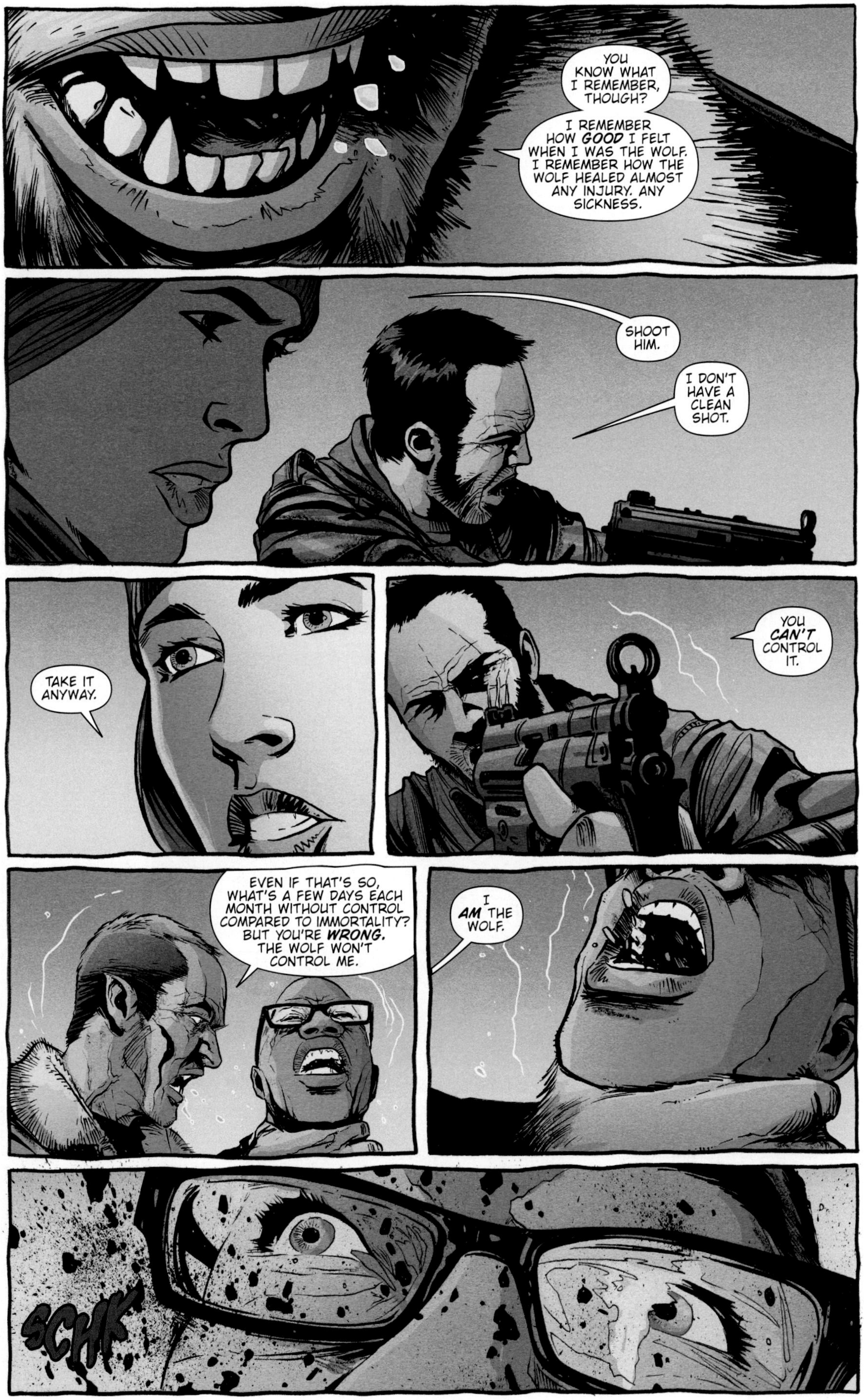
YOU KNOW WHAT I REMEMBER, THOUGH?
I REMEMBER HOW GOOD I FELT WHEN I WAS THE WOLF. I REMEMBER HOW THE WOLF HEALED ALMOST ANY INJURY. ANY SICKNESS.
SHOOT HIM.
I DON'T HAVE A CLEAN SHOT.
TAKE IT ANYWAY.
YOU CAN'T CONTROL IT.
EVEN IF THAT'S SO, WHAT'S A FEW DAYS EACH MONTH WITHOUT CONTROL COMPARED TO IMMORTALITY? BUT YOU'RE WRONG. THE WOLF WON'T CONTROL ME.
I AM THE WOLF.
SCHK

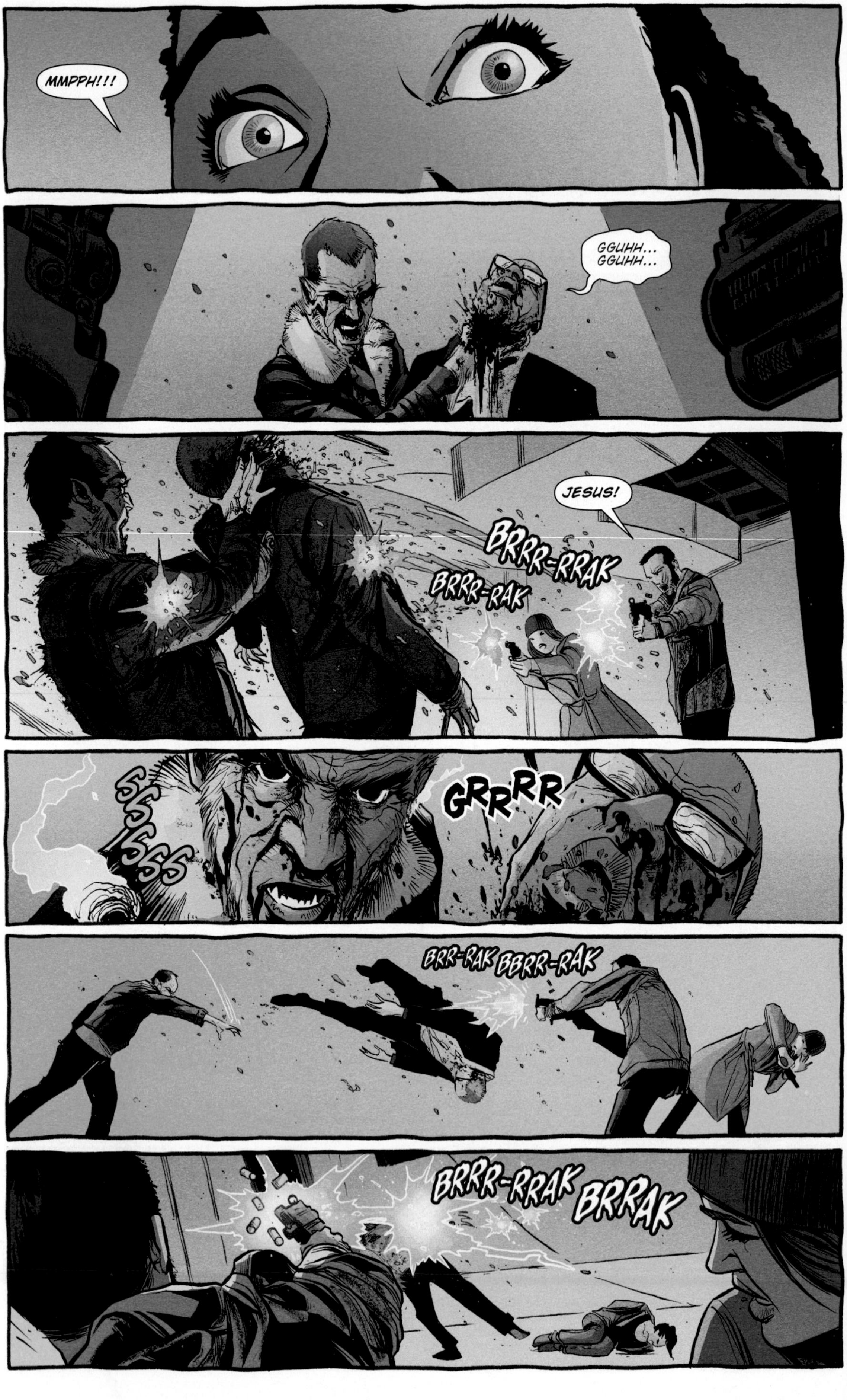
MMPPH!!!
GGUHH...
GGUHH...
JESUS!
BRRR-RRAK
BRRR-RAK
SSSSSS
GRRRR
BRR-RAK
BBRR-RAK
BRRR-RRAK
BRRAK

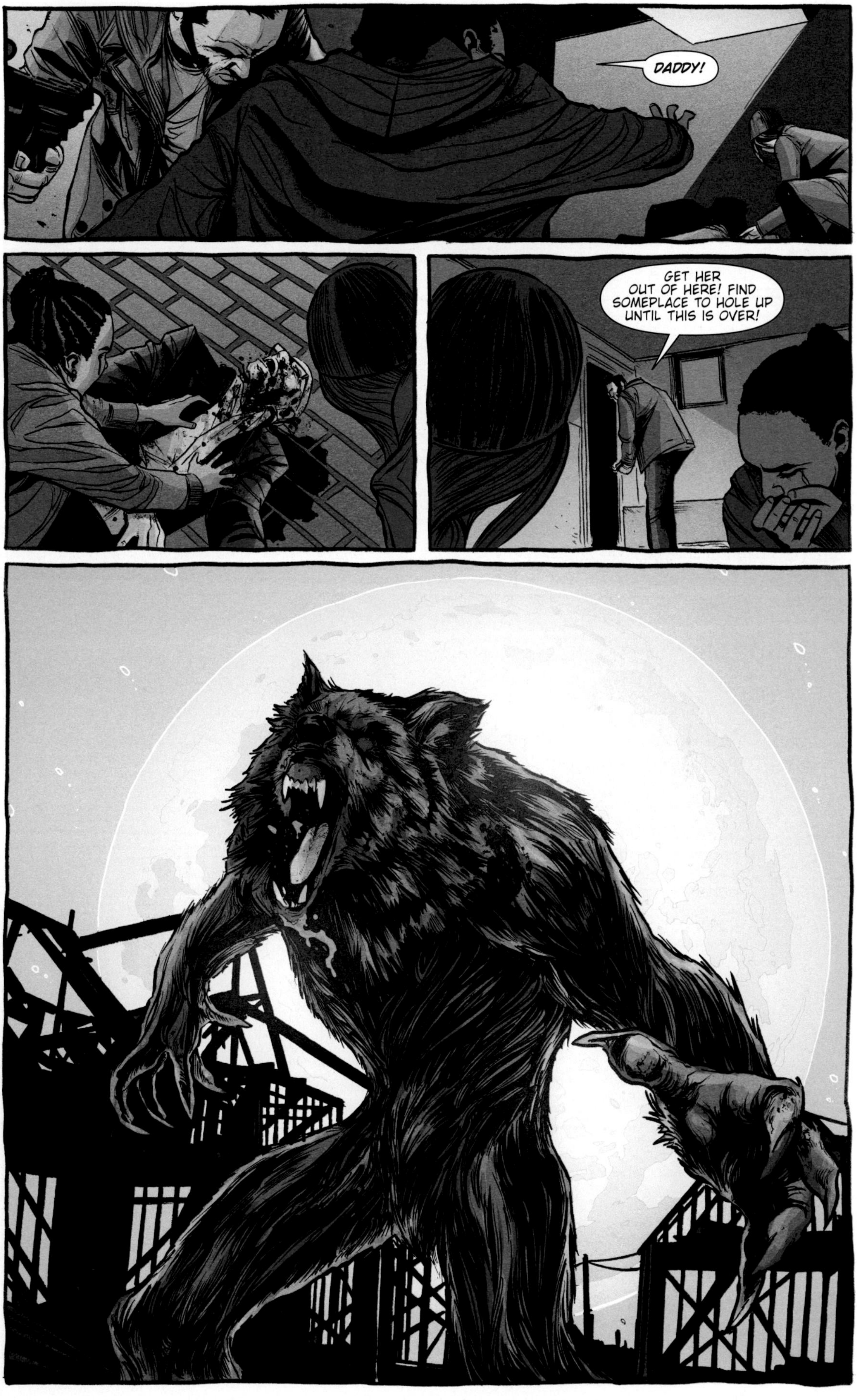
DADDY!
GET HER OUT OF HERE! FIND SOMEPLACE TO HOLE UP UNTIL THIS IS OVER!

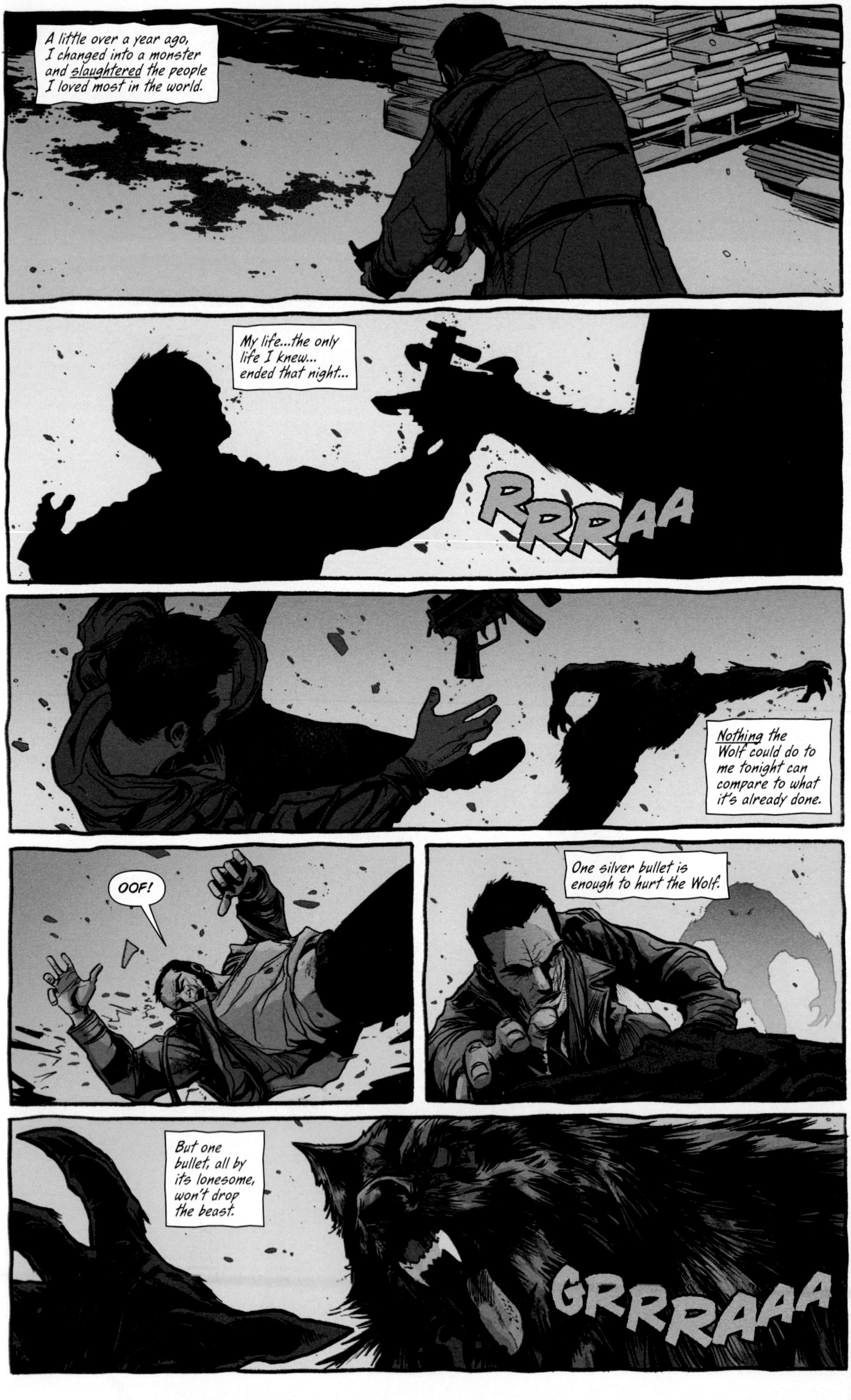
A little over a year ago, I changed into a monster and slaughtered the people I loved most in the world.
My life...the only life I knew... ended that night...
RRRRAA
Nothing the Wolf could do to me tonight can compare to what it's already done.
OOF!
One silver bullet is enough to hurt the Wolf.
But one bullet, all by its lonesome, won't drop the beast.
GRRRRAAA

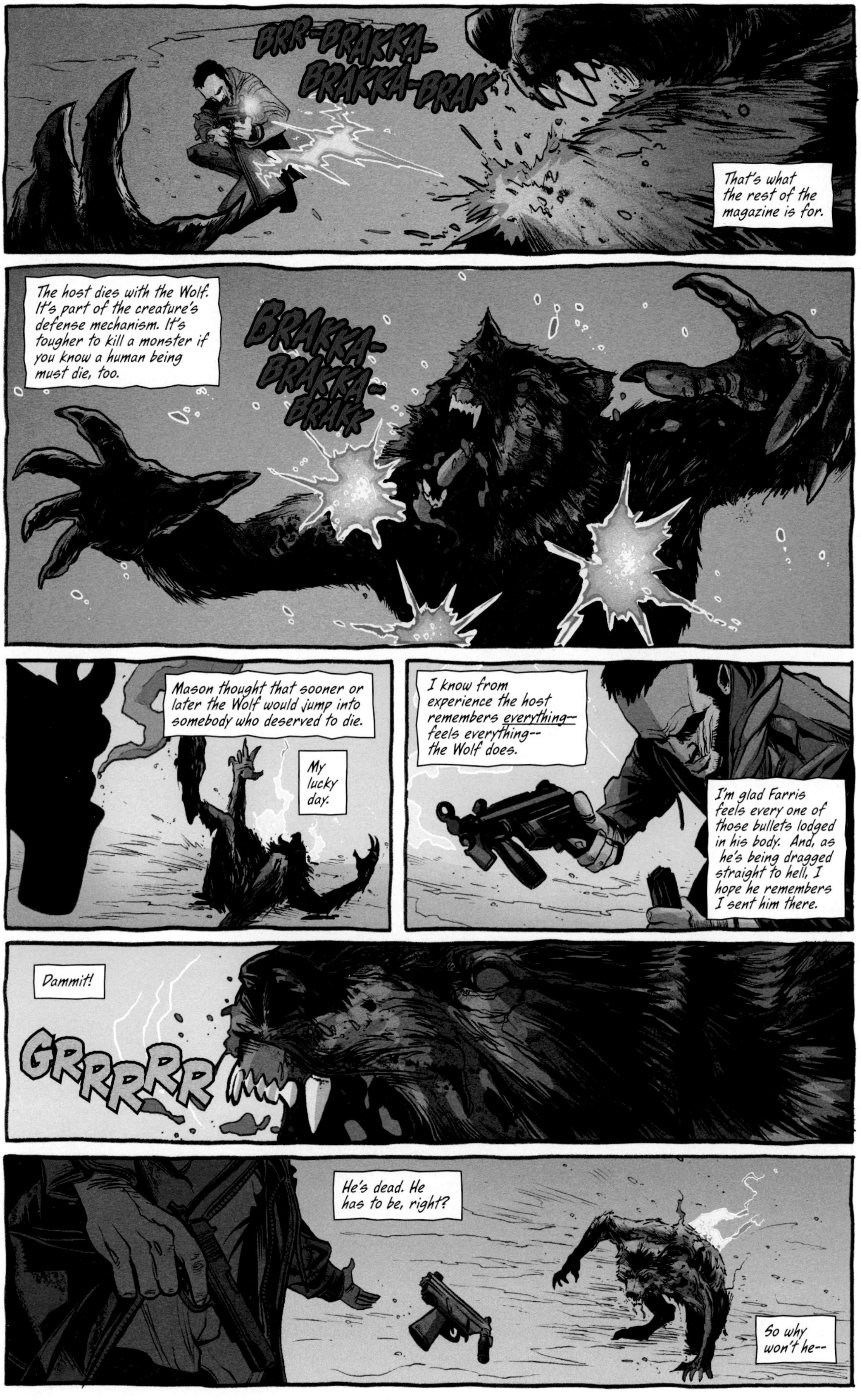
BRR-BRAKKA-BRAKKA-BRAK
That's what the rest of the magazine is for.
The host dies with the Wolf. It's part of the creature's defense mechanism. It's tougher to kill a monster if you know a human being must die, too.
BRAKKA-BRAKKA-BRAKK
Mason thought that sooner or later the Wolf would jump into somebody who deserved to die.
My lucky day.
I know from experience the host remembers everything-- feels everything-- the Wolf does.
I'm glad Farris feels every one of those bullets lodged in his body. And, as he's being dragged straight to hell, I hope he remembers I sent him there.
Dammit!
GRRRRR
He's dead. He has to be, right?
So why won't he--

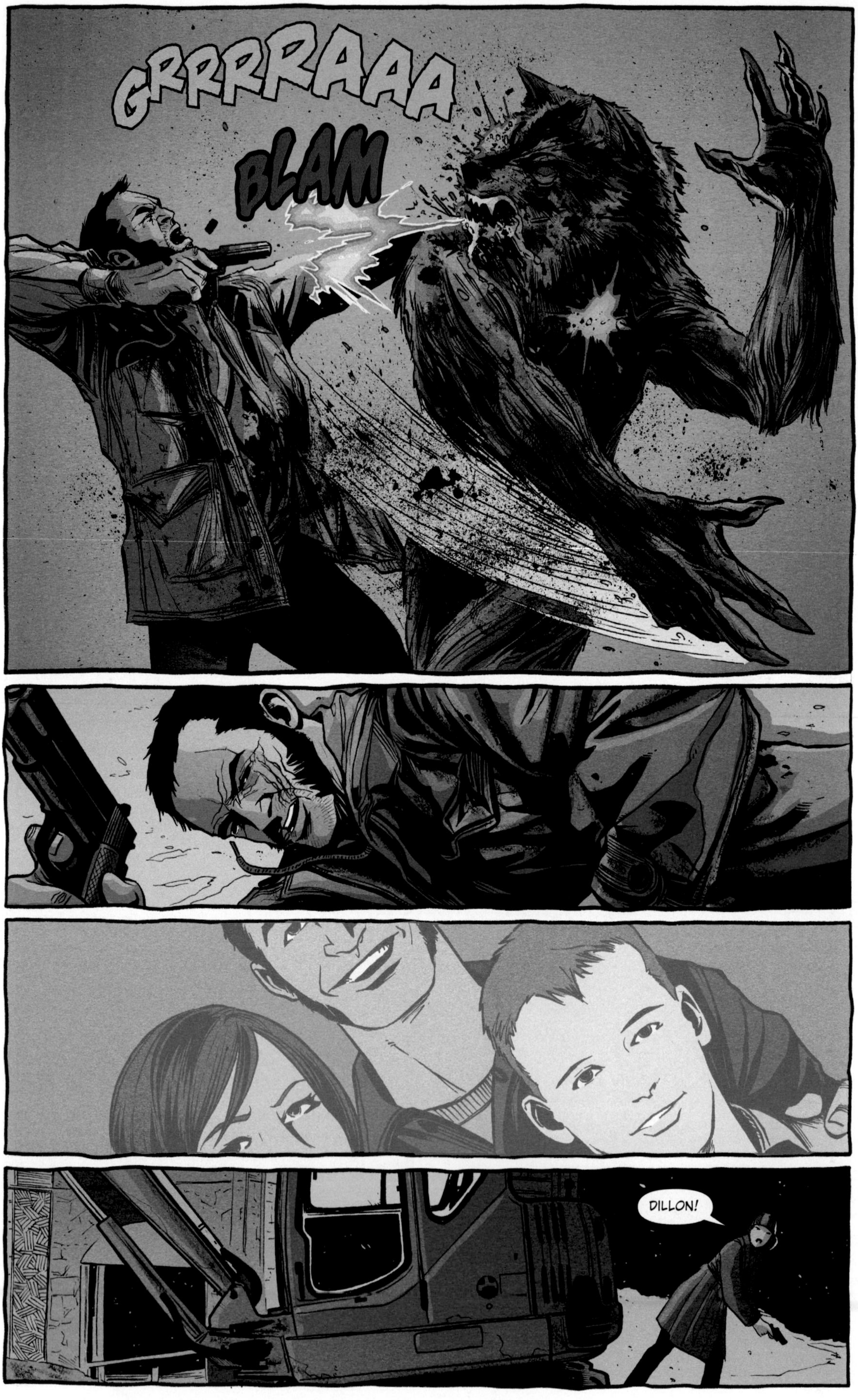
GRRRRAAA
BLAM
DILLON!

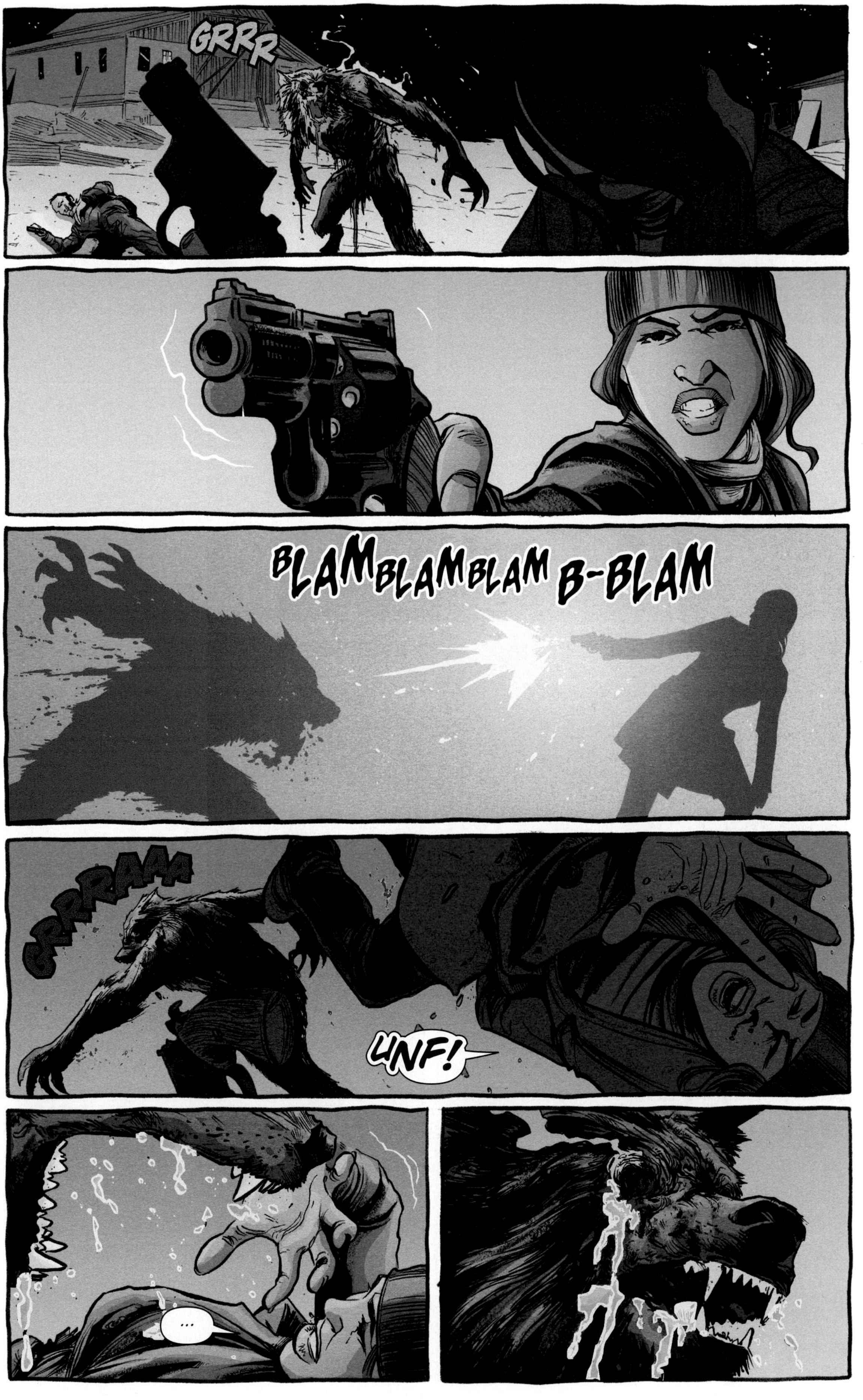
GRRR
BLAMBLAMBLAM B-BLAM
GRRRAAA
UNF!
...

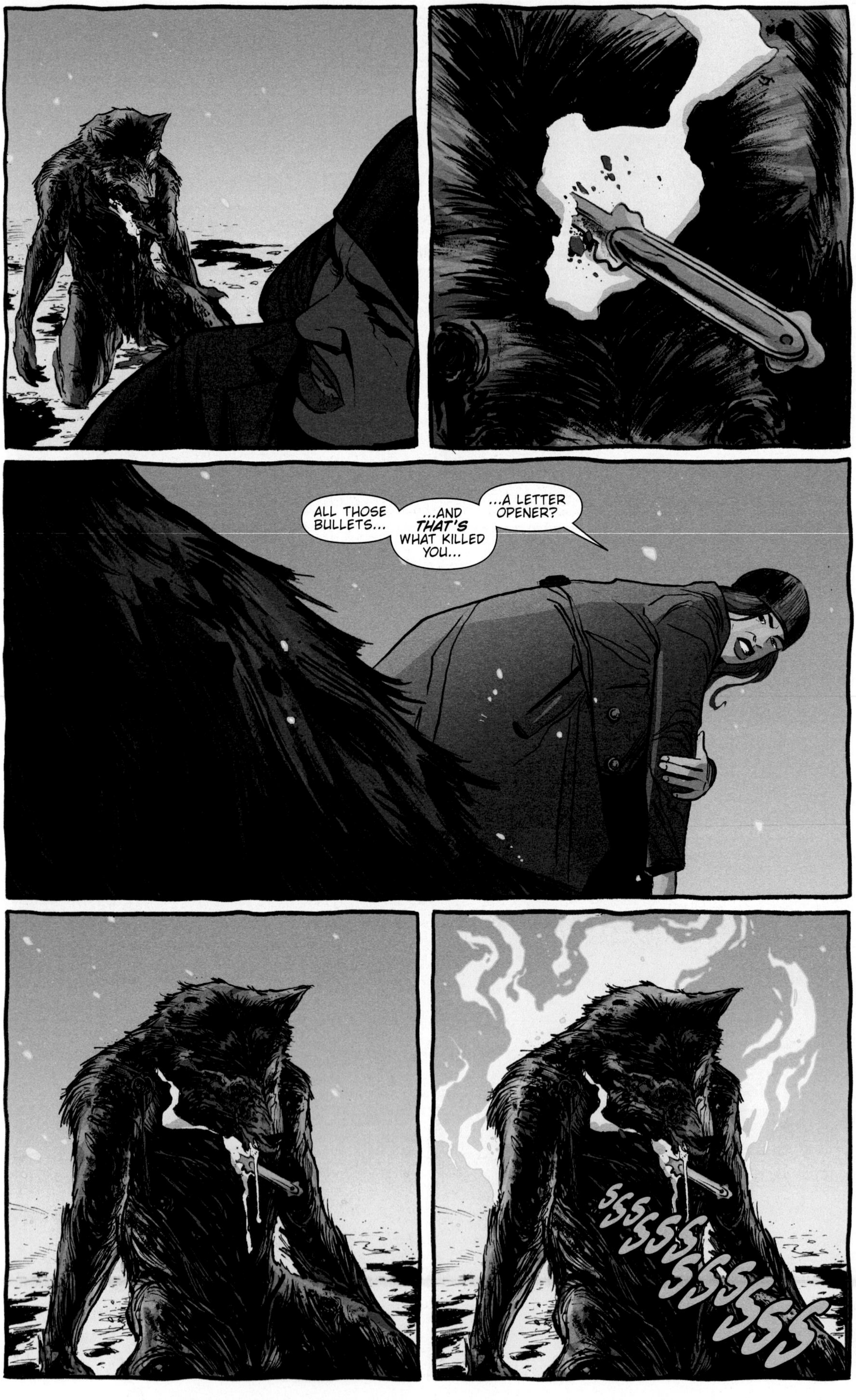
ALL THOSE BULLETS...
...AND *THAT'S* WHAT KILLED YOU...
...A LETTER OPENER?
SSSSSSSSSSSSSSSS

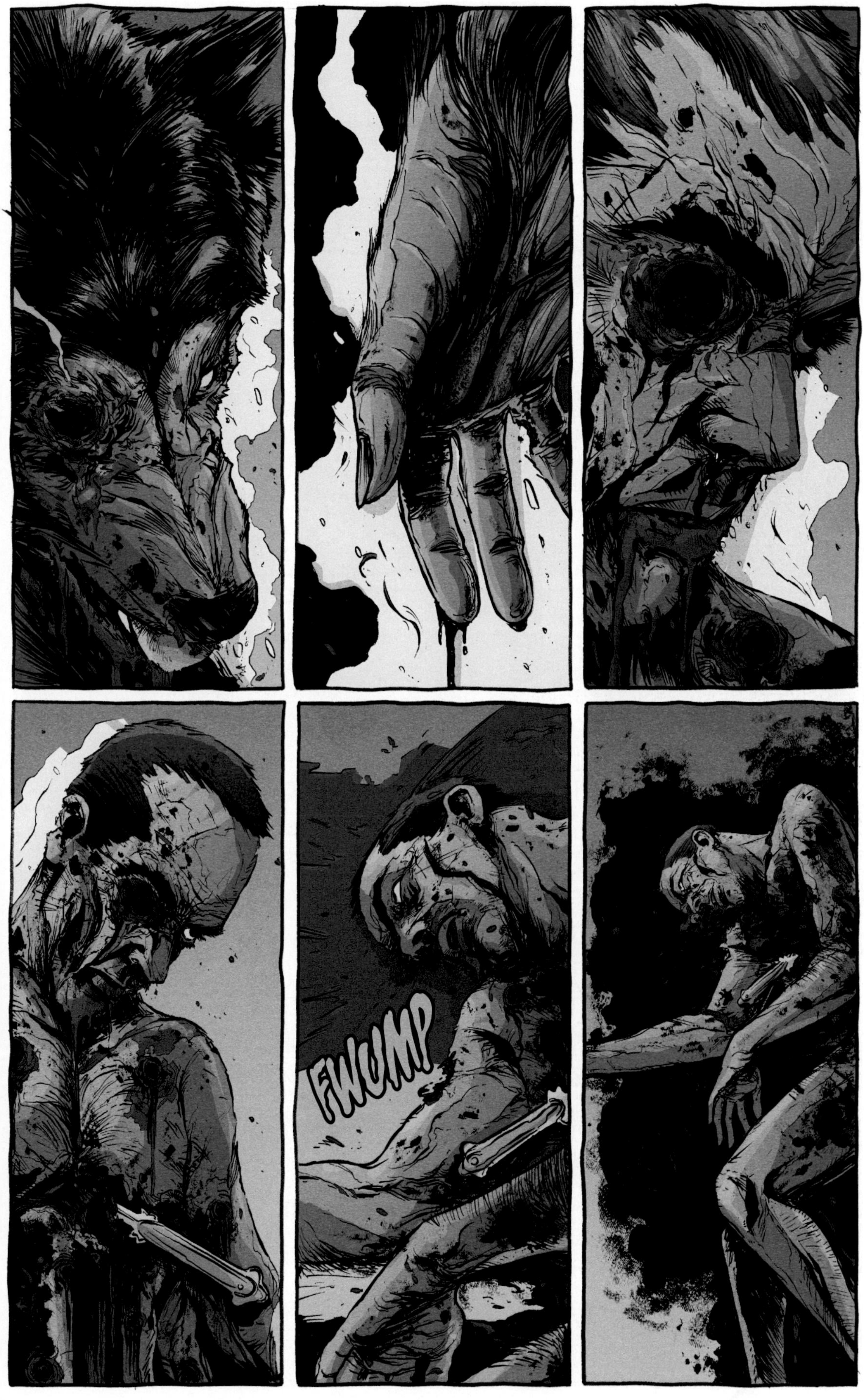
FWUMP

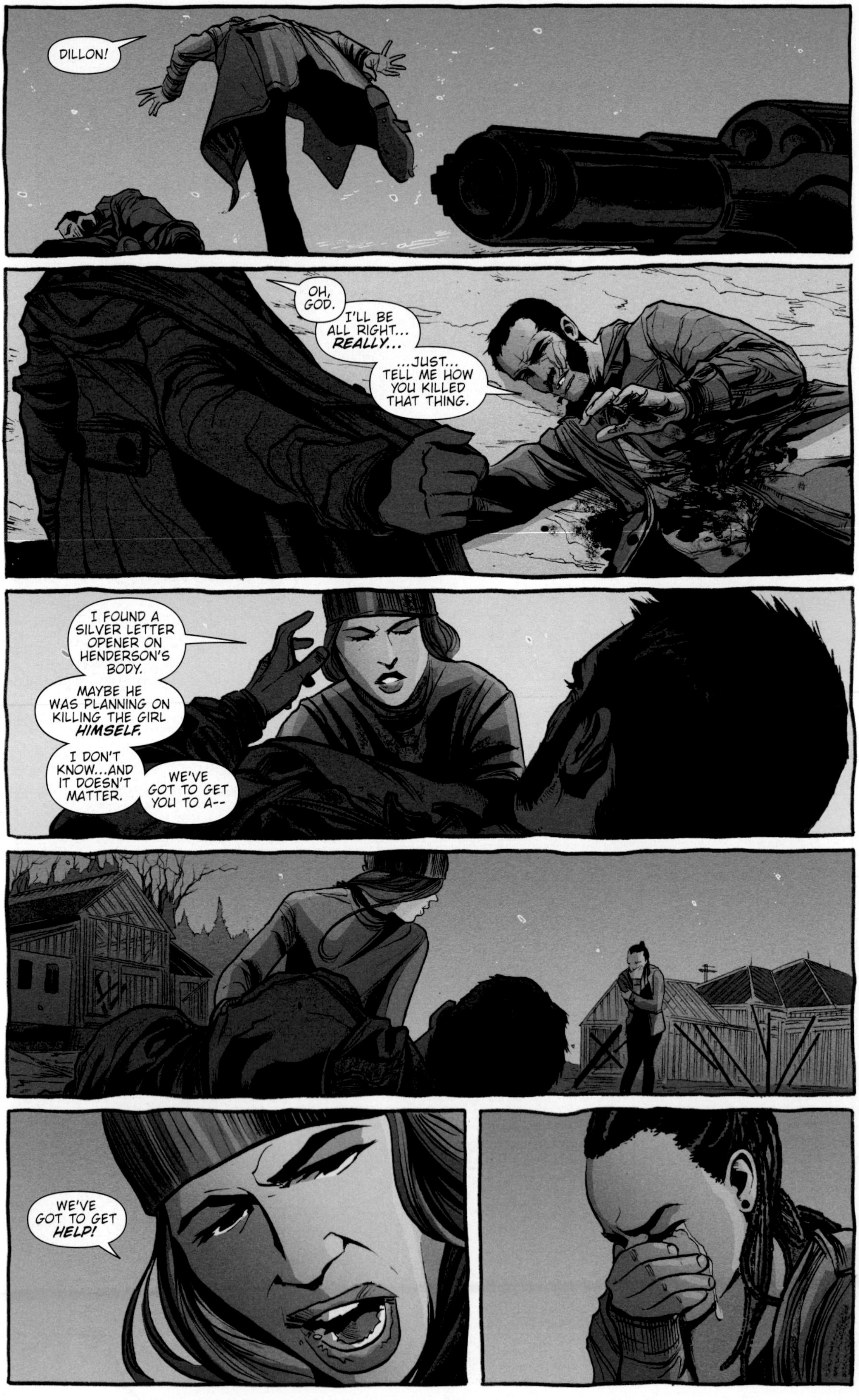
DILLON!
OH, GOD.
I'LL BE ALL RIGHT... REALLY...
...JUST... TELL ME HOW YOU KILLED THAT THING.
I FOUND A SILVER LETTER OPENER ON HENDERSON'S BODY.
MAYBE HE WAS PLANNING ON KILLING THE GIRL HIMSELF.
I DON'T KNOW...AND IT DOESN'T MATTER.
WE'VE GOT TO GET YOU TO A--
WE'VE GOT TO GET HELP!

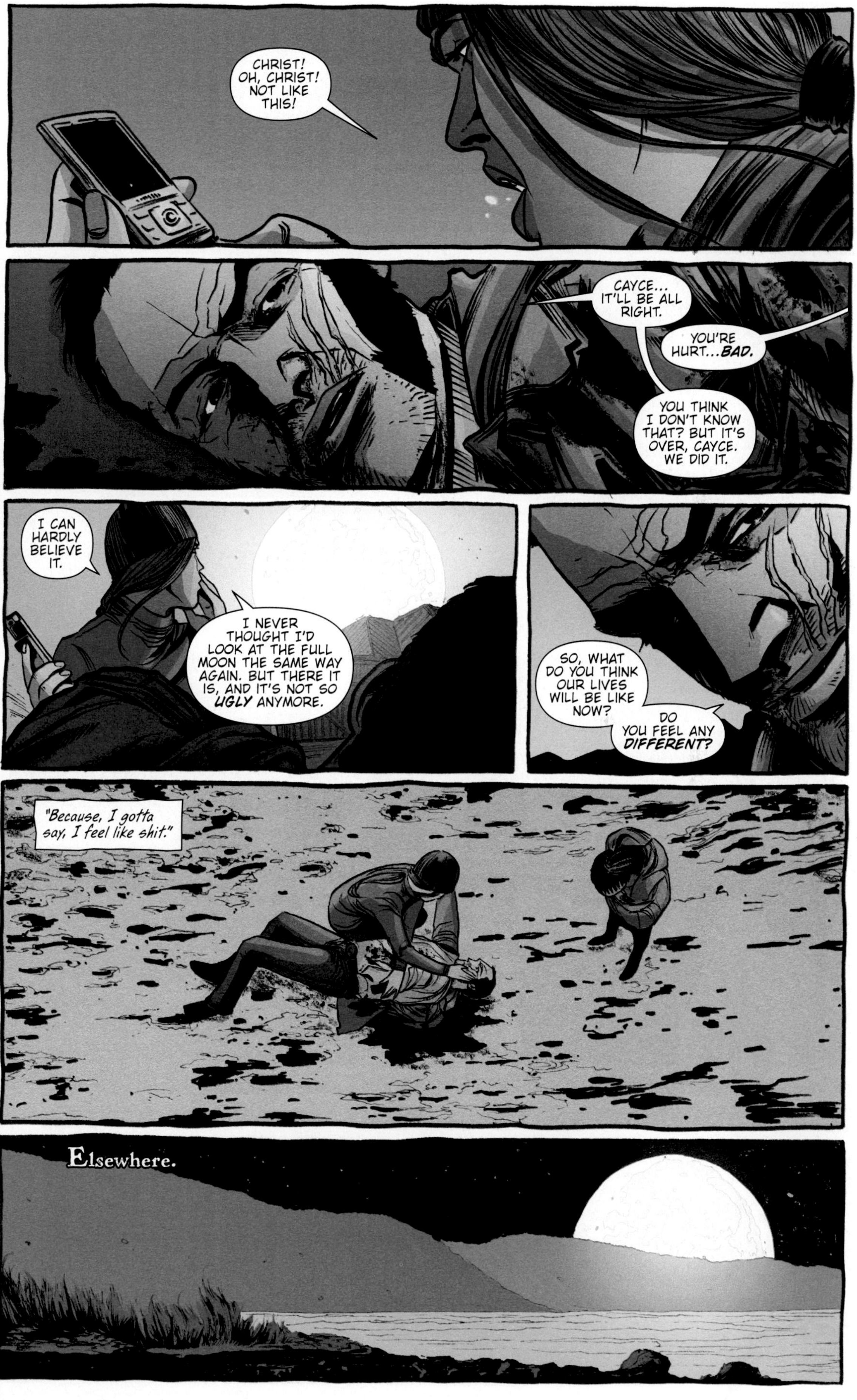
CHRIST! OH, CHRIST! NOT LIKE THIS!
CAYCE... IT'LL BE ALL RIGHT.
YOU'RE HURT...BAD.
YOU THINK I DON'T KNOW THAT? BUT IT'S OVER, CAYCE. WE DID IT.
I CAN HARDLY BELIEVE IT.
I NEVER THOUGHT I'D LOOK AT THE FULL MOON THE SAME WAY AGAIN. BUT THERE IT IS, AND IT'S NOT SO UGLY ANYMORE.
SO, WHAT DO YOU THINK OUR LIVES WILL BE LIKE NOW?
DO YOU FEEL ANY DIFFERENT?
"Because, I gotta say, I feel like shit."
Elsewhere.

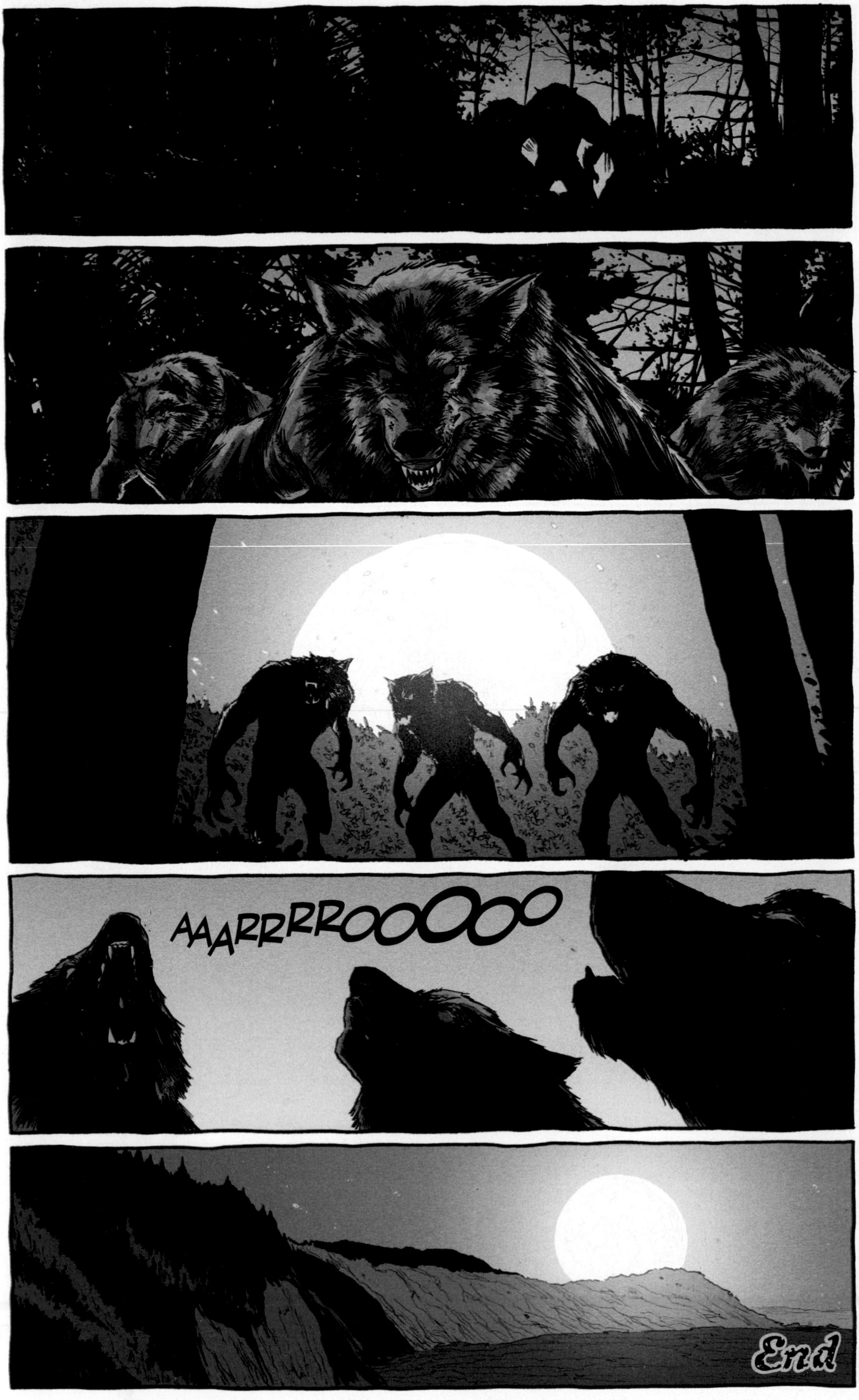
AAARRRROOOOOO
End

# BAD MOON RISING

PRELIMINARY ART AND LAYOUTS BY JEREMY HAUN

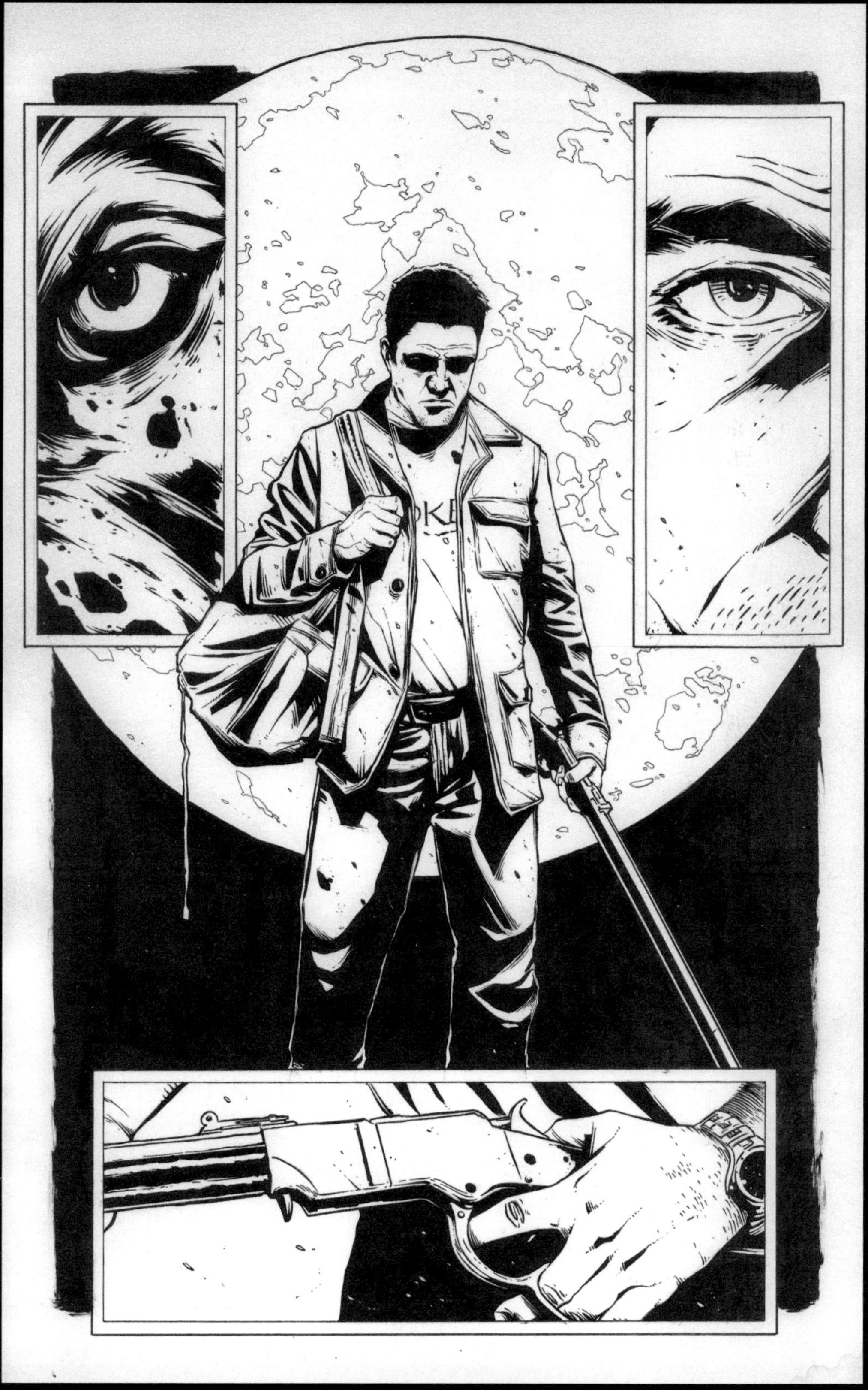

EARLY PROMOTIONAL PIECE.

THUMBNAILS AND FINAL ART FOR AN EARLY COVER IMAGE.

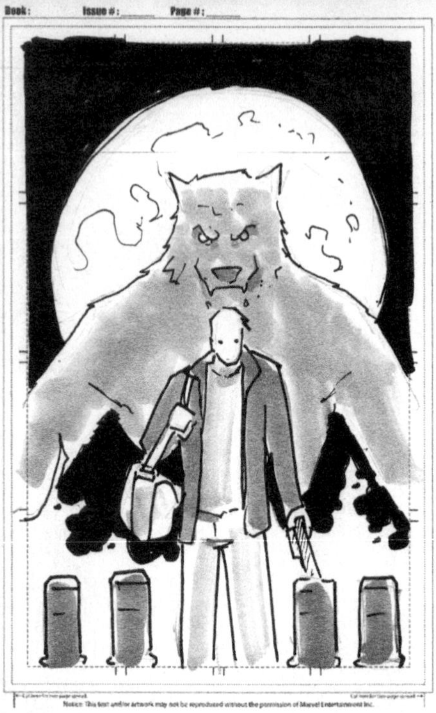
Book:
Issue #:
Page #:
Notice: This text and/or artwork may not be reproduced without the permission of Marvel Entertainment Inc.

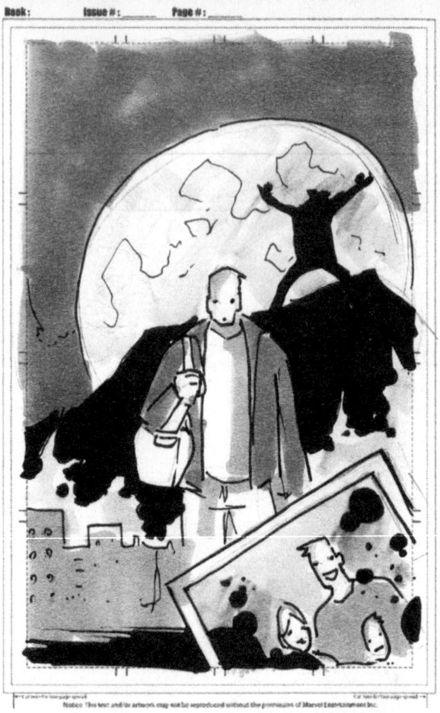
Book:
Issue #:
Page #:
Notice: This text and/or artwork may not be reproduced without the permission of Marvel Entertainment Inc.

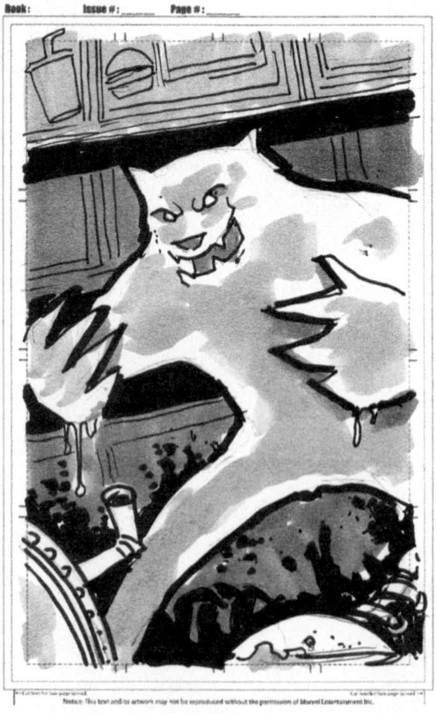
Book:
Issue #:
Page #:
Notice: This text and/or artwork may not be reproduced without the permission of Marvel Entertainment Inc.

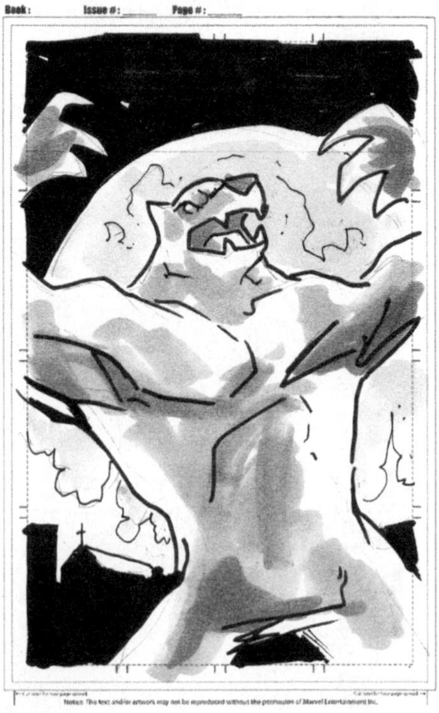
Book:
Issue #:
Page #:
Notice: This text and/or artwork may not be reproduced without the permission of Marvel Entertainment Inc.

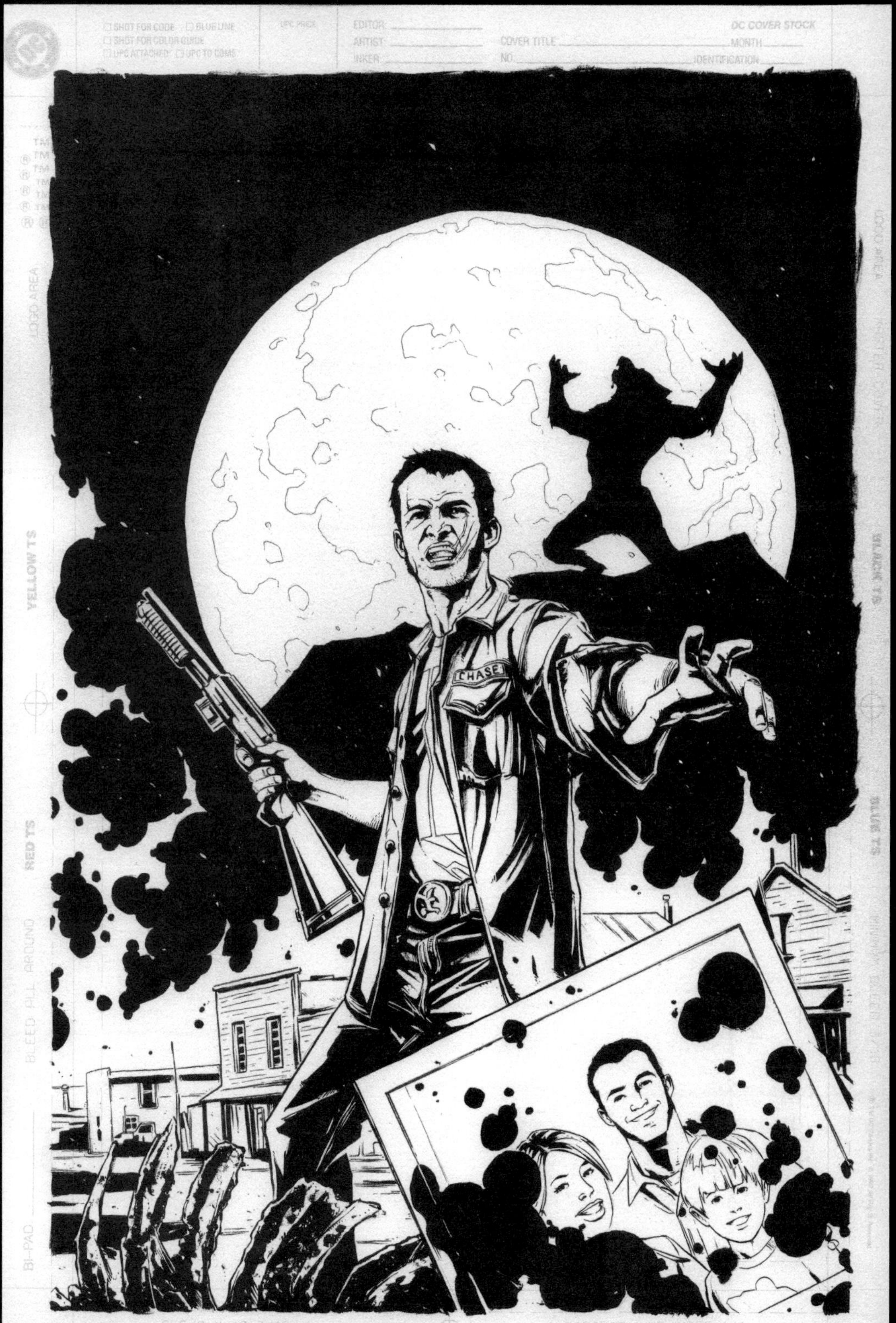
EDITOR
ARTIST
INKER
COVER TITLE
NO.
DC COVER STOCK
MONTH
IDENTIFICATION
LOGO AREA
YELLOW TS
RED TS
BLEED ALL AROUND
BI-PAD
BLACK TS
BLUE TS
CHASE
6 5/8 X 10 3/16
CLEARANCE LIVE IMAGE 1/4

THUMBNAIL LAYOUTS FOR ISSUE #5.

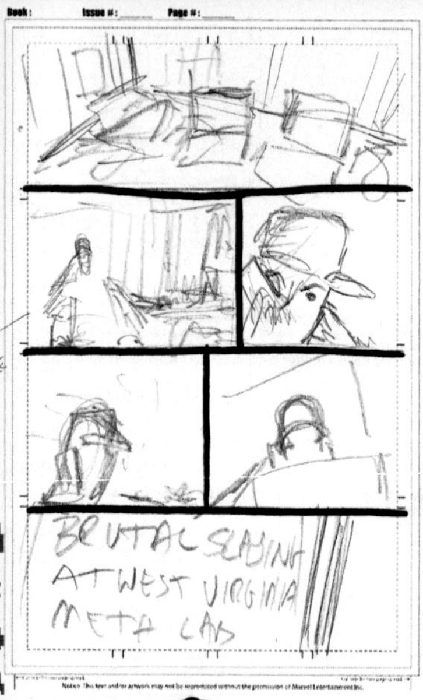
BRUTAL SLASHING
AT WEST VIRGINIA
META LAB

7

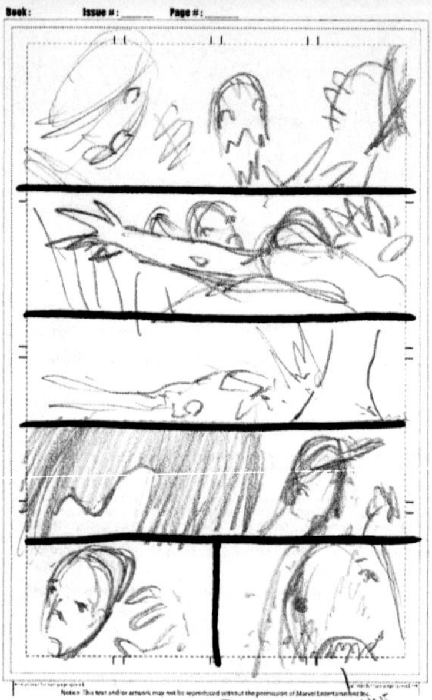

10

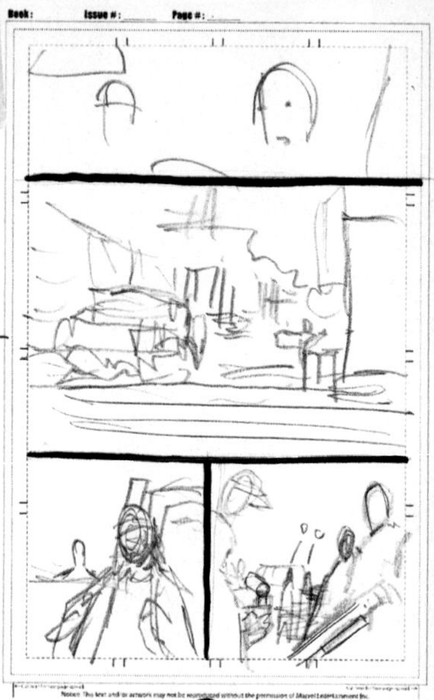

12

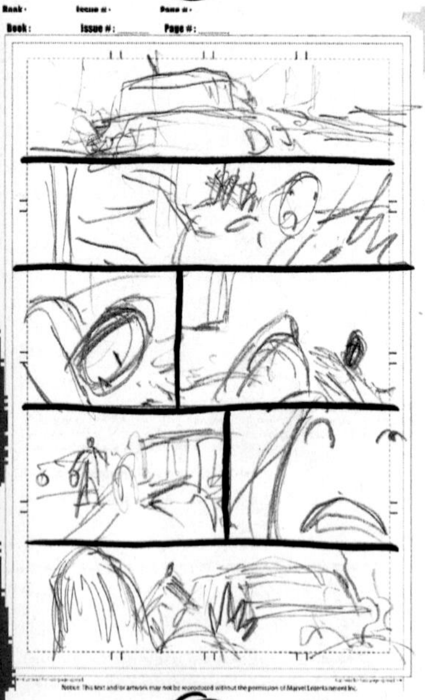

16

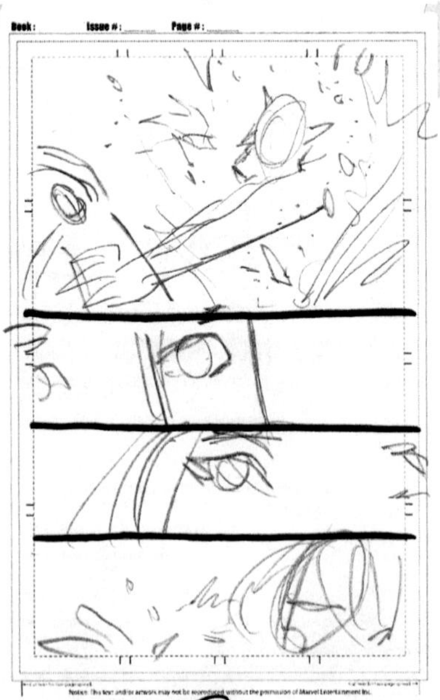

17

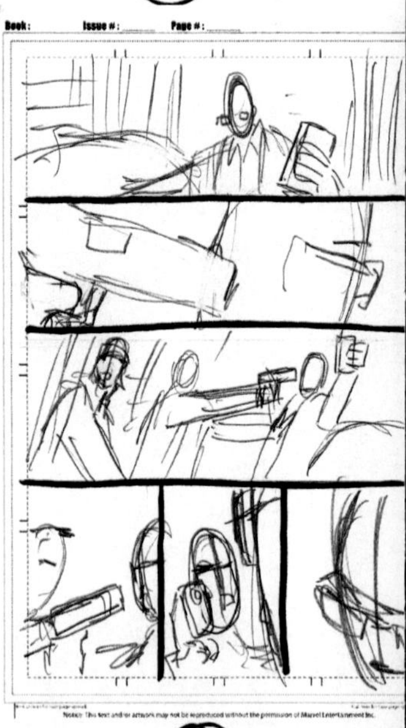

19

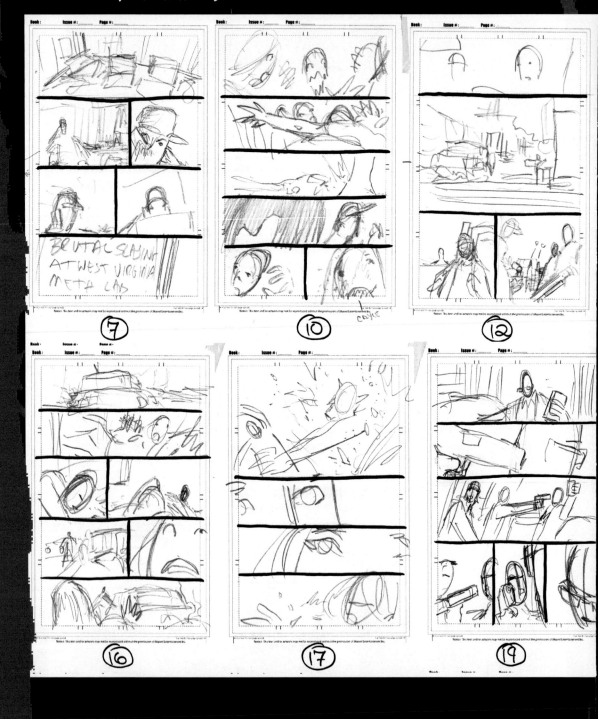

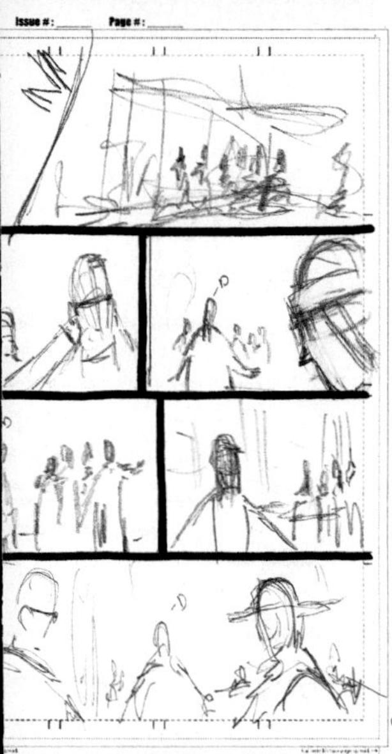
COFFEE IN HA

13

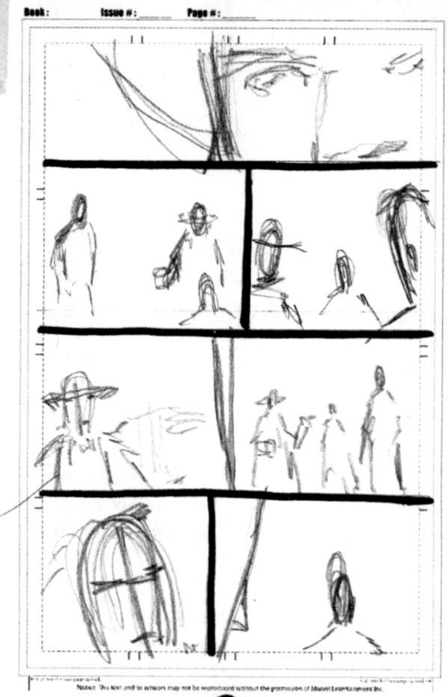

14

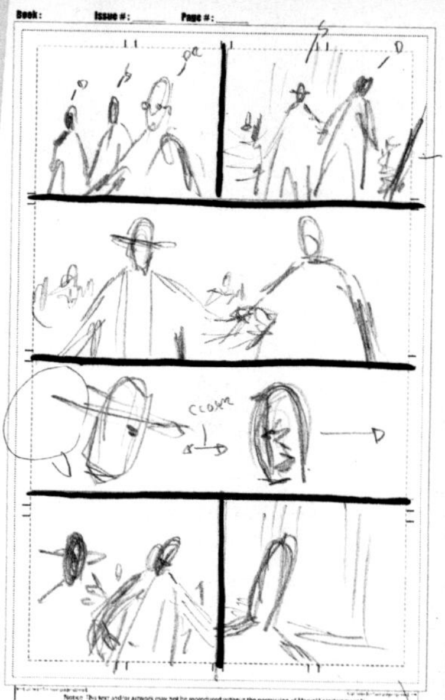
CLOSER

15

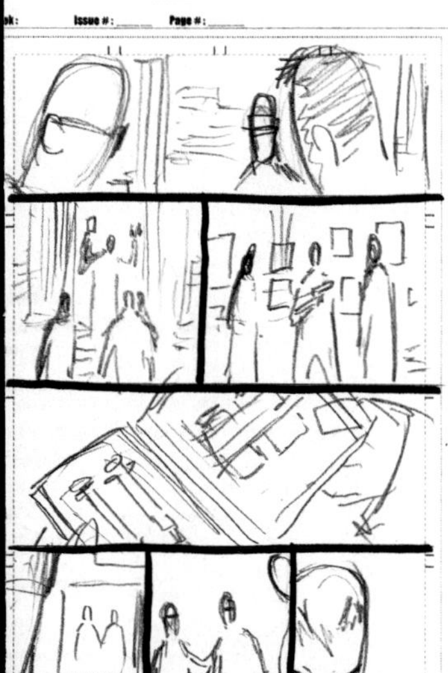
SLIGHT WORMS EYE

20

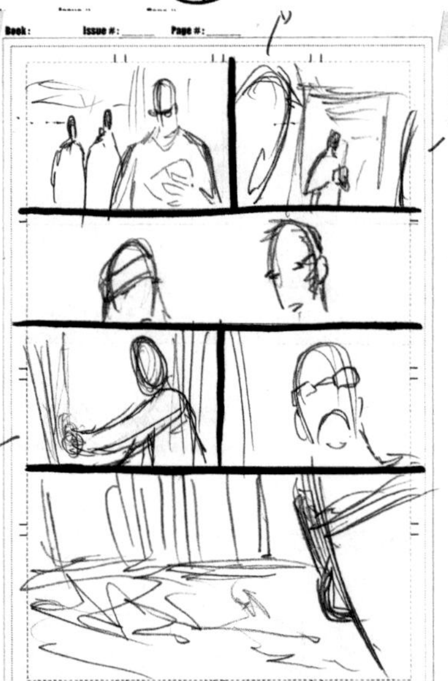

21

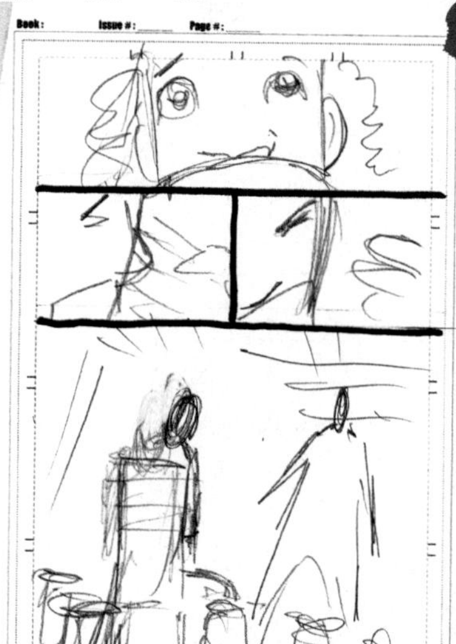
WORMS EYE

22

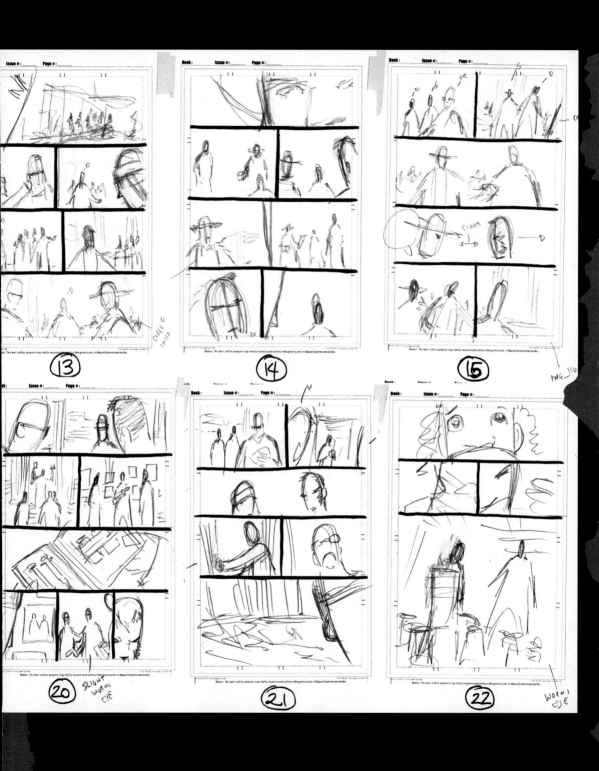

More early cover sketches.

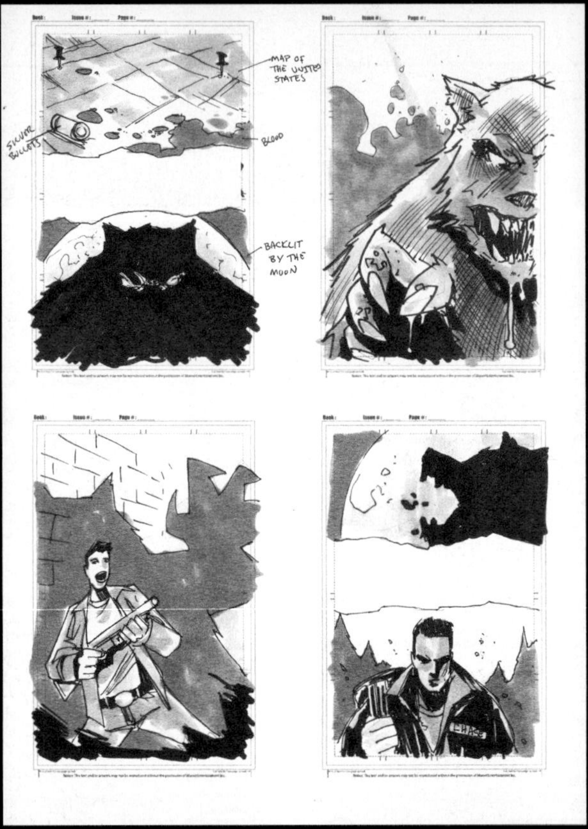

MAP OF THE UNITED STATES
SILVER BULLETS
BLOOD
BACKLIT BY THE MOON


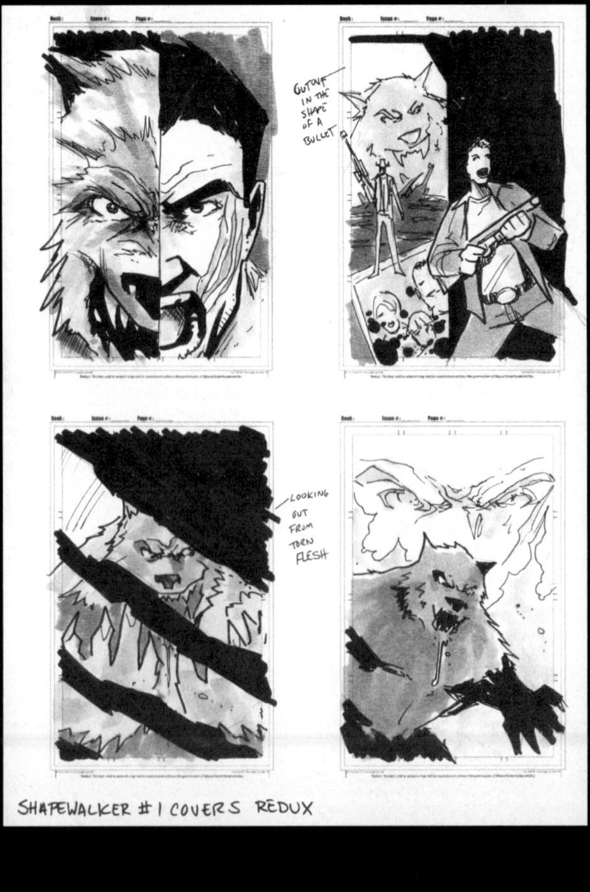

CUTOUT IN THE SHAPE OF A BULLET
LOOKING OUT FROM TORN FLESH
SHAPEWALKER #1 COVERS REDUX

Book: Issue #: Page #:

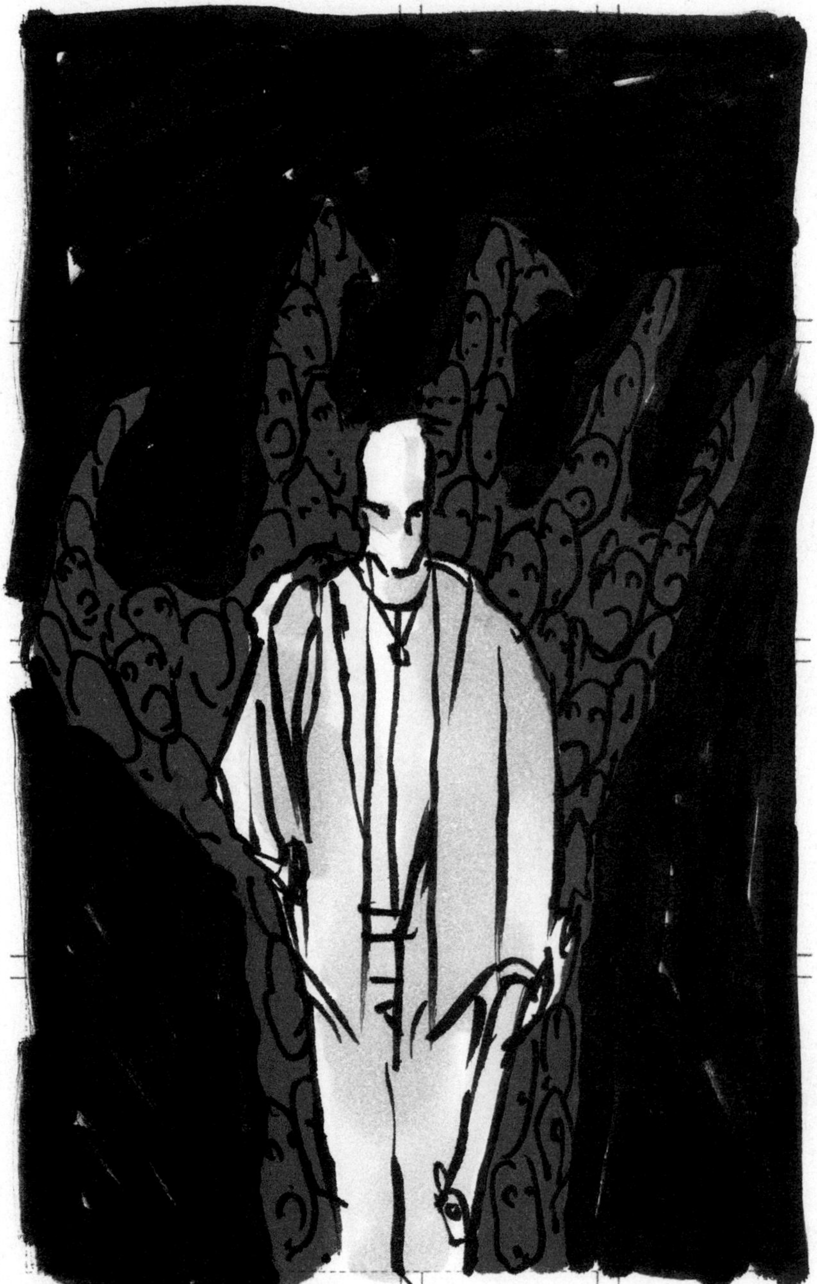



4

Final variant cover art for issue #1 (color by Lee Loughridge).

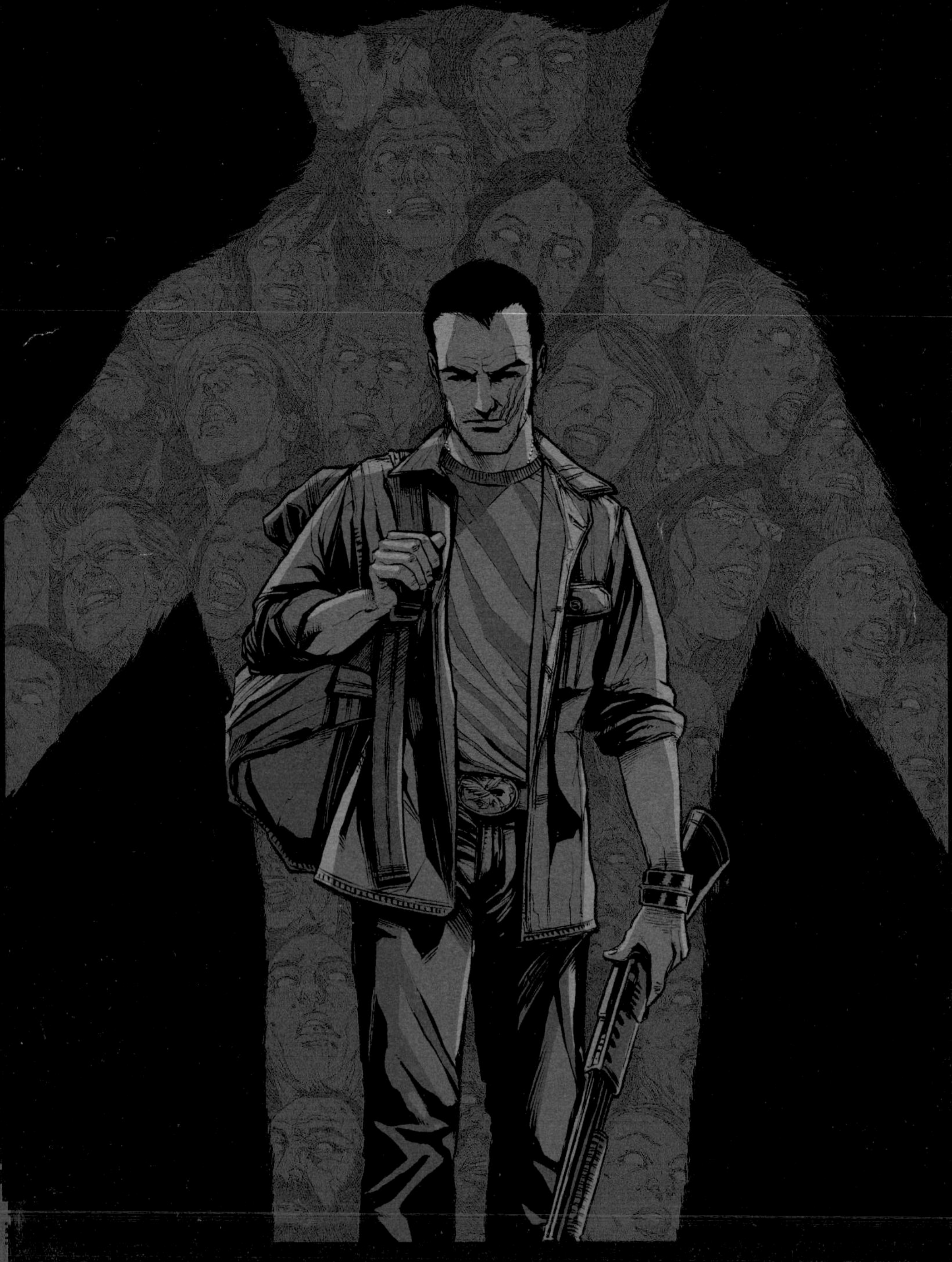